THE BOOK OF
Fairy and Folk Tales
OF IRELAND

THE BOOK OF
Fairy and Folk Tales
OF IRELAND

COMPILED BY

W.B. YEATS

BB **Bounty**
Books

Originally published by John Murray Publishers, London, in separate volumes:
Fairy and Folk Tales of the Irish Peasantry (1888) and *Irish Fairy Tales* (1892)

Design and arrangement copyright © Octopus Publishing Group Ltd 1994
The stories by Douglas Hyde are used by permission of the copyright holder.

This paperback edition first published in 2004 by Bounty Books,
a division of Octopus Publishing Group Ltd
Endeavour House
189 Shaftesbury Avenue
London WC2H 8JY

www.octopusbooks.co.uk

An Hachette UK Company
www.hachette.co.uk

Reprinted 2005, 2006, 2007, 2008, 2012

ISBN: 978-0-753723-23-4

A CIP catalogue record for this book is available from the British Library

Printed and bound by CPI Group (UK) Ltd, Croydon, CR0 4YY

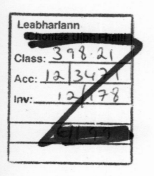

CONTENTS

Fairy and Folk Tales
of the Irish Peasantry

Inscribed to my mystical friend G. R.

INTRODUCTION

Dr Corbett, Bishop of Oxford and Norwich, lamented long ago the departure of the English fairies. "In Queen Mary's time" he wrote—

> "When Tom came home from labour,
>   Or Cis to milking rose,
> Then merrily, merrily went their tabor,
>   And merrily went their toes."

But now in the times of James, they had all gone, for "they were of the old profession", and "their songs were Ave Maries". In Ireland they are still extant, giving gifts to the kindly, and plaguing the surly. "Have you ever seen a fairy or such like?" I asked the old man in County Sligo. "Amn't I annoyed with them," was the answer. "Do the fishermen along here know anything of the mermaids?" I asked a woman of a village in County Dublin. "Indeed, they don't like to see them at all," she answered, "for they always bring bad weather." "Here is a man who believes in ghosts," said a foreign sea-captain, pointing to a pilot of my acquaintance. "In every house over there," said the pilot, pointing to his native village of Rosses, "there are several." Certainly that now old and much respected dogmatist, the Spirit of the Age, has in no manner made his voice heard down there. In a little while, for he has gotten a consumptive appearance of late, he will be covered over decently in his grave, and another will grow, old and much respected, in his place, and never be heard of down there, and after him another and another and another. Indeed, it is a question whether any of these personages will ever be heard of outside the newspaper offices and lecture-rooms and drawing-rooms and eel-pie houses of the cities, or if the Spirit of the Age is at any time more than a froth. At any rate, whole troops of their like will not change the

Celt much. Giraldus Cambrensis found the people of the western islands a trifle paganish. "How many gods are there?" asked a priest, a little while ago, of a man from the Island of Innistor. "There is one on Innistor; but this seems a big place," said the man, and the priest held up his hands in horror, as Giraldus had, just seven centuries before. Remember, I am not blaming the man; it is very much better to believe in a number of gods than in none at all, or think there is only one, but that he is a little sentimental and impracticable, and not constructed for the nineteenth century. The Celt, and his cromlechs, and his pillar-stones, these will not change much—indeed, it is doubtful if anybody at all changes at any time. In spite of hosts of deniers, and asserters, and wise-men, and professors, the majority still are averse to sitting down to dine thirteen at table, or being helped to salt, or walking under a ladder, or seeing a single magpie flirting his chequered tail. There are, of course, children of light who have set their faces against all this, though even a newspaper man, if you entice him into a cemetery at midnight, will believe in phantoms, for everyone is a visionary, if you scratch him deep enough. But the Celt is a visionary without scratching.

Yet, be it noticed, if you are a stranger, you will not readily get ghost and fairy legends, even in a western village. You must go adroitly to work, and make friends with the children, and the old men, with those who have not felt the pressure of mere daylight existence, and those with whom it is growing less, and will have altogether taken itself off one of these days. The old women are most learned, but will not so readily be got to talk, for the fairies are very secretive, and much resent being talked of; and are there not many stories of old women who were nearly pinched into their graves or numbed with fairy blasts?

At sea, when the nets are out and the pipes are lit, then will some ancient hoarder of tales become loquacious, telling his histories to the tune of the creaking of the boats. Holy-eve night, too, is a great time, and in old days many tales were to be heard at wakes. But the priests have set their faces against wakes.

In the *Parochial Survey of Ireland* it is recorded how the story-tellers used to gather together of an evening, and if any had a different version from the others, they would all recite theirs and vote, and the man who had varied would have to abide by their verdict. In this way stories have been handed down with such accuracy, that the long tale of Dierdre was, in the earlier decades of this century, told almost word for word, as in the very ancient MSS. in the Royal Dublin Society. In one case only it varied, and then the MS. was obviously wrong—a passage had been forgotten by the copyist. But this accuracy is rather in the folk and bardic tales than in the fairy legends, for these vary widely, being usually adapted to some neighbouring village or local fairy-seeing celebrity. Each county has usually some family, or personage, supposed to have been favoured or plagued, especially by the phantoms, as the Hackets of Castle Hacket, Galway, who had for their ancestor a fairy, or John-o'-Daly of Lisadell, Sligo, who wrote "Eilleen Aroon", the song the Scots have stolen and called "Robin Adair", and which Handel would sooner have written than all his oratorios,* and the "O'Donahue of Kerry". Round these men stories tended to group themselves, sometimes deserting more ancient heroes for the purpose. Round poets have they gathered especially, for poetry in Ireland has always been mysteriously connected with magic.

These folk tales are full of simplicity and musical occurrences, for they are the literature of a class for whom every incident in the old rut of birth, love, pain, and death has cropped up unchanged for centuries: who have steeped everything in the heart: to whom everything is a symbol. They have the spade over which man has leant from the beginning. The people of the cities have the machine, which is prose and a *parvenu*. They have few events. They can turn over the incidents of a long life as they sit by the fire. With us nothing has time to gather meaning, and too many things are occurring for even a big heart to hold. It is said the most eloquent people in the world are the Arabs, who have only the bare earth of the desert and a sky swept bare by the sun. "Wisdom has alighted upon three things," goes their proverb; "the hand of the Chinese, the brain of the Frank, and the tongue of the Arab." This, I take it, is the meaning of that simplicity sought for so much in these days by all the poets, and not to be had at any price.

The most notable and typical story-teller of my acquaintance is one Paddy Flynn, a little, bright-eyed, old man, living in a leaky one-roomed cottage of the village of B—, "The most gentle—i.e., fairy—place in the whole of the County Sligo," he says, though others claim that honour for Drumahair or for Drumcliff. A very pious old man, too! You may have some time to inspect his strange figure and ragged hair, if he happen to be in a devout humour, before he comes to the doings of the gentry. A strange devotion! Old tales of Columkill, and what he said to his mother. "How are you today, mother?" "Worse!" "May you be worse tomorrow"; and on the next day, "How are you today, mother?" "Worse!" "May

* He lived some time in Dublin, and heard it then.

you be worse tomorrow"; and on the next, "How are you today, mother?" "Better, thank God." "May you be better tomorrow." In which undutiful manner he will tell you Columkill inculcated cheerfulness. Then most likely he will wander off into his favourite theme—how the Judge smiles alike in rewarding the good and condemning the lost to unceasing flames. Very consoling does it appear to Paddy Flynn, this melancholy and apocalyptic cheerfulness of the Judge. Nor seems his own cheerfulness quite earthly—though a very palpable cheerfulness. The first time I saw him he was cooking mushrooms for himself; the next time he was asleep under a hedge, smiling in his sleep. Assuredly some joy not quite of this steadfast earth lightens in those eyes—swift as the eyes of a rabbit—among so many wrinkles, for Paddy Flynn is very old. A melancholy there is in the midst of their cheerfulness—a melancholy that is almost a portion of their joy, the visionary melancholy of purely instinctive natures and of all animals. In the triple solitude of age and eccentricity and partial deafness he goes about much pestered by children.

As to the reality of his fairy and spirit-seeing powers, not all are agreed. One day we were talking of the Banshee. "I have seen it", he said, "down there by the water 'batting' the river with its hands". He it was who said the fairies annoyed him.

Not that the Sceptic is entirely afar even from these western villages. I found him one morning as he bound his corn in a merest pocket-handkerchief of a field. Very different from Paddy Flynn—Scepticism in every wrinkle of his face, and a travelled man, too!—a foot-long Mohawk Indian tattooed on one of his arms to evidence the matter. "They who travel," says a neighbouring priest, shaking his head over him, and quoting Thomas Á'Kempis, "seldom come holy." I had mentioned ghosts to this Sceptic. "Ghosts," said he; "there are no such things at all, at all, but the gentry, they stand to reason; for the devil, when he fell out of heaven, took the weak-minded ones with him, and they were put into the waste places. And that's what the gentry are. But they are getting scarce now, because their time's over, ye see, and they're going back. But ghosts, no! And I'll tell ye something more I don't believe in—the fire of hell;" then, in a low voice, "that's only invented to give the priests and the parsons something to do." Thereupon this man, so full of enlightenment, returned to his corn-binding.

The various collectors of Irish folk-lore have, from our point of view, one great merit, and from the point of view of others, one great fault. They have made their

6

work literature rather than science, and told us of the Irish peasantry rather than of the primitive religion of mankind, or whatever else the folk-lorists are on the gad after. To be considered scientists they should have tabulated all their tales in forms like grocers' bills—item the fairy king, item the queen. Instead of this they have caught the very voice of the people, the very pulse of life, each giving what was most noticed in his day. Croker and Lover, full of the ideas of harum-scarum Irish gentility, saw everything humorised. The impulse of the Irish literature of their time came from a class that did not—mainly for political reasons—take the populace seriously, and imagined the country as a humorist's Arcadia; its passion, its gloom, its tragedy, they knew nothing of. What they did was not wholly false; they merely magnified an irresponsible type, found oftenest among boatmen, carmen, and gentlemen's servants, into the type of a whole nation, and created the stage Irishman. The writers of 'forty-eight, and the famine combined, burst their bubble. Their work had the dash as well as the shallowness of an ascendant and idle class, and in Croker is touched everywhere with beauty—a gentle Arcadian beauty. Carleton, a peasant born, has in many of his stories—I have been only able to give a few of the slightest—more especially in his ghost stories, a much more serious way with him, for all his humour. Kennedy, an old bookseller in Dublin, who seems to have had a something of genuine belief in the fairies, came next in time. He has far less literary faculty, but is wonderfully accurate, giving often the very words the stories were told in. But the best book since Croker is Lady Wilde's *Ancient Legends*. The humour has all given way to pathos and tenderness. We have here the innermost heart of the Celt in the moments he has grown to love through years of persecution, when, cushioning himself about with dreams, and hearing fairy-songs in the twilight, he ponders on the soul and on the dead. Here is the Celt, only it is the Celt dreaming.

Besides these are two writers of importance, who have published, so far, nothing in book shape—Miss Letitia Maclintock and Mr Douglas Hyde. Miss Maclintock writes accurately and beautifully the half Scottish dialect of Ulster; and Mr Douglas Hyde is now preparing a volume of folk tales in Gaelic, having taken them down, for the most part, word for word among the Gaelic speakers of Roscommon and Galway. He is, perhaps, most to be trusted of all. He knows the people thoroughly. Others see a phase of Irish life; he understands all its elements. His work is neither humorous nor mournful; it is simply life. I hope he may put some of his gatherings into ballads, for he is the last of our ballad-writers of the school of Walsh and

Callanan—men whose work seems fragrant with turf smoke. And this brings to mind the chap-books. They are to be found brown with turf smoke on cottage shelves, and are, or were, sold on every hand by the pedlars, but cannot be found in any library of this city of the Sassenach. *The Royal Fairy Tales, The Hibernian Tales,* and *The Legends of the Fairies* are the fairy literature of the people.

Several specimens of our fairy poetry are given. It is more like the fairy poetry of Scotland than of England. The personages of English fairy literature are merely, in most cases, mortals beautifully masquerading. Nobody ever believed in such fairies. They are romantic bubbles from Provence. Nobody ever laid new milk on their doorstep for them.

As to my own part in this book, I have tried to make it representative, as far as so few pages would allow, of every kind of Irish folk-faith. The reader will perhaps wonder that in all my notes I have not rationalised a single hobgoblin. I seek for shelter to the words of Socrates.*

"*Phædrus.* I should like to know, Socrates, whether the place is not somewhere here at which Boreas is said to have carried off Orithyia from the banks of the Ilissus?

"*Socrates.* That is the tradition.

"*Phædrus.* And is this the exact spot? The little stream is delightfully clear and bright; I can fancy that there might be maidens playing near.

"*Socrates.* I believe the spot is not exactly here, but about a quarter-of-a-mile lower down, where you cross to the temple of Artemis, and I think that there is some sort of an altar of Boreas at the place.

"*Phædrus.* I do not recollect; but I beseech you to tell me, Socrates, do you believe this tale?

"*Socrates.* The wise are doubtful, and I should not be singular if, like them, I also doubted. I might have a rational explanation that Orithyia was playing with Pharmacia, when a northern gust carried her over the neighbouring rocks; and this being the manner of her death, she was said to have been carried away by Boreas. There is a discrepancy, however, about the locality. According to another version of the story, she was taken from the Areopagus, and not from this place. Now I quite acknowledge that these allegories are very nice, but he is not to be envied who has to invent them; much labour and ingenuity will be required of him; and

---

* *Phædrus,* Jowett's translation (Clarendon Press).

when he has once begun, he must go on and rehabilitate centaurs and chimeras dire. Gorgons and winged steeds flow in apace and numberless other inconceivable and portentous monsters. And if he is sceptical about them, and would fain reduce them one after another to the rules of probability, this sort of crude philosophy will take up all his time. Now, I have certainly not time for such inquiries. Shall I tell you why? I must first know myself, as the Delphian inscription says; to be curious about that which is not my business, while I am still in ignorance of my own self, would be ridiculous. And, therefore, I say farewell to all this; the common opinion is enough for me. For, as I was saying, I want to know not about this, but about myself. Am I, indeed, a wonder more complicated and swollen with passion than the serpent Typho, or a creature of gentler and simpler sort, to whom nature has given a diviner and lowlier destiny?"

I have to thank Messrs Macmillan, and the editors of *Belgravia*, *All the Year Round*, and *Monthly Packet*, for leave to quote from Patrick Kennedy's Legendary *Fictions of the Irish Celts*, and Miss Maclintock's articles respectively; Lady Wilde, for leave to give what I would from her *Ancient Legends of Ireland* (Ward & Downey); and Mr Douglas Hyde, for his three unpublished stories, and for valuable and valued assistance in several ways; and also Mr Allingham, and other copyright holders, for their poems. Mr Allingham's poems are from *Irish Songs and Poems* (Reeves and Turner); Fergusson's, from Sealey, Bryers, & Walker's shilling reprint; my own and Miss O'Leary's from *Ballads and Poems of Young Ireland*, 1888, a little anthology published by Gill & Sons, Dublin.

W. B. YEATS

THE TROOPING FAIRIES

The Irish word for fairy is *sheehogue* [*sidheóg*], a diminutive of "shee" in *banshee*. Fairies are *deenee shee* [*daoine sidhe*] (fairy people).

Who are they? "Fallen angels who were not good enough to be saved, nor bad enough to be lost," say the peasantry. "The gods of the earth," says the Book of Armagh. "The gods of pagan Ireland," say the Irish antiquarians, "the *Tuatha De Danān*, who, when no longer worshipped and fed with offerings, dwindled away in the popular imagination, and now are only a few spans high."

And they will tell you, in proof, that the names of fairy chiefs are the names of old *Danān* heroes, and the places where they especially gather together, *Danān* burying-places, and that the *Tuatha De Danān* used also to be called the *slooa-shee* [*sheagh sidhe*] (the fairy host), or *Marcra shee* (the fairy cavalcade).

On the other hand, there is much evidence to prove them fallen angels. Witness the nature of the creatures, their caprice, their way of being good to the good and evil to the evil, having every charm but conscience—consistency. Beings so quickly offended that you must not speak much about them at all, and never call them anything but the "gentry", or else *daoine maithe*, which in English means good people, yet so easily pleased, they will do their best to keep misfortune away from you, if you leave a little milk for them on the window-sill over night. On the whole, the popular belief tells us most about them, telling us how they fell, and yet were not lost, because their evil was wholly without malice.

Are they "the gods of the earth"? Perhaps! Many poets, and all mystic and occult writers, in all ages and countries, have declared that behind the visible are chains on chains of conscious beings, who are not of heaven but of the earth, who have no inherent form but change according to their whim, or the mind that sees them. You cannot lift your hand without influencing and being influenced by hoards. The visible world is merely their skin. In dreams we go amongst them, and play with them, and combat with them. They are, perhaps, human souls in the crucible—these creatures of whim.

Do not think the fairies are always little. Everything is capricious about them, even their size. They seem to take what size or shape pleases them. Their chief occupations are feasting, fighting, and making love, and playing the most beautiful music. They have only one industrious person amongst them, the *lepracaun*—the shoemaker. Perhaps they wear their shoes out with dancing. Near the village of Ballisodare is a little woman who lived amongst them seven years. When she came home she had no toes—she had danced them off.

They have three great festivals in the year—May Eve, Midsummer Eve, November Eve. On May Eve, every seventh year, they fight all round, but mostly on the "Plain-a-Bawn" (wherever that is), for the harvest, for the best ears of grain belong to them. An old man told me he saw them fight once; they tore the thatch off a house in the midst of it all. Had anyone else been near they would merely have seen a great wind whirling everything into the air as it passed. When the wind makes the straws and leaves whirl as it passes, that is the fairies, and the peasantry take off their hats and say, "God bless them".

On Midsummer Eve, when the bonfires are lighted on every hill in honour of St John, the fairies are at their gayest, and sometimes steal away beautiful mortals to be their brides.

On November Eve they are at their gloomiest, for according to the old Gaelic reckoning, this is the first night of winter. This night they dance with the ghosts, and the *pooka* is abroad, and witches make their spells, and girls set a table with food in the name of the devil, that the fetch of their future lover may come through the window and eat of the food. After November Eve the blackberries are no longer wholesome, for the *pooka* has spoiled them.

When they are angry they paralyse men and cattle with their fairy darts.

When they are gay they sing. Many a poor girl has heard them, and pined away and died, for love of that singing. Plenty of the old beautiful tunes of Ireland are only their music, caught up by eavesdroppers. No wise peasant would hum "The Pretty Girl milking the Cow" near a fairy rath, for they are jealous, and do not like to hear their songs on clumsy mortal lips. Carolan, the last of the Irish bards, slept on a rath, and ever after the fairy tunes ran in his head, and made him the great man he was.

Do they die? Blake saw a fairy's funeral; but in Ireland we say they are immortal.

The Fairies

WILLIAM ALLINGHAM

Up the airy mountain,
  Down the rushy glen,
We daren't go a-hunting
  For fear of little men;
Wee folk, good folk,
  Trooping all together;
Green jacket, red cap,
And white owl's feather!

Down along the rocky shore
  Some make their home,
They live on crispy pancakes
  Of yellow tide-foam;
Some in the reeds
  Of the black mountain lake,
With frogs for their watch-dogs,
  All night awake.

High on the hill-top
  The old King sits;
He is now so old and grey
  He's nigh lost his wits.
With a bridge of white mist
  Columbkill he crosses,
On his stately journeys
  From Slieveleague to Rosses;

Or going up with music
  On cold starry nights,
To sup with the Queen
  Of the gay Northern Lights.

They stole little Bridget
For seven years long;
  When she came down again
  Her friends were all gone.
They took her lightly back,
  Between the night and morrow,
They thought that she was fast asleep,
  But she was dead with sorrow.

They have kept her ever since
  Deep within the lake,
On a bed of flag-leaves,
  Watching till she wake.

By the craggy hill-side,
  Through the mosses bare,
They have planted thorn-trees
  For pleasure here and there.
Is any man so daring
  As dig them up in spite,
He shall find their sharpest thorns
  In his bed at night.

Up the airy mountain,
  Down the rushy glen,
We daren't go a-hunting
  For fear of little men;
Wee folk, good folk,
  Trooping all together;
Green jacket, red cap,
  And white owl's feather!

Frank Martin And The Fairies

WILLIAM CARLETON

Martin was a thin, pale man, when I saw him, of a sickly look, and a constitution naturally feeble. His hair was a light auburn, his beard mostly unshaven, and his hands of a singular delicacy and whiteness, owing, I dare say, as much to the soft and easy nature of his employment as to his infirm health. In everything else he was as sensible, sober, and rational as any other man; but on the topic of fairies, the man's mania was peculiarly strong and immovable. Indeed, I remember that the expression of his eyes was singularly wild and hollow, and his long narrow temples sallow and emaciated.

Now, this man did not lead an unhappy life, nor did the malady he laboured under seem to be productive of either pain or terror to him, although one might be apt to imagine otherwise. On the contrary, he and the fairies maintained the most friendly intimacy, and their dialogues—which I fear were woefully one-sided ones—must have been a source of great pleasure to him, for they were conducted with much mirth and laughter, on his part at least.

"Well, Frank, when did you see the fairies?"

"Whist! there's two dozen of them in the shop (the weaving shop) this minute. There's a little ould fellow sittin' on the top of the sleys, an' all to be rocked while I'm weavin'. The sorrow's in them, but they're the greatest little skamers alive, so they are. See, there's another of them at my dressin' noggin.* Go out o' that, you *shingawn*; or, bad cess to me, if you don't, but I'll lave you a mark. Ha! cut, you thief you!"

"Frank, arn't you afeard o' them?"

"Is it me! Arra, what ud' I be afeard o' them for? Sure they have no power over me."

*The dressings are a species of sizy flummery, which is brushed into the yarn to keep the thread round and even, and to prevent it from being frayed by the friction of the reed.

"And why haven't they, Frank?"

"Because I was baptised against them."

"What do you mean by that?"

"Why, the priest that christened me was tould by my father, to put in the proper prayer against the fairies—an' a priest can't refuse it when he's asked—an' he did so. Begorra, it's well for me that he did—(let the tallow alone, you little glutton—see, there's a weeny thief o' them aitin' my tallow)—becaise, you see, it was their intention to make me king o' the fairies."

"Is it possible?"

"Devil a lie in it. Sure you may ax them, an' they'll tell you."

"What size are they, Frank?"

"Oh, little wee fellows, with green coats, an' the purtiest little shoes ever you seen. There's two of them—both ould acquaintances o' mine—runnin' along the yarn-beam. That ould fellow with the bob-wig is called Jim Jam, an' the other chap, with the three-cocked hat, is called Nickey Nick. Nickey plays the pipes. Nickey, give us a tune, or I'll malivogue you—come now, 'Lough Erne Shore'. Whist, now—listen!"

The poor fellow, though weaving as fast as he could all the time, yet bestowed every possible mark of attention to the music, and seemed to enjoy it as much as if it had been real.

But who can tell whether that which we look upon as a privation may not after all be a fountain of increased happiness, greater, perhaps, than any which we ourselves enjoy? I forget who the poet is who says—

"Mysterious are thy laws;
The vision's finer than the view;
Her landscape Nature never drew
So fair as Fancy draws."

Many a time, when a mere child, not more than six or seven years of age, have I gone as far as Frank's weaving-shop, in order, with a heart divided between curiosity and fear, to listen to his conversation with the good people. From morning till night his tongue was going almost as incessantly as his shuttle; and it was well known that at night, whenever he awoke out of his sleep, the first thing he did was to put out his hand, and push them, as it were, off his bed.

"Go out o' this, you thieves, you—go out o' this now, an' let me alone. Nickey, is this any time to be playing the pipes, and me wants to sleep? Go off, now—troth if yez do, you'll see what I'll give yez tomorrow. Sure I'll be makin' new dressin's; and if yez behave decently, maybe I'll lave yez the scrapin' o' the pot. There now. Och! poor things, they're dacent crathurs. Sure they're all gone, barrin' poor Red-cap, that doesn't like to lave me." And then the harmless monomaniac would fall back into what we trust was an innocent slumber.

About this time there was said to have occurred a very remarkable circumstance, which gave poor Frank a vast deal of importance among the neighbours. A man named Frank Thomas, the same in whose house Mickey M'Rorey held the first dance at which I ever saw him, as detailed in a former sketch; this man, I say, had a child sick, but of what complaint I cannot now remember, nor is it of any importance. One of the gables of Thomas's house was built against, or rather into, a Forth or Rath, called Towny, or properly Tonagh Forth. It was said to be haunted by the fairies, and what gave it a character peculiarly wild in my eyes was, that there were on the southern side of it two or three little green mounds, which were said to be the graves of unchristened children, over which it was considered dangerous and unlucky to pass. At all events, the season was mid-summer; and one evening about dusk, during the illness of the child, the noise of a hand-saw was heard upon the Forth. This was considered rather strange, and, after a little time, a few of those who were assembled at Frank Thomas's went to see who it could be that was sawing in such a place, or what they could be sawing at so late an hour, for every one knew that nobody in the whole country about them would dare to cut down the few white-thorns that grew upon the Forth. On going to examine, however, judge of their surprise, when, after surrounding and searching the whole place, they could discover no trace of either saw or sawyer. In fact, with the exception of themselves, there was no one, either natural or supernatural, visible. They then returned to the house, and had scarcely sat down, when it was heard again within ten yards of them. Another examination of the premises took place, but with equal success. Now, however, while standing on the Forth, they heard the sawing in a little hollow, about a hundred and fifty yards below them, which was completely exposed to their view, but they could see nobody. A party of them immediately went down to ascertain, if possible, what this singular noise and invisible labour could mean; but on arriving at the spot, they heard the sawing, to which were now added hammering, and the driving of

17

nails upon the Forth above, whilst those who stood on the Forth continued to hear it in the hollow. On comparing notes, they resolved to send down to Billy Nelson's for Frank Martin, a distance of only about eighty or ninety yards. He was soon on the spot, and without a moment's hesitation solved the enigma.

" 'Tis the fairies," said he. "I see them, and busy crathurs they are."

"But what are they sawing, Frank?"

"They are makin' a child's coffin," he replied; "they have the body already made, an' they're now nailin' the lid together."

That night the child died, and the story goes that on the second evening afterwards, the carpenter who was called upon to make the coffin brought a table out from Thomas's house to the Forth, as a temporary bench; and, it is said, that the sawing and hammering necessary for the completion of his task were precisely the same which had been heard the evening but one before—neither more nor less. I remember the death of the child myself, and the making of its coffin, but I think the story of the supernatural carpenter was not heard in the village for some months after its interment.

Frank had every appearance of a hypochondriac about him. At the time I saw him, he might be about thirty-four years of age, but I do not think, from the debility of his frame and infirm health, that he has been alive for several years. He was an object of considerable interest and curiosity, and often have I been present when he was pointed out to strangers as "the man that could see the good people".

The Priest's Supper

T. CROFTON CROKER

It is said by those who ought to understand such things, that the good people, or the fairies, are some of the angels who were turned out of heaven, and who landed on their feet in this world, while the rest of their companions, who had more sin to sink them, went down farther to a worse place. Be this as it may, there was a merry troop of the fairies, dancing and playing all manner of wild pranks, on a bright moonlight evening towards the end of September. The scene of their merriment was not far distant from Inchegeela, in the west of the county Cork—a poor village, although it had a barrack for soldiers; but great mountains and barren rocks, like those round about it, are enough to strike poverty into any place: however as the fairies can have everything they want for wishing, poverty does not trouble them much, and all their care is to seek out unfrequented nooks and places where it is not likely any one will come to spoil their sport.

On a nice green sod by the river's side were the little fellows dancing in a ring as gaily as may be, with their red caps wagging about at every bound in the moonshine, and so light were these bounds that the lobs of dew, although they trembled under their feet, were not disturbed by their capering. Thus did they carry on their gambols, spinning round and round, and twirling and bobbing and diving, and going through all manner of figures, until one of them chirped out,

> "Cease, cease, with your drumming,
> Here's an end to our mumming;
> By my smell
> I can tell
> A priest this way is coming!"

And away every one of the fairies scampered off as hard as they could, concealing themselves under the green leaves of the lusmore, where, if their little red caps should happen to peep out, they would only look like its crimson bells; and more hid themselves at the shady side of stones and brambles, and others under the bank of the river, and in holes and crannies of one kind or another.

The fairy speaker was not mistaken; for along the road, which was within view of the river, came Father Horrigan on his pony, thinking to himself that as it was so late he would make an end of his journey at the first cabin he came to. According to his determination, he stopped at the dwelling of Dermod Leary, lifted the latch, and entered with "My blessing on all here".

I need not say that Father Horrigan was a welcome guest wherever he went, for no man was more pious or better beloved in the country. Now it was a great trouble to Dermod that he had nothing to offer his reverence for supper as a relish to the potatoes, which "the old woman", for so Dermod called his wife, though she was not much past twenty, had down boiling in a pot over the fire; he thought of the net which he had set in the river, but as it had been there only a short time, the chances were against his finding a fish in it. "No matter," thought Dermod, "there can be no harm in stepping down to try; and maybe, as I want fish for the priest's supper, that one will be there before me."

Down to the river-side went Dermod, and he found in the net as fine a salmon as ever jumped in the bright waters of "the spreading Lee"; but as he was going to take it out, the net was pulled from him, he could not tell how or by whom, and away got the salmon, and went swimming along with the current as gaily as if nothing had happened.

Dermod looked sorrowfully at the wake which the fish had left upon the water, shining like a line of silver in the moonlight, and then, with an angry motion of his right hand, and a stamp of his foot, gave vent to his feelings by muttering, "May bitter bad luck attend you night and day for a blackguard schemer of a salmon, wherever you go! You ought to be ashamed of yourself, if there's any shame in you, to give me the slip after this fashion! And I'm clear in my own mind you'll come to no good, for some kind of evil thing or other helped you—did I not feel it pull the net against me as strong as the devil himself?"

"That's not true for you," said one of the little fairies who had scampered off at the approach of the priest, coming up to Dermod Leary with a whole throng of companions at his heels; "there was only a dozen and a half of us pulling against you."

20

Dermod gazed on the tiny speaker with wonder, who continued, "Make yourself noways uneasy about the priest's supper; for if you will go back and ask him one question from us, there will be as fine a supper as ever was put on a table spread out before him in less than no time."

"I'll have nothing at all to do with you," replied Dermod in a tone of determination; and after a pause he added, "I'm much obliged to you for your offer, sir, but I know better than to sell myself to you, or the like of you, for a supper; and more than that, I know Father Horrigan has more regard for my soul than to wish me to pledge it for ever, out of regard to anything you could put before him—so there's an end of the matter."

The little speaker, with a pertinacity not to be repulsed by Dermod's manner, continued, "Will you ask the priest one civil question for us?"

Dermod considered for some time, and he was right in doing so, but he thought that no one could come to harm out of asking a civil question. "I see no objection to do that same, gentlemen," said Dermod; "but I will have nothing in life to do with your supper—mind that."

"Then," said the little speaking fairy, whilst the rest came crowding after him from all parts, "go and ask Father Horrigan to tell us whether our souls will be saved at the last day, like the souls of good Christians; and if you wish us well, bring back word what he says without delay."

Away went Dermod to his cabin, where he found the potatoes thrown out on the table, and his good woman handing the biggest of them all, a beautiful laughing red apple, smoking like a hard-ridden horse on a frosty night, over to Father Horrigan.

"Please your reverence," said Dermod, after some hesitation, "may I make bold to ask your honour one question?"

"What may that be?" said Father Horrigan.

"Why, then, begging your reverence's pardon for my freedom, it is: If the souls of the good people are to be saved at the last day?"

"Who bid you ask me that question, Leary?" said the priest, fixing his eyes upon him very sternly, which Dermod could not stand before at all.

"I'll tell no lies about the matter, and nothing in life but the truth," said Dermod. "It was the good people themselves who sent me to ask the question, and there they are in thousands down on the bank of the river, waiting for me to go back with the answer."

21

"Go back by all means," said the priest, "and tell them, if they want to know, to come here to me themselves, and I'll answer that or any other question they are pleased to ask with the greatest pleasure in life."

Dermod accordingly returned to the fairies, who came swarming round about him to hear what the priest had said in reply; and Dermod spoke out among them like a bold man as he was: but when they heard that they must go to the priest, away they fled, some here and more there, and some this way and more that, whisking by poor Dermod so fast and in such numbers that he was quite bewildered.

When he came to himself, which was not for a long time, back he went to his cabin, and ate his dry potatoes along with Father Horrigan, who made quite light of the thing; but Dermod could not help thinking it a mighty hard case that his reverence, whose words had the power to banish the fairies at such a rate, should have no sort of relish to his supper, and that the fine salmon he had in the net should have been got away from him in such a manner.

The Fairy Well Of Lagnanay

SAMUEL FERGUSON

Mournfully, sing mournfully—
   "O listen, Ellen, sister dear:
Is there no help at all for me,
   But only ceaseless sigh and tear?
   Why did not he who left me here,
With stolen hope steal memory?
   O listen, Ellen, sister dear,
(Mournfully, sing mournfully)—
   I'll go away to Sleamish hill,
I'll pluck the fairy hawthorn-tree,
   And let the spirits work their will;
   I care not if for good or ill,
So they but lay the memory
   Which all my heart is haunting still!
(Mournfully, sing mournfully)—
   The Fairies are a silent race,
   And pale as lily flowers to see;
   I care not for a blanched face,
   For wandering in a dreaming place,
So I but banish memory:—
   I wish I were with Anna Grace!"
Mournfully, sing mournfully!

Hearken to my tale of woe—
   'Twas thus to weeping Ellen Con,
Her sister said in accents low,

Her only sister, Una bawn:
'Twas in their bed before the dawn,
And Ellen answered sad and slow,—
  "Oh Una, Una, be not drawn
(Hearken to my tale of woe)—
  To this unholy grief I pray,
Which makes me sick at heart to know,
  And I will help you if I may:
  —The Fairy Well of Lagnanay—
Lie nearer me, I tremble so,—
  Una, I've heard wise women say
(Hearken to my tale of woe)—
    That if before the dews arise,
True maiden in its icy flow
  With pure hand bathe her bosom thrice,
  Three lady-brackens pluck likewise,
And three times round the fountain go,
  She straight forgets her tears and sighs."
Hearken to my tale of woe!

All, alas! and well-away!
  "Oh, sister Ellen, sister sweet,
Come with me to the hill I pray,
  And I will prove that blessed freet!"
  They rose with soft and silent feet,
They left their mother where she lay,
  Their mother and her care discreet,
(All, alas and well-away!)
  And soon they reached the Fairy Well,
The mountain's eye, clear, cold and grey,
  Wide open in the dreary fell:
  How long they stood 'twere vain to tell,
At last upon the point of day,
  Bawn Una bares her bosom's swell,
(All, alas and well-away!)

24

Thrice o'er her shrinking breasts she laves
The gliding glance that will not stay
   Of subtly-streaming fairy waves:—
   And now the charm three brackens craves,
She plucks them in their fring'd array:—
   Now round the well her fate she braves,
All, alas! and well-away!

Save us all from Fairy thrall!
   Ellen sees her face the rim
Twice and thrice, and that is all—
   Fount and hill and maiden swim
   All together melting dim!
"Una! Una!" thou may'st call,
   Sister sad! but lith or limb
(Save us all from Fairy thrall!)
   Never again of Una bawn,
Where now she walks in dreamy hall,
   Shall eye of mortal look upon!
   Oh! can it be the guard was gone,
The better guard than shield or wall?
   Who knows on earth save Jurlagh Daune?
(Save us all from Fairy thrall!)
   Behold the banks are green and bare,
No pit is here wherein to fall:
   Aye—at the fount you well may stare,
   But nought save pebbles smooth is there,
And small straws twirling one and all.
   Hie thee home, and be thy pray'r,
Save us all from Fairy thrall.

Teig O'Kane (Tadhg O Cáthán) and the Corpse*

Literally Translated from the Irish by Douglas Hyde

[I found it hard to place Mr Douglas Hyde's magnificent story. Among the ghosts or the fairies? It is among the fairies on the grounds that all these ghosts and bodies were in no manner ghosts and bodies, but *pishogues*—fairy spells. One often hears of these visions of Ireland. I have met a man who had lived a wild life like the man in the story, till a vision came to him in County—— one dark night—in no way so terrible a vision as this, but sufficient to change his whole character. He will not go out at night. If you speak to him suddenly he trembles. He has grown timid and strange. He went to the bishop and was sprinkled with holy water. "It may have come as a warning," said the bishop; "yet great theologians are of opinion that no man ever saw an apparition, for no man would survive it."—ED.]

There was once a grown-up lad in the County Leitrim, and he was strong and lively, and the son of a rich farmer. His father had plenty of money, and he did not spare it on the son. Accordingly, when the boy grew up he liked sport better than work, and, as his father had no other children, he loved this one so much that he allowed him to do in everything just as it pleased himself. He was very extravagant, and he used to scatter the gold money as another person would scatter the white. He was seldom to be found at home, but if there was a fair, or a race, or a gathering within ten miles of him, you were dead certain to find him there. And he seldom spent a night in his father's house, but he used to be always out rambling, and, like Shawn Bwee long ago, there was——

---

*None of Mr Hyde's stories here given have been published before. They will be printed in the original Irish in his forthcoming *Leabhar Sgeulaigheachta* (Gill, Dublin).

26

"grádh gach cailin i mbrollach a léine,"

"the love of every girl in the breast of his shirt", and it's many's the kiss he got and he gave, for he was very handsome, and there wasn't a girl in the country but would fall in love with him, only for him to fasten his two eyes on her, and it was for that someone made this *rann* on him—

> "Feuch an rógaire 'g iarraidh póige,
>   Ni h-iongantas mór é a bheith mar atá
> Ag leanamhaint a gcómhnuidhe d'árnán na gráineóige
>   Anuas 's anios 's nna chodladh 'sa' lá."

i.e.—

> "Look at the rogue, its for kisses he's rambling,
>   It isn't much wonder, for that was his way;
> He's like an old hedgehog, at night he'll be scrambling
>   From this place to that, but he'll sleep in the day."

At last he became very wild and unruly. He wasn't to be seen day nor night in his father's house, but always rambling or going on his *kailee* (night-visit) from place to place and from house to house, so that the old people used to shake their heads and say to one another, "it's easy seen what will happen to the land when the old man dies; his son will run through it in a year, and it won't stand him that long itself".

He used to be always gambling and card-playing and drinking, but his father never minded his bad habits, and never punished him. But it happened one day that the old man was told that the son had ruined the character of a girl in the neighbourhood, and he was greatly angry, and he called the son to him, and said to him, quietly and sensibly—"Avic," says he, "you know I loved you greatly up to this, and I never stopped you from doing your choice thing whatever it was, and I kept plenty of money with you, and I always hoped to leave you the house and land, and all I had after myself would be gone; but I heard a story of you today that has disgusted me with you. I cannot tell you the grief that I felt when I heard such a thing of you, and I tell you now plainly that unless you marry that girl I'll leave house and land and everything to my brother's son. I never could leave it to anyone

27

who would make so bad a use of it as you do yourself, deceiving women and coaxing girls. Settle with yourself now whether you'll marry that girl and get my land as a fortune with her, or refuse to marry her and give up all that was coming to you; and tell me in the morning which of the two things you have chosen."

"Och! *Domnoo Sheery!* father, you wouldn't say that to me, and I such a good son as I am. Who told you I wouldn't marry the girl?" says he.

But his father was gone, and the lad knew well enough that he would keep his word too; and he was greatly troubled in his mind, for as quiet and as kind as the father was, he never went back of a word that he had once said, and there wasn't another man in the country who was harder to bend than he was.

The boy did not know rightly what to do. He was in love with the girl indeed, and he hoped to marry her some time or other, but he would much sooner have remained another while as he was, and follow on at his old tricks—drinking, sporting and playing cards; and, along with that, he was angry that his father should order him to marry, and should threaten him if he did not do it.

"Isn't my father a great fool," says he to himself. "I was ready enough, and only too anxious, to marry Mary; and now since he threatened me, faith I've a great mind to let it go another while."

His mind was so much excited that he remained between two notions as to what he should do. He walked out into the night at last to cool his heated blood, and went on to the road. He lit a pipe, and as the night was fine he walked and walked on, until the quick pace made him begin to forget his trouble. The night was bright, and the moon half full. There was not a breath of wind blowing, and the air was calm and mild. He walked on for nearly three hours, when he suddenly remembered that it was late in the night, and time for him to turn. "Musha! I think I forgot myself," says he; "it must be near twelve o'clock now."

The word was hardly out of his mouth, when he heard the sound of many voices, and the trampling of feet on the road before him. "I don't know who can be out so late at night as this, and on such a lonely road," said he to himself.

He stood listening, and he heard the voices of many people talking through other, but he could not understand what they were saying. "Oh, wirra!" says he, "I'm afraid. It's not Irish or English they have; it can't be they're Frenchmen!" He went on a couple of yards farther, and he saw well enough by the light of the moon a band of little people coming towards him, and they were carrying something big and heavy with them. "Oh, murder!" says he to himself, "sure it can't be that they're the good people that's in it!" Every *rib* of hair that was on his head stood up, and there fell a shaking on his bones, for he saw that they were coming to him fast.

He looked at them again, and perceived that there were about twenty little men in it, and there was not a man at all of them higher than about three feet or three feet and a half, and some of them were grey, and seemed very old. He looked again, but he could not make out what was the heavy thing they were carrying until they came up to him, and then they all stood round about him. They threw the heavy thing down on the road, and he saw on the spot that it was a dead body.

He became as cold as the Death, and there was not a drop of blood running in his veins when an old little grey *maneen* came up to him and said, "Isn't it lucky we met you, Teig O'Kane?"

Poor Teig could not bring out a word at all, nor open his lips, if he were to get the word for it, and so he gave no answer.

"Teig O'Kane," said the little grey man again, "isn't it timely you met us?"

Teig could not answer him.

"Teig O'Kane," says he, "the third time, isn't it lucky and timely that we met you?"

But Teig remained silent, for he was afraid to return an answer, and his tongue was as if it was tied to the roof of his mouth.

The little grey man turned to his companions, and there was joy in his bright little eye. "And now," says he, "Teig O'Kane hasn't a word, we can do with him what we please. Teig, Teig," says he, "you're living a bad life, and we can make a slave of you now, and you cannot withstand us, for there's no use in trying to go against us. Lift that corpse."

Teig was so frightened that he was only able to utter the two words, "I won't;" for as frightened as he was, he was obstinate and stiff, the same as ever.

"Teig O'Kane won't lift the corpse," said the little *maneen*, with a wicked little laugh, for all the world like the breaking of a *lock* or dry *kippeens*, and with a little harsh voice like the striking of a cracked bell. "Teig O'Kane won't lift the corpse—make him lift it;" and before the word was out of his mouth they had all gathered round poor Teig, and they all talking and laughing through other.

Teig tried to run from them, but they followed him, and a man of them stretched out his foot before him as he ran, so that Teig was thrown in a heap on the road. Then before he could rise up the fairies caught him, some by the hands and some by the feet, and they held him tight, in a way that he could not stir,

29

with his face against the ground. Six or seven of them raised the body then, and pulled it over to him, and left it down on his back. The breast of the corpse was squeezed against Teig's back and shoulders, and the arms of the corpse were thrown around Teig's neck. Then they stood back from him a couple of yards, and let him get up. He rose, foaming at the mouth and cursing, and he shook himself, thinking to throw the corpse off his back. But his fear and his wonder were great when he found that the two arms had a tight hold round his own neck, and that the two legs were squeezing his hips firmly, and that, however strongly he tried, he could not throw it off, any more than a horse can throw off its saddle. He was terribly frightened then, and he thought he was lost. "Ochone! for ever," said he to himself, "it's the bad life I'm leading that has given the good people this power over me. I promise to God and Mary, Peter and Paul, Patrick and Bridget, that I'll mend my ways for as long as I have to live, if I come clear out of this danger—and I'll marry the girl."

The little grey man came up to him again, and said he to him, "Now, Teig*een*," says he, "you didn't lift the body when I told you to lift it, and see how you were made to lift it; perhaps when I tell you to bury it you won't bury it until you're made to bury it!"

"Anything at all that I can do for your honour," said Teig, "I'll do it," for he was getting sense already, and if it had not been for the great fear that was on him, he never would have let that civil word slip out of his mouth.

The little man laughed a sort of laugh again. "You're getting quiet now, Teig," says he. "I'll go bail but you'll be quiet enough before I'm done with you. Listen to me now, Teig O'Kane, and if you don't obey me in all I'm telling you to do, you'll repent it. You must carry with you this corpse that is on your back to Teampoll-Démus, and you must bring it into the church with you, and make a grave for it in the very middle of the church, and you must raise up the flags and put them down again the very same way, and you must carry the clay out of the church and leave the place as it was when you came, so that no one could know that there had been anything changed. But that's not all. Maybe that the body won't be allowed to be buried in the church; perhaps some other man has the bed, and, if so, it's likely he won't share it with this one. If you don't get leave to bury it in Teampoll-Démus, you must carry it to Carrick-fhad-vic-Orus, and bury it in the churchyard there; and if you don't get it into that place, take it with you to Teampoll-Ronan; and if that churchyard is closed on you, take it to Imlogue-Fada;

and if you're not able to bury it there, you've no more to do than to take it to Kill-Breedya, and you can bury it there without hindrance. I cannot tell you what one of those churches is the one where you will have leave to bury that corpse under the clay, but I know that it will be allowed you to bury him at some church or other of them. If you do this work rightly, we will be thankful to you, and you will have no cause to grieve; but if you are slow or lazy, believe me we shall take satisfaction of you."

When the grey little man had done speaking, his comrades laughed and clapped their hands together. "Glic! Glic! Hwee! Hwee!" they all cried; "go on, go on, you have eight hours before you till daybreak, and if you haven't this man buried before the sun rises, you're lost." They struck a fist and a foot behind on him, and drove him on in the road. He was obliged to walk, and to walk fast, for they gave him no rest.

He thought himself that there was not a wet path, or a dirty *boreen*, or a crooked contrary road in the whole county, that he had not walked that night. The night was at times very dark, and whenever there would come a cloud across the moon he could see nothing, and then he used often to fall. Sometimes he was hurt, and sometimes he escaped, but he was obliged always to rise on the moment and to hurry on. Sometimes the moon would break out clearly, and then he would look behind him and see the little people following his back. And he heard them speaking amongst themselves, talking and crying out, and screaming like a flock of sea-gulls; and if he was to save his soul he never understood as much as one word of what they were saying.

He did not know how far he had walked, when at last one of them cried out to him, "Stop here!" He stood, and they all gathered round him.

"Do you see those withered trees over there?" says the old boy to him again. "Teampoll Démus is among those trees, and you must go in there by yourself, for we cannot follow you or go with you. We must remain here. Go on boldly."

Teig looked from him, and he saw a high wall that was in places half broken down, and an old grey church on the inside of the wall, and about a dozen withered old trees scattered here and there round it. There was neither leaf nor twig on any of them, but their bare crooked branches were stretched out like the arms of an angry man when he threatens. He had no help for it, but was obliged to go forward. He was a couple of hundred yards from the church, but he walked on, and never looked behind him until he came to the gate of the churchyard. The old gate was thrown down, and he had no difficulty in entering. He turned then to see if any of the little people were following him, but there came a cloud over the moon, and the night became so dark that he could see nothing. He went into the churchyard, and he walked up the old grassy pathway leading to the church. When he reached the door, he found it locked. The door was large and strong, and he did not know what to do. At last he drew out his knife with difficulty, and stuck it in the wood to try if it were not rotten, but it was not.

"Now," said he to himself, "I have no more to do; the door is shut, and I can't open it."

Before the words were rightly shaped in his own mind, a voice in his ear said to him, "Search for the key on the top of the door, or on the wall."

He started. "Who is that speaking to me?" he cried, turning round; but he saw no one. The voice said in his ear again, "Search for the key on the top of the door, or on the wall."

"What's that?" said he, and the sweat running from his forehead; "who spoke to me?"

"It's I, the corpse, that spoke to you!" said the voice.

"Can you talk?" said Teig.

"Now and again," said the corpse.

Teig searched for the key, and he found it on the top of the wall. He was too much frightened to say any more, but he opened the door wide, and as quickly as he could, and he went in, with the corpse on his back. It was as dark as pitch inside, and poor Teig began to shake and tremble.

"Light the candle," said the corpse.

Teig put his hand in his pocket, as well as he was able, and drew out a flint and steel. He struck a spark out of it, and lit a burnt rag he had in his pocket. He blew it until it made a flame, and he looked round him. The church was very ancient, and part of the wall was broken down. The windows were blown in or cracked, and the timber of the seats was rotten. There were six or seven old iron candlesticks left there still, and in one of these candlesticks Teig found the stump of an old candle, and he lit it. He was still looking round him on the strange and horrid place in which he found himself, when the cold corpse whispered in his ear, "Bury me now, bury me now; there is a spade and turn the ground." Teig looked from him, and he saw a spade lying beside the altar. He took it up, and he placed the blade under a flag that was in the middle of the aisle, and leaning all his weight on the

32

handle of the spade, he raised it. When the first flag was raised it was not hard to raise the others near it, and he moved three or four of them out of their places. The clay that was under them was soft and easy to dig, but he had not thrown up more than three or four shovelfuls, when he felt the iron touch something soft like flesh. He threw up three or four more shovelfuls from around it, and then he saw that it was another body that was buried in the same place.

"I am afraid I'll never be allowed to bury the two bodies in the same hole," said Teig, in his own mind. "You corpse, there on my back," says he, "will you be satisfied if I bury you down here?" But the corpse never answered him a word.

"That's a good sign," said Teig to himself. "Maybe he's getting quiet," and he thrust the spade down in the earth again. Perhaps he hurt the flesh of the other body, for the dead man that was buried there stood up in the grave, and shouted an awful shout. "Hoo! hoo!! hoo!!! Go! go!! go!!! or you're a dead, dead, dead man!" And then he fell back in the grave again. Teig said afterwards, that of all the wonderful things he saw that night, that was the most awful to him. His hair stood upright on his head like the bristles of a pig, the cold sweat ran off his face, and then came a tremor over all his bones, until he thought that he must fall.

But after a while he became bolder, when he saw that the second corpse remained lying quietly there, and he threw in the clay on it again, and he smoothed it overhead, and he laid down the flags carefully as they had been before. "It can't be that he'll rise up any more," said he.

He went down the aisle a little farther, and drew near to the door, and began raising the flags again, looking for another bed for the corpse on his back. He took up three or four flags and put them aside, and then he dug the clay. He was not long digging until he laid bare an old woman without a thread upon her but her shirt. She was more lively than the first corpse, for he had scarcely taken any of the clay away from about her, when she sat up and began to cry, "Ho, you *bodach* (clown)! Ha, you *bodach*! Where has he been that he got no bed?"

Poor Teig drew back, and when she found that she was getting no answer, she closed her eyes gently, lost her vigour and fell back quietly and slowly under the clay. Teig did to her as he had done to the man—he threw the clay back on her, and left the flags down overhead.

He began digging again near the door, but before he had thrown up more than a couple of shovelfuls, he noticed a man's hand laid bare by the spade. "By my soul, I'll go no farther, then," said he to himself; "what use is it for me?" And he

33

threw the clay in again on it, and settled the flags as they had been before.

He left the church then, and his heart was heavy enough, but he shut the door and locked it, and left the key where he found it. He sat down on a tombstone that was near the door, and began thinking. He was in great doubt what he should do. He laid his face between his two hands, and cried for grief and fatigue, since he was dead certain at this time that he never would come home alive. He made another attempt to loosen the hands of the corpse that were squeezed round his neck, but they were as tight as if they were clamped; and the more he tried to loosen them, the tighter they squeezed him. He was going to sit down once more, when the cold, horrid lips of the dead man said to him, "Carrick-fhad-vic-Orus," and he remembered the command of the good people to bring the corpse with him to that place if he should be unable to bury it where he had been.

He rose up, and looked about him. "I don't know the way," he said.

As soon as he had uttered the word, the corpse stretched out suddenly its left hand that had been tightened round his neck, and kept it pointing out, showing him the road he ought to follow. Teig went in the direction that the fingers were stretched, and passed out of the churchyard. He found himself on an old rutty, stony road, and he stood still again, not knowing where to turn. The corpse stretched out its bony hand a second time, and pointed out to him another road—not the road by which he had come when approaching the old church. Teig followed that road, and whenever he came to a path or road meeting it, the corpse always stretched out its hand and pointed with its fingers, showing him the way he was to take.

Many was the cross-road he turned down, and many was the crooked *boreen* he walked, until he saw from him an old burying-ground at last, beside the road, but there was neither church nor chapel nor any other building in it. The corpse squeezed him tightly, and he stood. "Bury me, bury me in the burying-ground," said the voice.

Teig drew over towards the old burying-place, and he was not more than about twenty yards from it, when, raising his eyes, he saw hundreds and hundreds of ghosts—men, women, and children—sitting on the top of the wall round about, or standing on the inside of it, or running backwards and forwards, and pointing at him, while he could see their mouths opening and shutting as if they were speaking, though he heard no word, nor any sound amongst them at all.

He was afraid to go forward, so he stood where he was, and the moment he stood, all the ghosts became quiet, and ceased moving. Then Teig understood that it was trying to keep him from going in, that they were. He walked a couple of yards forwards, and immediately the whole crowd rushed together towards the spot to which he was moving, and they stood so thickly together that it seemed to him that he never could break through them, even though he had a mind to try. But he had no mind to try it. He went back broken and dispirited, and when he had gone a couple of hundred yards from the burying-ground, he stood again, for he did not know what way he was to go. He heard the voice of the corpse in his ear, saying "Teampoll-Ronan", and the skinny hand was stretched out again, pointing him out the road.

As tired as he was, he had to walk, and the road was neither short nor even. The night was darker than ever, and it was difficult to make his way. Many was the toss he got, and many a bruise they left on his body. At last he saw Teampoll-Ronan from him in the distance, standing in the middle of the burying-ground. He moved over towards it, and thought he was all right and safe, when he saw no ghosts nor anything else on the wall, and he thought he would never be hindered now from leaving his load off him at last. He moved over to the gate, but as he was passing in, he tripped on the threshold. Before he could recover himself, something that he could not see seized him by the neck, by the hands, and by the feet, and bruised him, and shook him, and choked him, until he was nearly dead; and at last he was lifted up, and carried more than a hundred yards from that place, and then thrown down in an old dyke, with the corpse still clinging to him.

He rose up, bruised and sore, but feared to go near the place again, for he had seen nothing the time he was thrown down and carried away.

"You corpse, up on my back," said he, "shall I go over again to the churchyard?"—but the corpse never answered him. "That's a sign you don't wish me to try it again," said Teig.

He was now in great doubt as to what he ought to do, when the corpse spoke in his ear, and said, "Imlogue-Fada."

"Oh, murder!" said Teig, "must I bring you there? If you keep me long walking like this, I tell you I'll fall under you."

He went on, however, in the direction the corpse pointed out to him. He could not have told, himself, how long he had been going, when the dead man behind suddenly squeezed him, and said, "There!"

35

Teig looked from him, and he saw a little low wall, that was so broken down in places that it was no wall at all. It was in a great wide field, in from the road; and only for three or four great stones at the corners, that were more like rocks than stones, there was nothing to show that there was either graveyard or burying-ground there.

"Is this Imlogue-Fada? Shall I bury you here?" said Teig.

"Yes," said the voice.

"But I see no grave or gravestone, only this pile of stones," said Teig.

The corpse did not answer, but stretched out its long fleshless hand, to show Teig the direction in which he was to go. Teig went on accordingly, but he was greatly terrified, for he remembered what had happened to him at the last place. He went on, "with his heart in his mouth", as he said himself afterwards; but when he came to within fifteen or twenty yards of the little low square wall, there broke out a flash of lightning, bright yellow and red, with blue streaks in it, and went round about the wall in one course, and it swept by as fast as the swallow in the clouds, and the longer Teig remained looking at it the faster it went, till at last it became like a bright ring of flame round the old graveyard, which no one could pass without being burnt by it. Teig never saw, from the time he was born, and never saw afterwards, so wonderful or so splendid a sight as that was. Round went the flame, white and yellow and blue sparks leaping out from it as it went, and although at first it had been no more than a thin, narrow line, it increased slowly until it was at last a great broad band, and it was continually getting broader and higher, and throwing out more brilliant sparks, till there was never a colour on the ridge of the earth that was not to be seen in that fire; and lightning never shone and flame never flamed that was so shining and so bright as that.

Teig was amazed; he was half dead with fatigue, and he had no courage left to approach the wall. There fell a mist over his eyes, and there came a *soorawn* in his head, and he was obliged to sit down upon a great stone to recover himself. He could see nothing but the light, and he could hear nothing but the whirr of it as it shot round the paddock faster than a flash of lightning.

As he sat there on the stone, the voice whispered once more in his ear, "Kill-Breedya"; and the dead man squeezed him so tightly that he cried out. He rose again, sick, tired, and trembling, and went forwards as he was directed. The wind was cold, and the road was bad, and the load upon his back was heavy, and the night was dark, and he himself was nearly worn out, and if he had had very

36

much farther to go he must have fallen dead under his burden.

At last the corpse stretched out its hand, and said to him, "Bury me there."

"This is the last burying-place," said Teig in his own mind; "and the little grey man said I'd be allowed to bury him in some of them, so it must be this; it can't be but they'll let him in here."

The first faint streak of the *ring of day* was appearing in the east, and the clouds were beginning to catch fire, but it was darker than ever, for the moon was set, and there were no stars.

"Make haste, make haste!" said the corpse; and Teig hurried forward as well as he could to the graveyard, which was a little place on a bare hill, with only a few graves in it. He walked boldly in through the open gate, and nothing touched him, nor did he either hear or see anything. He came to the middle of the ground, and then stood up and looked round him for a spade or shovel to make a grave. As he was turning round and searching, he suddenly perceived what startled him greatly—a newly-dug grave right before him. He moved over to it, and looked down, and there at the bottom he saw a black coffin. He clambered down into the hole and lifted the lid, and found that (as he thought it would be) the coffin was empty. He had hardly mounted up out of the hole, and was standing on the brink, when the corpse, which had clung to him for more than eight hours, suddenly relaxed its hold of his neck, and loosened its shins from round his hips, and sank down with a *plop* into the open coffin.

Teig fell down on his two knees at the brink of the grave, and gave thanks to God. He made no delay then, but pressed down the coffin lid in its place, and threw in the clay over it with his two hands; and when the grave was filled up, he stamped and leaped on it with his feet, until it was firm and hard, and then he left the place.

The sun was fast rising as he finished his work, and the first thing he did was to return to the road, and look out for a house to rest himself in. He found an inn at last, and lay down upon a bed there, and slept till night. Then he rose up and ate a little, and fell asleep again till morning. When he awoke in the morning he hired a horse and rode home. He was more than twenty-six miles from home where he was, and he had come all that way with the dead body on his back in one night.

All the people at his own home thought that he must have left the country, and they rejoiced greatly when they saw him come back. Everyone began asking him where he had been, but he would not tell anyone except his father.

He was a changed man from that day. He never drank too much; he never lost his money over cards; and especially he would not take the world and be out late by himself of a dark night.

He was not a fortnight at home until he married Mary, the girl he had been in love with; and it's at their wedding the sport was, and it's he was the happy man from that day forward, and it's all I wish that we may be as happy as he was.

GLOSSARY: *Rann*, a stanza; *kailee* (*céilidhe*), a visit in the evening; *wirra* (*a mhuire*), "Oh, Mary!" an exclamation like the French *dame*; *rib*, a single hair (in Irish, *ribe*); *a lock* (*glac*), a bundle or wisp, or a little share of anything; *kippeen* (*cipín*), a rod or twig; *boreen* (*bóithrin*), a lane; *bodach*, a clown; *soorawn* (*suarán*), vertigo. *Avic* (*a Mhic*) = my son, or rather, Oh, son. Mic is the vocative of Mac.

Paddy Corcoran's Wife

WILLIAM CARLETON

Paddy Corcoran's wife was for several years afflicted with a kind of complaint which nobody could properly understand. She was sick, and she was not sick; she was well, and she was not well; she was as ladies wish to be who love their lords, and she was not as such ladies wish to be. In fact nobody could tell what the matter with her was. She had a gnawing at the heart which came heavily upon her husband; for, with the help of God, a keener appetite than the same gnawing amounted to could not be met with of a summer's day. The poor woman was delicate beyond belief, and had no appetite at all, so she hadn't barring a little relish for a mutton-chop, or a "staik", or a bit o' mait, anyway; for sure, God help her! she hadn't the laist inclination for the dhry pratie, or the dhrop o' sour buttermilk along wid it, especially as she was so poorly; and, indeed, for a woman in her condition—for, sick as she was, poor Paddy always was made to believe her in *that* condition—but God's will be done! she didn't care. A pratie an' a grain o' salt was a welcome to her—glory be to his name!—as the best roast an' boiled that ever was dressed; and why not? There was one comfort: she wouldn't be long wid him—long troublin' him; it matthered little what she got; but sure she knew herself, that from the gnawin' at her heart, she could never do good widout the little bit o' mait now and then; an', sure, if her own husband begridged it to her, who else had she a better right to expect it from?

Well, as we have said, she lay a bedridden invalid for long enough, trying doctors and quacks of all sorts, sexes, and sizes, and all without a farthing's benefit, until, at the long run, poor Paddy was nearly brought to the last pass in striving to keep her in "the bit o' mait". The seventh year was now on the point of closing, when, one harvest day, as she lay bemoaning her hard condition, on her bed beyond the kitchen fire, a little weeshy woman, dressed in a neat red cloak, comes in, and sitting down by the hearth, says:

"Well, Kitty Corcoran, you've had a long lair of it there on the broad o' yer back for seven years, an' you're jist as far from bein' cured as ever."

"Mavrone, ay" said the other; "in throth that's what I was this minnit thinkin' ov, and a sorrowful thought it's to me."

"It's yer own fau't, thin," says the little woman; "an', indeed, for that matter, it's yer fau't that ever you wor there at all."

"Arra, how is that?" asked Kitty; "sure I wouldn't be here if I could help it? Do you think it's a comfort or a pleasure to me to be sick and bedridden?"

"No," said the other, "I do not; but I'll tell you the truth: for the last seven years you have been annoying US. I am one o' the good people; an' as I have a regard for you, I'm come to let you know the raison why you've been sick so long as you are. For all the time you've been ill, if you'll take the thrubble to remimber, your childhre threwn out yer dirty wather afther dusk an' before sunrise, at the very time we're passin' yer door, which we pass twice a-day. Now, if you avoid this, if you throw it out in a different place, an' at a different time, the complaint you have will lave you: so will the gnawin' at the heart; an' you'll be as well as ever you wor. If you don't follow this advice, why, remain as you are, an' all the art o' man can't cure you." She then bade her good-bye, and disappeared.

Kitty, who was glad to be cured on such easy terms, immediately complied with the injunction of the fairy; and the consequence was, that the next day she found herself in as good health as ever she enjoyed during her life.

Cusheen Loo

Translated From The Irish By J. J. Callanan

[This song is supposed to have been sung by a young bride, who was forcibly detained in one of those forts which are so common in Ireland, and to which the good people are very fond of resorting. Under pretence of hushing her child to rest, she retired to the outside margin of the fort, and addressed the burthen of her song to a young woman whom she saw at a short distance, and whom she requested to inform her husband of her condition, and to desire him to bring the steel knife to dissolve the enchantment.]

> Sleep, my child! for the rustling trees,
> Stirr'd by the breath of summer breeze,
> And fairy songs of sweetest note,
> Around us gently float.
>
> Sleep! for the weeping flowers have shed
> Their fragrant tears upon thy head,
> The voice of love hath sooth'd thy rest,
> And thy pillow is a mother's breast.
>   Sleep, my child!
>
> Weary hath pass'd the time forlorn,
> Since to your mansion I was borne,
> Tho' bright the feast of its airy halls,
> And the voice of mirth resounds from its walls.
>   Sleep, my child!

Full many a maid and blooming bride
Within that splendid dome abide,—
And many a hoar and shrivell'd sage,
And many a matron bow'd with age.
                    Sleep, my child!

Oh! thou who hearest this song of fear,
To the mourner's home these tidings bear.
Bid him bring the knife of the magic blade,
At whose lightning-flash the charm will fade.
                    Sleep, my child!

Haste! for tomorrow's sun will see
The hateful spell renewed for me;
Nor can I from that home depart,
Till life shall leave my withering heart.
                    Sleep, my child!

Sleep, my child! for the rustling trees,
Stirr'd by the breath of summer breeze,
And fairy songs of sweetest note,
Around us gently float.

The White Trout; A Legend of Cong

S. LOVER

There was wanst upon a time, long ago, a beautiful lady that lived in a castle upon the lake beyant, and they say she was promised to a king's son, and they wor to be married, when all of a sudden he was murthered, the crathur (Lord help us), and threwn into the lake above, and so, of course, he couldn't keep his promise to the fair lady—and more's the pity.

Well, the story goes that she went out iv her mind, bekase av loosin' the king's son—for she was tendher-hearted, God help her, like the rest iv us!—and pined away after him, until at last, no one about seen her, good or bad; and the story wint that the fairies took her away.

Well, sir, in coorse o' time, the White Throut, God bless it, was seen in the sthrame beyant, and sure the people didn't know what to think av the crathur, seein' as how a *white* throut was never heard av afor, nor since; and years upon years the throut was there, just where you seen it this blessed minit, longer nor I can tell—aye throth, and beyant the memory o' th' ouldest in the village.

At last the people began to think it must be a fairy; for what else could it be?—and no hurt nor harm was iver put an the white throut, until some wicked sinners of sojers kem to these parts, and laughed at all the people, and gibed and jeered them for thinkin' o' the likes; and one o' them in partic'lar (bad luck to him; God forgi' me for saying it!) swore he'd catch the throut and ate it for his dinner—the blackguard!

Well, what would you think o' the villainy of the sojer? Sure enough he cotch the throut, and away wid him home, and puts an the fryin'-pan, and into it he pitches the purty little thing. The throut squeeled all as one as a christian crathur, and, my dear, you'd think the sojer id split his sides laughin'—for he was a harden'd villian; and when he thought one side was done, he turns it over to fry the other; and, what would you think, but the divil a taste of a burn was an it all at all; and

43

sure the sojer thought it was a *quare* throut that could not be briled. "But," says he, "I'll give it another turn by-and-by," little thinkin' what was in store for him, the haythen.

Well, when he thought that side was done he turns it agin, and lo and behould you, the divil a taste more done that side was nor the other. "Bad luck to me," says the sojer, "but that bates the world," says he; "but I'll thry you agin, my darlint," says he, "as cunnin' as you think yourself;" and so with that he turns it over, but not a sign of the fire was on the purty throut. "Well," says the desperate villain—(for sure, sir, only he was a desperate villain *entirely*, he might know he was doing a wrong thing, seein' that all his endeavours was no good)—"Well," says he, "my jolly little throut, maybe you're fried enough, though you don't seem over well dress'd; but you may be better than you look, like a singed cat, and a tit-bit afther all," says he; and with that he ups with his knife and fork to taste a piece o' the throut; but, my jew'l, the minit he puts his knife into the fish, there was a murtherin' screech, that you'd think the life id lave you if you hurd it, and away jumps the throut out av the fryin'-pan into the middle o' the flure; and an the spot where it fell, up riz a lovely lady—the beautifullest crathur that eyes ever seen, dressed in white, and a band o' goold in her hair, and a sthrame o' blood runnin' down her arm.

"Look where you cut me, you villain, " says she, and she held out her arm to him—and, my dear, he thought the sight id lave his eyes.

"Couldn't you lave me cool and comfortable in the river where you snared me, and not disturb me in my duty?" says she.

Well, he thrimbled like a dog in a wet sack, and at last he stammered out somethin', and begged for his life, and ax'd her ladyship's pardin, and said he didn't know she was on duty, or he was too good a sojer not to know betther nor to meddle wid her.

"I *was* on duty, then," says the lady; "I was watchin' for my true love that is comin' by wather to me," says she, "an' if he comes while I'm away, an' that I miss iv him, I'll turn you into a pinkeen, and I'll hunt you up and down for evermore, while grass grows or wather runs."

Well the sojer thought the life id lave him, at the thoughts iv his bein' turned into a pinkeen, and begged for mercy; and with that says the lady—

"Renounce your evil coorses," says she, "you villain, or you'll repint it too late;

be a good man for the futher, and go to your duty* reg'lar, and now," says she, "take me back and put me into the river again, where you found me."

"Oh, my lady," says the sojer, "how could I have the heart to drownd a beautiful lady like you?"

But before he could say another word, the lady was vanished, and there he saw the little throut an the ground. Well he put it in a clean plate, and away he runs for the bare life, for fear her lover would come while she was away; and he run, and he run, even till he came to the cave agin, and threw the throut into the river. The minit he did, the wather was as red as blood for a little while, by rayson av the cut, I suppose, until the sthrame washed the stain away; and to this day there's a little red mark an the the throut's side, where it was cut.[†]

Well, sir, from that day out the sojer was an altered man, and reformed his ways, and went to his duty reg'lar, and fasted three times a-week—though it was never fish he tuk an fastin' days, for afther the fright he got, fish id never rest an his stomach—savin' your presence.

But anyhow, he was an altered man, as I said before, and in coorse o' time he left the army, and turned hermit at last; and they say he *used to pray evermore for the soul of the White Throut.*

[These trout stories are common all over Ireland. Many holy wells are haunted by such blessed trout. There is a trout in a well on the border of Lough Gill, Sligo, that some paganish person put once on the gridiron. It carries the marks to this day. Long ago, the saint who sanctified the well put that trout there. Nowadays it is only visible to the pious, who have done due penance.]

---

*The Irish peasant calls his attendance at the confessional "going to his duty".
[†]The fish has really a red spot on its side.

The Fairy Thorn

An Ulster Ballad

SIR SAMUEL FERGUSON

"Get up, our Anna dear, from the weary spinning-wheel;
    For your father's on the hill, and your mother is asleep;
Come up above the crags, and we'll dance a highland-reel
    Around the fairy thorn on the steep."

At Anna Grace's door 'twas thus the maidens cried,
    Three merry maidens fair in kirtles of the green;
And Anna laid the rock and the weary wheel aside,
    The fairest of the four, I ween.

They're glancing through the glimmer of the quiet eve,
    Away in milky wavings of neck and ankle bare;
The heavy-sliding stream in its sleepy song they leave,
    And the crags in the ghostly air:

And linking hand in hand, and singing as they go,
    The maids along the hill-side have ta'en their fearless way,
Till they come to where the rowan trees in lonely beauty grow
    Beside the Fairy Hawthorn grey.

The Hawthorn stands between the ashes tall and slim,
    Like matron with her twin grand-daughters at her knee;
The rowan berries cluster o'er her low head grey and dim
    In ruddy kisses sweet to see.

The merry maidens four have ranged them in a row,
  Between each lovely couple a stately rowan stem,
And away in mazes wavy, like skimming birds they go,
  Oh, never caroll'd bird like them!

But solemn is the silence of the silvery haze
  That drinks away their voices in echoless repose,
And dreamily the evening has still'd the haunted braes,
  And dreamier the gloaming grows.

And sinking one by one, like lark-notes from the sky
  When the falcon's shadow saileth across the open shaw,
Are hush'd the maiden's voices, as cowering down they lie
  In the flutter of their sudden awe.

For, from the air above, the grassy ground beneath,
  And from the mountain-ashes and the old Whitethorn between,
A Power of faint enchantment doth through their beings breathe,
  And they sink down together on the green.

They sink together silent, and stealing side by side,
  They fling their lovely arms o'er their drooping necks so fair,
Then vainly strive again their naked arms to hide,
  For their shrinking necks again are bare.

Thus clasp'd and prostrate all, with their heads together bow'd,
  Soft o'er their bosom's beating—the only human sound—
They hear the silky footsteps of the silent fairy crowd,
  Like a river in the air, gliding round.

No scream can any raise, no prayer can any say,
  But wild, wild, the terror of the speechless three—
For they feel fair Anna Grace drawn silently away,
  By whom they dare not look to see.

They feel their tresses twine with her parting locks of gold
    And the curls elastic falling as her head withdraws;
They feel her sliding arms from their tranced arms unfold,
    But they may not look to see the cause:

For heavy on their senses the faint enchantment lies
    Through all that night of anguish and perilous amaze;
And neither fear nor wonder can ope their quivering eyes,
    Or their limbs from the cold ground raise,

Till out of night the earth has roll'd her dewy side,
    With every haunted mountain and streamy vale below;
When, as the mist dissolves in the yellow morning tide,
    The maidens' trance dissolveth so.

Then fly the ghastly three as swiftly as they may,
    And tell their tale of sorrow to anxious friends in vain—
They pined away and died within the year and day,
    And ne'er was Anna Grace seen again.

The Legend of Knockgrafton

T. CROFTON CROKER

There was once a poor man who lived in the fertile glen of Aherlow, at the foot of the gloomy Galtee mountains, and he had a great hump on his back: he looked just as if his body had been rolled up and placed upon his shoulders; and his head was pressed down with the weight so much that his chin, when he was sitting, used to rest upon his knees for support. The country people were rather shy of meeting him in any lonesome place, for though, poor creature, he was as harmless and as inoffensive as a new-born infant, yet his deformity was so great that he scarcely appeared to be a human creature, and some ill-minded persons had set strange stories about him afloat. He was said to have a great knowledge of herbs and charms; but certain it was that he had a mighty skilful hand in plaiting straws and rushes into hats and baskets, which was the way he made his livelihood.

Lusmore, for that was the nickname put upon him by reason of his always wearing a sprig of the fairy cap, or lusmore (the foxglove), in his little straw hat, would ever get a higher penny for his plaited work than any one else and perhaps that was the reason why some one, out of envy, had circulated the strange stories about him. Be that as it may, it happened that he was returning one evening from the pretty town of Cahir towards Cappagh, and as little Lusmore walked very slowly, on account of the great hump upon his back, it was quite dark when he came to the old moat of Knockgrafton, which stood on the right-hand side of his road. Tired and weary was he, and noways comfortable in his own mind at thinking how much farther he had to travel, and that he should be walking all the night; so he sat down under the moat to rest himself, and began looking mournfully enough upon the moon, which—

> "Rising in clouded majesty, at length
>   Apparent Queen, unveil'd her peerless light,
> And o'er the dark her silver mantle threw".

Presently there rose a wild strain of unearthly melody upon the ear of little Lusmore; he listened, and he thought that he had never heard such ravishing music before. It was like the sound of many voices, each mingling and blending with the other so strangely that they seemed to be one, though all singing different strains, and the words of the song were these—

Da Luan, Da Mort, Da Luan, Da Mort, Da Luan, Da Mort;

when there would be a moment's pause, and then the round of melody went on again.

Lusmore listened attentively, scarcely drawing his breath lest he might lose the slightest note. He now plainly perceived that the singing was within the moat; and though at first it had charmed him so much, he began to get tired of hearing the same sound sung over and over so often without any change; so availing himself of the pause when *Da Luan, Da Mort,* had been sung three times, he took up the tune, and raised it with the words *augus Da Dardeen*, and then went on singing with the voices inside of the moat, *Da Luan, Da Mort*, finishing the melody, when the pause again came, with *augus Da Dardeen*.

The fairies within Knockgrafton, for the song was a fairy melody, when they heard this addition to the tune, were so much delighted that, with instant resolve, it was determined to bring the mortal among them, whose musical skill so far exceeded theirs, and little Lusmore was conveyed into their company with the eddying speed of a whirlwind.

Glorious to behold was the sight that burst upon him as he came down through the moat, twirling round and round, with the lightness of a straw, to the sweetest music that kept time to his motion. The greatest honour was then paid him, for he was put above all the musicians, and he had servants tending upon him, and everything to his heart's content, and a hearty welcome to all; and, in short, he was made as much of as if he had been the first man in the land.

Presently Lusmore saw a great consultation going forward among the fairies, and, notwithstanding all their civility, he felt very much frightened, until one stepping out from the rest came up to him and said—

"Lusmore! Lusmore!
Doubt not, nor deplore,

> For the hump which you bore
> On your back is no more;
> Look down on the floor,
> And view it, Lusmore!"

When these words were said, poor little Lusmore felt himself so light, and so happy, that he thought he could have bounded at one jump over the moon, like the cow in the history of the cat and the fiddle; and he saw, with inexpressible pleasure, his hump tumble down upon the ground from his shoulders. He then tried to lift up his head, and he did so with becoming caution, fearing that he might knock it against the ceiling of the grand hall, where he was; he looked round and round again with the greatest wonder and delight upon everything, which appeared more and more beautiful; and, overpowered at beholding such a resplendent scene, his head grew dizzy, and his eyesight became dim. At last he fell into a sound sleep, and when he awoke he found it was broad daylight, the sun shining brightly, and the birds singing sweetly; and that he was lying just at the foot of the moat of Knockgrafton, with the cows and sheep grazing peaceably round about him. The first thing Lusmore did, after saying his prayers, was to put his hand behind to feel for his hump, but no sign of one was there on his back, and he looked at himself with great pride, for he had now become a well-shaped dapper little fellow, and more than that, found himself in a full suit of new clothes, which he concluded the fairies had made for him.

Towards Cappagh he went, stepping out as lightly, and springing up at every step as if he had been all his life a dancing-master. Not a creature who met Lusmore knew him without his hump, and he had a great work to persuade every one that he was the same man—in truth he was not, so far as the outward appearance went.

Of course it was not long before the story of Lusmore's hump got about, and a great wonder was made of it. Through the country, for miles round, it was the talk of every one high and low.

One morning, as Lusmore was sitting contented enough at his cabin door, up came an old woman to him, and asked him if he could direct her to Cappagh.

"I need give you no directions, my good woman," said Lusmore, "for this is Cappagh; and whom may you want here?"

"I have come," said the woman, "out of Decie's country, in the county of Waterford, looking after one Lusmore, who, I have heard tell, had his hump taken

51

off by the fairies; for there is a son of a gossip of mine who has got a hump on him that will be his death; and maybe, if he could use the same charm as Lusmore, the hump may be taken off him. And now I have told you the reason of my coming so far: 'tis to find out about this charm, if I can."

Lusmore, who was ever a good-natured little fellow, told the woman all the particulars, how he had raised the tune for the fairies at Knockgrafton, how his hump had been removed from his shoulders, and how he had got a new suit of clothes into the bargain.

The woman thanked him very much, and then went away quite happy and easy in her mind. When she came back to her gossip's house, in the county of Waterford, she told her everything that Lusmore had said, and they put the little hump-backed man, who was a peevish and cunning creature from his birth, upon a car, and took him all the way across the country. It was a long journey, but they did not care for that, so the hump was taken from off him; and they brought him, just at nightfall, and left him under the old moat of Knockgrafton.

Jack Madden, for that was the humpy man's name, had not been sitting there long when he heard the tune going on within the moat much sweeter than before; for the fairies were singing it the way Lusmore had settled their music for them, and the song was going on: *Da Luan, Da Mort, Da Luan, Da Mort, Da Luan, Da Mort, augus Da Dardeen*, without ever stopping. Jack Madden, who was in a great hurry to get quit of his hump, never thought of waiting until the fairies had done, or watching for a fit opportunity to raise the tune higher again than Lusmore had; so having heard them sing it over seven times without stopping, out he bawls, never minding the time or the humour of the tune, or how he could bring his words in properly, *augus Da Dardeen, augus Da Hena*, thinking that if one day was good two were better; and that if Lusmore had one new suit of clothes given him, he should have two.

No sooner had the words passed his lips than he was taken up and whisked into the moat with prodigious force; and the fairies came crowding round him with great anger, screeching and screaming, and roaring out, "Who spoiled our tune? who spoiled our tune?" and one stepped up to him above all the rest, and said—

"Jack Madden! Jack Madden!
Your words came so bad in
The tune we felt glad in;—

52

This castle you're had in,
That your life we may sadden;
Here's two humps for Jack Madden!"

And twenty of the strongest fairies brought Lusmore's hump, and put it down upon poor Jack's back, over his own, where it became fixed as firmly as if it was nailed on with twelve-penny nails, by the best carpenter that ever drove one. Out of their castle they then kicked him; and in the morning, when Jack Madden's mother and her gossip came to look after their little man, they found him half dead, lying at the foot of the moat, with the other hump upon his back. Well to be sure, how they did look at each other! but they were afraid to say anything, lest a hump might be put upon their own shoulders. Home they brought the unlucky Jack Madden with them, as downcast in their hearts and their looks as ever two gossips were; and what through the weight of his other hump, and the long journey, he died soon after, leaving, they say, his heavy curse to any one who would go to listen to fairy tunes again.

A Donegal Fairy

LETITIA MACLINTOCK

Ay, it's a bad thing to displeasure the gentry, sure enough—they can be unfriendly if they're angered, an' they can be the very best o' gude neighbours if they're treated kindly.

My mother's sister was her lone in the house one day, wi' a big pot o' water boiling on the fire, and ane o' the wee folk fell down the chimney, and slipped wi' his leg in the hot water.

He let a terrible squeal out o' him, an' in a minute the house was full o' wee crathurs pulling him out o' the pot, an' carrying him across the floor.

"Did she scald you?" my aunt heard them saying to him.

"Na, na, it was mysel' scalded my ainsel'," quoth the wee fellow.

"A weel, a weel," says they. "If it was your ainsel scalded yoursel', we'll say nothing, but if she had scalded you, we'd ha' made her pay."

Changelings

Sometimes the fairies fancy mortals, and carry them away into their own country, leaving instead some sickly fairy child, or a log of wood so bewitched that it seems to be a mortal pining away, and dying, and being buried. Most commonly they steal children. If you "over look a child", that is look on it with envy, the fairies have it in their power. Many things can be done to find out if a child's a changeling, but there is one infallible thing—lay it on the fire with this formula, "Burn, burn, burn—if of the devil, burn; but if of God and the saints, be safe from harm" (given by Lady Wilde). Then if it be a changeling it will rush up the chimney with a cry, for, according to Giraldus Cambrensis, "fire is the greatest of enemies to every sort of phantom, in so much that those who have seen apparitions fall into a swoon as soon as they are sensible of the brightness of fire".

Sometimes the creature is got rid of in a more gentle way. It is on record that once when a mother was leaning over a wizened changeling the latch lifted and a fairy came in, carrying home again the wholesome stolen baby. "It was the others," she said, "who stole it." As for her, she wanted her own child.

Those who are carried away are happy, according to some accounts, having plenty of good living and music and mirth. Others say, however, that they are continually longing for their earthly friends. Lady Wilde gives a gloomy tradition that there are two kinds of fairies—one kind merry and gentle, the other evil, and sacrificing every year a life to Satan, for which purpose they steal mortals. No other Irish writer gives this tradition—if such fairies there be, they must be among the solitary spirits—Pookas, Fir Darrigs, and the like.

The Brewery of Egg-Shells

T. CROFTON CROKER

Mrs Sullivan fancied that her youngest child had been exchanged by "fairies theft", and certainly appearances warranted such a conclusion; for in one night her healthy, blue-eyed boy had become shrivelled up into almost nothing, and never ceased squalling and crying. This naturally made poor Mrs Sullivan very unhappy; and all the neighbours, by way of comforting her, said that her own child was, beyond any kind of doubt, with the good people, and that one of themselves was put in his place.

Mrs Sullivan of course could not disbelieve what every one told her, but she did not wish to hurt the thing; for although its face was so withered, and its body wasted away to a mere skeleton, it had still a strong resemblance to her own boy. She, therefore, could not find it in her heart to roast it alive on the griddle, or to burn its nose off with the red-hot tongs, or to throw it out in the snow on the road-side, notwithstanding these, and several like proceedings, were strongly recommended to her for the recovery of her child.

One day who should Mrs Sullivan meet but a cunning woman, well known about the country by the name of Ellen Leah (or Grey Ellen). She had the gift, however she got it, of telling where the dead were, and what was good for the rest of their souls; and could charm away warts and wens, and do a great many wonderful things of the same nature.

"You're in grief this morning, Mrs Sullivan," were the first words of Ellen Leah to her.

"You may say that, Ellen," said Mrs Sullivan, "and good cause I have to be in grief, for there was my own fine child whipped off from me out of his cradle, without as much as 'by your leave' or 'ask your pardon', and an ugly dony bit of a shrivelled-up fairy put in his place; no wonder, then, that you see me in grief, Ellen."

"Small blame to you, Mrs Sullivan," said Ellen Leah, "but are you sure 'tis a fairy?"

"Sure!" echoed Mrs Sullivan, "sure enough I am to my sorrow, and can I doubt my own two eyes? Every mother's soul must feel for me!"

"Will you take an old woman's advice?" said Ellen Leah, fixing her wild and mysterious gaze upon the unhappy mother; and, after a pause, she added, "but maybe you'll call it foolish?"

"Can you get me back my child, my own child, Ellen?" said Mrs Sullivan with great energy.

"If you do as I bid you," returned Ellen Leah, "you'll know." Mrs Sullivan was silent in expectation, and Ellen continued, "Put down the big pot, full of water, on the fire, and make it boil like mad; then get a dozen new-laid eggs, break them, and keep the shells, but throw away the rest; when that is done, put the shells in the pot of boiling water, and you will soon know whether it is your own boy or a fairy. If you find that it is a fairy in the cradle, take the red-hot poker and cram it down his ugly throat, and you will not have much trouble with him after that I promise you."

Home went Mrs Sullivan, and did as Ellen Leah desired. She put the pot on the fire, and plenty of turf under it, and set the water boiling at such a rate, that if ever water was red-hot, it surely was.

The child was lying, for a wonder, quite easy and quiet in the cradle, every now and then cocking his eye, that would twinkle as keen as a star in a frosty night, over at the great fire, and the big pot upon it; and he looked on with great attention at Mrs Sullivan breaking the eggs and putting down the egg-shells to boil. At last he asked, with the voice of a very old man, "What are you doing mammy?"

Mrs Sullivan's heart, as she said herself, was up in her mouth ready to choke her, at hearing the child speak. But she contrived to put the poker in the fire, and to answer, without making any wonder at the words, "I'm brewing, *a vick*" (my son).

"And what are you brewing, mammy?" said the little imp, whose supernatural gift of speech now proved beyond question that he was a fairy substitute.

"I wish the poker was red," thought Mrs Sullivan; but it was a large one, and took a long time heating; so she determined to keep him in talk until the poker was in a proper state to thrust down his throat, and therefore repeated the question.

"Is it what I'm brewing, *a vick*," said she, "you want to know?"

"Yes, mammy: what are you brewing?" returned the fairy.

"Egg-shells, *a vick*," said Mrs Sullivan.

"Oh!" shrieked the imp, starting up in the cradle, and clapping his hands together, "I'm fifteen hundred years in the world, and I never saw a brewery of egg-shells before!" The poker was by this time quite red, and Mrs Sullivan, seizing it, ran furiously towards the cradle; but somehow or other her foot slipped, and she fell flat on the floor, and the poker flew out of her hand to the other end of the house. However, she got up without much loss of time and went to the cradle, intending to pitch the wicked thing that was in it into the pot of boiling water, when there she saw her own child in a sweet sleep, one of his soft round arms rested upon the pillow—his features were as placid as if their repose had never been disturbed, save the rosy mouth, which moved with a gentle and regular breathing.

The Fairy Nurse

EDWARD WALSH

Sweet babe! a golden cradle holds thee,
And soft the snow-white fleece enfolds thee;
In airy bower I'll watch thy sleeping,
Where branchy trees to the breeze are sweeping.
     Shuheen, sho, lulo lo!

When mothers languish broken-hearted,
When young wives are from husbands parted,
Ah! little think the keeners lonely,
They weep some time-worn fairy only.
     Shuheen, sho, lulo lo!

Within our magic halls of brightness,
Trips many a foot of snowy whiteness;
Stolen maidens, queens of fairy—
And kings and chiefs a sluagh-shee airy,
     Shuheen, sho, lulo lo!

Rest thee, babe! I love thee dearly,
And as thy mortal mother nearly;
Ours is the swiftest steed and proudest,
That moves where the tramp of the host is loudest.
     Shuheen, sho, lulo lo!

Rest thee, babe! for soon thy slumbers
Shall flee at the magic koelshie's* numbers;
In airy bower I'll watch thy sleeping,
Where branchy trees to the breeze are sweeping.
                    Shuheen, sho, lulo lo!

*Ceól-sidhe—i.e., fairy music.

Jamie Freel and the Young Lady

A Donegal Tale

MISS LETITIA MACLINTOCK

Down in Fannet, in times gone by, lived Jamie Freel and his mother. Jamie was the widow's sole support; his strong arm worked for her untiringly, and as each Saturday night came round, he poured his wages into her lap, thanking her dutifully for the halfpence which she returned him for tobacco.

He was extolled by his neighbours as the best son ever known or heard of. But he had neighbours, of whose opinion he was ignorant—neighbours who lived pretty close to him, whom he had never seen, who are, indeed, rarely seen by mortals, except on May eves and Halloweens.

An old ruined castle, about a quarter of a mile from his cabin, was said to be the abode of the "wee folk". Every Halloween were the ancient windows lighted up, and passers-by saw little figures flitting to and fro inside the building, while they heard the music of pipes and flutes.

It was well known that fairy revels took place; but nobody had the courage to intrude on them.

Jamie had often watched the little figures from a distance, and listened to the charming music, wondering what the inside of the castle was like; but one Halloween he got up and took his cap, saying to his mother, "I'm awa' to the castle to seek my fortune."

"What!" cried she, "would you venture there? you that's the poor widow's one son! Dinna be sae venturesome an' foolitch, Jamie! They'll kill you, an' then what'll come o' me?"

"Never fear, mother; nae harm 'ill happen me, but I maun gae."

He set out, and as he crossed the potato-field, came in sight of the castle, whose windows were ablaze with light, that seemed to turn the russet leaves, still clinging to the crabtree branches, into gold.

Halting in the grove at one side of the ruin, he listened to the elfin revelry, and the laughter and singing made him all the more determined to proceed.

Numbers of little people, the largest about the size of a child of five years old, were dancing to the music of flutes and fiddles, while others drank and feasted.

"Welcome, Jamie Freel! welcome, welcome, Jamie!" cried the company, perceiving their visitor. The word "Welcome" was caught up and repeated by every voice in the castle.

Time flew, and Jamie was enjoying himself very much, when his hosts said, "We're going to ride to Dublin tonight to steal a young lady. Will you come too, Jamie Freel?"

"Aye, that will I!" cried the rash youth, thirsting for adventure.

A troop of horses stood at the door. Jamie mounted and his steed rose with him into the air. He was presently flying over his mother's cottage, surrounded by the elfin troop, and on and on they went, over bold mountains, over little hills, over the deep Lough Swilley, over towns and cottages, when people were burning nuts, and eating apples, and keeping merry Halloween. It seemed to Jamie that they flew all round Ireland before they got to Dublin.

"This is Derry," said the fairies, flying over the cathedral spire; and what was said by one voice was repeated by all the the rest, till fifty little voices were crying out, "Derry! Derry! Derry!"

In like manner was Jamie informed as they passed over each town on the route, and at length he heard the silvery voices cry, "Dublin! Dublin!"

It was no mean dwelling that was to be honoured by the fairy visit, but one of the finest houses in Stephen's Green.

The troop dismounted near a window, and Jamie saw a beautiful face, on a pillow in a splendid bed. He saw the young lady lifted and carried away, while the stick which was dropped in her place on the bed took her exact form.

The lady was placed before one rider and carried a short way, then given another, and the names of the towns were cried out as before.

They were approaching home. Jamie heard "Rathmullan", "Milford", "Tamney", and then he knew they were near his own house.

"You've all had your turn at carrying the young lady, " said he. "Why wouldn't I get her for a wee piece?"

"Ay, Jamie," replied they, pleasantly, "you may take your turn at carrying her, to be sure."

Holding his prize very tightly, he dropped down near his mother's door.

"Jamie Freel, Jamie Freel! is that the way you treat us?" cried they, and they too dropped down near the door.

Jamie held fast, though he knew not what he was holding, for the little folk turned the lady into all sorts of strange shapes. At one moment she was a black dog, barking and trying to bite; at another, a glowing bar of iron, which yet had no heat; then, again, a sack of wool.

But still Jamie held her, and the baffled elves were turning away, when a tiny woman, the smallest of the party, exclaimed, "Jamie Freel has her awa' frae us, but he sall hae nae gude o' her, for I'll mak' her deaf and dumb," and she threw something over the young girl.

While they rode off disappointed, Jamie lifted the latch and went in.

"Jamie, man!" cried his mother, "you've been awa' all night; what have they done on you?"

"Naething bad, mother; I ha' the very best of gude luck. Here's a beautiful young lady I ha' brought you for company."

"Bless us an' save us!" exclaimed the mother, and for some minutes she was so astonished that she could not think of anything else to say.

Jamie told his story of the night's adventure, ending by saying, "Surely you wouldna have allowed me to let her gang with them to be lost forever?"

"But a *lady*, Jamie! How can a lady eat we'er poor diet, and live in we'er poor way? I ax you that, you foolitch fellow?"

"Weel, mother, sure it's better for her to be here nor over yonder," and he pointed in the direction of the castle.

Meanwhile, the deaf and dumb girl shivered in her light clothing, stepping close to the humble turf fire.

"Poor crathur, she's quare and handsome! Nae wonder they set their hearts on her," said the old woman, gazing at her guest with pity and admiration. "We maun dress her first; but what, in the name o' fortune, hae I fit for the likes o' her to wear?"

She went to her press in "the room", and took out her Sunday gown of brown drugget; she then opened a drawer and drew forth a pair of white stockings, a long snowy garment of fine linen, and a cap, her "dead dress", as she called it.

These articles of attire had long been ready for a certain triste ceremony, in which she would some day fill the chief part, and only saw the light occasionally, when they were hung out to air; but she was willing to give even these to the fair trembling visitor, who was turning in dumb sorrow and wonder from her to Jamie, and from Jamie back to her.

The poor girl suffered herself to be dressed, and then sat down on a "creepie" in the chimney corner, and buried her face in her hands.

"What'll we do to keep up a lady like thou?" cried the old woman.

"I'll work for you both, mother," replied the son.

"An' how could a lady live on we'er poor diet?" she repeated.

"I'll work for her," was all Jamie's answer.

He kept his word. The young lady was very sad for a long time, and tears stole down her cheeks many an evening while the old woman spun by the fire, and Jamie made salmon nets, an accomplishment lately acquired by him, in hopes of adding to the comfort of his guest.

But she was always gentle, and tried to smile when she perceived them looking at her; and by degrees she adapted herself to their ways and mode of life. It was not very long before she began to feed the pig, mash potatoes and meal for the fowls, and knit blue worsted socks.

So a year passed, and Halloween came round again. "Mother," said Jamie, taking down his cap, "I'm off to the ould castle to seek my fortune."

"Are you mad, Jamie?" cried his mother, in terror; "sure they'll kill you this time for what you done on them last year."

Jamie made light of her fears and went his way.

As he reached the crab-tree grove, he saw bright lights in the castle windows as before, and heard loud talking. Creeping under the window, he heard the wee folk say, "That was a poor trick Jamie Freel played us this night last year, when he stole the nice young lady from us."

"Ay," said the tiny woman, "an' I punished him for it, for there she sits, a dumb image by his hearth; but he does na' know that three drops out o' this glass I hold in my hand wad gie her her hearing and her speeches back again."

Jamie's heart beat fast as he entered the hall. Again he was greeted by a chorus of welcomes from the company—"Here comes Jamie Freel! welcome, welcome, Jamie!"

As soon as the tumult subsided, the little woman said, "You be to drink our health, Jamie, out o' this glass in my hand."

Jamie snatched the glass from her and darted to the door. He never knew how he reached his cabin, but he arrived there breathless, and sank on a stove by the fire.

"You're kilt surely this time, my poor boy," said his mother.

"No, indeed, better luck than ever this time!" and he gave the lady three drops of the liquid that still remained at the bottom of the glass, notwithstanding his mad race over the potato-field.

The lady began to speak, and her first words were words of thanks to Jamie.

The three inmates of the cabin had so much to say to one another, that long after cock-crow, when the fairy music had quite ceased, they were talking round the fire.

"Jamie," said the lady, "be pleased to get me paper and pen and ink, that I may write to my father, and tell him what has become of me."

She wrote, but weeks passed, and she received no answer. Again and again she wrote, and still no answer.

At length she said, "You must come with me to Dublin, Jamie, to find my father."

"I ha' no money to hire a car for you," he replied, "an' how can you travel to Dublin on your foot?"

But she implored him so much that he consented to set out with her, and walk all the way from Fannet to Dublin. It was not as easy as the fairy journey; but at last they rang the bell at the door of the house in Stephen's Green.

"Tell my father that his daughter is here," said she to the servant who opened the door.

"The gentleman that lives here has no daughter, my girl. He had one, but she died better nor a year ago."

"Do you not know me, Sullivan?"

"No, poor girl, I do not."

"Let me see the gentleman. I only ask to see him."

"Well, that's not much to ax; we'll see what can be done."

In a few moments the lady's father came to the door.

"Dear father," said she, "don't you know me?"

"How dare you call me father?" cried the old gentleman, angrily. "You are an impostor. I have no daughter."

"Look in my face, father, and surely you'll remember me."

65

"My daughter is dead and buried. She died a long, long time ago." The old gentleman's voice changed from anger to sorrow. "You can go," he concluded.

"Stop, dear father, till you look at this ring on my finger. Look at your name and mine engraved on it."

"It certainly is my daughter's ring; but I do not know how you came by it I fear in no honest way."

"Call my mother, *she* will be sure to know me," said the poor girl, who, by this time, was crying bitterly.

"My poor wife is beginning to forget her sorrow. She seldom speaks of her daughter now. Why should I renew her grief by reminding her of her loss?"

But the young lady persevered, till at last the mother was sent for.

"Mother," she began, when the old lady came to the door, "don't *you* know your daughter?"

"I have no daughter; my daughter died and was buried a long, long time ago."

"Only look in my face, and surely you'll know me."

The old lady shook her head.

"You have all forgotten me; but look at this mole on my neck. Surely, mother, you know me now?"

"Yes, yes," said the mother, "my Gracie had a mole on her neck like that; but then I saw her in her coffin, and saw the lid shut down upon her."

It became Jamie's turn to speak, and he gave the history of the fairy journey, of the theft of the young lady, of the figure he had seen laid in its place, of her life with his mother in Fannet, of last Halloween, and of the three drops that had released her from her enchantment.

She took up the story when he paused, and told how kind the mother and son had been to her.

The parents could not make enough of Jamie. They treated him with every distinction, and when he expressed his wish to return to Fannet, said they did not know what to do to show their gratitude.

But an awkward complication arose. The daughter would not let him go without her. "If Jamie goes, I'll go too," she said. "He saved me from the fairies, and has worked for me ever since. If it had not been for him, dear father and mother, you would never have seen me again. If he goes, I'll go too."

This being her resolution, the old gentleman said that Jamie should become his son-in-law. The mother was brought from Fannet in a coach and four, and there was a splendid wedding.

They all lived together in the grand Dublin house, and Jamie was heir to untold wealth at his father-in-law's death.

The Stolen Child

W. B. YEATS

Where dips the rocky highland
   Of Sleuth Wood in the lake,
There lies a leafy island
   Where flapping herons wake
The drowsy water-rats.
There we've hid our fairy vats
Full of berries,
And of reddest stolen cherries.
Come away, O, human child!
To the woods and waters wild
With a fairy hand in hand,
For the world's more full of weeping than you can understand.

Where the wave of moonlight glosses
   The dim grey sands with light,
Far off by farthest Rosses
   We foot it all the night,
Weaving olden dances,
Mingling hands, and mingling glances,
   Till the moon has taken flight;

To and fro we leap,
   And chase the frothy bubbles,
   While the world is full of troubles.
And is anxious in its sleep.
Come away! O, human child!

To the woods and waters wild,
With a fairy hand in hand,
For the world's more full of weeping than you can understand.

Where the wandering water gushes
   From the hills above Glen-Car,
In pools among the rushes,
   That scarce could bathe a star,
We seek for slumbering trout,
   And whispering in their ears;
     We give them evil dreams,
Leaning softly out
   From ferns that drop their tears
     Of dew on the young streams.
Come! O, human child!
To the woods and waters wild,
With a fairy hand in hand,
For the world's more full of weeping than you can understand.

Away with us, he's going,
   The solemn-eyed;
He'll hear no more the lowing
   Of the calves on the warm hill-side.
Or the kettle on the hob
   Sing peace into his breast;
Or see the brown mice bob
   Round and round the oatmeal chest.
For he comes, the human child,
To the woods and waters wild,
With a fairy hand in hand,
For the world's more full of weeping than he can understand.

The Merrow

The *Merrow*, or if you write it in the Irish, *Moruadh* or *Murrúghach*, from *muir*, sea, and *oigh*, a maid, is not uncommon, they say, on the wilder coasts. The fishermen do not like to see them, for it always means coming gales. The male *Merrows* (if you can use such a phrase—I have never heard the masculine of Merrow) have green teeth, green hair, pig's eyes, and red noses; but their women are beautiful, for all their fish tails and the little duck-like scale between their fingers. Sometimes they prefer, small blame to them, good-looking fishermen to their sea lovers. Near Bantry in the last century, there is said to have been a woman covered all over with scales like a fish, who was descended from such a marriage. Sometimes they come out of the sea, and wander about the shore in the shape of little hornless cows. They have, when in their own shape, a red cap, called a *cohullen druith*, usually covered with feathers. If this is stolen, they cannot again go down under the waves.

Red is the colour of magic in every country, and has been so from the very earliest times. The caps of fairies and magicians are well-nigh always red.

The Soul Cages

T. CROFTON CROKER

Jack Dogherty lived on the coast of the county Clare. Jack was a fisherman, as his father and grandfather before him had been. Like them, too, he lived all alone (but for the wife), and just in the same spot. People used to wonder why the Dogherty family were so fond of that wild situation, so far away from all human kind, and in the midst of huge shattered rocks, with nothing but the wide ocean to look upon. But they had their own good reasons for it.

The place was just the only spot on that part of the coast where anybody could well live. There was a neat little creek, where a boat might lie as snug as a puffin in her nest, and out from this creek a ledge of sunken rocks ran into the sea. Now when the Atlantic, according to custom, was raging with a storm, and a good westerly wind was blowing strong on the coast, many a richly-laden ship went to pieces on these rocks; and then the fine bales of cotton and tobacco, and such like things, and the pipes of wine and the puncheons of rum, and the casks of brandy, and the kegs of Hollands that used to come ashore! Dunbeg Bay was just like a little estate to the Doghertys.

Not but they were kind and humane to a distressed sailor, if ever one had the good luck to get to land; and many a time indeed did Jack put out in his little *corragh* (which, though not quite equal to honest Andrew Hennessy's canvas life-boat would breast the billows like any gannet), to lend a hand towards bringing off the crew from a wreck. But when the ship had gone to pieces, and the crew were all lost, who would blame Jack for picking up all he could find?

"And who is the worse of it?" said he. "For as to the king, God bless him! everybody knows he's rich enough already without getting what's floating in the sea."

Jack, though such a hermit, was a good-natured, jolly fellow. No other, sure, could ever have coaxed Biddy Mahony to quit her father's snug and warm house in the middle of the town of Ennis, and to go so many miles off to live among the rocks, with the seals and sea-gulls for next-door neighbours. But Biddy knew that Jack was the man for a woman who wished to be comfortable and happy; for to say nothing of the fish, Jack had the supplying of half the gentlemen's houses of the country with the Godsends that came into the bay. And she was right in her choice; for no woman ate, drank, or slept better, or made a prouder appearance at chapel on Sundays, than Mrs Dogherty.

Many a strange sight, it may well be supposed, did Jack see, and many a strange sound did he hear, but nothing daunted him. So far was he from being afraid of Merrows, or such beings, that the very first wish of his heart was to fairly meet with one. Jack had heard that they were mighty like Christians, and that luck had always come out of an acquaintance with them. Never, therefore, did he dimly discern the Merrows moving along the face of the waters in their robes of mist, but he made direct for them; and many a scolding did Biddy, in her own quiet way, bestow upon Jack for spending his whole day out at sea, and bringing home no fish. Little did poor Biddy know the fish Jack was after!

It was rather annoying to Jack that, though living in a place where the Merrows were as plenty as lobsters, he never could get a right view of one. What vexed him more was that both his father and grandfather had often and often seen them; and he even remembered hearing, when a child, how his grandfather, who was the first of the family that had settled down at the creek, had been so intimate with a Merrow that, only for fear of vexing the priest, he would have had him stand for one of his children. This, however, Jack did not well know how to believe.

Fortune at length began to think that it was only right that Jack should know as much as his father and grandfather did. Accordingly, one day when he had strolled a little farther than usual along the coast to the northward, just as he turned a point, he saw something, like to nothing he had ever seen before, perched upon a rock at a little distance out to sea. It looked green in the body, as well as he could discern at that distance, and he would have sworn, only the thing was impossible, that it had a cocked hat in its hand. Jack stood for a good half-hour straining his eyes, and wondering at it, and all the time the thing did not stir hand or foot. At last Jack's patience was quite worn out, and he gave a loud whistle and a hail, when the Merrow (for such it was) started up, put the cocked hat on its head, and dived down, head foremost, from the rock.

Jack's curiosity was now excited, and he constantly directed his steps towards the point; still he could never get a glimpse of the sea-gentleman with the cocked hat; and with thinking and thinking about the matter, he began at last to fancy he had been only dreaming. One very rough day, however, when the sea was running mountains high, Jack Dogherty determined to give a look at the Merrow's rock (for he had always chosen a fine day before), and then he saw the strange thing cutting capers upon the top of the rock, and then diving down, and then coming up, and then diving down again.

Jack had now only to choose his time (that is, a good blowing day), and he might see the man of the sea as often as he pleased. All this, however, did not satisfy him—"much will have more"; he wished now to get acquainted with the Merrow, and even in this he succeeded. One tremendous blustering day, before he got to the point whence he had a view of the Merrow's rock, the storm came on so furiously that Jack was obliged to take shelter in one of the caves which are so numerous along the coast; and there, to his astonishment, he saw sitting before him a thing with green hair, long green teeth, a red nose, and pig's eyes. It had a fish's tail, legs with scales on them, and short arms like fins. It wore no clothes, but had the cocked hat under its arm, and seemed engaged thinking very seriously about something.

Jack, with all his courage, was a little daunted; but now or never, thought he; so up he went boldly to the cogitating fishman, took off his hat, and made his best bow.

"Your servant, sir," said Jack.

"Your servant, kindly, Jack Dogherty," answered the Merrow.

"To be sure, then, how well your honour knows my name!" said Jack.

"Is it I not know your name, Jack Dogherty? Why man, I knew your grandfather long before he was married to Judy Regan, your grandmother! Ah, Jack, Jack, I was fond of that grandfather of yours; he was a mighty worthy man in his time: I never met his match above or below, before or since, for sucking in a shellful of brandy. I hope, my boy," said the old fellow, with a merry twinkle in his eyes, "I hope you're his own grandson!"

"Never fear me for that," said Jack; "if my mother had only reared me on brandy, 'tis myself that would be a sucking infant to this hour!"

"Well, I like to hear you talk so manly; you and I must be better acquainted, if it were only for your grandfather's sake. But, Jack, that father of yours was not the thing! he had no head at all."

73

"I'm sure," said Jack, "since your honour lives down under the water, you must be obliged to drink a power to keep any heat in you in such a cruel, damp, *could* place. Well, I've often heard of Christians drinking like fishes; and might I be so bold as ask where you get the spirits?"

"Where do you get them yourself, Jack?" said the Merrow, twitching his red nose between his forefinger and thumb.

"Hubbubboo," cries Jack "now I see how it is; but I suppose, sir, your honour has got a fine dry cellar below to keep them in."

"Let me alone for the cellar," said the Merrow, with a knowing wink of his left eye.

"I'm sure," continued Jack, "it must be mighty well worth the looking at."

"You may say that, Jack," said the Merrow; "and if you meet me here next Monday, just at this time of the day, we will have a little more talk with one another about the matter."

Jack and the Merrow parted the best friends in the world. On Monday they met, and Jack was not a little surprised to see that the Merrow had two cocked hats with him, one under each arm.

"Might I take the liberty to ask, sir," said Jack, "why your honour has brought the two hats with you today? You would not, sure, be going to give me one of them, to keep for the *curiosity* of the thing?"

"No, no, Jack," said he, "I don't get my hats so easily, to part with them that way; but I want you to come down and dine with me, and I brought you that hat to dive with."

"Lord bless and preserve us!" cried Jack, in amazement, "would you want me to go down to the bottom of the salt sea ocean? Sure, I'd be smothered and choked up with the water, to say nothing of being drowned! And what would poor Biddy do for me, and what would she say?"

"And what matter what she says, you *pinkeen*? Who cares for Biddy's squalling? It's long before your grandfather would have talked in that way. Many's the time he stuck that same hat on his head, and dived down boldly after me; and many's the snug bit of dinner and good shellful of brandy he and I have had together below, under the water."

"Is it really, sir, and no joke?" said Jack; "why, then, sorrow from me for ever and a day after, if I'll be a bit worse man nor my grandfather was! Here goes—but play me fair now. Here's neck or nothing!" cried Jack.

"That's your grandfather all over," said the old fellow; "so come along, then, and do as I do."

They both left the cave, walked into the sea, and then swam a piece until they got to the rock, The Merrow climbed to the top of it, and Jack followed him. On the far side it was as straight as the wall of a house, and the sea beneath looked so deep that Jack was almost cowed.

"Now, do you see, Jack," said the Merrow: "just put this hat on your head, and mind to keep your eyes wide open. Take hold of my tail, and follow after me, and you'll see what you'll see."

In he dashed, and in dashed Jack after him boldly. They went and they went, and Jack thought they'd never stop going. Many a time did he wish himself sitting at home by the fireside with Biddy. Yet where was the use of wishing now, when he was so many miles, as he thought, below the waves of the Atlantic? Still he held hard by the Merrow's tail, slippery as it was; and, at last, to Jack's great surprise, they got out of the water, and he actually found himself on dry land at the bottom of the sea. They landed just in front of a nice house that was slated very neatly with oyster shells! and the Merrow, turning about to Jack, welcomed him down.

Jack could hardly speak, what with wonder, and what with being out of breath with travelling so fast through the water. He looked about him and could see no living things, barring crabs and lobsters, of which there were plenty walking leisurely about on the sand. Overhead was the sea like a sky, and the fishes like birds swimming about in it.

"Why don't you speak, man?" said the Merrow: "I dare say you had no notion that I had such a snug little concern here as this? Are you smothered, or choked, or drowned, or are you fretting after Biddy, eh?"

"Oh! not myself indeed," said Jack, showing his teeth with a good-humoured grin; "but who in the world would ever have thought of seeing such a thing?"

"Well, come along, and let's see what they've got for us to eat?"

Jack really was hungry, and it gave him no small pleasure to perceive a fine column of smoke rising from the chimney, announcing what was going on within. Into the house he followed the Merrow, and there he saw a good kitchen, right well provided with everything. There was a noble dresser, and plenty of pots and pans, with two young Merrows cooking. His host then led him into the room, which was furnished shabbily enough. Not a table or a chair was there in it; nothing but planks and logs of wood to sit on, and eat off. There was, however, a good fire blazing upon the hearth—a comfortable sight to Jack.

"Come now, and I'll show you where I keep—you know what," said the Merrow, with a sly look; and opening a little door, he led Jack into a fine cellar, well filled with pipes, and kegs, and hogsheads, and barrels.

"What do you say to that, Jack Dogherty? Eh! may be a body can't live snug under the water?"

"Never the doubt of that," said Jack, with a convincing smack of his upper lip, that he really thought what he said.

They went back to the room, and found dinner laid. There was no tablecloth, to be sure—but what matter? It was not always Jack had one at home. The dinner would have been no discredit to the first house of the country on a fast day. The choicest of fish, and no wonder, was there. Turbots, and sturgeons, and soles, and lobsters, and oysters, and twenty other kinds, were on the planks at once, and plenty of the best of foreign spirits. The wines, the old fellow said, were too cold for his stomach.

Jack ate and drank till he could eat no more: then taking up a shell of brandy, "Here's to your honour's good health, sir," said he; "though, begging you pardon, it's mighty odd that as long as we've been acquainted I don't know your name yet."

"That's true, Jack," replied he; "I never thought of it before, but better late than never. My name's Coomara."

"And a mighty decent name it is," cried Jack, taking another shellfull: "here's to your good health, Coomara, and may ye live these fifty years to come!"

"Fifty years!" repeated Coomara; "I'm obliged to you, indeed! If you had said five hundred, it would have been something worth the wishing."

"By the laws, sir," cries Jack, "*youz* live to a powerful age here under the water! You knew my grandfather, and he's dead and gone better than these sixty years. I'm sure it must be a healthy place to live in."

"No doubt of it; but come, Jack, keep the liquor stirring."

Shell after shell did they empty, and to Jack's exceeding surprise, he found the drink never got into his head, owing, I suppose, to the sea being over them, which kept their noddles cool.

Old Coomara got exceedingly comfortable, and sung several songs; but Jack, if his life had depended on it, never could remember more than

"Rum fum boodle boo,
　Ripple dipple nitty dob;
Dumdoo doodle coo,
　Raffle taffle chittiboo!"

It was the chorus to one of them; and, to say the truth, nobody that I know has ever been able to pick any particular meaning out of it; but that, to be sure, is the case with many a song nowadays.

At length said he to Jack, "Now, my dear boy, if you follow me, I'll show you my *curiosities!*" He opened a little door, and led Jack into a large room, where Jack saw a great many odds and ends that Coomara had picked up at one time or another. What chiefly took his attention, however, were things like lobster-pots ranged on the ground along the wall.

"Well, Jack, how do you like my *curiosities?*" said old Coo.

"Upon my *sowkins,** sir," said Jack, "they're mighty well worth the looking at; but might I make so bold as to ask what these things like lobster-pots are?"

"Oh! the Soul Cages, is it?"

"The what? sir!"

"These things here that I keep the souls in."

"*Arrah!* what souls, sir?" said Jack, in amazement; "sure the fish have no souls in them?"

"Oh! no," replied Coo, quite coolly, "that they have not; but these are the souls of drowned sailors."

"The Lord preserve us from all harm!" muttered Jack, "how in the world did you get them?"

"Easily enough: I've only, when I see a good storm coming on, to set a couple of dozen of these, and then, when the sailors are drowned and the souls get out of them under the water, the poor things are almost perished to death, not being used to the cold; so they make into my pots for shelter, and then I have them snug, and fetch them home, and is it not well for them, poor souls, to get into such good quarters?"

Jack was so thunderstruck he did not know what to say, so he said nothing. They went back into the dining-room, and had a little more brandy, which was excellent, and then, as Jack knew that it must be getting late, and as Biddy might

*Sowkins, diminutive of soul.

be uneasy, he stood up, and said he thought it was time for him to be on the road.

"Just as you like, Jack," said Coo. "but take a *duc an durrus** before you go; you've a cold journey before you."

Jack knew better manners than to refuse the parting glass.

"I wonder," said he, "will I be able to make out my way home?"

"What should ail you," said Coo, "when I'll show you the way?"

Out they went before the house, and Coomara took one of the cocked hats, and put it upon Jack's head the wrong way, and then lifted him up on his shoulder that he might launch him up into the water.

"Now," says he, giving him a heave, "you'll come up just in the same spot you came down in; and, Jack, mind and throw me back the hat."

He canted Jack off his shoulder, and up he shot like a bubble—whirr, whirr, whiz—away he went up through the water, till he came to the very rock he had jumped off where he found a landing-place, and then in he threw the hat, which sunk like a stone.

The sun was just going down in the beautiful sky of a calm summer's evening. *Feascor* was seen dimly twinkling in the cloudless heaven, a solitary star, and the waves of the Atlantic flashed in a golden flood of light. So Jack, perceiving it was late, set off home; but when he got there, not a word did he say to Biddy of where he had spent his day.

The state of the poor souls cooped up in the lobster-pots gave Jack a great deal of trouble, and how to release them cost him a great deal of thought. He at first had a mind to speak to the priest about the matter. But what could the priest do, and what did Coo care for the priest? Besides, Coo was a good sort of an old fellow, and did not think he was doing any harm. Jack had a regard for him, too, and it also might not be much to his own credit if it were known that he used to go dine with Merrows. On the whole, he thought his best plan would be to ask Coo to dinner, and to make him drunk, if he was able, and then to take the hat and go down and turn up the pots. It was, first of all, necessary, however, to get Biddy out of the way; for Jack was prudent enough, as she was a woman, to wish to keep the thing secret from her.

Accordingly, Jack grew mighty pious all of a sudden, and said to Biddy that he thought it would be for the good of both their souls if she was to go and take her rounds at Saint John's Well, near Ennis. Biddy thought so too, and accordingly off

**Rectè, doech án dorrus*—door-drink or stirrup-cup.

she set one fine morning at day-dawn, giving Jack a strict charge to have an eye to the place. The coast being clear, away went Jack to the rock to give the appointed signal to Coomara, which was throwing a big stone into the water. Jack threw, and up sprang Coo!

"Good morning, Jack," said he; "what do you want with me?"

"Just nothing at all to speak about, sir," returned Jack, "only to come and take a bit of dinner with me, if I might make so free as to ask you, and sure I'm now after doing so."

"It's quite agreeable, Jack, I assure you; what's your hour?"

"Any time that's most convenient to you, sir—say one o'clock, that you may go home, if you wish, with the daylight."

"I'll be with you," said Coo, "never fear me."

Jack went home, and dressed a noble fish dinner, and got out plenty of his best foreign spirits, enough, for that matter, to make twenty men drunk. Just to the minute came Coo, with his cocked hat under his arm. Dinner was ready, they sat down, and ate and drank away manfully. Jack, thinking of the poor souls below in the pots, plied old Coo well with brandy, and encouraged him to sing, hoping to put him under the table, but poor Jack forgot that he had not the sea over his head to keep it cool. The brandy got into it, and did his business for him, and Coo reeled off home, leaving his entertainer as dumb as a haddock on a Good Friday.

Jack never woke till the next morning, and then he was in a sad way. "'Tis to no use for me thinking to make that old Rapparee drunk," said Jack, "and how in this world can I help the poor souls out of the lobster-pots?" After ruminating nearly the whole day, a thought struck him. "I have it," says he, slapping his knee; "I'll be sworn that Coo never saw a drop of *poteen*, as old as he is, and that's the *thing* to settle him! Oh! then, is not it well that Biddy will not be home these two days yet; I can have another twist at him."

Jack asked Coo again, and Coo laughed at him for having no better head, telling him he'd never come up to his grandfather.

"Well, but try me again," said Jack, "and I'll be bail to drink you drunk and sober, and drunk again."

"Anything in my power," said Coo, "to oblige you."

At this dinner Jack took care to have his own liquor well watered, and to give the strongest brandy he had to Coo. At last says he, "Pray, sir, did you ever drink any poteen?—any real mountain dew?"

"No," says Coo; "what's that, and where does it come from?"

"Oh, that's a secret," said Jack, "but it's the right stuff—never believe me again, if 'tis not fifty times as good as brandy or rum either. Biddy's brother just sent me a present of a little drop, in exchange for some brandy, and as you're an old friend of the family, I kept it to treat you with."

"Well, let's see what sort of thing it is," said Coomara.

The *poteen* was the right sort. It was first-rate, and had the real smack upon it. Coo was delighted: he drank and he sung *Rum bum boodle boo* over and over again; and he laughed and he danced, till he fell on the floor fast asleep. Then Jack, who had taken good care to keep himself sober, snapt up the cocked hat—ran off to the rock—leaped, and soon arrived at Coo's habitation.

All was as still as a churchyard at midnight—not a Merrow, old or young, was there. In he went and turned up the pots, but nothing did he see, only he heard a sort of a little whistle or chirp as he raised each of them. At this he was surprised, till he recollected what the priests had often said, that nobody living could see the soul, no more than they could see the wind or the air. Having now done all that he could for them, he set the pots as they were before, and sent a blessing after the poor souls to speed them on their journey wherever they were going. Jack now began to think of returning; he put the hat on, as was right, the wrong way; but when he got out he found the water so high over his head that he had no hopes of ever getting up into it, now that he had not old Coomara to give him a lift. He walked about looking for a ladder, but not one could he find, and not a rock was there in sight. At last he saw a spot where the sea hung rather lower than anywhere else, so he resolved to try there. Just as he came to it, a big cod happened to put down his tail. Jack made a jump and caught hold of it, and the cod, all in amazement, gave a bounce and pulled Jack up. The minute the hat touched the water away Jack was whisked, and up he shot like a cork, dragging the poor cod, that he forgot to let go, up with him tail foremost. He got to the rock in no time and without a moment's delay hurried home, rejoicing in the good deed he had done.

But, meanwhile, there was fine work at home; for our friend Jack had hardly left the house on his soul-freeing expedition, when back came Biddy from her soul-saving one to the well. When she entered the house and saw the things lying *thrie-na-helah** on the table before her—"Here's a pretty job!" said she; "that

*Tri-na-cheile, literally through other—i.e., higgledy-piggledy.

blackguard of mine—what ill-luck I had ever to marry him! He has picked up some vagabond or other, while I was praying for the good of his soul, and they've been drinking all the *poteen* that my own brother gave him, and all the spirits, to be sure, that he was to have sold to his honour." Then hearing an outlandish kind of grunt, she looked down, and saw Coomara lying under the table. "The Blessed Virgin help me," shouted she, "if he has not made a real beast of himself! Well, well, I've often heard of a man making a beast of himself with drink! Oh hone, oh hone!—Jack, honey, what will I do with you, or what will I do without you? How can any decent woman ever think of living with a beast?"

With such like lamentations Biddy rushed out of the house, and was going she knew not where, when she heard the well-known voice of Jack singing a merry tune. Glad enough was Biddy to find him safe and sound, and not turned into a thing that was like neither fish nor flesh. Jack was obliged to tell her all, and Biddy, though she had half a mind to be angry with him for not telling her before, owned that he had done a great service to the poor souls. Back they both went most lovingly to the house, and Jack wakened up Coomara; and, perceiving the old fellow to be rather dull, he bid him not to be cast down, for 'twas many a good man's case; said it all came of his not being used to the *poteen*, and recommended him, by way of cure, to swallow a hair of the dog that bit him. Coo, however, seemed to think he had had quite enough. He got up, quite out of sorts, and without having the manners to say one word in the way of civility, he sneaked off to cool himself by a jaunt through the salt water.

Coomara never missed the souls. He and Jack continued the best friends in the world, and no one, perhaps, ever equalled Jack for freeing souls from purgatory; for he contrived fifty excuses for getting into the house below the sea, unknown to the old fellow, and then turning up the pots and letting out the souls. It vexed him, to be sure, that he could never see them; but as he knew the thing to be impossible, he was obliged to be satisfied.

Their intercourse continued for several years. However, one morning, on Jack's throwing in a stone as usual, he got no answer. He flung another, and another, still there was no reply. He went away, and returned the following morning, but it was to no purpose. As he was without the hat, he could not go down to see what had become of old Coo, but his belief was, that the old man, or the old fish, or whatever he was, had either died, or had removed from that part of the country.

Flory Cantillon's Funeral

T. CROFTON CROKER

The ancient burial-place of the Cantillon family was on an island in Ballyheigh Bay. This island was situated at no great distance from the shore, and at a remote period was overflowed in one of the encroachments which the Atlantic has made on that part of the coast of Kerry. The fishermen declare they have often seen the ruined walls of an old chapel beneath them in the water, as they sailed over the clear green sea of a sunny afternoon. However this may be, it is well-known that the Cantillons were, like most other Irish families, strongly attached to their ancient burial-place; and this attachment led to the custom, when any of the family died, of carrying the corpse to the seaside, where the coffin was left on the shore within reach of the tide. In the morning it had disappeared, being, as was traditionally believed, conveyed away by the ancestors of the deceased to their family tomb.

Connor Crowe, a county Clare man, was related to the Cantillons by marriage. "Connor Mac in Cruagh, of the seven quarters of Breintragh," as he was commonly called, and a proud man he was of the name. Connor, be it known, would drink a quart of salt water, for its medicinal virtues, before breakfast; and for the same reason, I suppose, double that quantity of raw whiskey between breakfast and night, which last he did with as little inconvenience to himself as any man in the barony of Moyferta; and were I to add Clanderalaw and Ibrickan, I don't think I should say wrong.

On the death of Florence Cantillon, Connor Crowe was determined to satisfy himself about the truth of this story of the old church under the sea: so when he heard the news of the old fellow's death, away with him to Ardfert, where Flory was laid out in high style, and a beautiful corpse he made.

Flory had been as jolly and as rollicking a boy in his day as ever was stretched, and his wake was in every respect worthy of him. There was all kind of entertainment, and all sort of diversion at it, and no less than three girls got husbands there—more luck to them. Everything was as it should be; all that side of the country, from Dingle to Tarbert, was at the funeral. The Keen was sung long and bitterly; and, according to the family custom, the coffin was carried to Ballyheigh strand, where it was laid upon the shore, with a prayer for the repose of the dead.

The mourners departed, one group after another, and at last Connor Crowe was left alone. He then pulled out his whiskey bottle, his drop of comfort, as he called it, which he required, being in grief; and down he sat upon a big stone that was sheltered by a projecting rock, and partly concealed from view, to await with patience the appearance of the ghostly undertakers.

The evening came on mild and beautiful. He whistled an old air which he had heard in his childhood, hoping to keep idle fears out of his head; but the wild strain of that melody brought a thousand recollections with it, which only made the twilight appear more pensive.

"If 'twas near the gloomy tower of Dunmore, in my own sweet country, I was," said Connor Crowe, with a sigh, "one might well believe that the prisoners, who were murdered long ago there in the vaults under the castle, would be the hands to carry off the coffin out of envy, for never a one of them was buried decently, nor had as much as a coffin amongst them all. 'Tis often, sure enough, I have heard lamentations and great mourning coming from the vaults of Dunmore Castle; but," continued he, after fondly pressing his lips to the mouth of his companion and silent comforter, the whiskey bottle, "didn't I know all the time well enough, 'twas the dismal sounding waves working through the cliffs and hollows of the rocks, and fretting themselves to foam. Oh, then, Dunmore Castle, it is you that are the gloomy-looking tower on a gloomy day, with the gloomy hills behind you; when one has gloomy thoughts on their heart, and sees you like a ghost rising out of the smoke made by the kelp burners on the strand, there is, the Lord save us! as fearful a look about you as about the Blue Man's Lake at midnight. Well, then, anyhow," said Connor, after a pause, "is it not a blessed night, though surely the moon looks mighty pale in the face? St Senan himself between us and all kinds of harm."

It was, in truth, a lovely moonlight night; nothing was to be seen around the dark rocks, and the white pebbly beach, upon which the sea broke with a hoarse and melancholy murmur. Connor, notwithstanding his frequent draughts, felt rather queerish, and almost began to repent his curiosity. It was certainly a solemn sight to behold the black coffin resting upon the white strand. His imagination gradually converted the deep moaning of old ocean into a mournful wail for the dead, and from the shadowy recesses of the rocks he imaged forth strange and visionary forms.

As the night advanced, Connor became weary with watching. He caught himself more than once in the act of nodding, when suddenly giving his head a shake, he would look towards the black coffin. But the narrow house of death remained unmoved before him.

It was long past midnight, and the moon was sinking into the sea, when he heard the sound of many voices, which gradually became stronger, above the heavy and monotonous roll of the sea. He listened, and presently could distinguish a Keen of exquisite sweetness, the notes of which rose and fell with the heaving of the waves, whose deep murmur mingled with and supported the strain!

The Keen grew louder and louder, and seemed to approach the beach, and then fell into a low, plaintive wail. As it ended Connor beheld a number of strange and, in the dim light, mysterious-looking figures emerge from the sea, and surround the coffin, which they prepared to launch into the water.

"This comes of marrying with the creatures of earth," said one of the figures, in a clear, yet hollow tone.

"True," replied another, with a voice still more fearful, "our king would never have commanded his gnawing white-toothed waves to devour the rocky roots of the island cemetery, had not his daughter, Durfulla, been buried there by her mortal husband!"

"But the time will come," said a third, bending over the coffin,

"When mortal eye—our work shall spy,
And mortal ear—our dirge shall hear."

"Then," said a fourth, "our burial of the Cantillons is at an end for ever!"

As this was spoken the coffin was borne from the beach by a retiring wave, and the company of sea people prepared to follow it; but at the moment one chanced to discover Connor Crowe, as fixed with wonder and as motionless with fear as the stone on which he sat.

"The time is come," cried the unearthly being, "the time is come; a human eye looks on the forms of ocean, a human ear has heard their voices. Farewell to the

84

Cantillons; the sons of the sea are no longer doomed to bury the dust of the earth!"

One after the other turned slowly round, and regarded Connor Crowe, who still remained as if bound by a spell. Again arose their funeral song; and on the next wave they followed the coffin. The sound of the lamentation died away, and at length nothing was heard but the rush of waters. The coffin and the train of sea people sank over the old churchyard, and never since the funeral of old Flory Cantillon have any of the family been carried to the strand of Ballyheigh, for conveyance to their rightful burial-place, beneath the waves of the Atlantic.

THE SOLITARY FAIRIES

Lepracaun Cluricaun Far Darrig

"The name *Lepracaun*," Mr Douglas Hyde writes to me, "is from the Irish *leith brog*—i.e., the One-shoemaker, since he is generally seen working at a single shoe. It is spelt in Irish *leith bhrogan*, or *leith phrogan, and* is in some places pronounced Luchryman, as O'Kearney writes it in that very rare book, the *Feis Tigh Chonain*."

The Lepracaun, Cluricaun, and *Far Darrig*. Are these one spirit in different moods and shapes? Hardly two Irish writers are agreed. In many things these three fairies, if three, resemble each other. They are withered, old, and solitary, in every way unlike the sociable spirits of the first sections. They dress with all unfairy homeliness, and are, indeed, most sluttish, slouching, jeering, mischievous phantoms. They are the great practical jokers among the good people.

The *Lepracaun* makes shoes continually, and has grown very rich. Many treasure-crocks, buried of old in war-time, has he now for his own. In the early part of this century, according to Croker, in a newspaper office in Tipperary, they used to show a little shoe forgotten by a Lepracaun.

The *Cluricaun*, (*Clobhair-ceann*, in O'Kearney) makes himself drunk in gentlemen's cellars. Some suppose he is merely the Lepracaun on a spree. He is almost unknown in Connaught and the north.

The *Far Darrig (fear dearg)*, which means the Red Man, for he wears a red cap and coat, busies himself with practical joking, especially with gruesome joking. This he does, and nothing else.

The *Fear-Gorta* (Man of Hunger) is an emaciated phantom that goes through the land in famine time, begging an alms and bringing good luck to the giver.

There are other solitary fairies, such as the House-spirit and the *Water-sheerie*, own brother to the English Jack-o'-Lantern; the *Pooka* and the *Banshee*—concerning these presently; the *Dallahan*, or headless phantom—one used to stand in a Sligo street on dark nights till lately; the Black Dog, a form, perhaps, of the *Pooka*. The ships at the Sligo quays are haunted sometimes by this spirit, who announces his presence by a sound like the flinging of all "the tin porringers in the world" down into the hold. He even follows them to sea.

The Leanhaun Shee (fairy mistress), seeks the love of mortals. If they refuse, she must be their slave; if they consent, they are hers, and can only escape by finding another to take their place. The fairy lives on their life, and they waste away. Death is no escape from her. She is the Gaelic muse, for she gives inspiration to those she persecutes. The Gaelic poets die young, for she is restless, and will not let them remain long on earth—this malignant phantom.

Besides these are divers monsters—the *Augh-iska*, the Waterhorse, the Payshtha (*píast-bestia*), the Lake-dragon, and such like; but whether these be animals, fairies, or spirits, I know not.

The Lepracaun; or Fairy Shoemaker

WILLIAM ALLINGHAM

I

Little Cowboy, what have you heard,
    Up on the lonely rath's green mound?
Only the plaintive yellow bird*
    Sighing in sultry fields around,
Chary, chary, chary, chee-ee!—
    Only the grasshopper and the bee?—
      "Tip-tap, rip-rap,
      Tick-a-tack-too!
Scarlet leather, sewn together,
    This will make a shoe.
Left, right, pull it tight;
    Summer days are warm;
Underground in winter,
    Laughing at the storm!"
Lay your ear close to the hill.
Do you not catch the tiny clamour,
Busy click of an elfin hammer,
Voice of the Lepracaun singing shrill
    As he merrily plies his trade?
      He's a span
      And a quarter in height.
Get him in sight, hold him tight,
      And you're a made
      Man!

*"Yellow bird", the yellow-bunting, or *yorlin*.

II

You watch your cattle the summer day,
Sup on potatoes, sleep in the hay;
   How would you like to roll in your carriage.
   Look for a duchess's daughter in marriage?
Seize the Shoemaker—then you may!
     "Big boots a-hunting,
     Sandals in the hall,
   White for a wedding-feast,
     Pink for a ball.
   This way, that way,
     So we make a shoe;
   Getting rich every stitch,
     Tick-tack-too!"
Nine-and-ninety treasure-crocks
This keen miser-fairy hath,
Hid in mountains, woods, and rocks,
Ruin and round-tow'r, cave and rath,
   And where the cormorants build;
     From times of old
     Guarded by him;
     Each of them fill'd
     Full to the brim
       With gold!

III

I caught him at work one day, myself,
   In the castle-ditch, where foxglove grows,—
A wrinkled, wizen'd and bearded Elf,
   Spectacles stuck on his pointed nose,
   Silver buckles to his hose,

Leather apron—shoe in his lap—
   "Rip-rap, tip-tap,
   Tick-tack-too!
(A grasshopper on my cap!
   Away the moth flew!)
Buskins for a fairy prince,
   Brogues for his son,—
Pay me well, pay me well,
   When the job is done!"
The rogue was mine, beyond a doubt.
I stared at him; he stared at me;
"Servant, Sir!" "Humph!" says he,
   And pull'd a snuff-box out.
He took a long pinch, look'd better pleased,
   The queer little Lepracaun;
Offer'd the box with a whimsical grace,—
Pouf! he flung the dust in my face,
   And, while I sneezed,
     Was gone!

Master and Man

T. CROFTON CROKER

Billy Mac Daniel was once as likely a young man as ever shook his brogue at a patron,* emptied a quart, or handled a shillelagh; fearing for nothing but the want of drink; caring for nothing but who should pay for it; and thinking of nothing but how to make fun over it; drunk or sober, a word and a blow was ever the way with Billy Mac Daniel; and a mighty easy way it is of either getting into or of ending a dispute. More is the pity that, through the means of his thinking, and fearing, and caring for nothing, this same Billy Mac Daniel fell into bad company; for surely the good people are the worst of all company any one could come across.

It so happened that Billy was going home one clear frosty night not long after Christmas; the moon was round and bright; but although it was as fine a night as heart could wish for, he felt pinched with cold. "By my word," chattered Billy, "a drop of good liquor would be no bad thing to keep a man's soul from freezing in him; and I wish I had a full measure of the best."

"Never wish it twice, Billy," said a little man in a three-cornered hat, bound all about with gold lace, and with great silver buckles in his shoes, so big that it was a wonder how he could carry them, and he held out a glass as big as himself, filled with as good liquor as ever eye looked on or lip tasted.

"Success, my little fellow," said Billy Mac Daniel, nothing daunted, though well he knew the little man to belong to the *good people*; "here's your health, any way, and thank you kindly; no matter who pays for the drink;" and he took the glass and drained it to the very bottom without ever taking a second breath to it.

"Success," said the little man; "and you're heartily welcome, Billy; but don't think to cheat me as you have done others—out with your purse and pay me like a gentleman."

*A festival held in honour of some patron saint.

"Is it I pay you?" said Billy; "could I not just take you up and put you in my pocket as easily as a blackberry?"

"Billy Mac Daniel," said the little man, getting very angry, "you shall be my servant for seven years and a day, and that is the way I will be paid; so make ready to follow me."

When Billy heard this he began to be very sorry for having used such bold words towards the little man; and he felt himself, yet could not tell how, obliged to follow the little man the live-long night about the country, up and down, and over hedge and ditch, and through bog and brake, without any rest.

When morning began to dawn the little man turned round to him and said, "You may now go home, Billy, but on your peril don't fail to meet me in the Fort-field tonight; or if you do it may be the worse for you in the long run. If I find you a good servant, you will find me an indulgent master."

Home went Billy Mac Daniel; and though he was tired and weary enough, never a wink of sleep could he bet for thinking of the little man; but he was afraid not to do his bidding, so up he got in the evening, and away he went to the Fort-field. He was not long there before the little man came towards him and said, "Billy, I want to go a long journey tonight; so saddle one of my horses, and you may saddle another for yourself, as you are to go along with me, and may be tired after your walk last night."

Billy thought this very considerate of his master, and thanked him accordingly: "But," said he, "if I may be so bold, sir, I would ask which is the way to your stable, for never a thing do I see but the fort here, and the old thorn tree in the corner of the field, and the stream running at the bottom of the hill, with the bit of bog over against us."

"Ask no questions, Billy," said the little man, "but go over to that bit of a bog, and bring me two of the strongest rushes you can find."

Billy did accordingly, wondering what the little man would be at; and he picked two of the stoutest rushes he could find, with a little bunch of brown blossom stuck at the side of each, and brought them back to his master.

"Get up, Billy," said the little man, taking one of the rushes from him and striding across it.

"Where shall I get up, please your honour?" said Billy.

"Why, upon horseback, like me, to be sure," said the little man.

"Is it after making a fool of me you'd be," said Billy, "bidding me get a horseback upon that bit of rush? May be you want to persuade me that the rush I pulled but a while ago out of the bog over there is a horse?"

"Up! up! and no words," said the little man, looking very angry; "the best horse you ever rode was but a fool to it." So Billy, thinking all this was in joke, and fearing to vex his master, straddled across the rush. "Borram! Borram! Borram!" cried the little man three times (which, in English, means to become great), and Billy did the same after him; presently the rushes swelled up into fine horses, and away they went full speed; but Billy, who had put the rush between his legs, without much minding how he did it, found himself sitting on horseback the wrong way, which was rather awkward, with his face to the horse's tail; and so quickly had his steed started off with him that he had no power to turn round, and there was therefore nothing for it but to hold on by the tail.

At last they came to their journey's end, and stopped at the gate of a fine house. "Now, Billy," said the little man, "do as you see me do, and follow me close; but as you did not know your horse's head from his tail, mind that your own head does not spin round until you can't tell whether you are standing on it or on your heels: for remember that old liquor, though able to make a cat speak, can make a man dumb."

The little man then said some queer kind of words, out of which Billy could make no meaning; but he contrived to say them after him for all that; and in they both went through the keyhole of the door, and through one key-hole after another, until they got into the wine-cellar, which was well stored with all kinds of wine.

The little man fell to drinking as hard as he could, and Billy, noway disliking the example, did the same. "The best of masters are you surely," said Billy to him; "no matter who is the next; and well pleased will I be with your service if you continue to give me plenty to drink."

"I have made no bargain with you," said the little man, "and will make none; but up and follow me." Away they went, through key-hole after key-hole; and each mounting upon the rush which he left at the hall door, scampered off, kicking the clouds before them like snow-balls, as soon as the words, "Borram, Borram, Borram", had passed their lips.

When they came back to the Fort-field the little man dismissed Billy, bidding him to be there the next night at the same hour. Thus did they go on, night after night, shaping their course one night here, and another night there; sometimes north, and sometimes east, and sometimes south, until there was not a gentleman's wine-cellar in all Ireland they had not visited, and could tell the flavour of every wine in it as well, ay, better than the butler himself.

One night when Billy Mac Daniel met the little man as usual in the Fort-field, and was going to the bog to fetch the horses for their journey, his master said to him, "Billy, I shall want another horse tonight, for may be we may bring back more company than we take." So Billy, who now knew better than to question any order given to him by his master, brought a third rush, much wondering who it might be that would travel back in their company, and whether he was about to have a fellow-servant. "If I have," thought Billy, "he shall go and fetch the horses from the bog every night; for I don't see why I am not, every inch of me, as good a gentleman as my master."

Well, away they went, Billy leading the third horse, and never stopped until they came to a snug farmer's house, in the county Limerick, close under the old castle of Carrigogunniel, that was built, they say, by the great Brian Boru. Within the house there was great carousing going forward, and the little man stopped outside for some time to listen; then turning round all of a sudden, said, "Billy, I will be a thousand years old tomorrow!"

"God bless us, sir," said Billy; "will you?"

"Don't say these words again, Billy," said the little old man, "or you will be my ruin for ever. Now Billy, as I will be a thousand years in the world tomorrow, I think it is full time for me to get married."

"I think so too, without any kind of doubt at all," said Billy, "if ever you mean to marry."

"And to that purpose," said the little man, "have I come all the way to Carrigogunniel; for in this house, this very night, is young Darby Riley going to be married to Bridget Rooney; and as she is a tall and comely girl, and has come of decent people, I think of marrying her myself, and taking her off with me."

"And what will Darby Riley say to that?" said Billy.

"Silence!" said the little man, putting on a mighty severe look; "I did not bring you here with me to ask questions;" and without holding further argument, he began saying the queer words which had the power of passing him through the key-hole as free as air, and which Billy thought himself mighty clever to be able to say after him.

In they both went; and for the better viewing the company, the little man perched himself up as nimbly as a cocksparrow upon one of the big beams which went across the house over all their heads, and Billy did the same upon another facing him; but not being much accustomed to roosting in such a place, his legs hung down as untidy as may be, and it was quite clear he had not taken pattern after the way in which the little man had bundled himself up together. If the little man had been a tailor all his life he could not have sat more contentedly upon his haunches.

There they were, both master and man, looking down upon the fun that was going forward; and under them were the priest and piper, and the father of Darby Riley, with Darby's two brothers and his uncle's son; and there were both the father and the mother of Bridget Rooney, and proud enough the old couple were that night of their daughter, as good right they had; and her four sisters, with bran new ribbons in their caps, and her three brothers all looking as clean and as clever as any three boys in Munster, and there were uncles and aunts, and gossips and cousins enough besides to make a full house of it; and plenty was there to eat and drink on the table for every one of them, if they had been double the number.

Now it happened, just as Mrs Rooney had helped his reverence to the first cut of the pig's head which was placed before her, beautifully bolstered up with white savoys, that the bride gave a sneeze, which made every one at table start, but not a soul said "God bless us". All thinking that the priest would have done so, as he ought if he had done his duty, no one wished to take the word out of his mouth, which, unfortunately, was preoccupied with pig's head and greens. And after a moment's pause the fun and merriment of the bridal feast went on without the pious benediction.

Of this circumstance both Billy and his master were no inattentive spectators from their exalted stations. "Ha!" exclaimed the little man, throwing one leg from under him with a joyous flourish, and his eye twinkled with a strange light, whilst his eyebrows became elevated into the curvature of Gothic arches; "Ha!" said he, leering down at the bride, and then up at Billy, "I have half of her now, surely. Let her sneeze but twice more, and she is mine, in spite of priest, mass-book, and Darby Riley."

Again the fair Bridget sneezed; but it was so gently, and she blushed so much, that few except the little man took, or seemed to take any notice; and no one thought of saying "God bless us".

Billy all this time regarded the poor girl with a most rueful expression of countenance; for he could not help thinking what a terrible thing it was for a nice young girl of nineteen, with large blue eyes, transparent skin, and dimpled cheeks, suffused with health and joy, to be obliged to marry an ugly little bit of a man, who was a thousand years old, barring a day.

At this critical moment the bride gave a third sneeze, and Billy roared out with all his might, "God save us!" Whether this exclamation resulted from his soliloquy, or from the mere force of habit, he never could tell exactly himself; but no sooner was it uttered than the little man, his face glowing with rage and disappointment, sprung from the beam on which he had perched himself, and shrieking out in the shrill voice of a cracked bagpipe, "I discharge you from my service, Billy Mac Daniel—take *that* for your wages," gave poor Billy a most furious kick in the back, which sent his unfortunate servant sprawling upon his face and hands right in the middle of the supper-table.

If Billy was astonished, how much more so was every one of the company into which he was thrown with so little ceremony. But when they heard his story, Father Cooney laid down his knife and fork, and married the young couple out of hand with all speed; and Billy Mac Daniel danced the Rinka at their wedding, and plenty he did drink at it too, which was what he thought more of than dancing.

Far Darrig in Donegal

MISS LETITIA MACLINTOCK

Pat Diver, the tinker, was a man well-accustomed to a wandering life, and to strange shelters; he had shared the beggar's blanket in smoky cabins; he had crouched beside the still in many a nook and corner where poteen was made on the wild Innishowen mountains; he had even slept on the bare heather, or on the ditch, with no roof over him but the vault of heaven; yet were all his nights of adventure tame and commonplace when compared with one especial night.

During the day preceding that night, he had mended all the kettles and saucepans in Moville and Greencastle, and was on his way to Culdaff, when night overtook him on a lonely mountain road.

He knocked at one door after another asking for a night's lodging, while he jingled the halfpence in his pocket, but was everywhere refused.

Where was the boasted hospitality of Innishowen, which he had never before known to fail? It was of no use to be able to pay when the people seemed so churlish. Thus thinking, he made his way towards a light a little farther on, and knocked at another cabin door.

An old man and woman were seated one at each side of the fire.

"Will you be pleased to give me a night's lodging, sir?" asked Pat respectfully.

"Can you tell a story?" returned the old man.

"No, then, sir, I canna say I'm good at story-telling," replied the puzzled tinker.

"Then you maun just gang farther, for none but them that can tell a story will get in here."

This reply was made in so decided a tone that Pat did not attempt to repeat his appeal, but turned away reluctantly to resume his weary journey.

"A story, indeed," muttered he. "Auld wives fables to please the weans!"

As he took up his bundle of tinkering implements, he observed a barn standing rather behind the dwelling-house, and, aided by the rising moon, he made his way towards it.

It was a clean, roomy barn, with a piled-up heap of straw in one corner. Here was a shelter not to be despised; so Pat crept under the straw and was soon asleep.

He could not have slept very long when he was awakened by the tramp of feet, and, peeping cautiously through a crevice in his straw covering, he saw four immensely tall men enter the barn, dragging a body which they threw roughly upon the floor.

They next lighted a fire in the middle of the barn, and fastened the corpse by the feet with a great rope to a beam in the roof. One of them began to turn it slowly before the fire. "Come on," said he, addressing a gigantic fellow, the tallest of the four—"I'm tired; you be to tak' your turn."

"Faix an' troth, I'll no' turn him," replied the big man.

"There's Pat Diver in under the straw, why wouldn't he tak' his turn?"

With hideous clamour the four men called the wretched Pat, who, seeing there was no escape, thought it was his wisest plan to come forth as he was bidden.

"Now, Pat," said they, "you'll turn the corpse, but if you let him burn you'll be tied up there and roasted in his place."

Pat's hair stood on end, and the cold perspiration poured from his forehead, but there was nothing for it but to perform his dreadful task.

Seeing him fairly embarked in it, the tall men went away.

Soon, however, the flames rose so high as to singe the rope, and the corpse fell with a great thud upon the fire, scattering the ashes and embers, and extracting a howl of anguish from the miserable cook, who rushed to the door, and ran for his life.

He ran on until he was ready to drop with fatigue, when, seeing a drain overgrown with tall, rank grass, he thought he would creep in there and lie hidden till morning.

But he was not many minutes in the drain before he heard the heavy tramping again, and the four men came up with their burthen, which they laid down on the edge of the drain.

"I'm tired," said one, to the giant; "it's your turn to carry him a piece now."

"Faix and troth, I'll no' carry him," replied he, "but there's Pat Diver in the drain, why wouldn't he come out and tak' his turn?"

"Come out, Pat, come out," roared all the men, and Pat, almost dead with fright, crept out.

He staggered on under weight of the corpse until he reached Kiltown Abbey, a ruin festooned with ivy, where the brown owl hooted all night long, and the forgotten dead slept around the walls under dense, matted tangles of brambles and ben-weed.

No one ever buried there now, but Pat's tall companions turned into the wild graveyard, and began digging a grave.

Pat, seeing them thus engaged, thought he might once more try to escape, and climbed up into a hawthorn tree in the fence, hoping to be hidden in the boughs.

"I'm tired," said the man who was digging the grave; "here, take the spade," addressing the big man, "it's your turn."

"Faix an' troth, it's no' my turn," replied he, as before. "There's Pat Diver in the tree, why wouldn't he come down and tak' his turn?"

Pat came down to take the spade, but just then the cocks in the little farmyards and cabins round the abbey began to crow, and the men looked at one another.

"We must go," said they, "and well is it for you, Pat Diver, that the cocks crowed, for if they had not, you'd just ha' been bundled into that grave with the corpse."

Two months passed, and Pat had wandered far and wide over the county Donegal, when he chanced to arrive at Raphoe during a fair.

Among the crowd that filled the Diamond he came suddenly on the big man.

"How are you, Pat Diver?" said he, bending down to look into the tinker's face.

"You've the advantage of me, sir, for I havna' the pleasure of knowing you," faltered Pat.

"Do you not know me, Pat?" Whisper—"When you go back to Innishowen, you'll have a story to tell!"

The Pooka

The Pooka, *rectè* Púca, seems essentially an animal spirit. Some derive his name from *poc*, a he-goat; and speculative persons consider him the forefather of Shakespeare's "Puck". On solitary mountains and among old ruins he lives, "grown monstrous with much solitude", and is of the race of the nightmare. "In the MS. story, called 'Mac-na-Michomhairle', of uncertain authorship," writes me Mr Douglas Hyde, "we read that 'out of a certain hill in Leinster, there used to emerge as far as his middle, a plump, sleek, terrible steed, and speak in human voice to each person about November-day, and he was accustomed to give intelligent and proper answers to such as consulted him concerning all that would befall them until the November of next year. And the people used to leave gifts and presents at the hill until the coming of Patrick and the holy clergy.' This tradition appears to be a cognate one with that of the Púca." Yes! unless it were merely an *augh-iska [each-uisgé]*, or Water-horse. For these, we are told, were common once, and used to come out of the water to gallop on the sands and in the fields, and people would often go between them and the marge and bridle them, and they would make the finest of horses if only you could keep them away from the sight of the water; but if once they saw a glimpse of the water, they would plunge in with their rider, and tear him to pieces at the bottom. It being a November spirit, however, tells in favour of the Pooka, for November-day is sacred to the Pooka. It is hard to realise that wild, staring phantom grown sleek and civil.

He has many shapes—is now a horse, now an ass, now a bull, now a goat, now an eagle. Like all spirits, he is only half in the world of form.

The Piper and the Púca

DOUGLAS HYDE

Translated literally from the Irish of the *Leabhar Sgeulaigheachta*

In the old times, there was a half fool living in Dunmore, in the county Galway, and although he was excessively fond of music, he was unable to learn more than one tune, and that was the "Black Rogue". He used to get a good deal of money from the gentlemen, for they used to get sport out of him. One night the piper was coming home from a house where there had been a dance, and he half drunk. When he came to a little bridge that was up by his mother's house, he squeezed the pipes on, and began playing the "Black Rogue" (an rógaire dubh). The Púca came behind him, and flung him up on his own back. There were long horns on the Púca, and the piper got a good grip of them, and then he said—

"Destruction on you, you nasty beast, let me home. I have a ten-penny piece in my pocket for my mother, and she wants snuff."

"Never mind your mother," said the Púca, "but keep your hold. If you fall, you will break your neck and your pipes." Then the Púca said to him, "Play up for me the 'Shan Van Vocht' (an t-seann-bhean bhocht)."

"I don't know it," said the piper.

"Never mind whether you do or you don't," said the Púca. "Play up, and I'll make you know."

The piper put wind in his bag, and he played such music as made himself wonder.

"Upon my word, you're a fine music-master," says the piper then; "but tell me where you're for bringing me."

"There's a great feast in the house of the Banshee, on the top of Croagh Patric tonight," says the Púca, "and I'm for bringing you there to play music, and, take my word, you'll get the price of your trouble."

"By my word, you'll save me a journey, then," says the piper, "for Father William put a journey to Croagh Patric on me, because I stole the white gander from him last Martinmas."

The Púca rushed him across hills and bogs and rough places, till he brought him to the top of Croagh Patric. Then the Púca struck three blows with his foot, and a great door opened, and they passed in together, into a fine room.

The piper saw a golden table in the middle of the room, and hundreds of old women (cailleacha) sitting round about it. The old woman rose up, and said, "A hundred thousand welcomes to you, you Púca of November (na Samhna). Who is this you have brought with you?"

"The best piper in Ireland," says the Púca.

One of the old women struck a blow on the ground, and a door opened in the side of the wall, and what should the piper see coming out but the white gander which he had stolen from Father William.

"By my conscience, then," says the piper, "myself and my mother ate every taste of that gander, only one wing, and I gave that to Moy-rua (Red Mary), and it's she told the priest I stole his gander."

The gander cleaned the table, and carried it away, and the Púca said, "Play up music for these ladies."

The piper played up, and the old women began dancing, and they were dancing till they were tired. Then the Púca said to pay the piper, and every old woman drew out a gold piece, and gave it to him.

"By the tooth of Patric," said he, "I'm as rich as the son of a lord."

"Come with me," says the Púca, "and I'll bring you home."

They went out then, and just as he was going to ride on the Púca, the gander came up to him, and gave him a new set of pipes. The Púca was not long until he brought him to Dunmore, and he threw the piper off at the little bridge, and then he told him to go home, and says to him, "You have two things now that you never had before—you have sense and music" (ciall agus ceól).

The piper went home, and he knocked at his mother's door, saying, "Let me in, I'm as rich as a lord, and I'm the best piper in Ireland."

"You're drunk," said the mother.

"No, indeed," says the piper, "I haven't drunk a drop."

The mother let him in, and he gave her the gold pieces, and, "Wait now," says he, "till you hear the music, I'll play."

He buckled on the pipes, but instead of music, there came a sound as if all the geese and ganders in Ireland were screeching together. He awakened the neighbours and they all were mocking him, until he put on the old pipes, and then he played melodious music for them; and after that he told them all he had gone through that night.

The next morning, when his mother went to look at the gold pieces, there was nothing there but the leaves of a plant.

The piper went to the priest, and told him his story, but the priest would not believe a word from him, until he put the pipes on him, and then the screeching of the ganders and geese began.

"Leave my sight, you thief," said the priest.

But nothing would do the piper till he would put the old pipes on him to show the priest that his story was true.

He buckled on the old pipes, and he played melodious music, and from that day till the day of his death, there was never a piper in the county Galway was as good as he was.

Daniel O'Rourke

T. CROFTON CROKER

People may have heard of the renowned adventures of Daniel O'Rourke, but how few are there who know that the cause of all his perils, above and below, was neither more nor less than having slept under the walls of the Pooka's tower. I knew the man well. He lived at the bottom of Hungry Hill, just at the right-hand side of the road as you go towards Bantry. An old man was he, at the time he told me the story, with grey hair and a red nose; and it was on the 25th of June 1813 that I heard it from his own lips, as he sat smoking his pipe under the old poplar tree, on as fine an evening as ever shone from the sky. I was going to visit the caves in Dursey Island, having spent the morning at Glengariff.

"I am often *axed* to tell it, sir," said he, "so that this is not the first time. The master's son, you see, had come from beyond foreign parts in France and Spain, as young gentlemen used to go before Buonaparte or any such was heard of; and sure enough there was a dinner given to all the people on the ground, gentle and simple, high and low, rich and poor. The *ould* gentlemen were the gentlemen after all, saving your honour's presence. They'd swear at a body a little, to be sure, and, may be, give one a cut of a whip now and then, but we were no losers by it in the end; and they were so easy and civil, and kept such rattling houses, and thousands of welcomes; and there was no grinding for rent, and there was hardly a tenant on the estate that did not taste of his landlord's bounty often and often in a year; but now it's another thing. No matter for that, sir, for I'd better be telling you my story.

"Well, we had everything of the best, and plenty of it; and we ate, and we drank, and we danced, and the young master by the same token danced with Peggy Barry, from the Bohereen—a lovely young couple they were, though they are both low enough now. To make a long story short, I got, as a body may say, the same thing as tipsy almost, for I can't remember ever at all, no ways, how it was I left the place;

only I did leave it, that's certain. Well, I thought, for all that, in myself, I'd just step to Molly Cronohan's, the fairy woman, to speak a word about the bracket heifer that was bewitched; and so as I was crossing the stepping-stones of the ford of Ballyashenogh, and was looking up at the stars and blessing myself—for why? it was Lady-day—I missed my foot, and souse I fell into the water. 'Death alive!' thought I, 'I'll be drowned now!' However, I began swimming, swimming away for the dear life, till at last I got ashore, somehow or other, but never the one of me can tell how, upon a *dissolute* island.

"I wandered and wandered about there, without knowing where I wandered, until at last I got into a big bog. The moon was shining as bright as day, or your fair lady's eyes, sir (with your pardon for mentioning her), and I looked east and west, and north and south, and every way, and nothing did I see but bog, bog, bog—I could never find out how I got into it; and my heart grew cold with fear, for sure and certain I was that it would be my *berrin* place. So I sat down, upon a stone which, as good luck would have it, was close by me, and I began to scratch my head, and sing the *Ullagone*—when all of a sudden the moon grew black, and I looked up, and saw something for all the world as if it was moving down between me and it, and I could not tell what it was. Down it came with a pounce, and looked at me full in the face; and what was it but an eagle? as fine a one as ever flew from the kingdom of Kerry. So he looked at me in the face, and says he to me, 'Daniel O'Rourke,' says he, 'how do you do?' 'Very well, I thank you, sir,' says I; 'I hope you're well;' wondering out of my senses all the time how an eagle came to speak like a Christian. 'What brings you here, Dan,' says he. 'Nothing at all, sir,' says I; 'only I wish I was safe home again.' 'Is it out of the island you want to go, Dan?' says he. ''Tis, sir, says I: so I up and told him how I had taken a drop too much, and fell into the water; how I swam to the island; and how I got into the bog and did not know my way out of it. 'Dan,' says he, after a minute's thought, 'though it is very improper for you to get drunk on Lady-day, yet as you are a decent sober man, who 'tends mass well, and never fling stones at me or mine, nor cries out after us in the fields—my life for yours,' says he; 'so get up on my back, and grip me well for fear you'd fall off, and I'll fly you out of the bog.' 'I am afraid,' says I, 'your honour's making game of me; for who ever heard of riding a horseback on an eagle before?' ' 'Pon the honour of a gentleman,' says he, putting his right foot on his breast, 'I am quite in earnest: and so now either take my offer or starve in the bog—besides, I see that your weight is sinking the stone.'

105

"It was true enough as he said, for I found the stone every minute going from under me. I had no choice; so thinks I to myself, faint heart never won fair lady, and this is fair persuadance. 'I thank your honour,' says I 'for the loan of your civility; and I'll take your kind offer.' I therefore mounted upon the back of the eagle, and held him tight enough by the throat, and up he flew in the air like a lark. Little I knew the trick he was going to serve me. Up—up—up, God knows how far up he flew. 'Why then,' said I to him—thinking he did not know the right road home—very civilly, because why? I was in his power entirely 'sir,' says I, 'please your honour's glory, and with humble submission to your better judgment, if you'd fly down a bit, you're now just over my cabin, and I could be put down there, and many thanks to your worship.'

" '*Arrah*, Dan,' said he, 'do you think me a fool? Look down in the next field, and don't you see two men and a gun? By my word it would be no joke to be shot this way, to oblige a drunken blackguard that I picked up off of a *could* stone in a bog.' 'Bother you,' said I to myself, but I did not speak out, for where was the use? Well, sir, up he kept, flying, flying, and I asking him every minute to fly down, and all to no use. 'Where in the world are you going, sir?' says I to him. 'Hold your tongue, Dan,' says he: 'mind your own business, and don't be interfering with the business of other people.' 'Faith, this is my business I think,' says I. 'Be quiet, Dan,' says he: so I said no more.

"At last where should we come to, but to the moon itself. Now you can't see it from this, but there is, or there was in my time, a reaping-hook sticking out of the side of the moon, this way (drawing the figure thus ⚯ on the ground with the end of his stick).

" 'Dan,' said the eagle, 'I'm tired with this long fly; I had no notion 'twas so far.' 'And my lord, sir,' said I, 'who in the world *axed* you to fly so far—was it I? did not I beg and pray and beseech you to stop half an hour ago?' 'There's no use talking, Dan,' said he; 'I'm tired bad enough, so you must get off, and sit down on the moon until I rest myself.' 'Is it sit down on the moon?' said I; 'is it upon that little round thing, then? why, then, sure I'd fall off in a minute, and be kilt and spilt, and smashed all to bits; you are a vile deceiver—so you are.' 'Not at all, Dan,' said he; 'you can catch fast hold of the reaping-hook that's sticking out of the side of the moon, and 'twill keep you up.' 'I won't then,' said I. 'May be not,' said he, quite quiet. 'If you don't, my man, I shall just give you a shake, and one slap of my wing, and send you down to the ground, where every bone in your body will be smashed as small as a drop of dew on a cabbage in the morning.' 'Why, then, I'm in a fine way,' said I to myself, 'ever to have come along with the likes of you;' and so giving him a hearty curse in Irish, for fear he'd know what I said, I got off his back with a heavy heart, took hold of the reaping-hook, and sat down upon the moon, and a mighty cold seat it was, I can tell you that.

"When he had me there fairly landed, he turned about on me, and said, 'Good morning to you, Daniel O'Rourke,' said he; 'I think I've nicked you fairly now. You robbed my nest last year' ('twas true enough for him, but how he found out is hard to say), 'and in return you are freely welcome to cool your heels dangling upon the moon like a cockthrow.'

" 'Is that all, and is this the way you leave me, you brute, you,' says I. 'You ugly unnatural *baste*, and is this the way you serve me at last? Bad luck to yourself, with your hook'd nose, and to all your breed, you blackguard.' 'Twas all to no manner of use; he spread out his great big wings, burst out a laughing, and flew away like lightning. I bawled after him to stop; but I might have called and bawled for ever, without his minding me. Away he went, and I never saw him from that day to this—sorrow fly away with him! You may be sure I was in a disconsolate condition, and kept roaring out for the bare grief, when all at once a door opened right in the middle of the moon, creaking on its hinges as if it had not been opened for a month before, I suppose they never thought of greasing 'em, and out there walks—who do you think but the man in the moon himself? I knew him by his bush.

" 'Good morrow to you, Daniel O'Rourke,' said he; 'how do you do?' 'Very well, thank your honour,' said I. 'I hope your honour's well.' 'What brought you here, Dan?' said he. So I told him how I was a little overtaken in liquor at the master's, and how I was cast on a *dissolute* island, and how I lost my way in the bog, and how the thief of an eagle promised to fly me out of it, and how, instead of that, he had fled me up to the moon.

" 'Dan,' said the man in the moon, taking a pinch of snuff when I was done, 'you must not stay here.' 'Indeed, sir,' says I, ' 'tis much against my will I'm here at all; but how am I to go back?' 'That's your business,' said he; 'Dan, mine is to tell you that here you must not stay; so be off in less than no time.' 'I'm doing no harm,' says I, 'only holding on hard by the reaping-hook, lest I fall off.' 'That's what you must not do, Dan,' says he. 'Pray, sir,' says I, 'may I ask how many you are in family, that you would not give a poor traveller lodging: I'm sure 'tis not often you're troubled with strangers coming to see you, for 'tis a long way.' 'I'm by myself, Dan,'

107

says he; 'but you'd better let go'. 'Indeed I will not,' says I, 'I needs the grip, and the more you bids me, the more I won't let go;—so I will.' 'You had better, Dan,' says he again. 'Why, then, my little fellow,' says I, taking the whole weight of him with my eye from head to foot, 'there are two words to that bargain; and I'll not budge, but you may if you like.' 'We'll see how that is to be,' says he; and back he went, giving the door such a great bang after him (for it was plain he was huffed) that I thought the moon and all would fall down with it.

"Well, I was preparing myself to try strength with him, when back again he comes, with the kitchen cleaver in his hand, and, without saying a word, he gives two bangs to the handle of the reaping-hook that was keeping me up, and *whap*! it came in two. 'Good morning to you, Dan,' says the spiteful little old blackguard, when he saw me cleanly falling down with a bit of the handle in my hand; 'I thank you for your visit, and fair weather after you, Daniel.' I had not time to make any answer to him, for I was tumbling over and over, and rolling and rolling, at the rate of a fox-hunt. 'God help me!' says I, 'but this is a pretty pickle for a decent man to be seen in at this time of night: I am now sold fairly.' The word was not out of my mouth when whiz! what should fly by close to my ear but a flock of wild geese, all the way from my own bog of Ballyasheenogh, else how should they know *me*? The *ould* gander, who was their general, turning about his head, cried out to me, 'Is that you, Dan?' 'The same,' said I, not a bit daunted now at what he said, for I was by this time used to all kinds of *bedevilment*, and, besides, I knew him of *ould*. 'Good morrow to you,' says he, 'Daniel O'Rourke; how are you in health this morning?' 'Very well, sir,' says I, 'I thank you kindly,' drawing my breath, for I was mightily in want of some. 'I hope your honour's the same.' 'I think 'tis falling you are, Daniel,' says he. 'You may say that, sir,' says I. 'And where are you going all the way so fast?' said the gander. So I told him how I had taken the drop, and how I came on the island, and how I lost my way in the bog, and how the thief of an eagle flew me up to the moon, and how the man in the moon turned me out. 'Dan,' said he, 'I'll save you: put out your hand and catch me by the leg, and I'll fly you home.' 'Sweet is your hand in a pitcher of honey, my jewel,' says I, though all the time I thought within myself that I don't much trust you; but there was no help, so I caught the gander by the leg, and away I and the other geese flew after him as fast as hops.

"We flew, and we flew, and we flew, until we came right over the wide ocean. I knew it well, for I saw Cape Clear to my right hand, sticking up out of the water.

'Ah, my lord,' said I to the goose, for I thought it best to keep a civil tongue in my head any way, 'fly to land if you please.' 'It is impossible, you see, Dan,' said he, 'for a while, because you see we are going to Arabia.' 'To Arabia!' said I; 'that's surely some place in foreign parts, far away. Oh! Mr Goose: why then, to be sure, I'm a man to be pitied among you.' 'Whist, whist, you fool,' said he, 'hold your tongue; I tell you Arabia is a very decent sort of place, as like West Carbery as one egg is like another, only there is a little more sand there.'

"Just as we were talking, a ship hove in sight, scudding so beautiful before the wind. 'Ah! then, sir,' said I, 'will you drop me on the ship, if you please?' 'We are not fair over it,' said he; 'if I dropped you now you would go splash into the sea.' 'I would not,' says I; 'I know better than that, for it is just clean under us, so let me drop now at once.'

" 'If you must, you must,' said he; 'there, take your own way;' and he opened his claw, and faith he was right—sure enough I came down plump into the very bottom of the salt sea! Down to the very bottom I went, and I gave myself up then for ever, when a whale walked up to me, scratching himself after his night's sleep, and he looked me full in the face, and never the word did he say, but lifting up his tail, he splashed me all over again with the cold salt water till there wasn't a dry stitch upon my whole carcass! and I heard somebody saying—'twas a voice I knew, too—'Get up you drunken brute, off o' that'; and with that I woke up, and there was Judy with a tub full of water, which she was splashing all over me—for, rest her soul! though she was a good wife, she never could bear to see me in drink, and had a bitter hand of her own.

" 'Get up,' said she again: 'and of all places in the parish would no place sarve your turn to lie down upon but under the ould walls of Carrigapooka? an uneasy resting I am sure you had of it.' And sure enough I had: for I was fairly bothered out of my senses with eagles, and men of the moons, and flying ganders, and whales, driving me through bogs, and up to the moon, and down to the bottom of the green ocean. If I was in drink ten times over, long would it be before I'd lie down in the same spot again, I know that."

The Kildare Pooka*

PATRICK KENNEDY

Mr H— R—, when he was alive, used to live a good deal in Dublin, and he was once a great while out of the country on account of the "ninety-eight" business. But the servants kept on in the big house at Rath—all the same as if the family was at home. Well, they used to be frightened out of their lives after going to their beds with the banging of the kitchen-door, and the clattering of fire-irons, and the pots and plates and dishes. One evening they sat up ever so long, keeping one another in heart with telling stories about ghosts and fetches, and that when—what would you have it?—the little scullery boy that used to be sleeping over the horses, and could not get room at the fire, crept into the hot hearth, and when he got tired listening to the stories, sorra fear him, but he fell dead asleep.

Well and good, after they were all gone and the kitchen fire raked up, he was woke with the noise of the kitchen door opening, and the trampling of an ass on the kitchen floor. He peeped out, and what should he see but a big ass, sure enough, sitting on his curabingo and yawning before the fire. After a little he looked about him, and began scratching his ears as if he was quite tired, and says he, "I may as well begin first as last." The poor boy's teeth began to chatter in his head, for says he, "Now he's goin' to ate me;" but the fellow with the long ears and tail on him had something else to do. He stirred the fire, and then he brought in a pail of water from the pump, and filled a big pot that he put on the fire before he went out. He then put in his hand—foot, I mean—into the hot hearth, and pulled out the little boy. He let a roar out of him with the fright, but the pooka only looked at him, and thrust out his lower lip to show how little he valued him, and then he pitched him into his pew again.

Well, he then lay down before the fire till he heard the boil coming on the water, and maybe there wasn't a plate, or a dish, or a spoon on the dresser that he

Legendary Fictions of the Irish Celts—Macmillan.

didn't fetch and put into the pot, and wash and dry the whole bilin' of 'em as well as e'er a kitchen-maid from that to Dublin town. He then put all of them up on their places on the shelves; and if he didn't give a good sweepin' to the kitchen, leave it till again. Then he comes and sits fornent the boy, let down one of his ears, and cocked up the other, and gave a grin. The poor fellow strove to roar out, but not a dheeg 'ud come out of the throat. The last thing the pooka done was to rake up the fire, and walk out, giving such a slap o' the door, that the boy thought the house couldn't help tumbling down.

Well, to be sure if there wasn't a hullabulloo next morning when the poor fellow told his story! They could talk of nothing else the whole day. One said one thing, another said another, but a fat, lazy scullery girl said the wittiest thing of all. "Musha!" says she, "if the pooka does be cleaning up everything that way when we are asleep, what should we be slaving ourselves for doing his work?" "*Shu gu dheine*,"* says another; "them's the wisest words you ever said, Kauth; it's meeself won't contradict you."

So said, so done. Not a bit of a plate or dish saw a drop of water that evening, and not a besom was laid on the floor, and every one went to bed soon after sundown. Next morning everything was as fine as fine in the kitchen, and the lord mayor might eat his dinner off the flags. It was great ease to the lazy servants, you may depend, and everything went on well till a foolhardy gag of a boy said he would stay up one night and have a chat with the pooka.

He was a little daunted when the door was thrown open and the ass marched up to the fire.

"An' then, sir," says he, at last, picking up courage, "if it isn't taking a liberty, might I ax who you are, and why you are so kind as to do half of the day's work for the girls every night?" "No liberty at all," says the pooka, says he: "I'll tell you, and welcome. I was a servant in the time of Squire R.'s father, and was the laziest rogue that ever was clothed and fed, and done nothing for it. When my time came for the other world, this is the punishment was laid on me—to come here and do all this labour every night, and then go out in the cold. It isn't so bad in the fine weather; but if you only knew what it is to stand with your head between your legs, facing the storm, from midnight to sunrise, on a bleak winter night." "And could we do anything for your comfort, my poor fellow?" says the boy. "Musha, I don't know," says the pooka; "but I think a good quilted frieze coat would help to keep

*Meant for *seadh go deimhin*—i.e., yes, indeed.

111

the life in me them long nights." "Why then, in troth, we'd be the ungratefullest of people if we didn't feel for you."

To make a long story short, the next night but two the boy was there again; and if he didn't delight the poor pooka holding up a fine warm coat before him, it's no mather! Betune the pooka and the man, his legs was got into the four arms of it, and it was buttoned down the breast and the belly, and he was so pleased he walked up to the glass to see how he looked. "Well," says he, "it's a long lane that has no turning. I am much obliged to you and your fellow-servants. You have made me happy at last. Good-night to you."

So he was walking out, but the other cried, "Och! sure your going too soon. What about the washing and sweeping?" "Ah, you may tell the girls that they must now get their turn. My punishment was to last till I was thought worthy of a reward for the way I done my duty. You'll see me no more." And no more they did, and right sorry they were for having been in such a hurry to reward the ungrateful pooka.

The Banshee

The *banshee* (from *ban* [*bean*], a woman, and *shee* [*sidhe*], a fairy) is an attendant fairy that follows the old families, and none but them, and wails before a death. Many have seen her as she goes wailing and clapping her hands. The keen [*caoine*], the funeral cry of the peasantry, is said to be an imitation of her cry.[7] When more than one banshee is present, and they wail and sing in chorus, it is for the death of some holy or great one. An omen that sometimes accompanies the banshee is the *coach-a-bower* (*cóiste-bodhar*)—an immense black coach, mounted by a coffin, and drawn by headless horses driven by a *Dullahan*. It will go rumbling to your door, and if you open it, according to Croker, a basin of blood will be thrown in your face. These headless phantoms are found elsewhere than in Ireland. In 1807 two of the sentries stationed outside St James's Park died of fright. A headless woman, the upper part of her body naked, used to pass at midnight and scale the railings. After a time the sentries were stationed no longer at the haunted spot. In Norway the heads of corpses were cut off to make their ghosts feeble. Thus came into existence the *Dullahans*, perhaps; unless, indeed, they are descended from that Irish giant who swam across the Channel with his head in his teeth.—ED.

How Thomas Connolly Met The Banshee

J. TODHUNTER

Aw, the banshee, sir? Well, sir, as I was striving to tell ye I was going home from work one day, from Mr Cassidy's that I tould ye of, in the dusk o' the evening. I had more nor a mile—aye, it was nearer two mile—to thrack to, where I was lodgin' with a dacent widdy woman I knew, Biddy Maguire be name, so as to be near me work.

It was the first week in November, an' a lonesome road I had to travel, an' dark enough, wid threes above it; an' about halfways there was a bit of a brudge I had to cross, over one o' them little sthrames that runs into the Doddher. I walked on in the middle iv the road, for there was no toe-path at that time, Misther Harry, nor for many a long day afther that; but, as I was sayin', I walked along till I come nigh upon the brudge, where the road was a bit open, an' there, right enough, I seen the hog's back o' the ould-fashioned brudge that used to be there till it was pulled down, an' a white mist steamin' up out o' the wather all around it.

Well, now, Misther Harry, often as I'd passed by the place before, that night it seemed sthrange to me, an' like a place ye might see in a dhrame; an as' I come up to it I began to feel a cowld wind blowin' through the hollow o' me heart. "Musha Thomas," sez I to meself, "is it yerself that's in it?" sez I; "or, if it is, what's the matter wid ye at all, at all?" sez I; so I put a bould face on it, an' I made a shruggle to set one leg afore the other, ontil I came to the rise o' the bridge. And there, God be good to us!in a cantle o' the wall I seen an ould woman, as I thought, sittin' on her hunkers, all crouched together, an' her head bowed down, seemin'ly in the greatest affliction.

Well, sir, I pitied the ould craythur, an thought I wasn't worth a thraneen, for the mortial fright I was in, I up an' sez to her, "That's a cowld lodgin' for ye, ma'am." Well, the sorra ha'porth she sez to that, nor tuk no more notice o' me than if I hadn't let a word out o' me, but kep' rockin' herself to an' fro, as if her heart was

114

breakin'; so I sez to her again, "Eh, ma'am, is there anythin' the matther wid ye?" An' I made for to touch her on the showldher, on'y somethin' stopt me, for as I looked closer at her I saw she was no more an ould woman nor she was an ould cat. The first thing I tuk notice to, Misther Harry, was her hair, that was sthreelin' down over her showldhers, an' a good yard on the ground on aich side of her. O, be the hoky farmer, but that was the hair! The likes of it I never seen on mortial woman, young or ould, before nor sense. It grew as sthrong out of her as out of e'er a young slip of a girl ye could see; but the colour of it was a misthery to describe. The first squint I got of it I thought it was silvery grey, like an ould crone's; but when I got up beside her I saw, be the glance o' the sky, it was a soart iv an Iscariot colour, an' a shine out of it like floss silk. It ran over her showldhers and the two shapely arms she was lanin' her head on, for all the world like Mary Magdalen's in a picther; and then I persaved that the grey cloak and the green gownd undhernaith it was made of no earthly matarial I ever laid eyes on. Now, I needn't tell ye, sir, that I seen all this in the twinkle of a bed-post—long as I take to make the narration of it. So I made a step back from her, an' "The Lord be betune us an' harm!" sez I, out loud, an' wid that I blessed meself. Well Misther Harry, the word wasn't out o' me mouth afore she turned her face on me. Aw, Misther Harry, but 'twas that was the awfullest apparation ever I seen, the face of her as she looked up at me! God forgive me for sayin' it, but 'twas more like the face of the 'Axy Homo' beyand in Marlboro Sthreet Chapel nor like any face I could mintion—as pale as a corpse, an' a most o' freckles on it, like the freckles on a turkey's egg; an' the two eyes sewn in wid thread, from the terrible power o' crying the' had to do; an' such a pair iv eyes as the' wor, Misther Harry, as blue as two forget-me nots, an' as cowld as the moon in a bog-hole of a frosty night, an' a dead-an'-live look in them that sent a cowld shiver through the marra o' me bones. Be the mortial! ye could ha' rung a tay cupful o' cowld paspiration out o' the hair o' me head that minute, so ye could. Well, I thought the life 'ud lave me intirely when she riz up from her hunkers, till, bedad! she looked mostly as tall as Nelson's Pillar; an' wid the two eyes gazin' back at me, an' her two arms stretched out before hor, an' a keine out of her that riz the hair o' me scalp till it was as stiff as the hog's bristles in a new hearth broom, away she glides—glides round the angle o' the brudge, an' down with her into the sthrame that ran undhernaith it. 'Twas then I began to suspect what she was. "Wisha, Thomas!" says I to meself, sez I; an' I made a great struggle to get me two legs into a throt, in spite o' the spavin o' fright the pair o' them wor in; an' how I brought meself home that same night the Lord in heaven only knows, for I never could tell; but I must ha' tumbled agin the door, and shot in head foremost into the middle o' the flure, where I lay in a dead swoon for mostly an hour; and the first I knew was Mrs Maguire stannin' over me with a jorum o' punch she was pourin' down me throath (throat), to bring back the life into me, an' me head in a pool of cowld wather she dashed over me in her first fright. "Arrah, Mister Connolly," shashee, "what ails ye?" shashee, "to put the scare on a lone woman like that?" shashee. "Am I in this world or the next?" sez I. "Musha! where else would ye be on'y here in my kitchen?" shashee. "O, glory be to God!" sez I, "but I thought I was in Purgathory at the laste, not to mintion an uglier place," sez I, "only it's too cowld I find meself, an' not too hot," sez I. "Faix, an' maybe ye wor more nor half-ways there, on'y for me, shashee; but what's come to you at all, at all? Is it your fetch ye seen, Mister Connolly?" "Aw, naboclish!"* sez I. "Never mind what I seen," sez I. So be degrees I began to come to a little; an' that's the way I met the banshee, Misther Harry!

"But how did you know it really was the banshee after all, Thomas?"

"Begor, sir, I knew the apparation of her well enough; but 'twas confirmed by a sarcumstance that occurred the same time. There was a Misther O'Nales was come on a visit, ye must know, to a place in the neighbourhood—one o' the ould O'Nales iv the county Tyrone, a rale ould Irish family—an' the banshee was heard keening round the house that same night, be more then one that was in it; an' sure enough, Misther Harry, he was found dead in his bed the next mornin'. So if it wasn't the banshee I seen that time, I'd like to know what else it could a' been."

*Na bac leis—i.e., don't mind it.

116

A Lamentation

For the Death of Sir Maurice Fitzgerald, Knight, of Kerry, who was killed in
Flanders, 1642

From The Irish, By Clarence Mangan

There was lifted up one voice of woe,
    One lament of more than mortal grief,
Through the wide South to and fro,
    For a fallen Chief.
In the dead of night that cry thrilled through me,
    I looked out upon the midnight air?
My own soul was all as gloomy,
    As I knelt in prayer.

O'er Loch Gur, that night, once—twice—yea, thrice—
    Passed a wail of anguish for the Brave
That half curled into ice
    Its moon-mirroring wave.
Then uprose a many-toned wild hymn in
    Choral swell from Ogra's dark ravine,
And Mogeely's Phantom Women
    Mourned the Geraldine!

Far on Carah Mona's emerald plains
    Shrieks and sighs were blended many hours,
And Fermoy in fitful strains
    Answered from her towers.
Youghal, Keenalmeaky, Eemokilly,
    Mourned in concert, and their piercing *keen*

117

Woke wondering life the stilly
    Glens of Inchiqueen.

From Loughmoe to yellow Dunanore
    There was fear; the traders of Tralee
Gathered up their golden store,
    And prepared to flee;
For, in ship and hall from night till morning,
    Showed the first faint beamings of the sun,
All the foreigners heard the warning
    Of the Dreaded One!

"This," they spake, "portendeth death to us,
    If we fly not swiftly from our fate!"
Self-conceited idiots! thus
    Ravingly to prate!
Not for base-born higgling Saxon trucksters
    Ring laments like those by shore and sea!
Not for churls with souls like hucksters
    Waileth our Banshee!

For the high Milesian race alone
    Ever flows the music of her woe!
For slain heir to bygone throne,
    And for Chief laid low!
Hark! . . . Again, methinks, I hear her weeping
    Yonder! is she near me now, as then?
Or was but the night-wind sweeping
    Down the hollow glen?

The Banshee Of The Mac Carthys

T. CROFTON CROKER

Charles Mac Carthy was, in the year 1749, the only surviving son of a very numerous family. His father died when he was little more than twenty, leaving him the Mac Carthy estate, not much encumbered, considering that it was an Irish one. Charles was gay, handsome, unfettered either by poverty, a father, or guardians, and therefore was not, at the age of one-and-twenty, a pattern of regularity and virtue. In plain terms, he was an exceedingly dissipated—I fear I may say debauched, young man. His companions were, as may be supposed, of the higher classes of the youth in his neighbourhood, and, in general, of those whose fortunes were larger than his own, whose dispositions to pleasure were, therefore, under still less restrictions, and in whose example he found at once an incentive and an apology for his irregularities. Besides, Ireland, a place to this day not very remarkable for the coolness and steadiness of its youth, was then one of the cheapest countries in the world in most of those articles which money supplies for the indulgence of the passions. The odious exciseman,—with his portentous book in one hand, his unrelenting pen held in the other, or stuck beneath his hat-band, and the inkbottle ("black emblem of the informer") dangling from his waistcoat-button—went not then from ale-house to ale-house, denouncing all those patriotic dealers in spirits, who preferred selling whiskey, which had nothing to do with English laws (but to elude them), to retailing that poisonous liquor, which derived its name from the British "Parliament" that compelled its circulation among a reluctant people. Or if the gauger—recording angel of the law—wrote down the peccadillo of a publican, he dropped a tear upon the word, and blotted it out for ever! For, welcome to the tables of their hospitable neighbours, the guardians of the excise, where they existed at all, scrupled to abridge those luxuries which they freely shared; and thus the competition in the market between the smuggler, who incurred little hazard, and the personage

119

ycleped fair trader, who enjoyed little protection, made Ireland a land flowing, not merely with milk and honey, but with whiskey and wine. In the enjoyments supplied by these, and in the many kindred pleasures to which frail youth is but too prone, Charles Mac Carthy indulged to such a degree, that just about the time when he had completed his four-and-twentieth year, after a week of great excesses, he was seized with a violent fever, which, from its malignity, and the weakness of his frame, left scarcely a hope of his recovery. His mother, who had at first made many efforts to check his vices, and at last had been obliged to look on at his rapid progress to ruin in silent despair, watched day and night at his pillow. The anguish of parental feeling was blended with that still deeper misery which those only know who have striven hard to rear in virtue and piety a beloved and favourite child; have found him grow up all that their hearts could desire, until he reached manhood; and then, when their pride was highest, and their hopes almost ended in the fulfilment of their fondest expectations, have seen this idol of their affections plunge headlong into a course of reckless profligacy, and, after a rapid career of vice, hang upon the verge of eternity, without the leisure or the power of repentance. Fervently she prayed that, if his life could not be spared, at least the delirium, which continued with increasing violence from the first few hours of his disorder, might vanish before death, and leave enough of light and of calm for making his peace with offended Heaven. After several days, however, nature seemed quite exhausted, and he sunk into a state too like death to be mistaken for the repose of sleep. His face had that pale, glossy, marble look, which is in general so sure a symptom that life has left its tenement of clay. His eyes were closed and sunk; the lids having that compressed and stiffened appearance which seemed to indicate that some friendly hand had done its last office. The lips, half closed and perfectly ashy, discovered just so much of the teeth as to give to the features of death their most ghastly, but most impressive look. He lay upon his back, with his hands stretched beside him, quite motionless; and his distracted mother, after repeated trials, could discover not the least symptom of animation. The medical man who attended, having tried the usual modes for ascertaining the presence of life, declared at last his opinion that it was flown, and prepared to depart from the house of mourning. His horse was seen to come to the door. A crowd of people who were collected before the windows, or scattered in groups on the lawn in front, gathered around when the door opened. These were tenants, fosterers, and poor relations of the family, with others attracted by affection, or by that interest which partakes of curiosity, but is something more, and which collects the lower ranks round a house where a human being is in his passage to another world. They saw the professional man come out from the hall door and approach his horse; and while slowly, and with a melancholy air, he prepared to mount, they clustered round him with inquiring and wistful looks. Not a word was spoken, but their meaning could not be misunderstood; and the physician, when he had got into his saddle, and while the servant was still holding the bridle as if to delay him, and was looking anxiously at his face as if expecting that he would relieve the general suspense, shook his head, and said in a low voice, "It's all over, James;" and moved slowly away. The moment he had spoken, the women present, who were very numerous, uttered a shrill cry, which, having been sustained for about half a minute, fell suddenly into a full, loud, continued, and discordant but plaintive wailing, above which occasionally were heard the deep sounds of a man's voice, sometimes in deep sobs, sometimes in more distinct exclamations of sorrow. This was Charles's foster-brother, who moved about the crowd, now clapping his hands, now rubbing them together in an agony of grief. The poor fellow had been Charles's playmate and companion when a boy, and afterwards his servant; had always been distinguished by his peculiar regard, and loved his young master as much, at least, as he did his own life.

When Mrs Mac Carthy became convinced that the blow was indeed struck, and that her beloved son was sent to his last account, even in the blossoms of his sin, she remained for some time gazing with fixedness upon his cold features; then, as if something had suddenly touched the string of her tenderest affections, tear after tear trickled down her cheeks, pale with anxiety and watching. Still she continued looking at her son, apparently unconscious that she was weeping, without once lifting her handkerchief to her eyes, until reminded of the sad duties which the custom of the country imposed upon her, by the crowd of females belonging to the better class of the peasantry, she now, crying audibly, nearly filled the apartment. She then withdrew, to give directions for the ceremony of waking, and for supplying the numerous visitors of all ranks with the refreshments usual on these melancholy occasions. Though her voice was scarcely heard, and though no one saw her but the servants and one or two old followers of the family, who assisted her in the necessary arrangements, everything was conducted with the greatest regularity; and though she made no effort to check her sorrows they never once suspended her attention, now more than ever required to preserve order in her household, which, in this season of calamity, but for her would have been all confusion.

The night was pretty far advanced; the boisterous lamentations which had prevailed during part of the day in and about the house had given place to a solemn and mournful stillness; and Mrs Mac Carthy, whose heart, notwithstanding her long fatigue and watching, was yet too sore for sleep, was kneeling in fervent prayer in a chamber adjoining that of her son. Suddenly her devotions were disturbed by an unusual noise, proceeding from the persons who were watching round the body. First there was a low murmur, then all was silent, as if the movements of those in the chamber were checked by a sudden panic, and then a loud cry of terror burst from all within. The door of the chamber was thrown open, and all who were not overturned in the press rushed wildly into the passage which led to the stairs, and into which Mrs Mac Carthy's room opened. Mrs Mac Carthy made her way through the crowd into her son's chamber, where she found him sitting up in the bed, and looking vacantly around, like one risen from the grave. The glare thrown upon his sunk features and thin lathy frame gave an unearthly horror to his whole aspect. Mrs Mac Carthy was a woman of some firmness; but she was a woman, and not quite free from the superstitions of her country. She dropped on her knees, and, clasping her hands, began to pray aloud. The form before her moved only its lips, and barely uttered "Mother"; but though the pale lips moved, as if there was a design to finish the sentence, the tongue refused its office. Mrs Mac Carthy sprung forward, and catching the arms of her son, exclaimed, "Speak! in the name of God and His saints, speak! are you alive?"

He turned to her slowly, and said, speaking still with apparent difficulty, "Yes, my mother, alive, and—but sit down and collect yourself; I have that to tell which will astonish you still more than what you have seen." He leaned back upon his pillow, and while his mother remained kneeling by the bedside, holding one of his hands clasped in hers, and gazing on him with the look of one who distrusted all her senses, he proceeded: "Do not interrupt me until I have done. I wish to speak while the excitement of returning life is upon me, as I know I shall soon need much repose. Of the commencement of my illness I have only a confused recollection; but within the last twelve hours I have been before the judgment-seat of God. Do not stare incredulously on me—'tis as true as have been my crimes, and as, I trust, shall be repentance. I saw the awful Judge arrayed in all the terrors which invest him when mercy gives place to justice. The dreadful pomp of offended

122

omnipotence, I saw—I remember. It is fixed here; printed on my brain in characters indelible; but it passeth human language. What I *can* describe I *will*—I may speak it briefly. It is enough to say, I was weighed in the balance, and found wanting. The irrevocable sentence was upon the point of being pronounced; the eye of my Almighty Judge, which had already glanced upon me, half spoke my doom; when I observed the guardian saint, to whom you so often directed my prayers when I was a child, looking at me with an expression of benevolence and compassion. I stretched forth my hands to him, and besought his intercession. I implored that one year, one month, might be given to me on earth to do penance and atonement for my transgressions. He threw himself at the feet of my Judge, and supplicated for mercy. Oh! never—not if I should pass through ten thousand successive states of being—never, for eternity, shall I forget the horrors of that moment, when my fate hung suspended—when an instant was to decide whether torments unutterable were to be my portion for endless ages! But Justice suspended its decree, and Mercy spoke in accents of firmness, but mildness, 'Return to that world in which thóu hast lived but to outrage the laws of Him who made that world and thee. Three years are given thee for repentance; when these are ended, thou shalt again stand here, to be saved or lost for ever.' I heard no more; I saw no more, until I awoke to life, the moment before you entered."

Charles's strength continued just long enough to finish these last words, and on uttering them he closed his eyes, and lay quite exhausted. His mother, though, as was before said, somewhat disposed to give credit to supernatural visitations, yet hesitated whether or not she should believe that, although awakened from a swoon which might have been the crisis of his disease, he was still under the influence of delirium. Repose, however, was at all events necessary, and she took immediate measures that he should enjoy it undisturbed. After some hours' sleep, he awoke refreshed, and thenceforward gradually but steadily recovered.

Still he persisted in his account of the vision, as he had at first related it; and his persuasion of its reality had an obvious and decided influence on his habits and conduct. He did not altogether abandon the society of his former associates, for his temper was not soured by his reformation; but he never joined in their excesses, and often endeavoured to reclaim them. How his pious exertions succeeded, I have never learnt; but of himself it is recorded that he was religious without ostentation, and temperate without austerity; giving a practical proof that vice may be exchanged for virtue, without the loss of respectability, popularity, or happiness.

Time rolled on, and long before the three years were ended the story of his vision was forgotten, or, when spoken of, was usually mentioned as an instance proving the folly of believing in such things. Charles's health, from the temperance and regularity of his habits, became more robust than ever. His friends, indeed, had often occasion to rally him upon a seriousness and abstractedness of demeanour, which grew upon him as he approached the completion of his seven-and-twentieth year, but for the most part his manner exhibited the same animation and cheerfulness for which he had always been remarkable. In company he evaded every endeavour to draw from him a distinct opinion on the subject of the supposed prediction; but among his own family it was well known that he still firmly believed it. However, when the day had nearly arrived on which the prophecy was, if at all, to be fulfilled, his whole appearance gave such promise of a long and healthy life, that he was persuaded by his friends to ask a large party to an entertainment at Spring House, to celebrate his birthday. But the occasion of this party,and the circumstances which attended it, will be best learned from a perusal of the following letters, which have been carefully preserved by some relations of his family. The first is from Mrs Mac Carthy to a lady, a very near connection and valued friend of her's who lived in the county of Cork, at about fifty miles' distance from Spring House.

TO MRS BARRY, CASTLE BARRY

Spring House, Tuesday morning,
October 15th, 1752

My dearest Mary,
    I am afraid I am going to put your affection for your old friend and kinswoman to a severe trial. A two days' journey at this season, over bad roads and through a troubled country, it will indeed require friendship such as yours to persuade a sober woman to encounter. But the truth is, I have, or fancy I have, more than usual cause for wishing you near me. You know my son's story. I can't tell you how it is, but as next Sunday approaches, when the prediction of his dream, or vision, will be proved false or true, I feel a sickening of the heart, which I cannot suppress, but which your presence, my dear Mary, will soften, as it has done so many of my sorrows. My nephew, James Ryan, is to be married to Jane Osborne (who, you know, is my son's ward), and the bridal entertainment will take place here on Sunday next,

124

though Charles pleaded hard to have it postponed for a day or two longer. Would to God—but no more of this till we meet. Do prevail upon yourself to leave your good man for *one* week, if his farming concerns will not admit of his accompanying you; and come to us, with the girls, as soon before Sunday as you can.

Ever my dear Mary's attached cousin and friend,

ANN MAC CARTHY

Although this letter reached Castle Barry early on Wednesday, the messenger having travelled on foot over bog and moor, by paths impassable to horse or carriage, Mrs Barry, who at once determined on going, had so many arrangements to make for the regulation of her domestic affairs (which, in Ireland, among the middle orders of the gentry, fall soon into confusion when the mistress of the family is away), that she and her two young daughters were unable to leave until late on the morning of Friday. The eldest daughter remained to keep her father company, and superintend the concerns of the household. As the travellers were to journey in an open one-horse vehicle, called a jaunting-car (still used in Ireland), and as the roads, bad at all times, were rendered still worse by the heavy rains, it was their design to make two easy stages—to stop about midway the first night, and reach Spring House early on Saturday evening. This arrangement was now altered, as they found that from the lateness of their departure they could proceed, at the utmost, no farther than twenty miles on the first day; and they, therefore, purposed sleeping at the house of a Mr Bourke, a friend of theirs, who lived at somewhat less than that distance from Castle Barry. They reached Mr Bourke's in safety after a rather disagreeable ride. What befell them on their journey the next day to Spring House, and after their arrival there, is fully recounted in a letter from the second Miss Barry to her eldest sister.

Spring House, Sunday evening,
20th October, 1752

Dear Ellen,

As my mother's letter, which encloses this, will announce to you briefly the sad intelligence which I shall here relate more fully, I think it better to go regularly through the recital of the extraordinary events of the last two days.

The Bourkes kept us up so late on Friday night that yesterday was pretty far advanced before we could begin our journey, and the day closed when we were nearly fifteen miles distant from this place. The roads were excessively deep, from the heavy rains of the last week, and we proceeded so slowly that, at last, my mother resolved on passing the night at the house of Mr Bourke's brother (who lives about a quarter-of-a-mile off the road), and coming here to breakfast in the morning. The day had been windy and showery, and the sky looked fitful, gloomy, and uncertain. The moon was full, and at times shone clear and bright; at others it was wholly concealed behind the thick, black, and rugged masses of clouds that rolled rapidly along, and were every moment becoming larger, and collecting together as if gathering strength for a coming storm. The wind, which blew in our faces, whistled bleakly along the low hedges of the narrow road, on which we proceeded with difficulty from the number of deep sloughs, and which afforded not the least shelter, no plantation being within some miles of us. My mother, therefore, asked Leary, who drove the jaunting-car, how far we were from Mr Bourke's? "'Tis about ten spades from this to the cross, and we have then only to turn to the left into the avenue, ma'am." "Very well, Leary; turn up to Mr Bourke's as soon as you reach the cross roads." My mother had scarcely spoken these words, when a shriek, that made us thrill as if our very hearts were pierced by it, burst from the hedge to to the right of our way. If it resembled anything earthly it seemed the cry of a female, struck by a sudden and mortal blow, and giving out her life in one long deep pang of expiring agony. "Heaven defend us!" exclaimed my mother. "Go you over the hedge, Leary, and save that woman, if she is not yet dead, while we run back to the hut we have just passed, and alarm the village near it." "Woman!" said Leary, beating the horse violently, while his voice trembled, "that's no woman; the sooner we get on, ma'am, the better"; and he continued his efforts to quicken the horse's pace. We saw nothing. The moon was hid. It was quite dark, and we had been for some time expecting a heavy fall of rain. But just as Leary had spoken, and had succeeded in making the horse trot briskly forward, we distinctly heard a loud clapping of hands, followed by a succession of screams, that seemed to denote the last excess of despair and anguish, and to issue from a person running forward inside the hedge, to keep pace with our progress. Still we saw nothing; until, when we were within about ten yards of the place where an avenue branched off to Mr Bourke's to the left, and the road turned to Spring House on the right, the moon started suddenly from behind a cloud, and enabled us to see, as plainly as I now see this paper, the figure of a tall, thin woman, with uncovered head, and long hair that floated round her shoulders, attired in something which seemed either a loose white cloak or a sheet thrown hastily about her. She stood on the corner hedge, where the road on which we were met that which leads to Spring House, with her face towards us, her left hand pointing to this place, and her right arm waving rapidly and violently as if to draw us on in that direction. The horse had stopped, apparently frightened at the sudden presence of the figure, which stood in the manner I have described, still uttering the same piercing cries, for about half a minute. It then leaped upon the road, disappeared from our view for one instant, and the next was seen standing upon a high wall a little way up the avenue on which we purposed going, still pointing towards the road to Spring House, but in an attitude of defiance and command, as if prepared to oppose our passage up the avenue. The figure was now quite silent, and its garments, which had been flown loosely in the wind, were closely wrapped around it. "Go on, Leary, to Spring House, in God's name!" said my mother; "whatever world it belongs to, we will provoke it no longer." "'Tis the Banshee, ma'am," said Leary; "and I would not, for what my life is worth, go anywhere this blessed night but to Spring House. But I'm afraid there's something bad going forward, or *she* would not send us there." So saying, he drove forward; and as we turned on the road to the right, the moon suddenly withdrew its light, and we saw the apparition no more; but we heard plainly a prolonged clapping of hands, gradually dying away, as if it issued from a person rapidly retreating. We proceeded as quickly as the badness of the roads and the fatigue of the poor animal that drew us would allow, and arrived here about eleven o'clock last night. The scene which awaited us you have learned from my mother's letter. To explain it fully, I must recount to you some of the transactions which took place here during the last week.

You are aware that Jane Osborne was to have been married this day to James Ryan, and that they and their friends have been here for the last week. On Tuesday last, the very day on the morning of which cousin Mac Carthy despatched the letter inviting us here, the whole of the company were walking about the grounds a little before dinner. It seems that an unfortunate creature, who had been seduced by James Ryan, was seen prowling in the neighbourhood in a moody, melancholy state for some days previous. He had separated from her several months, and, they say, had provided for her rather handsomely; but she had been seduced by the promise of his marrying her; and the shame of her unhappy condition, uniting with disappointment and jealousy, had disordered her intellects. During the whole forenoon of this Tuesday she had been walking in the plantations near Spring House, with her cloak folded tight round her, the hood nearly covering her face; and she had avoided conversing with or even meeting any of the family.

Charles Mac Carthy, at the time I mentioned, was walking between James Ryan and another, at a little distance from the rest, on a gravel path, skirting a shrubbery. The whole party was thrown into the utmost consternation by the report of a pistol, fired from a thickly-planted part of the shrubbery which Charles and his companions had just passed. He fell instantly, and it was found that he had been wounded in the leg. One of the party was a medical man. His assistance was immediately given, and, on examining, he declared that the injury was very slight, that no bone was broken, it was merely a flesh wound, and that it would certainly be well in a few days. "We shall know more by Sunday," said Charles, as he was carried to his chamber. His wound was immediately dressed, and so slight was the inconvenience which it gave that several of his friends spent a portion of the evening in his apartment.

On inquiry, it was found that the unlucky shot was fired by the poor girl I just mentioned. It was also manifest that she had aimed, not at Charles, but at the destroyer of her innocence and happiness, who was walking beside him. After a fruitless search for her through the grounds, she walked into the house of her own accord, laughing and dancing, and singing wildly, and every moment exclaiming that she had at last killed Mr Ryan. When she heard that it was Charles, and not Mr Ryan, who was shot, she fell into a violent fit, out of which, after working convulsively for some time, she sprung to the door, escaped from the crowd that pursued her, and could never be taken until last night, when she was brought here, perfectly frantic, a little before our arrival.

Charles's wound was thought of such little consequence that the preparations went forward, as usual, for the wedding entertainment on Sunday. But on Friday night he grew restless and feverish, and on Saturday (yesterday) morning felt so ill that it was deemed necessary to obtain additional medical advice. Two physicians and a surgeon met in consultation about twelve o'clock in the day, and the dreadful intelligence was announced, that unless a change, hardly hoped for, took place before night, death must happen within twenty-four hours after. The wound, it seems, had been too tightly bandaged, and otherwise injudiciously treated. The physicians were right in their anticipations. No favourable symptom appeared, and long before we reached Spring House every ray of hope had vanished. The scene we witnessed on our arrival would have wrung the heart of a demon. We heard briefly at the gate that Mr Charles was upon his death-bed. When we reached the house, the information was confirmed by the servant who opened the door. But just as we entered we were horrified by the most appalling screams issuing from the staircase. My mother thought she heard the voice of poor Mrs Mac Carthy, and sprung forward. We followed, and on ascending a few steps of the stairs, we found a young woman, in a state of frantic passion, struggling furiously with two men-servants, whose united strength was hardly sufficient to prevent her rushing upstairs over the body of Mrs Mac Carthy, who was lying in strong hysterics upon the steps. This, I afterwards discovered, was the unhappy girl I before described, who was attempting to gain access to Charles's room, to "get his forgiveness", as she said, "before he went away to accuse her for having killed him". This wild idea was mingled with another, which seemed to dispute with the former possession of her mind. In one sentence she called on Charles to forgive her, in the next she would denounce James Ryan as the murderer, both of Charles and her. At length she was torn away; and the last words I heard her scream were, "James Ryan, 'twas you killed him, and not I—'twas you killed him, and not I."

Mrs Mac Carthy, on recovering, fell into the arms of my mother, whose presence seemed a great relief to her. She wept—the first tears, I was told, that she had shed since the fatal accident. She conducted us to Charles's room, who, she said, had desired to see us the moment of our arrival, as he found his end approaching, and wished to devote the last hours of his existence to uninterrupted prayer and meditation. We found him perfectly calm, resigned, and even cheerful. He spoke of the awful event which was at hand with courage and confidence, and treated it as a doom for which he had been preparing ever since his former remarkable illness, and which he never once doubted was truly foretold to him. He bade us farewell with the air of one who was about to travel a short and easy journey; and we left him with impressions which, notwithstanding all their anguish, will, I trust, never entirely forsake us.

Poor Mrs Mac Carthy—but I am just called away. There seems a slight stir in the family; perhaps—

The above letter was never finished. The enclosure to which it more than once alludes told the sequel briefly, and it is all that I have further learned of the family of Mac Carthy. Before the sun had gone down upon Charles's seven-and-twentieth birthday, his soul had gone to render its last account to its Creator.

GHOSTS

Ghosts, or as they are called in Irish, *Thevshi* or *Tash* (*taidhbhse*, *tais*), live in a state intermediary between this life and the next. They are held there by some earthly longing or affection, or some duty unfulfilled, or anger against the living. "I will haunt you", is a common threat; and one hears such phrases as, "She will haunt him, if she has any good in her". If one is sorrowing greatly after a dead friend, a neighbour will say, "Be quiet now, you are keeping him from his rest"; or, in the Western Isles, according to Lady Wilde, they will tell you, "You are waking the dog that watches to devour the souls of the dead". Those who die suddenly, more commonly than others, are believed to become haunting Ghosts. They go about moving the furniture, and in every way trying to attract attention.

When the soul has left the body, it is drawn away, sometimes, by the fairies. I have a story of a peasant who once saw, sitting in a fairy rath, all who had died for years in his village. Such souls are considered lost. If a soul eludes the fairies, it may be snapped up by the evil spirits. The weak souls of young children are in especial danger. When a very young child dies, the western peasantry sprinkle the threshold with the blood of a chicken, that the spirits may be drawn away to the blood. A Ghost is compelled to obey the commands of the living. "The stable-boy up at Mrs G——'s there," said an old countryman, "met the master going round the yards after he had been two days dead, and told him to be away with him to the lighthouse, and haunt that; and there he is far out to sea still, sir. Mrs G—— was quite wild about it, and dismissed the boy." A very desolate lighthouse poor devil of a Ghost! Lady Wilde considers it is only the spirits who are too bad for heaven, and too good for hell, who are thus plagued. They are compelled to obey some one they have wronged.

The souls of the dead sometimes take the shapes of animals. There is a garden at Sligo where the gardener sees a previous owner in the shape of a rabbit. They will sometimes take the forms of insects, especially butterflies. If you see one fluttering near a corpse, that is the soul, and is a sign of its having entered upon immortal happiness. The author of the *Parochial Survey of Ireland, 1814*, heard a woman say to a child who was chasing a butterfly, "How do you know it is not the soul of your grandfather". On November eve the dead are abroad, and dance with the fairies.

As in Scotland, the fetch is commonly believed in. If you see the double, or fetch, of a friend in the morning, no ill follows; if at night, he is about to die.

A Dream

WILLIAM ALLINGHAM

I heard the dogs howl in the moonlight night;
I went to the window to see the sight;
All the Dead that ever I knew
   Going one by one and two by two.

On they pass'd, and on they pass'd;
Townsfellows all, from first to last;
Born in the moonlight of the lane,
   Quench'd in the heavy shadow again.

Schoolmates, marching as when we play'd
At soldiers once—but now more staid;
Those were the strangest sight to me
   Who were drown'd, I knew, in the awful sea.

Straight and handsome folk; bent and weak, too;
Some that I loved, and gasp'd to speak to;
Some but a day in their churchyard bed;
   Some that I had not known were dead.

A long, long crowd—where each seem'd lonely,
Yet of them all there was one, one only,
Raised a head or look'd my way.
   She linger'd a moment,—she might not stay.

How long since I saw that fair pale face!
Ah! Mother dear! might I only place
My head on thy breast, a moment to rest,
   While thy hand on my tearful cheek were prest!

On, on, a moving bridge they made
Across the moon-stream, from shade to shade,
Young and old, women and men;
   Many long-forgot, but remember'd then.

And first there came a bitter laughter;
A sound of tears the moment after;
And then a music so lofty and gay,
That every morning, day by day,
   I strive to recall it if I may.

Grace Connor

MISS LETITIA MACLINTOCK

Thady and Grace Connor lived on the borders of a large turf bog, in the parish of Clondevaddock, where they could hear the Atlantic surges thunder in upon the shore, and see the wild storms of winter sweep over the Muckish mountain, and his rugged neighbours. Even in summer the cabin by the bog was dull and dreary enough.

Thady Connor worked in the fields, and Grace made a livelihood as a pedlar, carrying a basket of remnants of cloth, calico, drugget, and frieze about the country. The people rarely visited any large town, and found it convenient to buy from Grace, who was welcomed in many a lonely house, where a table was hastily cleared, that she might display her wares. Being considered a very honest woman, she was frequently entrusted with commissions to the shops in Letterkenny and Ramelton. As she set out towards home, her basket was generally laden with little gifts for her children.

"Grace, dear," would one of the kind housewives say, "here's a farrel* of oaten cake, wi' a taste o' butter on it; tak' it wi' you for the weans;" or, "Here's half-a-dozen of eggs; you've a big family to support."

Small Connors of all ages crowded round the weary mother, to rifle her basket of these gifts. But her thrifty, hard life came suddenly to an end. She died after an illness of a few hours, and was waked and buried as handsomely as Thady could afford.

Thady was in bed the night after the funeral, and the fire still burned brightly, when he saw his departed wife across the room and bend over the cradle. Terrified, he muttered rapid prayers, covered his face with the blanket; and on looking up again the appearance was gone.

*When a large, round, flat griddle cake is divided into triangular cuts, each of these cuts is called a farrel, farli or parli.

Next night he lifted the infant out of the cradle, and laid it behind him in the bed, hoping thus to escape his ghostly visitor; but Grace was presently in the room, and stretching over him to wrap up her child. Shrinking and shuddering, the poor man exclaimed, "Grace, woman, what is it brings you back? What is it you want wi' me?"

"I want naething fae you, Thady, but to put thon wean back in her cradle," replied the spectre, in a tone of scorn. "You're too feared for me, but my sister Rose willna be feared for me—tell her to meet me tomorrow evening, in the old wallsteads."

Rose lived with her mother, about a mile off, but she obeyed her sister's summons without the least fear, and kept the strange tryste in due time.

"Rose, dear," she said, as she appeared before her sister in the old wallsteads, "my mind's oneasy about them twa' red shawls that's in the basket. Matty Hunter and Jane Taggart paid me for them, an' I bought them wi' their money, Friday was eight days. Gie them the shawls the morrow. An' old Mosey M'Corkell gied me the price o' a wiley coat; it's in under the other things in the basket. An' now farewell; I can get to my rest."

"Grace, Grace, bide a wee minute," cried the faithful sister, as the dear voice grew fainter, and the dear face began to fade—"Grace, darling! Thady? The children? One word mair!" but neither cries nor tears could further detain the spirit hastening to its rest!

A Legend of Tyrone

ELLEN O'LEARY

Crouched round a bare hearth in hard, frosty weather,
Three lonely helpless weans cling close together;
Tangled those gold locks, once bonnie and bright—
There's no one to fondle the baby tonight.

"My mammie I want; oh! my mammie I want!"
The big tears stream down with the low wailing chant.
Sweet Eily's slight arms enfold the gold head:
"Poor weeny Willie, sure mammie is dead—

And daddie is crazy from drinking all day—
Come down, holy angels, and take us away!"
Eily and Eddie keep kissing and crying—
Outside, the weird winds are sobbing and sighing.

All in a moment the children are still,
Only a quick coo of gladness from Will.
The sheeling no longer seems empty or bare,
For, clothed in soft raiment, the mother stands there.

They gather around her, they cling to her dress;
She rains down soft kisses for each shy caress.
Her light, loving touches smooth out tangled locks,
And, pressed to her bosom, the baby she rocks.

He lies in his cot, there's a fire on the hearth;
To Eily and Eddy 'tis heaven on earth,
For mother's deft fingers have been everywhere;
She lulls them to rest in the low *suggaun** chair.

They gaze open-eyed, then the eyes gently close,
As petals fold into the heart of a rose,
But ope soon again in awe, love, but no fear,
And fondly they murmur, "Our mammie is here."

She lays them down softly, she wraps them around;
They lie in sweet slumbers, she starts at a sound,
The cock loudly crows, and the spirit's away—
The drunkard steals in at the dawning of day.

Again and again, 'tween the dark and the dawn,
Glides in the dead mother to nurse Willie Bawn:
Or is it an angel who sits by the hearth?
An angel in heaven, a mother on earth.

*Chair made of twisted straw ropes.

The Black Lamb*

LADY WILDE

It is a custom amongst the people, when throwing away water at night, to cry out in a loud voice, "Take care of the water"; or literally, from the Irish, "Away with yourself from the water"—for they say that the spirits of the dead last buried are then wandering about, and it would be dangerous if the water fell on them.

One dark night a woman suddenly threw out a pail of boiling water without thinking of the warning words. Instantly a cry was heard, as of a person in pain, but no one was seen. However, the next night a black lamb entered the house, having the back all fresh scalded, and it lay down moaning by the hearth and died. Then they all knew that this was the spirit that had been scalded by the woman, and they carried the dead lamb out reverently, and buried it deep in the earth. Yet every night at the same hour it walked again into the house, and lay down, moaned, and died; and after this had happened many times, the priest was sent for, and finally, by the strength of his exorcism, the spirit of the dead was laid to rest; the black lamb appeared no more. Neither was the body of the dead lamb found in the grave when they searched for it, though it had been laid by their own hands deep in the earth, and covered with clay.

*Ancient Legends of Ireland.

Song of the Ghost

ALFRED PERCIVAL GRAVES

When all were dreaming
  But Pastheen Power,
A light came streaming
  Beneath her bower:
A heavy foot
  At her door delayed,
A heavy hand
  On the latch was laid.

"Now who dare venture,
  At this dark hour,
Unbid to enter
  My maiden bower?"
"Dear Pastheen, open
  The door to me,
And your true lover
  You'll surely see."

"My own true lover,
  So tall and brave,
Lives exiled over
  The angry wave."
"Your true love's body
  Lies on the bier,
His faithful spirit
  Is with you here."

"His look was cheerful,
    His voice was gay;
Your speech is fearful,
    Your face is grey;
And sad and sunken
    Your eye of blue,
But Patrick, Patrick,
    Alas! 'tis you!"

Ere dawn was breaking
    She heard below
The two cocks shaking
    Their wings to crow.
"Oh, hush you, hush you,
    Both red and grey,
Or will you hurry
    My love away.

"Oh, hush your crowing,
    Both grey and red,
Or he'll be going
    To join the dead;
Or, cease from calling
    His ghost to the mould,
And I'll come crowning
    Your combs with gold."

When all were dreaming
    But Pastheen Power,
A light went streaming
    From out her bower;
And on the morrow,
    When they awoke,
They knew that sorrow
    Her heart had broke.

The Radiant Boy

MRS CROW

Captain Stewart, afterwards Lord Castlereagh, when he was a young man, happened to be quartered in Ireland. He was fond of sport, and one day the pursuit of game carried him so far that he lost his way. The weather, too, had become very rough, and in this strait he presented himself at the door of a gentleman's house, and sending in his card, requested shelter for the night. The hospitality of the Irish country gentry is proverbial; the master of the house received him warmly; said he feared he could not make him so comfortable as he could have wished, his house being full of visitors already, added to which, some strangers, driven by the inclemency of the night, had sought shelter before him, but such accommodation as he could give he was heartily welcome to; whereupon he called his butler, and committing the guest to his good offices, told him he must put him up somewhere, and do the best he could for him. There was no lady, the gentleman being a widower.

Captain Stewart found the house crammed, and a very jolly party it was. His host invited him to stay, and promised him good shooting if he would prolong his visit a few days: and, in fine, he thought himself extremely fortunate to have fallen into such pleasant quarters.

At length, after an agreeable evening, they all retired to bed, and the butler conducted him to a large room, almost divested of furniture, but with a blazing turf fire in the grate, and a shake-down on the floor, composed of cloaks and other heterogeneous materials.

Nevertheless, to the tired limbs of Captain Stewart, who had had a hard day's shooting, it looked very inviting; but before he lay down, he thought it advisable to take off some of the fire, which was blazing up the chimney in what he thought an alarming manner. Having done this, he stretched himself on his couch and soon fell asleep.

He believed he had slept about a couple of hours when he awoke suddenly, and was startled by such a vivid light in the room that he thought it on fire, but on turning to look at the grate he saw the fire was out, though it was from the chimney the light proceeded. He sat up in bed, trying to discover what it was, when he perceived the form of a beautiful naked boy, surrounded by a dazzling radiance. The boy looked at him earnestly, and then the vision faded, and all was dark. Captain Stewart, so far from supposing what he had seen to be of a spiritual nature, had no doubt that the host, or the visitors, had been trying to frighten him. Accordingly, he felt indignant at the liberty, and on the following morning, when he appeared at breakfast, he took care to evince his displeasure by the reserve of his demeanour, and by announcing his intention to depart immediately. The host expostulated, reminding him of his promise to stay and shoot. Captain Stewart coldly excused himself, and, at length, the gentleman seeing something was wrong, took him aside, and pressed for an explanation; whereupon Captain Stewart, without entering into particulars, said he had been made the victim of a sort of practical joking that he thought quite unwarrantable with a stranger.

The gentleman considered this not impossible amongst a parcel of thoughtless young men, and appealed to them to make an apology; but one and all, on honour, denied the impeachment. Suddenly a thought seemed to strike him; he clapt his hand to his forehead, uttered an exclamation, and rang the bell.

"Hamilton," said he to the butler; "where did Captain Stewart sleep last night?"

"Well, sir," replied the man; "you know every place was full—the gentlemen were lying on the floor, three or four in a room—so I gave him the Boy's Room; but I lit a blazing fire to keep him from coming out."

"You were very wrong," said the host; "you know I have positively forbidden you to put anyone there, and have taken the furniture out of the room to ensure its not being occupied." Then, retiring with Captain Stewart, he informed him, very gravely of the nature of the phenomena he had seen; and at length, being pressed for further information, he confessed that there *existed* a tradition in the family, that whoever the "Radiant boy" appeared to will rise to the summit of power; and when he has reached the climax, will die a violent death, and I must say, he added, that the records that have been kept of his appearance go to confirm this persuasion.

The Fate of Frank M'Kenna

WILLIAM CARLETON

There lived a man named M'Kenna at the hip of one of the mountainous hills which divide the county of Tyrone from that of Monaghan. This M'Kenna had two sons, one of whom was in the habit of tracing hares of a Sunday whenever there happened to be a fall of snow. His father, it seems, had frequently remonstrated with him upon what he considered to be a violation of the Lord's day, as well as for his general neglect of mass. The young man, however, though otherwise harmless and inoffensive, was in this matter quite insensible to paternal reproof, and continued to trace whenever the avocations of labour would allow him. It so happened that upon a Christmas morning, I think in the year 1814, there was a deep fall of snow, and young M'Kenna, instead of going to mass, got down his cock-stick—which is a staff much thicker and heavier at one end than at the other—and prepared to set out on his favourite amusement. His father, seeing this, reproved him seriously, and insisted that he should attend prayers. His enthusiasm for the sport, however, was stronger than his love of religion, and he refused to be guided by his father's advice. The old man during the altercation got warm; and on finding that the son obstinately scorned his authority, he knelt down and prayed that if the boy persisted in following his own will, he might never return from the mountains unless as a corpse. The imprecation, which was certainly as harsh as it was impious and senseless, might have startled many a mind from a purpose that was, to say the least of it, at variance with religion and the respect due to a father. It had no effect, however, upon the son, who is said to have replied, that whether he ever returned or not, he was determined on going; and go accordingly he did. He was not, however, alone, for it appears that three or four of the neighbouring young men accompanied him. Whether their sport was good or otherwise, is not to the purpose, neither am I able to say; but the story goes that towards the latter part of the day they started a larger and darker hare than any they had ever seen, and that she kept dodging on before them bit by bit, leading them to suppose that every succeeding cast of the clock-stick would bring her down. It was observed afterwards that she also led them into the recesses of the mountains, and that although they tried to turn her course homewards, they could not succeed in doing so. As evening advanced, the companions of M'Kenna began to feel the folly of pursuing her farther, and to perceive the danger of losing their way in the mountains should night or a snow-storm come upon them. They therefore proposed to give over the chase and return home; but M'Kenna would not hear of it. "If you wish to go home, you may," said he; "as for me, I'll never leave the hills till I have her with me." They begged and entreated of him to desist and return, but all to no purpose: he appeared to be what the Scots call *fey*—that is, to act as if he were moved by some impulse that leads to death, and from the influence of which a man cannot withdraw himself. At length, on finding him invincibly obstinate, they left him pursuing the hare directly into the heart of the mountains, and returned to their respective homes.

In the meantime one of the most terrible snow-storms ever remembered in that part of the country came on, and the consequence was, that the self-willed young man, who had equally trampled on the sanctities of religion and parental authority, was given over for lost. As soon as the tempest became still, the neighbours assembled in a body and proceeded to look for him. The snow, however, had fallen so heavily that not a single mark of a footstep could be seen. Nothing but one wide waste of white undulating hills met the eye wherever it turned, and of M'Kenna no trace whatever was visible or could be found. His father now remembering the unnatural character of his imprecation, was nearly distracted; for although the body had not yet been found, still by every one who witnessed the sudden rage of the storm and who knew the mountains, escape or survival was felt to be impossible. Every day for about a week large parties were out among the hill-ranges seeking him, but to no purpose. At length there came a thaw, and his body was found on a snow-wreath, lying in a supine posture within a circle which he had drawn around him with his cock-stick. His prayer-book lay opened upon his mouth, and his hat was pulled down so as to cover it and his face. It is unnecessary to say that the rumour of his death, and of the circumstances under which he left home, created a most extraordinary sensation in the country—a sensation that was the greater in proportion to the uncertainty occasioned by his not having been found either alive or dead. Some affirmed that he had crossed the mountains, and was seen in Monaghan; others, that he had been seen in Clones, in Emyvale, in Five-mile-town; but despite of all these agreeable reports, the melancholy truth was at length made clear by the appearance of the body as just stated.

Now, it so happened that the house nearest the spot where he lay was inhabited by a man named Daly, I think—but of the name I am not certain—who was a herd or care-taker to Dr Porter, then Bishop of Clogher. The situation of this house was the most lonely and desolate-looking that could be imagined. It was at least two miles distant from any human habitation, being surrounded by one wide and dreary waste of dark moor. By this house lay the route of those who had found the corpse, and I believe the door of it was borrowed for the purpose of conveying it home. Be this as it may, the family witnessed the melancholy procession as it passed slowly through the mountains, and when the place and circumstances are all considered, we may admit that to ignorant and superstitious people, whose minds, even upon ordinary occasions, were strongly affected by such matters, it was a sight calculated to leave behind it a deep, if not a terrible impression. Time soon proved that it did so.

An incident is said to have occurred at the funeral in fine keeping with the wild spirit of the whole melancholy event. When the procession had advanced to a place called Mullaghtinny, a large dark-coloured hare, which was instantly recognised, by those who had been out with him on the hills, as the identical one that led him to his fate, is said to have crossed the roads about twenty yards or so before the coffin. The story goes, that a man struck it on the side with a stone, and that the blow, which would have killed any ordinary hare, not only did it no injury, but occasioned a sound to proceed from the body resembling the hollow one emitted by an empty barrel when struck.

In the meantime the interment took place, and the sensation began, like every other, to die away in the natural progress of time, when, behold, a report ran abroad like wild-fire that, to use the language of the people, "Frank M'Kenna was *appearing*!"

One night, about a fortnight after his funeral, the daughter of Daly, the herd, a girl about fourteen, while lying in bed saw what appeared to be the likeness of M'Kenna, who had been lost. She screamed out, and covering her head with the bed-clothes, told her father and mother that Frank M'Kenna was in the house. This alarming intelligence naturally produced great terror; still, Daly, who, notwithstanding his belief in such matters, possessed a good deal of moral courage, was cool enough to rise and examine the house, which consisted of only one apartment. This gave the daughter some courage, who, on finding that her father could not see him, ventured to look out, and she *then* could see nothing of him herself. She very soon fell asleep, and her father attributed what she saw to fear, or some accidental combination of shadows proceeding from the furniture, for it was a clear moonlight night. The light of the following day dispelled a great deal of their apprehensions, and comparatively little was thought of it until evening again advanced, when the fears of the daughter began to return. They appeared to be prophetic, for she said when night came that she knew he would appear again; and accordingly at the same hour he did so. This was repeated for several successive nights, until the girl, from the very hardihood of terror, began to become so far familiarised to the spectre as to venture to address it.

"In the name of God!" she asked, "what is troubling you, or why do you appear to me instead of to some of your own family or relations?"

The ghost's answer alone might settle the question involved in the authenticity of its appearance, being, as it was, an account of one of the most ludicrous missions that ever a spirit was despatched upon.

"I'm not allowed," said he, "to spake to any of my friends, for I parted wid them in anger; but I'm come to tell you that they are quarrelin' about my breeches—a new pair that I got made for Christmas day; an' as I was comin' up to thrace in the mountains, I thought the ould one 'ud do betther, an' of coorse I didn't put the new pair an me. My raison for appearin'," he added, "is, that you may tell my friends that none of them is to wear them—they must be given in charity."

This serious and solemn intimation from the ghost was duly communicated to the family, and it was found that the circumstances were exactly as it had represented them. This, of course, was considered as sufficient proof of the truth of its mission. Their conversations now became not only frequent, but quite friendly and familiar. The girl became a favourite with the spectre, and the spectre, on the other hand, soon lost all his terrors in her eyes. He told her that whilst his friends were bearing home his body, the handspikes or poles on which they carried him had cut his back, and *occasioned him great pain*! The cutting of the back also was known to be true, and strengthened, of course, the truth and authenticity of their dialogues. The whole neighbourhood was now in a commotion with this story of the apparition, and persons incited by curiosity began to visit the girl in order to satisfy themselves of the truth of what they had heard. Everything, however,

147

was corroborated, and the child herself, without any symptoms of anxiety or terror, artlessley related her conversations with the spirit. Hitherto their interviews had been all nocturnal, but now that the ghost found his footing made good, he put a hardy face on, and ventured to appear by daylight. The girl also fell into states of syncope, and while the fits lasted, long conversations with him upon the subject of God, the blessed Virgin, and Heaven, took place between them. He was certainly an excellent moralist, and gave the best advice. Swearing, drunkenness, theft,and every evil propensity of our nature, were declaimed against with a degree of spectral eloquence quite surprising. Common fame had now a topic dear to her heart, and never was a ghost made more of by his best friends than she made of him. The whole country was in a tumult, and I well remember the crowds which flocked to the lonely little cabin in the mountains, now the scene of matters so interesting and important. Not a single day passed in which I should think from ten to twenty, thirty, or fifty persons, were not present at these singular interviews. Nothing else was talked of, thought of, and, as I can well testify, dreamt of. I would myself have gone to Daly's were it not for a confounded misgiving I had, that perhaps the ghost might take such a fancy of appearing to *me*, as he had taken to cultivate an intimacy with the girl; and it so happens, that when I see the face of an individual nailed down in the coffin—chilling and gloomy operation!—I experience no particular wish to look upon it again.

The spot where the body of M'Kenna was found is now marked by a little heap of stones, which has been collected since the melancholy event of his death. Every person who passes it throws a stone upon the heap; but why this old custom is practised, or what it means, I do not know, unless it be simply to mark the spot as a visible means of preserving the memory of the occurrence.

Daly's house, the scene of the supposed apparition, is now a shapeless ruin, which could scarcely be seen were it not for the green spot that once was a garden, and which now shines at a distance like an emerald, but with no agreeable or pleasing associations. It is a spot which no solitary schoolboy will ever visit, nor indeed would the unflinching believer in the popular nonsense of ghosts wish to pass it without a companion. It is, under any circumstances, a gloomy and barren place; but when looked upon in connection with what we have just recited, it is lonely, desolate, and awful.

WITCHES, FAIRY DOCTORS

Witches and fairy doctors receive their power from opposite dynasties; the witch from evil spirits and her own malignant will; the fairy doctor from the fairies, and a something—a temperament—that is born with him or her. The first is always feared and hated.[9] The second is gone to for advice, and is never worse than mischievous. The most celebrated fairy doctors are sometimes people the fairies loved and carried away, and kept with them for seven years; not that those the fairies' love are always carried off—they may merely grow silent and strange, and take to lonely wanderings in the "gentle" places. Such will, in after-times, be great poets or musicians, or fairy doctors; they must not be confused with those who have a *Lianhaun shee* [*leannán-sidhe*], for the *Lianhaun shee* lives upon the vitals of its chosen, and they waste and die. She is of the dreadful solitary fairies. To her have belonged the greatest of the Irish poets, from Oisin down to the last century.

Those we speak of have for their friends the trooping fairies—the gay and sociable populace of raths and caves. Great is their knowledge of herbs and spells. These doctors, when the butter will not come on the milk, or the milk will not come from the cow, will be sent for to find out if the cause be in the course of common nature or if there has been witchcraft. Perhaps some old hag in the shape of a hare has been milking the cattle. Perhaps some user of "the dead hand" has drawn away the butter to her own churn. Whatever it be, there is the counter-charm. They will give advice, too, in cases of suspected changelings, and prescribe for the "fairy blast" (when the fairy strikes anyone a tumour rises, or they become paralysed. This is called a "fairy blast" or a "fairy stroke"). The fairies are, of course, visible to them, and many a new-built house have they bid the owner pull down because it lay on the fairies' road. Lady Wilde thus describes one who lived in Innis Sark:—"He never touched beer, spirits, or meat in all his life, but has lived entirely on bread, fruit, and vegetables. A man who knew him thus describes him—'Winter and summer his dress is the same—merely a flannel shirt and coat. He will pay his share at a feast, but neither eats nor drinks of the food and drink set before him. He speaks no English, and never could be made to learn the English tongue, though he says it might be used with great effect to curse one's enemy. He holds a burial-ground sacred, and would not carry away so much as a leaf of ivy from a grave. And he maintains that the people are right to keep to their ancient usages, such as never to dig a grave on a Monday, and to carry the coffin three times round the grave, following the course of the sun, for then the dead rest in peace. Like the people, also, he holds suicides as accursed; for they believe that all its dead turn over on their faces if a suicide is laid amongst them.

" 'Though well off, he never, even in his youth, thought of taking a wife; nor was he ever known to love a woman. He stands quite apart from life, and by this means holds his power over the mysteries. No money will tempt him to impart his knowledge to another, for if he did he would be struck dead—so he believes. He would not touch a hazel stick, but carries an ash wand, which he holds in his hands when he prays, laid across his knees; and the whole of his life is devoted to works of grace and charity, and though now an old man, he has never had a day's sickness. No one has ever seen him in a rage, nor heard an angry word from his lips but once, and then being under great irritation, he recited the Lord's Prayer backwards as an imprecation on his enemy. Before his death he will reveal the mystery of his power, but not till the hand of death is on him for certain.' " When he does reveal it, we may be sure it will be to one person only—his successor. There are several such doctors in County Sligo, really well up in herbal medicine by all accounts, and my friends find them in their own counties. All these things go on merrily. The spirit of the age laughs in vain, and is itself only a ripple to pass, or already passing away.

The spells of the witch are altogether different; they smell of the grave. One of the most powerful is the charm of the dead hand. With a hand cut from a corpse they, muttering words of power, will stir a well and skim from its surface a neighbour's butter.

A candle held between the fingers of the dead hand can never be blown out. This is useful to robbers, but they appeal for the suffrage of the lovers likewise, for they can make love-potions by drying and grinding into powder the liver of a black cat. Mixed with tea, and poured from a black teapot, it is infallible. There are many stories of its success in quite recent years, but, unhappily, the spell must be continually renewed, or all the love may turn into hate. But the central notion of witchcraft everywhere is the power to change into some fictitious form, usually in Ireland a hare or a cat. Long ago a wolf was the favourite. Before Giraldus Cambrensis came to Ireland, a monk wandering in a forest at night came upon two wolves, one of whom was dying. The other entreated him to give the dying wolf the last sacrament. He said the mass, and paused when he came to the viaticum. The other, on seeing this, tore the skin from the breast of the dying wolf, laying bare the form of an old woman. Thereon the monk gave the sacrament. Years afterwards he confessed the matter, and when Giraldus visited the country, was being tried by the synod of the bishops. To give the sacrament to an animal was a great sin. Was it a human being or an animal? On the advice of Giraldus they sent the monk, with papers describing the matter, to the Pope for his decision. The result is not stated.

Giraldus himself was of opinion that the wolf-form was an illusion, for, as he argued, only God can change the form. His opinion coincides with tradition, Irish and otherwise.

It is the notion of many who have written about these things that magic is mainly the making of such illusions. Patrick Kennedy tells a story of a girl who, having in her hand a sod of grass containing, unknown to herself, a four-leaved shamrock, watched a conjurer at a fair. Now, the four-leaved shamrock guards its owner from all *pishogues* (spells), and when the others were staring at a cock carrying along the roof of a shed a huge beam in its bill, she asked them what they found to wonder at in a cock with a straw. The conjurer begged from her the sod of grass, to give to his horse, he said. Immediately she cried out in terror that the beam would fall and kill somebody.

This, then, is to be remembered—the form of an enchanted thing is a fiction and a caprice.

Bewitched Butter (Donegal)

MISS LETITIA MACLINTOCK

Not far from Rathmullen lived, last spring, a family called Hanlon; and in a farm-house, some fields distant, people named Dogherty. Both families had good cows, but the Hanlons were fortunate in possessing a Kerry cow that gave more milk and yellower butter than the others.

Grace Dogherty, a young girl, who was more admired than loved in the neighbourhood, took much interest in the Kerry cow, and appeared one night at Mrs Hanlon's door with the modest request—

"Will you let me milk your Moiley* cow?"

"An' why wad you wish to milk wee Moiley, Grace, dear," inquired Mrs Hanlon.

"Oh, just becase you're sae throng at the present time."

"Thank you kindly, Grace, but I'm no too throng to do my ain work. I'll no trouble you to milk."

The girl turned away with a discontented air; but the next evening, and the next, found her at the cow-house door with the same request.

At length Mrs Hanlon, not knowing well how to persist in her refusal, yielded, and permitted Grace to milk the Kerry cow.

She soon had reason to regret her want of firmness. Moiley gave no milk to her owner.

When this melancholy state of things lasted for three days, the Hanlons applied to a certain Mark McCarrion, who lived near Binion.

"That cow has been milked by someone with an evil eye," said he. "Will she give you a wee drop, do you think? The full of a pint measure wad do."

"Oh, ay, Mark, dear; I'll get that much milk frae her, any way."

---

*In Connaught called a "mweeal" cow—i.e., a cow without horns. Irish *maol*, literally, blunt. When the new hammerless breech-loaders came into use two or three years ago, Mr Douglas Hyde heard a Connaught gentleman speak of them as the "mweeal" guns, because they had no cocks.

"Weel, Mrs Hanlon, lock the door, an' get nine new pins that was never used in clothes, an' put them into a saucepan wi' the pint o' milk. Set them on the fire, an' let them come to the boil."

The nine pins soon began to simmer in Moiley's milk.

Rapid steps were heard approaching the door, agitated knocks followed, and Grace Dogherty's high-toned voice was raised in eager entreaty.

"Let me in, Mrs Hanlon!" she cried. "Tak off that cruel pot! Tak out them pins, for they're pricking holes in my heart, an' I'll never offer to touch milk of yours again."

[There is hardly a village in Ireland where the milk is not thus believed to have been stolen times upon times. There are many counter-charms. Sometimes the coulter of a plough will be heated red-hot, and the witch will rush in, crying out that she is burning. A new horse-shoe or donkey-shoe, heated and put under the churn, with three straws, if possible, stolen at midnight from over the witches' door, is quite infallible.-ED.]

A Queen's County Witch*

It was about eighty years ago, in the month of May, that a Roman Catholic clergyman, near Rathdowney, in the Queen's County, was awakened at midnight to attend a dying man in a distant part of the parish. The priest obeyed without a murmur, and having performed his duty to the expiring sinner, saw him depart this world before he left the cabin. As it was yet dark, the man who had called on the priest offered to accompany him home, but he refused, and set forward on his journey alone. The grey dawn began to appear over the hills. The good priest was highly enraptured with the beauty of the scene, and rode on, now gazing intently at every surrounding object, and again cutting with his whip at the bats and big beautiful night-flies which flitted ever and anon from hedge to hedge across his lonely way. Thus engaged, he journeyed on slowly, until the nearer approach of sunrise began to render objects completely discernible, when he dismounted from his horse, and slipping his arm out of the rein, and drawing forth his "Breviary" from his pocket, he commenced reading his "morning office" as he walked leisurely along.

He had not proceeded very far, when he observed his horse, a very spirited animal, endeavouring to stop on the road, and gazing intently into a field on one side of the way where there were three or four cows grazing. However, he did not pay any particular attention to this circumstance, but went on a little farther, when the horse suddenly plunged with great violence, and endeavoured to break away by force. The priest with great difficulty succeeded in restraining him, and, looking at him more closely, observed him shaking from head to foot, and sweating profusely. He now stood calmly, and refused to move from where he was, nor could threats or entreaty induce him to proceed. The father was greatly astonished, but recollecting to have often heard of horses labouring under affright being induced

*Dublin University Magazine, 1839.

154

to go by blindfolding them, he took out his handkerchief and tied it across his eyes. He then mounted, and, striking him gently, he went forward without reluctance, but still sweating and trembling violently. They had not gone far, when they arrived opposite a narrow path or bridle-way, flanked at either side by a tall, thick hedge, which led from the high road to the field where the cows were grazing. The priest happened by chance to look into the lane, and saw a spectacle which made the blood curdle in his veins. It was the legs of a man from the hips downwards, without head or body, trotting up the avenue at a smart pace. The good father was very much alarmed, but, being a man of strong nerve, he resolved, come what might, to stand, and be further acquainted with this singular spectre. He accordingly stood, and so did the headless apparition, as if afraid to approach him. The priest observing this, pulled back a little from the entrance of the avenue, and the phantom again resumed its progress. It soon arrived on the road, and the priest now had sufficient opportunity to view it minutely. It wore yellow buckskin breeches, tightly fastened at the knees with green ribbon; it had neither shoes nor stockings on, and its legs were covered with long, red hairs, and all full of wet, blood, and clay, apparently contracted in its progress through the thorny hedges. The priest, although very much alarmed, felt eager to examine the phantom, and for this purpose summoned all his philosophy to enable him to speak to it. The ghost was now a little ahead, pursuing its march at its usual brisk trot, and the priest urged on his horse speedily until he came up with it, and thus addressed it—

"Hilloa, friend! who art thou, or whither art thou going so early?"

The hideous spectre made no reply, but uttered a fierce and superhuman growl, or "Umph".

"A fine morning for ghosts to wander abroad," again said the priest.

Another "Umph" was the reply.

"Why don't you speak?"

"Umph."

"You don't seem disposed to be very loquacious this morning."

"Umph," again.

The good man began to feel irritated at the obstinate silence of his unearthly visitor, and said, with some warmth—

"In the name of all that's sacred, I command you to answer me, Who art thou, or where art thou travelling?"

Another "Umph", more loud and more angry than before, was the only reply.

"Perhaps," said the father, "a taste of whipcord might render you a little more communicative"; and so saying, he struck the apparition a heavy blow with his whip on the breech.

The phantom uttered a wild and unearthly yell, and fell forward on the road, and what was the priest's astonishment when he perceived the whole place running over with milk. He was struck dumb with amazement; the prostrate phantom still continued to eject vast quantities of milk from every part; the priest's head swam, his eyes got dizzy; a stupor came all over him for some minutes, and on his recovering, the frightful spectre had vanished, and in its stead he found stretched on the road, and half drowned in milk, the form of Sarah Kennedy, an old woman of the neighbourhood, who had been long notorious in that district for her witchcraft and superstitious practices, and it was now discovered that she had, by infernal aid, assumed that monstrous shape, and was employed that morning in sucking the cows of the village. Had a volcano burst forth at his feet, he could not be more astonished; he gazed awhile in silent amazement—the old woman groaning, and writhing convulsively.

"Sarah," said he, at length, "I have long admonished you to repent of your evil ways, but you were deaf to my entreaties; and now, wretched woman, you are surprised in the midst of your crimes."

"Oh, father, father," shouted the unfortunate woman, "can you do nothing to save me? I am lost; hell is open for me, and legions of devils surround me this moment, waiting to carry my soul to perdition."

The priest had not power to reply; the old wretch's pains increased; her body swelled to an immense size; her eyes flashed as if on fire, her face was black as night, her entire form writhed in a thousand different contortions; her outcries were appalling, her face sunk, her eyes closed, and in a few minutes she expired in the most exquisite tortures.

The priest departed homewards, and called at the next cabin to give notice of the strange circumstances. The remains of Sarah Kennedy were removed to her cabin, situate at the edge of a small wood at a little distance. She had long been a resident in that neighbourhood, but still she was a stranger, and came there no one knew from whence. She had no relation in that country but one daughter, now advanced in years, who resided with her. She kept one cow, but sold more butter, it was said, than any farmer in the parish, and it was generally suspected that she acquired it by devilish agency, as she never made a secret of being intimately acquainted with sorcery and fairyism. She professed the Roman Catholic religion, but never complied with the practices enjoined by that church, and her remains were denied Christian sepulture, and were buried in a sand-pit near her own cabin.

On the evening of her burial, the villagers assembled and burned her cabin to the earth. Her daughter made her escape, and never after returned.

The Witch Hare

MR AND MRS S.C. HALL

I was out thracking hares meeself, and I seen a fine puss of a thing hopping, hopping in the moonlight, and whacking her ears about, now up, now down, and winking her great eyes, and—"Here goes," says I, and the thing was so close to me that she turned round and looked at me, and then bounced back, as well as to say, do your worst! So I had the least grain in life of *blessed powder left*, and I put it in the gun—and bang at her! My jewel the scritch she gave would frighten a rigment, and a mist, like, came betwixt me and her, and I seen her no more; but when the mist wint off I saw blood on the spot where she had been, and I followed its track, and at last it led me—whist, whisper—right up to Katey MacShane's door; and when I was at the thrashold, I heerd a murnin' within, a great murnin', and a groanin', and I opened the door, and there she was herself, sittin' quite content in the shape of a woman, and the black cat that was sittin' by her rose up its back and spit at me; but I went on never heedin', and asked the ould—how she was and what ailed her.

"Nothing," sis she.

"What's that on the floor?" sis I.

"Oh," she says, "I was cuttin' a billet of wood," she says, "wid the reaping hook," she says, "an' I've wounded meself in the leg," she says, "and that's drops of my precious blood," she says.

Bewitched Butter (Queen's County)*

About the commencement of the last century there lived in the vicinity of the once famous village of Aghavoe† a wealthy farmer, named Bryan Costigan. This man kept an extensive dairy and a great many milch cows, and every year made considerable sums by the sale of milk and butter. The luxuriance of the pasture lands in this neighbourhood has always been proverbial; and, consequently, Bryan's cows were the finest and most productive in the country, and his milk and butter the richest and sweetest, and brought the highest price at every market at which he offered these articles for sale.

Things continued to go on thus prosperously with Bryan Costigan, when, one season, all at once, he found his cattle declining in appearance, and his dairy almost entirely profitless. Bryan, at first, attributed this change to the weather, or some such cause, but soon found or fancied reasons to assign to a far different source. The cows, without any visible disorder, daily declined, and were scarcely able to crawl about on their pasture: many of them, instead of milk, gave nothing but blood; and the scanty quantity of milk which some of them continued to supply was so bitter that even the pigs would not drink it; whilst the butter which it produced was of such a bad quality, and stunk so horribly, that the very dogs would not eat it. Bryan applied for remedies to all the quacks and "fairy-women" in the country—but in vain. Many of the impostors declared that the mysterious malady in his cattle went beyond *their* skill; whilst others, although they found no difficulty in tracing it to superhuman agency, declared that they had no control in the

*Dublin University Magazine, 1839.
†*Aghavoe*—"the field of kine"—a beautiful and romantic village near Borris-in-Ossory, in the Queen's County. It was once a place of considerable importance, and for centuries the episcopal seat of the diocese of Ossory, but for ages back it has gone to decay, and is now remarkable for nothing but the magnificent ruins of a priory of the Dominicans, erected here at an early period by St Canice, the patron saint of Ossory.

matter, as the charm under the influence of which his property was made away with, was too powerful to be dissolved by anything less than the special interposition of Divine Providence. The poor farmer became almost distracted; he saw ruin staring him in the face; yet what was he to do? Sell his cattle and purchase others! No; that was out of the question, as they looked so miserable and emaciated, that no one would even take them as a present, whilst it was also impossible to sell to a butcher, as the flesh of one which he killed for his own family was as black as a coal, and stunk like any putrid carrion.

The unfortunate man was thus completely bewildered. He knew not what to do; he became moody and stupid; his sleep forsook him by night, and all day he wandered about the fields, amongst his "fairy-striken" cattle like a maniac.

Affairs continued in this plight, when one very sultry evening in the latter days of July, Bryan Costigan's wife was sitting at her own door, spinning at her wheel, in a very gloomy and agitated state of mind. Happening to look down the narrow green lane which led from the high road to her cabin, she espied a little old woman barefoot, and enveloped in an old scarlet cloak, approaching slowly, with the aid of a crutch which she carried in one hand, and a cane or walking-stick in the other. The farmer's wife felt glad at seeing the odd-looking stranger; she smiled, and yet she knew not why, as she neared the house. A vague and indefinable feeling of pleasure crowded on her imagination; and, as the old woman gained the threshold, she bade her "welcome" with a warmth which plainly told that her lips gave utterance but to the genuine feelings of her heart.

"God bless this good house and all belonging to it," said the stranger as she entered.

"God save you kindly, and you are welcome, whoever you are," replied Mrs Costigan.

"Hem, I thought so," said the old woman with a significant grin. "I thought so, or I wouldn't trouble you."

The farmer's wife ran, and placed a chair near the fire for the stranger; but she refused, and sat on the ground near where Mrs C. had been spinning. Mrs Costigan had now time to survey the old hag's person minutely. She appeared of great age; her countenance was extremely ugly and repulsive; her skin was rough and deeply embrowned as if from long exposure to the effects of some tropical climate; her forehead was low, narrow, and indented with a thousand wrinkles; her long grey hair fell in matted elf-locks from beneath a white linen skull-cap; her eyes were bleared, blood-shotten, and obliquely set in their sockets, and her voice was croaking, tremulous, and, at times, partially inarticulate. As she squatted on the floor, she looked round the house with an inquisitive gaze; she peered pryingly from corner to corner, with an earnestness of look, as if she had the faculty, like the Argonaut of old, to see through the very depths of the earth, whilst Mrs C. kept watching her motions with mingled feelings of curiosity, awe, and pleasure.

"Mrs," said the old woman, at length breaking silence, "I am dry with the heat of the day; can you give me a drink?"

"Alas!" replied the farmer's wife, "I have no drink to offer you except water, else you would have no occasion to ask me for it."

"Are you not the owner of the cattle I see yonder?" said the old hag, with a tone of voice and manner of gesticulation which plainly indicated her foreknowledge of the fact.

Mrs Costigan replied in the affirmative, and briefly related to her every circumstance connected with the affair, whilst the old woman still remained silent, but shook her grey head repeatedly; and still continued gazing round the house with an air of importance and self-sufficiency.

When Mrs C. had ended, the old hag remained a while as if in a deep reverie: at length she said—

"Have you any of the milk in the house?"

"I have," replied the other.

"Show me some of it."

She filled a jug from a vessel and handed it to the old sybil, who smelled it, then tasted it, and spat out what she had taken on the floor.

"Where is your husband?" she asked.

"Out in the fields," was the reply.

"I must see him."

A messenger was despatched for Bryan, who shortly after made his appearance.

"Neighbour," said the stranger, "your wife informs me that your cattle are going against you this season."

"She informs you right," said Bryan.

"And why have you not sought a cure?"

"A cure!" re-echoed the man; "why, woman, I have sought cures until I was heart-broken, and all in vain; they get worse every day."

"What will you give me if I cure them for you?"

"Anything in our power," replied Bryan and his wife, both speaking joyfully, and with a breath.

"All I will ask from you is a silver sixpence, and that you will do everything which I will bid you," said she.

The farmer and his wife seemed astonished at the moderation of her demand. They offered her a large sum of money.

"No," said she, "I don't want your money; I am no cheat, and I would not even take sixpence, but that I can do nothing till I handle some of your silver."

The sixpence was immediately given her, and the most implicit obedience promised to her injunctions by both Bryan and his wife, who already began to regard the old beldame as their tutelary angel.

The hag pulled off a black silk ribbon or fillet which encircled her head inside her cap, and gave it to Bryan, saying—

"Go, now, and the first cow you touch with this ribbon, turn her into the yard, but be sure don't touch the second, nor speak a word until you return; be also careful not to let the ribbon touch the ground, for, if you do, all is over."

Bryan took the talismanic ribbon, and soon returned, driving a red cow before him.

The old hag went out, and, approaching the cow, commenced pulling hairs out of her tail, at the same time singing some verses in the Irish language in a low, wild, and unconnected strain. The cow appeared restive and uneasy, but the old witch still continued her mysterious chant until she had the ninth hair extracted. She then ordered the cow to be drove back to her pasture, and again entered the house.

"Go, now," said she to the woman, "and bring me some milk from every cow in your possession."

She went, and soon returned with a large pail filled with a frightful-looking mixture of milk, blood, and corrupt matter. The old woman got it into the churn, and made preparations for churning.

"Now," she said, "you both must churn, make fast the door and windows, and let there be no light but from the fire; do not open your lips until I desire you, and by observing my directions, I make no doubt but, ere the sun goes down, we will find out the infernal villain who is robbing you."

Bryan secured the doors and windows, and commenced churning. The old sorceress sat down by a blazing fire which had been specially lighted for the occasion, and commenced singing the same wild song which she had sung at the

162

pulling of the cow-hairs, and after a little time she cast one of the nine hairs into the fire, still singing her mysterious strain, and watching, with intense interest, the witching process.

A loud cry, as if from a female in distress, was now heard approaching the house; the old witch discontinued her incantations, and listened attentively. The crying voice approached the door.

"Open the door quickly," shouted the charmer.

Bryan unbarred the door, and all three rushed out in the yard, when they heard the same cry down the *boreheen*, but could see nothing.

"It is all over," shouted the old witch; "something has gone amiss, and our charm for the present is ineffectual."

They now turned back quite crest-fallen, when, as they were entering the door, the sybil cast her eyes downwards, and perceiving a piece of horse-shoe nailed on the threshold,* she vociferated—

"Here I have it; no wonder our charm was abortive. The person that was crying abroad is the villain who has your cattle bewitched; I brought her to the house, but she was not able to come to the door on account of that horse-shoe. Remove it instantly, and we will try our luck again."

Bryan removed the horse-shoe from the doorway, and by the hag's directions placed it on the floor under the churn, having previously reddened it in the fire.

They again resumed their manual operations. Bryan and his wife began to churn, and the witch again to sing her strange verses, and casting her cow-hairs into the fire until she had them all nearly exhausted. Her countenance now began to exhibit evident traces of vexation and disappointment. She got quite pale, her teeth gnashed, her hand trembled, and as she cast the ninth and last hair into the fire, her person exhibited more the appearance of a female demon than a human being.

Once more the cry was heard, and an aged red-haired woman† was seen approaching the house quickly.

"Ho, ho!" roared the sorceress, "I knew it would be so; my charm has succeeded;

---

*It was once a common practice in Ireland to nail a piece of horseshoe on the threshold of the door, as a preservative against the influence of the fairies, who, it is thought, dare not enter any house thus guarded. This custom, however, is much on the wane, but still it is prevalent in some of the more uncivilised districts of the country.

†Red-haired people are thought to possess magic power.

my expectations are realised, and here she comes, the villain who has destroyed you."

"What are we to do now?" asked Bryan.

"Say nothing to her," said the hag; "give her whatever she demands, and leave the rest to me."

The woman advanced screeching vehemently, and Bryan went out to meet her. She was a neighbour, and she said that one of her best cows was drowning in a pool of water—that there was no one at home but herself, and she implored Bryan to go rescue the cow from destruction.

Bryan accompanied her without hesitation; and having rescued the cow from her perilous situation, was back again in a quarter of an hour.

It was now sunset, and Mrs Costigan set about preparing supper.

During supper they reverted to the singular transactions of the day. The old witch uttered many a fiendish laugh at the success of her incantations, and inquired who was the woman whom they had so curiously discovered.

Bryan satisfied her in every particular. She was the wife of a neighbouring farmer; her name was Rachel Higgins; and she had been long suspected to be on familiar terms with the spirit of darkness. She had five or six cows; but it was observed by her sapient neighbours that she sold more butter every year than other farmers' wives who had twenty. Bryan had, from the commencement of the decline in his cattle, suspected her for being the aggressor, but as he had no proof, he held his peace.

"Well," said the old beldame, with a grim smile, "it is not enough that we have merely discovered the robber; all is in vain, if we do not take steps to punish her for the past, as well as to prevent her inroads for the future."

"And how will that be done?" said Bryan.

"I will tell you; as soon as the hour of twelve o'clock arrives tonight, do you go to the pasture, and take a couple of swift-running dogs with you; conceal yourself in some place convenient to the cattle; watch them carefully; and if you see anything, whether man or beast, approach the cows, set on the dogs, and if possible make them draw the blood of the intruder; then ALL will be accomplished. If nothing approaches before sunrise, you may return, and we will try something else."

Convenient there lived the cow-herd of a neighbouring squire. He was a hardy, courageous young man, and always kept a pair of ferocious bull-dogs. To him Bryan applied for assistance, and he cheerfully agreed to accompany him, and, moreover, proposed to fetch a couple of his master's best greyhounds, as his own dogs, although extremely fierce and bloodthirsty, could not be relied on for swiftness. He promised Bryan to be with him before twelve o'clock, and they parted.

Bryan did not seek sleep that night; he sat up anxiously awaiting the midnight hour. It arrived at last, and his friend, the herdsman, true to his promise, came at the time appointed. After some further admonitions from the *Collough*, they departed. Having arrived at the field, they consulted as to the best position they could choose for concealment. At last they pitched on a small brake of fern, situated at the extremity of the field, adjacent to the boundary ditch, which was thickly studded with large, old white-thorn bushes. Here they crouched themselves, and made the dogs, four in number, lie down beside them, eagerly expecting the appearance of their as yet unknown and mysterious visitor.

Here Bryan and his comrade continued a considerable time in nervous anxiety, still nothing approached, and it became manifest that morning was at hand; they were beginning to grow impatient, and were talking of returning home, when on a sudden they heard a rushing sound behind them, as if proceeding from something endeavouring to force a passage through the thick hedge in their rear. They looked in that direction, and judge of their astonishment, when they perceived a large hare in the act of springing from the ditch, and leaping on the ground quite near them. They were now convinced that this was the object which they had so impatiently expected, and they were resolved to watch her motions narrowly.

After arriving to the ground, she remained motionless for a few moments, looking around her sharply. She then began to skip and jump in a playful manner; now advancing at a smart pace towards the cows, and again retreating precipitately, but still drawing nearer and nearer at each sally. At length she advanced up to the next cow, and sucked her for a moment; then on to the next, and so respectively to every cow on the field—the cows all the time lowing loudly, and appearing extremely frightened and agitated. Bryan, from the moment the hare commenced sucking the first, was with difficulty restrained from attacking her; but his more sagacious companion suggested to him, that it was better to wait until she would have done, as she would then be much heavier, and more unable to effect her escape than at present. And so the issue proved; for being now done sucking them all, her belly appeared enormously distended, and she made her exit slowly and apparently with difficulty. She advanced towards the hedge where she had entered, and as she arrived just at the clump of ferns where her foes were crouched, they started up with a fierce yell, and hallooed the dogs upon her path.

The hare started off at a brisk pace, squirting up the milk she had sucked from her mouth and nostrils, and the dogs making after her rapidly. Rachel Higgins's cabin appeared, through the grey morning twilight, at a little distance; and it was evident that puss seemed bent on gaining it, although she made a considerable circuit through the fields in the rear. Bryan and his comrade, however, had their thoughts, and made towards the cabin by the shortest route, and had just arrived as the hare came up, panting and almost exhausted, and the dogs at her very scut. She ran round the house, evidently confused and disappointed at the presence of the men, but at length made for the door. In the bottom of the door was a small, semi-circular aperture, resembling those cut in fowl-house doors for the ingress and egress of poultry. To gain this hole, puss now made a last and desperate effort, and had succeeded in forcing her head and shoulders through it, when the foremost of the dogs made a spring and seized her violently by the haunch. She uttered a loud and piercing scream, and struggled desperately to free herself from his gripe, and at last succeeded, but not until she left a piece of her rump in his teeth. The men now burst open the door; a bright turf fire blazed on the hearth, and the whole floor was streaming with blood. No hare, however, could be found, and the men were more than ever convinced that it was old Rachel, who had, by the assistance of some demon, assumed the form of the hare, and they now determined to have her if she were over the earth. They entered the bed-room, and heard some smothered groaning, as if proceeding from some one in extreme agony. They went to the corner of the room from whence the moans proceeded, and there, beneath a bundle of freshly-cut rushes, found the form of Rachel Higgins, writhing in the most excruciating agony, and almost smothered in a pool of blood. The men were astounded; they addressed the wretched old woman, but she either could not, or would not answer them. Her wound still bled copiously; her tortures appeared to increase, and it was evident that she was dying. The aroused family thronged around her with cries and lamentations; she did not seem to heed them, she got worse and worse, and her piercing yells fell awfully on the ears of the bystanders. At length she expired, and her corpse exhibited a most appalling spectacle, even before the spirit had well departed.

Bryan and his friend returned home. The old hag had been previously aware of the fate of Rachel Higgins, but it was not known by what means she acquired her supernatural knowledge. She was delighted at the issue of her mysterious operations. Bryan pressed her much to accept of some remuneration for her services, but she utterly rejected such proposals. She remained a few days at his house, and at length took her leave and departed, no one knew whither.

Old Rachel's remains were interred that night in the neighbouring churchyard. Her fate soon became generally known, and her family, ashamed to remain in their native village, disposed of their property, and quitted the country for ever. The story, however, is still fresh in the memory of the surrounding villagers; and often, it is said, amid the grey haze of a summer twilight, may the ghost of Rachel Higgins, in the form of a hare, be seen scudding over her favourite and well-remembered haunts.

The Horned Women*

LADY WILDE

A rich woman sat up late one night carding and preparing wool, while all the family and servants were asleep. Suddenly a knock was given at the door, and a voice called—"Open! open!"

"Who is there?" said the woman of the house.

"I am the Witch of the one Horn," was answered.

The mistress, supposing that one of her neighbours had called and required assistance, opened the door, and a woman entered, having in her hand a pair of wool carders, and bearing a horn on her forehead, as if growing there. She sat down by the fire in silence, and began to card the wool with violent haste. Suddenly she paused, and said aloud: "Where are the women? they delay too long."

Then a second knock came to the door, and a voice called as before, "Open! open!"

The mistress felt herself constrained to rise and open to the call, and immediately a second witch entered, having two horns on her forehead, and in her hand a wheel for spinning wool.

"Give me place," she said, "I am the Witch of the two Horns," and she began to spin as quick as lightning.

And so the knocks went on, and the call was heard, and the witches entered, until at last twelve women sat round the fire—the first with one horn, the last with twelve horns.

And they carded the thread, and turned their spinning wheels, and wound and wove.

All singing together an ancient rhyme, but no word did they speak to the mistress of the house. Strange to hear, and frightful to look upon, were these twelve women, with their horns and their wheels; and the mistress felt near to death, and

Ancient Legends of Ireland.

she tried to rise that she might call for help, but she could not move, nor could she utter a word or a cry, for the spell of the witches was upon her.

Then one of them called to her in Irish, and said—

"Rise, woman, and make us a cake." Then the mistress searched for a vessel to bring water from the well that she might mix the meal and make the cake, but she could find none.

And they said to her, "Take a sieve and bring water in it."

And she took the sieve and went to the well; but the water poured from it, and she could fetch none for the cake, and she sat down by the well and wept.

Then a voice came by her and said, "Take yellow clay and moss, and bind them together, and plaster the sieve so that it will hold."

This she did, and the sieve held water for the cake; and the voice said again—

"Return, and when thou comest to the north angle of the house, cry aloud three times and say, 'The mountain of the Fenian women and the sky over it is all on fire'."

And she did so.

When the witches inside heard the call, a great and terrible cry broke from their lips, and they rushed forth with wild lamentations and shrieks, and fled away to Slievenamon,* where was their chief abode. But the Spirit of the Well bade the mistress of the house to enter and prepare her home against the enchantments of witches if they returned again.

And first, to break their spells, she sprinkled the water in which she had washed her child's feet (the feet-water) outside the door on the threshold; secondly, she took the cake which the witches had made in her absence of meal mixed with the blood drawn from the sleeping family, and she broke the cake in bits, and placed a bit in the mouth of each sleeper, and they were restored; and she took the cloth they had woven and placed it half in and half out of the chest with the padlock; and lastly, she secured the door with a great crossbeam fastened in the jambs, so that they could not enter, and having done these things she waited.

Not long were the witches in coming back, and they raged and called for vengeance.

"Open, open!" they screamed, "open, feet-water!"

"I cannot," said the feet-water, "I am scattered on the ground, and my path is down to the Lough."

*Sliábh-na-mban—i.e., mountains of the women.

"Open, open, wood and trees and beam!" they cried to the door.

"I cannot," said the door, "for the beam is fixed in the jambs and I have no power to move."

"Open, open, cake that we have made and mingled with blood!" they cried again.

"I cannot," said the cake, "for I am broken and bruised, and my blood is on the lips of the sleeping children."

Then the witches rushed through the air with great cries, and fled back to Slievenamon, uttering strange curses on the Spirit of the Well, who had wished their ruin; but the woman and the house were left in peace, and a mantle dropped by one of the witches in her flight was kept hung up by the mistress as a sign of the night's awful contest; and this mantle was in possession of the same family from generation to generation for five hundred years after.

The Witches' Excursion*

PATRICK KENNEDY

Shemus Rua† (Red James) awakened from his sleep one night by noises in his kitchen. Stealing to the door, he saw half-a-dozen old women sitting round the fire, jesting and laughing, his old housekeeper, Madge, quite frisky and gay, helping her sister crones to cheering glasses of punch. He began to admire the impudence and imprudence of Madge, displayed in the invitation and the riot, but recollected on the instant her officiousness in urging him to take a comfortable posset, which she had brought to his bedside just before he fell asleep. Had he drunk it, he would have been just now deaf to the witches' glee. He heard and saw them drink his health in such a mocking style as nearly to tempt him to charge them, besom in hand, but he restrained himself.

The jug being emptied, one of them cried out, "Is it time to be gone?" and at the same moment, putting on a red cap, she added—

> "By yarrow and rue,
> And my red cap too,
> Hie over to England."

Making use of a twig which she held in her hand as a steed, she gracefully soared up the chimney, and was rapidly followed by the rest. But when it came to the house-keeper, Shemus interposed. "By your leave, ma'am," said he, snatching twig and cap. "Ah, you desateful ould crocodile! If I find you here on my return, there'll be wigs on the green—

---

*Fictions of the Irish Celts.

†Irish, Séumus Ruadh. The Celtic organs are unable to pronounce the letter j, hence they make Shon or Shawn of John, or Shamus of James, etc.

'By yarrow and rue,
And my red cap too,
Hie over to England'."

The words were not out of his mouth when he was soaring above the ridge pole, and swiftly ploughing the air. He was careful to speak no word (being somewhat conversant with witch-lore), as the result would be a tumble, and the immediate return of the expedition.

In a very short time they had crossed the Wicklow hills, the Irish Sea, and the Welsh mountains, and were charging, at whirlwind speed, the hall door of a castle. Shemus, only for the company in which he found himself, would have cried out for pardon, expecting to be *mummy* against the hard oak door in a moment; but, all bewildered, he found himself passing through the keyhole, along a passage, down a flight of steps, and through a cellar-door key-hole before he could form any clear idea of his situation.

Waking to the full consciousness of his position, he found himself sitting on a stallion, plenty of lights glimmering round, and he and his companions, with full tumblers of frothing wine in hand, hob-nobbing and drinking healths as jovially and recklessly as if the liquor was honestly come by, and they were sitting in *Shemus's* own kitchen. The red birrédh* has assimilated *Shemus's* nature for the time being to that of his unholy companions. The heady liquors soon got into their brains, and a period of unconsciousness succeeded the ecstasy, the head-ache, the turning round of the barrels, and the "scattered sight" of poor Shemus. He woke up under the impression of being roughly seized, and shaken, and dragged upstairs, and subjected to a disagreeable examination by the lord of the castle, in his state parlour. There was much derision among the whole company, gentle and simple, on hearing Shemus's explanation, and, as the thing occurred in the dark ages, the unlucky Leinster man was sentenced to be hung as soon as the gallows could be prepared for the occasion.

The poor Hibernian was in the cart proceeding on his last journey, with a label on his back, and another on his breast, announcing him as the remorseless villain who for the last month had been draining the casks in my lord's vault every night, He was surprised to hear himself addressed by his name, and in his native tongue,

*Irish, *Birreud*—i.e., a cap.

by an old woman in the crowd. "Ach, Shemus, alanna! is it going to die you are in a strange place without your *cappen d'yarrag?*"* These words infused hope and courage into the poor victim's heart. He turned to the lord and humbly asked leave to die in his red cap, which he supposed had dropped from his head in the vault. A servant was sent for the head-piece, and Shemus felt lively hope warming his heart while placing it on his head. On the platform he was graciously allowed to address the spectators, which he proceeded to do in the usual formula composed for the benefit of flying stationers—"Good people all, a warning take by me;" but when he had finished the line, "My parents reared me tenderly," he unexpectedly added—"By yarrow and rue," etc., and the disappointed spectators saw him shoot up obliquely through the air in the style of a sky-rocket that had missed its aim. It is said that the lord took the circumstance much to heart, and never afterwards hung a man for twenty-four hours after his offence.

*Irish, *caipín dearg*—i.e., red cap.

The Confessions of Tom Bourke

T. CROFTON CROKER

Tom Bourke lives in a low, long farm-house, resembling in outward appearance a large barn, placed at the bottom of the hill, just where the new road strikes off from the old one, leading from the town of Kilworth to that of Lismore. He is of a class of persons who are a sort of black swans in Ireland: he is a wealthy farmer. Tom's father had, in the good old times, when a hundred pounds were no inconsiderable treasure, either to lend or spend, accommodated his landlord with that sum, at interest; and obtained as a return for his civility a long lease about half-a-dozen times more valuable than the loan which procured it. The old man died worth several hundred pounds, the greater part of which, with his farm, he bequeathed to his son, Tom. But besides all this, Tom received from his father, upon his deathbed, another gift, far more valuable than worldly riches, greatly as he prized and is still known to prize them. He was invested with the privilege, enjoyed by few of the sons of men, of communicating with those mysterious beings called "the good people".

Tom Bourke is a little, stout, healthy, active man, about fifty-five years of age. His hair is perfectly white, short and bushy behind, but rising in front erect and thick above his forehead, like a new clothes-brush. His eyes are of that kind which I have often observed with persons of a quick, but limited intellect—they are small, grey, and lively. The large and projecting eyebrows under, or rather within, which they twinkle, give them an expression of shrewdness and intelligence, if not of cunning. And this is very much the character of the man. If you want to make a bargain with Tom Bourke you must act as if you were a general besieging a town, and make your advances a long time before you can hope to obtain possession; if you march up boldly, and tell him at once your object, you are for the most part sure to have the gates closed in your teeth. Tom does not wish to part with what you wish to obtain; or another person has been speaking to him for the whole of the last week. Or, it may be, your proposal seems to meet the most favourable reception. "Very well, sir"; "That's true, sir"; "I'm very thankful to your honour" and other expressions of kindness and confidence greet you in reply to every sentence; and you part from him wondering how he can have obtained the character which he universally bears, of being a man whom no one can make anything of in a bargain. But when you next meet him the flattering illusion is dissolved: you find you are a great deal further from your object than you were when you thought you had almost succeeded; his eye and his tongue express a total forgetfulness of what the mind within never lost sight of for an instant; and you have to begin operations afresh, with the disadvantage of having put your adversary completely upon his guard.

Yet, although Tom Bourke is, whether from supernatural revealings, or (as many will think more probable) from the tell-truth experience, so distrustful of mankind, and so close in his dealings with them, he is no misanthrope. No man loves better the pleasures of the genial board. The love of money, indeed, which is with him (and who will blame him?) a very ruling propensity, and the gratification which it has received from habits of industry, sustained throughout a pretty long and successful life, have taught him the value of sobriety, during these seasons, at least, when a man's business requires him to keep possession of his senses. He has, therefore, a general rule, never to get drunk but on Sundays. But in order that it should be a general one to all intents and purposes, he takes a method which, according to better logicians than he is, always proves the rule. He has many exceptions; among these, of course, are the evenings of all the fair and market-days that happen in his neighbourhood; so also all the days in which funerals, marriages, and christenings take place among his friends within many miles of him. As to this last class of exceptions, it may appear at first very singular, that he is much more punctual in his attendance at the funerals than at the baptisms or weddings of his friends. This may be construed as an instance of disinterested affection for departed worth, very uncommon in this selfish world. But I am afraid that the motives which lead Tom Bourke to pay more court to the dead than the living are precisely those which lead to the opposite conduct in the generality of mankind—a hope of future benefit and a fear of future evil. For the good people, who are a race as powerful as they are capricious, have their favourites among those who inhabit this world; often show their affection by easing the objects of it from the load of this burdensome life; and frequently reward or punish the living according to the degree of reverence paid to the obsequies and the memory of the elected dead.

Some may attribute to the same cause the apparently humane and charitable actions which Tom, and indeed the other members of his family, are known frequently to perform. A beggar has seldom left their farm-yard with an empty wallet, or without obtaining a night's lodging, if required, with a sufficiency of potatoes and milk to satisfy even an Irish beggar's appetite; in appeasing which, account must usually be taken of the auxiliary jaws of a hungry dog, and of two or three still more hungry children, who line themselves well within, to atone for their nakedness without. If one of the neighbouring poor be seized with a fever, Tom will often supply the sick wretch with some untenanted hut upon one of his two large farms (for he has added one to his patrimony, or will send his labourers to construct a shed at a hedge-side, and supply straw for a bed while the disorder continues. His wife, remarkable for the largeness of her dairy, and the goodness of everything it contains, will furnish milk for whey; and their good offices are frequently extended to the family of the patient, who are, perhaps, reduced to the extremity of wretchedness, by even the temporary suspension of a father's or a husband's labour.

If much of this arises from the hopes and fears to which I above alluded, I believe much of it flows from a mingled sense of compassion and of duty, which is sometimes seen to break from an Irish peasant's heart, even where it happens to be enveloped in a habitual covering of avarice and fraud; and which I once heard speak in terms not to be misunderstood: "When we get a deal, 'tis only fair we should give back a little of it."

It is not easy to prevail on Tom to speak of those good people, with whom he is said to hold frequent and intimate communications. To the faithful, who believe in their power, and their occasional delegation of it to him, he seldom refuses, if properly asked, to exercise his high prerogative when any unfortunate being is *struck* in his neighbourhood. Still he will not be won unsued: he is at first difficult of persuasion, and must be overcome by a little gentle violence. On these occasions he is unusually solemn and mysterious, and if one word of reward be mentioned he at once abandons the unhappy patient, such a proposition being a direct insult to his supernatural superiors. It is true that, as the labourer is worthy of his hire, most persons gifted as he is do not scruple to receive a token of gratitude from the patients or their friends *after* their recovery. It is recorded that a very handsome gratuity was once given to a female practitioner in this occult science, who deserves to be mentioned, not only because she was a neighbour and a rival of Tom's, but from the singularity of a mother deriving her name from her son. Her son's name was Owen, and she was always called *Owen sa vauher* (Owen's mother). This person was, on the occasion to which I have alluded, *persuaded* to give her assistance to a young girl who had lost the use of her right leg; *Owen sa vauher* found the cure a difficult one. A journey of about eighteen miles was essential for the purpose, probably to visit one of the good people, who resided at that distance; and this journey could only be performed by *Owen sa vauher* travelling upon the back of a white hen. The visit, however, was accomplished; and at a particular hour, according to the prediction of this extraordinary woman, when the hen and her rider were to reach their journey's end, the patient was seized with an irresistible desire to dance, which she gratified with the most perfect freedom of the diseased leg, much to the joy of her anxious family. The gratuity in this case was, as it surely ought to have been, unusually large, from the difficulty of procuring a hen willing to go so long a journey with such a rider.

To do Tom Bourke justice, he is on these occasions, as I have heard from many competent authorities, perfectly disinterested. Not many months since he recovered a young woman (the sister of a tradesman living near him), who had been struck speechless after returning from a funeral, and had continued so for several days. He steadfastly refused receiving any compensation, saying that even if he had not as much as would buy him his supper, he could take nothing in this case, because the girl had offended at the funeral of one of the *good people* belonging to his own family, and though he would do her a kindness, he could take none from her.

About the time this last remarkable affair took place, my friend Mr Martin, who is a neighbour of Tom's, had some business to transact with him, which it was exceedingly difficult to bring to a conclusion. At last Mr Martin, having tried all quiet means, had recourse to a legal process, which brought Tom to reason, and the matter was arranged to their mutual satisfaction, and with perfect good-humour between the parties. The accommodation took place after dinner at Mr Martin's house, and he invited Tom to walk into the parlour and take a glass of punch, made of some excellent *poteen*, which was on the table: he had long wished to draw out his highly-endowed neighbour on the subject of his supernatural powers, and as Mrs Martin, who was in the room, was rather a favourite of Tom's, this seemed a good opportunity.

"Well, Tom," said Mr Martin, "that was a curious business of Molly Dwyer's, who recovered her speech so suddenly the other day."

"You may say that, sir," replied Tom Bourke; "but I had to travel far for it: no matter for that now. Your health, ma'am," said he, turning to Mrs Martin.

"Thank you, Tom. But I am told you had some trouble once in that way in your own family," said Mrs Martin.

"So I had, ma'am; trouble enough: but you were only a child at that time."

"Come, Tom," said the hospitable Mr Martin, interrupting him, "take another tumbler;" and he then added, "I wish you would tell us something of the manner in which so many of your children died. I am told they dropped off, one after another, by the same disorder, and that your eldest son was cured in a most extraordinary way, when the physicians had given him over."

" 'Tis true for you, sir," returned Tom; "your father, the doctor (God be good to him, I won't belie him in his grave), told me, when my fourth boy was a week sick, that himself and Dr Barry did all that man could do for him; but they could not keep him from going after the rest. No more they could, if the people that took away the rest wished to take him too. But they left him; and sorry to the heart I am I did not know before why they were taking my boys from me; if I did, I would not be left trusting to two of 'em now."

"And how did you find it out, Tom?" inquired Mr Martin.

"Why, then, I'll tell you, sir," said Bourke. "When your father said what I told you, I did not know very well what to do. I walked down the little *bohereen** you know, sir, that goes to the river-side near Dick Heafy's ground; for 'twas a lonesome place, and I wanted to think of myself. I was heavy, sir, and my heart got weak in me, when I thought I was to lose my little boy; and I did not well know how to face his mother with the news, for she doated down upon him. Besides, she never got the better of all she cried at his brother's *berrin†* the week before. As I was going down the *bohereen* I met an old *bocough*, that used to come about the place once or twice a-year, and used always to sleep in our barn while he staid in the neighbourhood. So he asked me how I was. 'Bad enough, Shamous,'‡ says I. 'I'm sorry for your trouble,' says he; 'but you're a foolish man, Mr Bourke. Your son would be well enough if you would only do what you ought with him.' 'What more

Bohereen, or *bogheen*, i.e., a green lane.
†*Berrin*, burying.
‡*Shamous*, James.

can I do with him, Shamous?' says I; 'the doctors give him over.' 'The doctors know no more what ails him than they do what ails a cow when she stops her milk,' says Shamous; 'but go to such a one,' telling me his name, 'and try what he'll say to you.' "

"And who was that, Tom?" asked Mr Martin.

"I could not tell you that, sir," said Bourke, with a mysterious look; "howsomever, you often saw him, and he does not live far from this. But I had a trial of him before; and if I went to him at first, maybe I'd have now some of them that's gone, and so Shamous often told me. Well, sir, I went to this man, and he came with me to the house. By course, I did everything as he bid me. According to his order, I took the little boy out of the dwelling-house immediately, sick as he was, and made a bed for him and myself in the cow-house. Well, sir, I lay down by his side in the bed, between two of the cows, and he fell asleep. He got into a perspiration, saving your presence, as if he was drawn through the river, and breathed hard, with a great *impression* on his chest, and was very bad—very bad entirely through the night. I thought about twelve o'clock he was going at last, and I was just getting up to go call the man I told you of; but there was no occasion. My friends were getting the better of them that wanted to take him away from me. There was nobody in the cow-house but the child and myself. There was only one halfpenny candle lighting it, and that was stuck in the wall at the far end of the house. I had just enough of light where we were lying to see a person walking or standing near us: and there was no more noise than it was a churchyard, except the cows chewing the fodder in the stalls.

Just as I was thinking of getting up, as I told you—I won't belie my father, sir, he was a good father to me—I saw him standing at the bedside, holding out his right hand to me, and leaning his other on the stick he used to carry when he was alive, and looking pleasant and smiling at me, all as if he was telling me not to be afeard, for I would not lose the child. 'Is that you, father?' says I. He said nothing. 'If that's you,' says I again, 'for the love of them that's gone, let me catch your hand.' And so he did, sir; and his hand was as soft as a child's. He stayed about as long as you'd be going from this to the gate below at the end of the avenue, and then went away. In less than a week the child was as well as if nothing ever ailed him; and there isn't tonight a healthier boy of nineteen, from this blessed house to the town of Ballyporeen, across the Kilworth mountains."

"But I think, Tom," said Mr Martin, "it appears as if you are more indebted to your father than to the man recommended to you by Shamous; or do you suppose it was he who made favour with your enemies among the good people, and that then your father—"

"I beg your pardon, sir," said Bourke, interrupting him; "but don't call them my enemies. 'Twould not be wishing to me for a good deal to sit by when they are called so. No offence to you, sir. Here's wishing you a good health and long life."

"I assure you," returned Mr Martin, "I meant no offence, Tom; but was it not as I say?"

"I can't tell you that, sir," said Bourke; "I'm bound down, sir. Howsoever, you may be sure the man I spoke of and my father, and those they know, settled it between them."

There was a pause, of which Mrs Martin took advantage to inquire of Tom whether something remarkable had not happened about a goat and a pair of pigeons, at the time of his son's illness—circumstances often mysteriously hinted at by Tom.

"See that, now," said he, turning to Mr Martin, "how well she remembers it! True for you, ma'am. The goat I gave the mistress, your mother, when the doctors ordered her goats' whey?"

Mrs Martin nodded assent, and Tom Bourke continued, "Why then, I'll tell you how that was. The goat was as well as e'er goat ever was, for a month after she was sent to Killaan, to your father's. The morning after the night I just told you of, before the child woke, his mother was standing at the gap leading out of the barn-yard into the road, and she saw two pigeons flying from the town of Kilworth off the church down towards her. Well, they never stopped, you see, till they came to the house on the hill at the other side of the river, facing our farm. They pitched upon the chimney of that house, and after looking about them for a minute or two, they flew straight across the river, and stopped on the ridge of the cow-house where the child and I were lying. Do you think they came there for nothing, sir?"

"Certainly not, Tom," returned Mr Martin.

"Well, the woman came in to me, frightened, and told me. She began to cry. 'Whisht, you fool?' says I; ' 'tis all for the better.' 'Twas true for me. What do you think, ma'am; the goat that I gave your mother, that was seen feeding at sunrise that morning by Jack Cronin, as merry as a bee, dropped down dead without anybody knowing why, before Jack's face; and at that very moment he saw two pigeons fly from the top of the house out of the town, towards the Lismore road.

'Twas at the same time my woman saw them, as I just told you."

" 'Twas very strange, indeed, Tom," said Mr Martin; "I wish you could give us some explanation of it."

"I wish I could, sir," was Tom Bourke's answer; "but I'm bound down. I can't tell but what I'm allowed to tell, any more than a sentry is let walk more than his rounds."

"I think you said something of having had some former knowledge of the man that assisted in the cure of your son," said Mr Martin.

"So I had, sir," returned Bourke. "I had a trial of that man. But that's neither here nor there. I can't tell you anything about that, sir. But would you like to know how he got his skill?"

"Oh! very much, indeed," said Mr Martin.

"But you can tell us his Christian name, that we may know him better through the story," added Mrs Martin.

Tom Bourke paused for a minute to consider this proposition.

"Well, I believe that I may tell you that, anyhow; his name is Patrick. He was always a smart, 'cute* boy, and would be a great clerk if he stuck to it. The first time I knew him, sir, was at my mother's wake. I was in great trouble, for I did not know where to bury her. Her people and my father's people—I mean their friends, sir, among the *good people*—had the greatest battle that was known for many a year, at Dunmanwaycross, to see to whose churchyard she'd be taken. They fought for three nights, one after another, without being able to settle it. The neighbours wondered how long before I buried my mother; but I had my reasons, though I could not tell them at that time. Well, sir, to make my story short, Patrick came on the fourth morning and told me he settled the business, and that day we buried her in Kilcrumper churchyard, with my father's people."

"He was a valuable friend, Tom," said Mrs Martin, with difficulty suppressing a smile. "But you were about to tell how he became so skilful."

"So I will and welcome," replied Bourke. "Your health, ma'am. I'm drinking too much of this punch, sir; but to tell the truth, I never tasted the like of it; it goes down one's throat like sweet oil. But what was I going to say? Yes—well—Patrick, many a long year ago, was coming home from a *berrin* late in the evening, and walking by the side of a river, opposite the big inch,† near Ballyhefaan ford. He

*'*Cute*, acute.
†Inch, low meadow ground near a river.

181

had taken a drop, to be sure; but he was only a little merry, as you may say, and knew very well what he was doing. The moon was shining, for it was in the month of August, and the river was as smooth and as bright as a looking-glass. He heard nothing for a long time but the fall of the water at the mill weir about a mile down the river, and now and then the crying of the lambs on the other side of the river. All at once there was a noise of a great number of people laughing as if they'd break their hearts, and of a piper playing among them. It came from the inch at the other side of the ford, and he saw, through the mist that hung over the river, a whole crowd of people dancing on the inch. Patrick was as fond of a dance, as he was of a glass, and that's saying enough for him; so he whipped off his shoes and stockings, and away with him across the ford. After putting on his shoes and stockings at the other side of the river he walked over to the crowd, and mixed with them for some time without being minded. He thought, sir, that he'd show them better dancing than any of themselves, for he was proud of his feet, sir, and a good right he had, for there was not a boy in the same parish could foot a double or treble with him. But pwah! his dancing was no more to theirs than mine would be to the mistress' there. They did not seem as if they had a bone in their bodies, and they kept it up as if nothing could tire them. Patrick was 'shamed within himself, for he thought he had not his fellow in all the country round; and was going away, when a little old man, that was looking at the company bitterly, as if he did not like what was going on, came up to him. 'Patrick,' says he. Patrick started, for he did not think anybody there knew him. 'Patrick,' says he, 'you're discouraged, and no wonder for you. But you have a friend near you. I'm your friend, and your father's friend, and I think worse* of your little finger than I do of all that are here, though they think no one is as good as themselves. Go into the ring and call for a lilt. Don't be afeard. I tell you the best of them did not do it as well as you shall, if you will do as I bid you.' Patrick felt something within him as if he ought not to gainsay the old man. He went into the ring, and called the piper to play up the best double he had. And sure enough, all that the others were able for was nothing to him! He bounded like an eel, now here and now there, as light as a feather, although the people could hear the music answered by his steps, that beat time to every turn of it, like the left foot of the piper. He first danced a hornpipe on the ground. Then they got a table, and he danced a treble on it that drew down shouts from the whole company.

*Worse, more.

182

At last he called for a trencher; and when they saw him, all as if he was spinning on it like a top, they did not know what to make of him. Some praised him for the best dancer that ever entered a ring; others hated him because he was better than themselves; although they had good right to think themselves better than him or any other man that ever went the long journey."

"And what was the cause of his great success?" inquired Mr Martin.

"He could not help it, sir," replied Tom Bourke. "They that could make him do more than that made him do it. Howsomever, when he had done, they wanted him to dance again, but he was tired, and they could not persuade him. At last he got angry, and swore a big oath, saving your presence, that he would not dance a step more; and the word was hardly out of his mouth when he found himself all alone, with nothing but a white cow grazing by his side."

"Did he ever discover why he was gifted with these extraordinary powers in the dance, Tom?" said Mr Martin.

"I'll tell you that too, sir," answered Bourke, "when I come to it. When he went home, sir, he was taken with a shivering and went to bed; and the next day they found he had got the fever, or something like it, for he raved like as if he was mad. But they couldn't make out what it was he was saying, though he talked constant. The doctors gave him over. But it's little they knew what ailed him. When he was, as you may say, about ten days sick, and everybody thought he was going, one of the neighbours came in to him with a man, a friend of his, from Ballinlacken, that was keeping with him some time before. I can't tell you his name either, only it was Darby. The minute Darby saw Patrick he took a little bottle, with the juice of herbs in it, out of his pocket, and gave Patrick a drink of it. He did the same every day for three weeks, and then Patrick was able to walk about, as stout and as hearty as ever he was in his life. But he was a long time before he came to himself; and he used to walk the whole day sometimes by the ditch-side, talking to himself, like as if there was someone along with him. And so there was, surely, or he wouldn't be the man he is today."

"I suppose it was from some such companion he learned his skill," said Mr Martin.

"You have it all now, sir," replied Bourke. "Darby told him his friends were satisfied with what he did the night of the dance; and though they couldn't hinder the fever, they'd bring him over it, and teach him more than many knew beside him. And so they did. For you see, all the people he met on the inch that night were friends of a different faction; only the old man that spoke to him, he was a friend of Patrick's family, and it went again his heart, you see, that the others were so light and active, and he was bitter in himself to hear 'em boasting how they'd dance with any set in the whole country round. So he gave Patrick the gift that night, and afterwards gave him the skill that makes him the wonder of all that know him. And to be sure it was only learning he was at that time when he was wandering in his mind after the fever."

"I have heard many strange stories about that inch near Ballyhefaan ford," said Mr Martin. " 'Tis a great place for the good people, isn't it, Tom?"

"You may say that, sir," returned Bourke. "I could tell you a great deal about it. Many a time I sat for as good as two hours by moonlight, at th' other side of the river, looking at 'em playing goal as if they'd break their hearts over it; with their coats and waistcoats off, and white handkerchiefs on the heads of one party, and red ones on th' other, just as you'd see on a Sunday in Mr Simming's big field. I saw 'em one night play till the moon set, without one party being able to take the ball from th' other. I'm sure they were going to fight, only 'twas near morning. I'm told your grandfather, ma'am used to see 'em there too," said Bourke, turning to Mrs Martin.

"So I have been told, Tom," replied Mrs Martin. "But don't they say that the churchyard of Kilcrumper is just as favourite a place with the good people as Ballyhefaan inch?"

"Why, then, maybe you never heard, ma'am, what happened to Davy Roche in that same churchyard," said Bourke; and turning to Mr Martin, added, " 'Twas a long time before he went into your service, sir. He was walking home, of an evening, from the fair of Kilcumber, a little merry, to be sure, after the day, and he came up with a berrin. So he walked along with it, and thought it very queer that he did not know a mother's soul in the crowd but one man, and he was sure that man was dead many years afore. Howsomever, he went on with the berrin till they came to Kilcrumper churchyard; and faith, he went in and stayed with the rest, to see the corpse buried. As soon as the grave was covered, what should they do but gather about a piper that *come* along with 'em, and fall to dancing as if it was a wedding. Davy longed to be among 'em (for he hadn't a bad foot of his own, that time, whatever he may now); but he was loth to begin, because they all seemed strange to him, only the man I told you that he thought was dead. Well, at last this man saw what Davy wanted, and came up to him. 'Davy,' says he, 'take out a partner, and show what you can do, but take care and don't offer to kiss her.' 'That I won't.' says Davy, 'although her lips were made of honey.' And with that he made his bow to the *purtiest* girl in the ring, and he and she began to dance. 'Twas a jig they danced, and they did it to th' admiration, do you see, of all that were there. 'Twas all very well till the jig was over; but just as they had done, Davy, for he had a drop in, and was warm with the dancing, forgot himself, and kissed his partner, according to custom. The smack was no sooner off of his lips, you see, than he was left alone in the churchyard, without a creature near him, and all he could see was the tall tombstones. Davy said they seemed as if they were dancing too, but I suppose that was only the wonder that happened him, and he being a little in drink. Howsomever, he found it was a great many hours later than he thought it; 'twas near morning when he came home; but they couldn't get a word out of him till the next day, when he woke out of a dead sleep about twelve o'clock.''

When Tom had finished the account of Davy Roche and the berrin, it became quite evident that spirits, of some sort, were working too strong within him to admit of his telling many more tales of the good people. Tom seemed conscious of this. He muttered for a few minutes broken sentences concerning churchyards, river-sides, leprechauns, and *dina magh*,* which were quite unintelligible, perhaps, to himself, certainly to Mr Martin and his lady. At length he made a slight motion of the head upwards, as if he would say, "I can talk no more"; stretched his arm on the table, upon which he placed the empty tumbler slowly, and with the most knowing and cautious air; and rising from his chair, walked, or rather rolled, to the parlour door. Here he turned round to face his host and hostess; but after various ineffectual attempts to bid them good-night, the words, as they rose, being always choked by a violent hiccup, while the door, which he held by the handle, swung to and fro, carrying his unyielding body along with it, he was obliged to depart in silence. The cow-boy, sent by Tom's wife, who knew well what sort of allurement detained him when he remained out after a certain hour, was in attendance to conduct his master home. I have no doubt that he returned without meeting any material injury, as I know that within the last month he was, to use his own words, "as stout and hearty a man as any of his age in the county Cork."

Daoine maithe, i.e., the good people.

The Pudding Bewitched

WILLIAM CARLETON

"Moll Roe Rafferty was the son—daughter I mane—of ould Jack Rafferty, who was remarkable for a habit he had of always wearing his head undher his hat; but indeed the same family was a quare one, as everybody knew that was acquainted wid them. It was said of them—but whether it was thrue or not I won't undhertake to say, for 'fraid I'd tell a lie—that whenever they didn't wear shoes or boots they always went barefooted; but I heard aftherwards that this was disputed, so rather than say anything to injure their character, I'll let that pass. Now, ould Jack Rafferty had two sons, Paddy and Molly—hut! what are you all laughing at?—I mane a son and daughter, and it was generally believed among the neighbours that they were brother and sisther, which you know might be thrue or it might not: but that's a thing that, wid the help o' goodness, we have nothing to say to. Troth there was many ugly things put out on them that I don't wish to repate, such that neither Jack nor his son Paddy ever walked a perch without puttin' one foot afore the other like a salmon; an' I know it was whispered about, that whinever Moll Roe slep', she had an out-of-the-way custom of keepin' her eyes shut. If she did, however, for that matther the loss was her own; for sure we all know that when one comes to shut their eyes they can't see as far before them as another.

"Moll Roe was a fine young bouncin' girl, large and lavish, wid a purty head o' hair on her like scarlet, that bein' one of the raisons why she was called *Roe*, or red; her arms an' cheeks were much the colour of the hair, an' her saddle nose was the purtiest thing of its kind that ever was on a face. Her fists—for, thank goodness, she was well sarved wid them too—had a strong simularity to two thumpin' turnips, reddened by the sun; an' to keep all right and tight, she had a temper as fiery as her head—for indeed, it was well known that all the Rafferties were *warm*-hearted. Howandiver, it appears that God gives nothing in vain, and of coorse the same fists, big and red as they were, if all that is said about them is thrue, were not so

186

much given to her for ornament as use. At laist, takin' them in connection wid her lively temper, we have it upon good authority, that there was no danger of their getting blue-moulded for want of practice. She had a twist, too, in one of her eyes that was very becomin' in its way, and made her poor husband, when she got him, take it into his head that she could see round a corner. She found him out in many quare things, widout doubt; but whether it was owin' to that or not, I wouldn't undertake to say *for fraid I'd tell a lie.*

"Well, begad, anyhow it was Moll Roe that was the *dilsy.** It happened that there was a nate vagabone in the neighbourhood, just as much overburdened wid beauty as herself, and he was named Gusty Gillespie. Gusty, the Lord guard us, was what they call a black-mouth Prosbytarian, and wouldn't keep Christmas-day, the blagard, except what they call 'ould style'. Gusty was rather good-lookin' when seen in the dark, as well as Moll herself; and, indeed, it was purty well known that—accordin' as the talk went—it was in nightly meetings that they had an opportunity of becomin' detached to one another. The quensequence was, that in due time both families began to talk very seriously as to what was to be done. Moll's brother, Pawdien O'Rafferty, gave Gusty the best of two choices. What they were it's not worth spakin' about; but at any rate *one* of them was a poser, an' as Gusty knew his man, he soon came to his senses. Accordianly everything was deranged for their marriage, and it was appointed that they should be spliced by the Rev. Samuel M'Shuttle, the Prosbytarian parson, on the following Sunday.

"Now this was the first marriage that had happened for a long time in the neighbourhood betune a black-mouth an' a Catholic, an' of coorse there was strong objections on both sides against it; an' begad, only for one thing, it would never 'a tuck place at all. At any rate, faix, there was one of the bride's uncles, ould Harry Connolly, a fairy-man, who could cure all complaints wid a secret he had, and as he didn't wish to see his niece married upon sich a fellow, he fought bitterly against the match. All Moll's friends, however, stood up for the marriage barrin' him, an' of coorse the Sunday was appointed, as I said, that they were to be dove-tailed together.

"Well, the day arrived, and Moll, as became her, went to mass, and Gusty to meeting, afther which they were to join one another in Jack Rafferty's, where the priest, Father M'Sorley, was to slip up afther mass to take his dinner wid them, and

*Perhaps from Irish dilse—i.e., love.

187

to keep Misther M'Shuttle, who was to marry them, company. Nobody remained at home but ould Jack Rafferty an' his wife, who stopped to dress the dinner, for, to tell the truth, it was to be a great let-out entirely. Maybe, if all was known, too, that Father M'Sorley was to give them a cast of his office over an' above the ministher, in regard that Moll's friends were not altogether satisfied at the kind of marriage which M'Shuttle could give them. The sorrow may care about that—splice here—splice there—all I can say is, that when Mrs Rafferty was goin' to tie up a big bag pudden, in walks Harry Connolly, the fairy-man, in a rage, and shouts out,—'Blood and blunderbushes, what are yez here for?'

" 'Arrah why, Harry? Why, avick?'

" 'Why, the sun's in the suds and the moon in the high Horicks; there's a clipstick comin' an, an' there you're both as unconsarned as if it was about to rain mether. Go out and cross yourselves three times in the name o' the four Mandromarvins, for as prophecy says:—Fill the pot, Eddy, supernaculum—a blazing star's a rare spectaculum. Go out both of you and look at the sun, I say, an' ye'll see the condition he's in—off!'

"Begad, sure enough, Jack gave a bounce to the door, and his wife leaped like a two-year-ould, till they were both got on a stile beside the house to see what was wrong in the sky.

" 'Arrah, what is it, Jack,' said she; 'can you see anything?'

" 'No,' says he, 'sorra the full o' my eye of anything I can spy, barrin' the sun himself, that's not visible in regard of the clouds. God guard us! I doubt there's something to happen.'

" 'If there wasn't, Jack, what 'ud put Harry, that knows so much, in the state he's in?'

" 'I doubt it's this marriage,' said Jack: 'betune ourselves, it's not over an' above religious for Moll to marry a black-mouth, an' only for—; but it can't be helped now, though you see not a taste o' the sun willin' to show his face upon it.'

" 'As to that,' says the wife, winkin' wid both her eyes, 'if Gusty's satisfied wid Moll, it's enough. I know who'll carry the whip hand, anyhow; but in the manetime let us ax Harry 'ithin what ails the sun.'

"Well, they accordianly went in an' put the question to him:

" 'Harry, what's wrong, ahagur? What is it now, for if anybody alive knows, 'tis yourself?'

" 'Ah!' said Harry, screwin' his mouth wid a kind of a dhry smile, 'the sun has a hard twist o' the cholic; but never mind that, I tell you you'll have a merrier weddin' than you think, that's all;' and havin' said this, he put on his hat and left the house.

"Now, Harry's answer relieved them very much, and so, afther calling to him to be back for the dinner, Jack sat down to take a shough o' the pipe, and the wife lost no time in tying up the pudden and puttin' it in the pot to be boiled.

"In this way things went on well enough for a while, Jack smokin' away, an' the wife cookin' and dhressin' at the rate of a hunt. At last, Jack, while sittin', as I said, contentedly at the fire, thought he could persave an odd dancin' kind of motion in the pot that puzzled him a good deal.

" 'Katty,' said he, 'what the dickens is in this pot on the fire?'

" 'Nerra thing but the big pudden. Why do you ax?' says she.

" 'Why,' said he, 'if ever a pot tuck it into its head to dance a jig, and this did. Thundher and sparbles, look at it!'

"Begad, it was thrue enough; there was the pot bobbin' up an' down and from side to side, jiggin' it away as merry as a grig; an' it was quite aisy to see that it wasn't the pot itself, but what was inside of it, that brought about the hornpipe.

" 'Be the hole o' my coat,' shouted Jack, 'there's something alive in it, or it would never cut sich capers!'

" 'Be gorra, there is, Jack; something sthrange entirely has got into it. Wirra, man alive, what's to be done?'

"Jist as she spoke, the pot seemed to cut the buckle in prime style, and afther a spring that 'ud shame a dancin'-masther, off flew the lid, and out bounced the pudden itself, hoppin', as nimble as a pea on a drum-head, about the floor. Jack blessed himself, and Katty crossed herself. Jack shouted, and Katty screamed. 'In the name of goodness, keep your distance; no one here injured you!'

"The pudden, however, made a set at him, and Jack lepped first on a chair and then on the kitchen table to avoid it. It then danced towards Katty, who was now repatin' her prayers at the top of her voice, while the cunnin' thief of a pudden was hoppin' and jiggin' it round her, as if it was amused at her distress.

" 'If I could get the pitchfork,' said Jack, 'I'd dale wid it—by goxty I'd thry its mettle.'

" 'No, no,' shouted Katty, thinkin' there was a fairy in it; 'let us spake it fair. Who knows what harm it might do? Aisy now,' said she to the pudden, 'aisy, dear; don't harm honest people that never meant to offend you. It wasn't us—no, in

189

troth, it was ould Harry Connolly that bewitched you; pursue *him* if you wish, but spare a woman like me; for, whisper, dear, I'm not in a condition to be frightened—troth I'm not.'

"The pudden, bedad, seemed to take her at her word, and danced away from her towards Jack, who, like the wife believin' there was a fairy in it, an' that spakin' it fair was the best plan, thought he would give it a soft word as well as her.

" 'Plase your honour,' said Jack, 'she only spaiks the truth; an', upon my voracity, we both feels much oblaiged to your honour for your quietness. Faith, it's quite clear that if you weren't a gentlemanly pudden all out, you'd act otherwise. Ould Harry, the rogue, is your mark; he's jist gone down the road there, and if you go fast you'll overtake him. Be me song, your dancin' masther did his duty, anyhow. Thank your honour! God speed you, an' may you never meet wid a parson or alderman in your thravels!'

"Jist as Jack spoke the pudden appeared to take the hint, for it quietly hopped out, and as the house was directly on the road-side, turned down towards the bridge, the very way that ould Harry went. It was very natural, of coorse, that Jack and Katty should go out to see how it intended to thravel; and, as the day was Sunday, it was but natural, too, that a greater number of people than usual were passin' the road. This was a fact; and when Jack and his wife were seen followin' the pudden, the whole neighbourhood was soon up and afther it.

" 'Jack Rafferty, what is it? Katty, ahagur, will you tell us what it manes?'

" 'Why,' replied Katty, 'it's my big pudden that's bewitched, an' it's now hot foot pursuin'—;' here she stopped, not wishin' to mention her brother's name—'*some one* or other that surely put *pishogues* an it.'*

"This was enough; Jack, now seein' that he had assistance, found his courage comin' back to him; so says he to Katty, 'Go home,' says he, 'an' lose no time in makin' another pudden as good, an' here's Paddy Scanlan's wife, Bridget, says she'll let you boil it on her fire, as you'll want our own to dress the rest o' the dinner: and Paddy himself will lend me a pitchfork, for purshuin to the morsel of that same pudden will escape till I let the wind out of it, now that I've the neighbours to back an' support me,' says Jack.

"This was agreed to, and Katty went back to prepare a fresh pudden, while Jack an' half the townland pursued the other wid spades, graips, pitchforks, scythes, flails, and all possible description of instruments. On the pudden went, however,

*Put it under fairy influence.

190

at the rate of about six Irish miles an hour, an' sich a chase never was seen. Catholics, Prodestants, an' Prosbytarians, were all afther it, armed, as I said, an' bad end to the thing but its own activity could save it. Here it made a hop, and there a prod was made at it; but off it went, an' some one, as eager to get a slice at it on the other side, got the prod instead of the pudden. Big Frank Farrell, the miler of Ballyboulteen, got a prod backwards that brought a hullabaloo out of him you might hear at the other end of the parish. One got a slice of a scythe, another a whack of a flail, a third a rap of a spade that made him look nine ways at wanst.

" 'Where is it goin'?' asked one. 'My life for you, it's on it's way to Meeting. Three cheers for it if it turns to Carntaul.' 'Prod the sowl out of it, if it's a Prodestan',' shouted the others; 'if it turns to the left, slice it into pancakes. We'll have no Prodestan' puddens here.'

"Begad, by this time the people were on the point of beginnin' to have a regular fight about it, when, very fortunately, it took a short turn down a little by-lane that led towards the Methodist praichin-house, an' in an instant all parties were in an uproar against it as a Methodist pudden. 'It's a Wesleyan,' shouted several voices; 'an' by this an' by that, into a Methodist chapel it won't put a foot today, or we'll lose a fall. Let the wind out of it. Come boys, where's your pitchforks?'

"The divle purshuin to the one of them, however, ever could touch the pudden, an' jist when they thought they had it up against the gavel of the Methodist chapel, begad it gave them the slip, and hops over to the left, clane into the river, and sails away before all their eyes as light as an egg-shell.

"Now, it so happened that a little below this place, the demesne-wall of Colonel Bragshaw was built up to the very edge of the river on each side of its banks; and so findin' there was a stop put to their pursuit of it; they went home again, every man, woman, and child of them, puzzled to think what the pudden was at all, what it meant, or where it was goin'! Had Jack Rafferty an' his wife been willin' to let out the opinion they held about Harry Connolly bewitchin' it, there is no doubt of it but poor Harry might be badly trated by the crowd, when their blood was up. They had sense enough, howandiver, to keep that to themselves, for Harry bein' an' ould bachelor, was a kind friend to the Raffertys. So, of coorse, there was all kinds of talk about it—some guessin' this, and some guessin' that—one party sayin' the pudden was of there side, another party denyin' it, an' insistin' it belonged to them, an' so on.

"In the manetime, Katty Rafferty, for 'fraid the dinner might come short, went home and made another pudden much about the same size as the one that had escaped, and bringin' it over to their next neighbour, Paddy Scanlan's, it was put into a pot and placed on the fire to boil, hopin' that it might be done in time, espishilly as they were to have the ministher, who loved a warm slice of a good pudden as well as e'er a gintleman in Europe.

"Anyhow, the day passed; Moll and Gusty were made man an' wife, an' no two could be more lovin'. Their friends that had been asked to the widdin' were saunterin' about in pleasant little groups till dinner-time, chattin' an' laughin'; but, above all things, sthrivin' to account for the figaries of the pudden; for, to tell the truth, its adventures had now gone through the whole parish.

"Well, at any rate, dinner-time was dhrawin' near, and Paddy Scanlan was sittin' comfortably wid his wife at the fire, the pudden boilen before their eyes, when in walks Harry Connolly, in a flutter, shoutin'—'Blood an' blunderbushes, what are yez here for?'

" 'Arra, why Harry—why, avick?' said Mrs Scanlan.

" 'Why,' said Harry, 'the sun's in the suds an' the moon in the high Horicks! Here's a clipstick comin' an, an' there you sit as unconsarned as if it was about to rain mether! Go out both of you, an' look at the sun, I say, and ye'll see the condition he's in—off!'

" 'Ay, but, Harry, what's that rowled up in the tail of your cothamore* (big coat)?'

" 'Out wid yez,' said Harry, 'an' pray against the clipstick—the sky's fallin'!'

"Begad, it was hard to say whether Paddy or the wife got out first, they were so much alarmed by Harry's wild thin face an' piercin' eyes; so out they went to see what was wondherful in the sky, an' kep' lookin' an' lookin' in every direction, but not a thing was to be seen, barrin' the sun shinin' down wid great good-humour, an' not a single cloud in the sky.

"Paddy an' the wife now came in laughin', to scould Harry, who, no doubt, was a great wag in his way when he wished. 'Musha, bad scran to you, Harry—.' They had time to say no more, howandiver, for, as they were goin' into the door, they met him comin' out of it wid a reek of smoke out of his tail like a lime-kiln.

" 'Harry,' shouted Bridget, 'my sowl to glory, but the tail of your cothamore's a-fire—you'll be burned. Don't you see the smoke that's out of it?'

" 'Cross yourselves three times,' said Harry, widout stoppin,' or even lookin'

*Irish, *cóta mór*.

behind him, 'for, as the prophecy says—Fill the pot, Eddy—.' They could hear no more, for Harry appeared to feel like a man that carried something a great deal hotter than he wished, as anyone might see by the liveliness of his motions, and the quare faces he was forced to make as he went along.

" 'What the dickens is he carryin' in the skirts of his big coat?' asked Paddy.

" 'My sowl to happiness, but maybe he has stole the pudden,' said Bridget, 'for it's known that many a sthrange thing he does.'

"They immediately examined the pot, but found that the pudden was there as safe as tuppence, an' this puzzled them the more, to think what it was he could be carryin' about wid him in the manner he did. But little they knew what he had done while they were sky-gazin'!

"Well, anyhow, the day passed and the dinner was ready, an' no doubt but a fine gatherin' there was to partake of it. The Prosbytarian ministher met the Methodist praicher—a divilish stretcher of an appetite he had, in throth—on their way to Jack Rafferty's, an' as he knew he could take the liberty, why he insisted on his dinin' wid him; for, afther all, begad, in thim times the clargy of all descriptions lived upon the best footin' among one another, not all as one as now—but no matther. Well, they had nearly finished their dinner, when Jack Rafferty himself axed Katty for the pudden; but, jist as he spoke, in it came as big as a mess-pot.

" 'Gintlemen,' said he, 'I hope none of you will refuse tastin' a bit of Katty's pudden; I don't mane the dancin' one that tuck to its thravels today, but a good solid fellow that she med since.'

" 'To be sure we won't,' replied the priest; 'so, Jack, put a thrifle on them three plates at your right hand, and send them over here to the clargy, an' maybe,' he said, laughin'—for he was a droll good-humoured man—'maybe, Jack, we won't set you a proper example.'

" 'Wid a heart an' a half, yer reverence an' gintlemen; in troth, it's not a bad example ever any of you set us at the likes, or ever will set us, I'll go bail. An' sure I only wish it was betther fare I had for you; but we're humble people, gintlemen, and so you can't expect to meet here what you would in higher places.'

" 'Betther a male of herbs,' said the Methodist praicher, 'where pace is—.' He had time to go no farther, however; for much to his amazement, the priest and the ministher started up from the table jist as he was goin' to swallow the first spoonful of the pudden, and before you could say Jack Robinson, started away at a lively jig down the floor.

"At this moment a neighbour's son came runnin' in, an' tould them that the parson was comin' to see the new-married couple, an' wish them all happiness; an' the words were scarcely out of his mouth when he made his appearance. What to think he knew not, when he saw the ministher footing it away at the rate of a weddin'. He had very little time, however, to think; for, before he could sit down, up starts the Methodist praicher, and clappin' his two fists in his sides chimes in in great style along wid him.

" 'Jack Rafferty,' says he—and, by the way, Jack was his tenant—'what the dickens does all this mane?' says he; 'I'm amazed!'

" 'The not a particle o' me can tell you,' says Jack; 'but will your reverence jist taste a morsel o' pudden, merely that the young couple may boast that you ait at their weddin'; for sure if *you* wouldn't, *who* would?'

" 'Well,' says he, 'to gratify them I will; so just a morsel. But, Jack, this bates Bannagher,' says he again, puttin' the spoonful o' pudden into his mouth, 'has there been dhrink here?'

" 'Oh, the divle a *spudh*,' says Jack, 'for although there's plinty in the house, faith, it appears the gintlemen wouldn't wait for it. Unless they tuck it elsewhere, I can make nothin' of this.'

"He had scarcely spoken, when the parson, who was an active man, cut a caper a yard high, an' you could bless yourself, the three clargy were hard at work dancin', as if for a wager. Begad, it would be unpossible for me to tell you the state the whole meetin' was in when they seen this. Some were hoarse wid laughin'; some turned up their eyes wid wondher; many thought them mad, an' others thought they had turned up their little fingers a thrifle too often.

" 'Be goxty, it's a burnin' shame,' said one, 'to see three black-mouth clargy in sich a state at this early hour!' 'Thundher an' ounze, what's over them at all?' says others; 'why, one would think they're bewitched. Holy Moses, look at the caper the Methodist cuts! An' as for the Recther, who would think he could handle his feet at such a rate! Be this an' be that, he cuts the buckle, and does the threblin' step aiquil to Paddy Horaghan, the dancin' masther himself? An' see! Bad cess to the morsel of the parson that's not hard at *Peace upon a trancher*, an' it of a Sunday too Whirroo, gintlemen, the fun's in yez afther all—whish! more power to yez!'

"The sorra's own fun they had, an' no wondher; but judge of what they felt, when all at once they saw ould Jack Rafferty himself bouncin' in among them, and footing it away like the best o' them. Begad, no play could come up to it, an' nothin' could be heard but laughin', shouts of encouragement, and clappin' of hands like mad. Now the minute Jack Rafferty left the chair where he had been carvin' the pudden, ould Harry Connolly comes over and claps himself down in his place, in ordher to send it round, of coorse; an' he was scarcely sated, when who should make his appearance but Barney Hartigan, the piper. Barney, by the way, had been sent for early in the day, but bein' from home when the message for him went, he couldn't come any sooner.

" 'Begorra,' said Barney, 'you're airly at the work, gintlemen! but what does this mane? But, divle may care, yez shan't want the music while there's a blast in the pipes, anyhow!' So sayin' he gave them *Jig Polthogue, an' after that Kiss my Lady*, in his best style.

"In the manetime the fun went on thick an' threefold, for it must be remembered that Harry, the ould knave, was at the pudden; an' maybe he didn't sarve it about in double quick time too. The first he helped was the bride, and, before you could say chopstick, she was at it hard an' fast before the Methodist praicher, who gave a jolly spring before her that threw them into convulsions. Harry liked this, and made up his mind soon to find partners for the rest; so he accordianly sent the pudden about like lightnin'; an' to make a long story short, barrin' the piper himself, there wasn't a pair o' heels in the house but was as busy at the dancin' as if their lives depinded on it.

" 'Barney,' says Harry, 'just taste a morsel o' this pudden; divle the such a bully of a pudden ever you ett; here, your sowl! thry a snig of it—it's beautiful.'

" 'To be sure I will,' says Barney. 'I'm not the boy to refuse a good thing; but Harry, be quick, for you know my hands is engaged, an' it would be a thousand pities not to keep them in music, an' they so well inclined. Thank you, Harry; begad that is a famous pudden; but blood an' turnips, what's this for?'

"The word was scarcely out of his mouth when he bounced up, pipes an' all, an dashed into the middle of the party. 'Hurroo, your sowls, let us make a night of it! The Ballyboulteen boys for ever! Go it, your reverence—turn your partner—heel an' toe, ministher. Good! Well done again—Whish! Hurroo! Here's for Ballyboulteen an' the sky over it!'

"Bad luck to the sich a set was seen together in this world, or will again, I suppose. The worst, however, wasn't come yet, for jist as they were in the very heat an' fury of the dance, what do you think comes hoppin' in among them but another pudden, as nimble an' merry as the first! That was enough; they all had heard of—the ministhers among the rest—an' most o' them had seen the other pudden, and knew that there must be a fairy in it, sure enough. Well, as I said, in it comes to the thick o' them; but the very appearance of it was enough. Off the three clargy danced, and off the whole weddiners danced afther them, every one makin' the best of their way home; but not a sowl of them able to break out of step, if they were to be hanged for it. Throth it wouldn't lave a laugh in you to see the parson dancin' down the road on his way home, and the ministher and Methodist praicher cuttin' the buckle as they went along in the opposite direction. To make short work of it, they all danced home at last, wid scarce a puff of wind in them; the bride and bridegroom danced away to bed; an' now, boys, come an' let us dance the *Horo Lheig* in the barn 'idout. But you see, boys, before we go, an' in ordher that I may make everything plain, I had as good tell you that Harry, in crossing the bridge of Ballyboulteen, a couple of miles below Squire Bragshaw's demesne-wall, saw the pudden floatin' down the river—the truth is he was waitin' for it; but be this as it may, he took it out, for the wather had made it as clane as a new pin, and tuckin' it up in the tail of his big coat, contrived, as you all guess, I suppose, to change it while Paddy Scanlan an' the wife were examinin' the sky; an' for the other, he contrived to bewitch it in the same manner, by gettin' a fairy to go into it, for, indeed, it was purty well known that the same Harry was hand an' glove wid the *good people*. Others will tell you that it was half a pound of quicksilver he put into it; but that doesn't stand to raison. At any rate, boys, I have tould you the adventures of the Mad Pudden of Ballyboulteen; but I don't wish to tell you many other things about it that happened—*for fraid I'd tell a lie.*"*

---

*Some will insist that a fairy-man or fairy-woman has the power to bewitch a pudding by putting a fairy into it; whilst others maintain that a competent portion of quicksilver will make it dance over half the parish.

TÍR-NA-N-OG

There is a country called Tír-na-n-Og, which means the Country of the Young, for age and death have not found it; neither tears nor loud laughter have gone near it. The shadiest boskage covers it perpetually. One man has gone there and returned. The bard, Oisin, who wandered away on a white horse, moving on the surface of the foam with his fairy Niamh, lived there three hundred years, and then returned looking for his comrades. The moment his foot touched the earth his three hundred years fell on him, and he was bowed double, and his beard swept the ground. He described his sojourn in the Land of Youth to Patrick before he died. Since then many have seen it in many places; some in the depths of lakes, and have heard rising therefrom a vague sound of bells; more have seen it far off on the horizon, as they peered out from the western cliffs. Not three years ago a fisherman imagined that he saw it. It never appears unless to announce some national trouble.

There are many kindred beliefs. A Dutch pilot, settled in Dublin, told M. De La Boullage Le Cong, who travelled in Ireland in 1614, that round the poles were many islands; some hard to be approached because of the witches who inhabit them and destroy by storms those who seek to land. He had once, off the coast of Greenland, in sixty-one degrees of latitude, seen and approached such an island only to see it vanish. Sailing in an opposite direction, they met with the same island, and sailing near, were almost destroyed by a furious tempest.

According to many stories, Tír-na-n-Og is the favourite dwelling of the fairies. Some say it is triple—the island of the living, the island of victories, and an underwater land.

The Legend of O'Donoghue*

T. CROFTON CROKER

In an age so distant that the precise period is unknown, a chieftain named O'Donoghue ruled over the country which surrounds the romantic Lough Lean, now called the lake of Killarney. Wisdom, beneficence, and justice distinguished his reign, and the prosperity and happiness of his subjects were their natural results. He is said to have been as renowned for his war-like exploits as for his pacific virtues; and as a proof that his domestic administration was not the less rigorous because it was mild, a rocky island is pointed out to strangers, called "O'Donoghue's Prison", in which this prince once confined his own son for some act of disorder and disobedience.

His end—for it cannot correctly be called his death—was singular and mysterious. At one of those splendid feasts for which his court was celebrated, surrounded by the most distinguished of his subjects, he was engaged in a prophetic relation of the events which were to happen in ages yet to come. His auditors listened, now wrapt in wonder, now fired with indignation, burning with shame, or melted into sorrow, as he faithfully detailed the heroism, the injuries, the crimes, and the miseries of their descendants. In the midst of his predictions he rose slowly from his seat, advanced with a solemn, measured, and majestic tread to the shore of the lake, and walked forward composedly upon its unyielding surface. When he had nearly reached the centre he paused for a moment, then, turning slowly round, looked toward his friends, and waving his arms to them with the cheerful air of one taking a short farewell, disappeared from their view.

The memory of the good O'Donoghue has been cherished by successive generations with affectionate reverence; and it is believed that at sunrise, on every May-day morning, the anniversary of his departure, he revisits his ancient domains: a favoured few only are in general permitted to see him, and this distinction is always an omen of good fortune to the beholders; when it is granted

*Fairy Legends of the South of Ireland.

199

to many it is a sure token of an abundant harvest—a blessing, the want of which during this prince's reign was never felt by his people.

Some years have elapsed since the last appearance of O'Donoghue. The April of that year had been remarkably wild and stormy; but on May-morning the fury of the elements had altogether subsided. The air was hushed and still; and the sky, which was reflected in the serene lake, resembled a beautiful but deceitful countenance, whose smiles, after the most tempestuous emotions, tempt the stranger to believe that it belongs to a soul which no passion has ever ruffled.

The first beams of the rising sun were just gilding the lofty summit of Glenaa, when the waters near the eastern shore of the lake became suddenly and violently agitated, though all the rest of its surface lay smooth and still as a tomb of polished marble, the next morning a foaming wave darted forward, and, like a proud high-crested war-horse, exulting in his strength, rushed across the lake toward Toomies mountain. Behind this wave appeared a stately warrior fully armed, mounted upon a milk-white steed; his snowy plume waved gracefully from a helmet of polished steel, and at his back fluttered a light blue scarf. The horse, apparently exulting in his noble burden, sprung after the wave along the water, which bore him up like firm earth, while showers of spray that glittered brightly in the morning sun were dashed up at every bound.

The warrior was O'Donoghue; he was followed by numberless youths and maidens, who moved lightly and unconstrained over the watery plain, as the moonlight fairies glide through the fields of air; they were linked together by garlands of delicious spring flowers, and they timed their movements to strains of enchanting melody. When O'Donoghue had nearly reached the western side of the lake, he suddenly turned his steed, and directed his course along the wood-fringed shore of Glenaa, preceded by the huge wave that curled and foamed up as high as the horse's neck, whose fiery nostrils snorted above it. The long train of attendants followed with playful deviations the track of their leader, and moved on with unabated fleetness to their celestial music, till gradually, as they entered the narrow strait between Glenaa and Dinis, they became involved in the mists which still partially floated over the lakes, and faded from the view of the wondering beholders: but the sound of their music still fell upon the ear, and echo, catching up the harmonious strains, fondly repeated and prolonged them in soft and softer tones, till the last faint repetition died away, and the hearers awoke as from a dream of bliss.

Rent-Day

"Oh, ullagone! ullagone! this is a wide world, but what will we do in it, or where will we go?" muttered Bill Doody, as he sat on a rock by the Lake of Killarney. "What will we do? Tomorrow's rent-day, and Tim the Driver swears if we don't pay our rent, he'll cant every *ha'perth* we have; and then sure enough, there's Judy and myself, and the poor *grawls*,* will be turned out to starve on the high-road, for the never a halfpenny of rent have I!—Oh hone, that ever I should live to see this day!"

Thus did Bill Doody bemoan his hard fate, pouring his sorrows to the reckless waves of the most beautiful of lakes, which seemed to mock his misery as they rejoiced beneath the cloudless sky of a May morning. That lake, glittering in sunshine, sprinkled with fairy isles of rock and verdure, and bounded by giant hills of ever-varying hues, might, with its magic beauty, charm all sadness but despair; for alas,

> "How ill the scene that offers rest
> And heart that cannot rest agree!"

Yet Bill Doody was not so desolate as he supposed; there was one listening to him he little thought of, and help was at hand from a quarter he could not have expected.

"What's the matter with you, my poor man?" said a tall, portly-looking gentleman, at the same time stepping out of a furze-brake. Now Bill was seated on a rock that commanded the view of a large field. Nothing in the field could be concealed from him, except this furze-brake, which grew in a hollow near the margin of the lake. He was, therefore, not a little surprised at the gentleman's

*Children.

201

sudden appearance, and began to question whether the personage before him belonged to this world or not. He, however, soon mustered courage sufficient to tell him how his crops had failed, how some bad member had charmed away his butter, and how Tim the Driver threatened to turn him out of the farm if he didn't pay up every penny of the rent by twelve o'clock next day.

"A sad story, indeed," said the stranger; "but surely, if you represented the case to your landlord's agent, he won't have the heart to turn you out."

"Heart, your honour; where would an agent get a heart!" exclaimed Bill. "I see your honour does not know him; besides, he has an eye on the farm this long time for a fosterer of his own; so I expect no mercy at all, only to be turned out."

"Take this, my poor fellow, take this," said the stranger, pouring a purse full of gold into Bill's old hat, which in his grief he had flung on the ground. "Pay the fellow your rent, but I'll take care it shall do him no good. I remember the time when things went otherwise in this country, when I would have hung up such a fellow in the twinkling of an eye!"

These words were lost upon Bill, who was insensible to everything but the sight of the gold, and before he could unfix his gaze, and lift up his head to pour out his hundred thousand blessings, the stranger was gone. The bewildered peasant looked around in search of his benefactor, and at last he thought he saw him riding on a white horse a long way off on the lake.

"O'Donoghue, O'Donoghue!" shouted Bill; "the good, the blessed O'Donoghue!" and he ran capering like a madman to show Judy the gold, and to rejoice her heart with the prospect of wealth and happiness.

The next day Bill proceeded to the agent's; not sneakingly, with his hat in his hand, his eyes fixed on the ground, and his knees bending under him; but bold and upright, like a man conscious of his independence.

"Why don't you take off your hat, fellow? don't you know you are speaking to a magistrate?" said the agent.

"I know I'm not speaking to the king, sir," said Bill; "and I never takes off my hat but to them I can respect and love. The Eye that sees all knows I've no right either to respect or love an agent!"

"You scoundrel!" retorted the man in office, biting his lips with rage at such an unusual and unexpected opposition, "I'll teach you how to be insolent again; I have the power, remember."

"To the cost of the country, I know you have," said Bill, who still remained with his head as firmly covered as if he was Lord Kingsdale himself.

"But come," said the magistrate; "have you got the money for me? this is rent-day. If there's one penny of it wanting, or the running gale that's due, prepare to turn out before night, for you shall not remain another hour in possession."

"There is your rent," said Bill, with an unmoved expression of tone and countenance; "you'd better count it, and give me a receipt in full for the running gale and all."

The agent gave a look of amazement at the gold; for it was gold—real guineas! and not bits of dirty ragged small notes, that are not fit to light one's pipe with. However willing the agent may have been to ruin, as he thought, the unfortunate tenant, he took up the gold, and handed the receipt to Bill, who strutted off with it as proud as a cat of her whiskers.

The agent going to his desk shortly after, was confounded at beholding a heap of gingerbread cakes instead of the money he had deposited there. He raved and swore, but all to no purpose; the gold had become gingerbread cakes, just marked like the guineas, with the king's head; and Bill had the receipt in his pocket; so he saw there was no use in saying anything about the affair, as he would only get laughed at for his pains.

From that hour Bill Doody grew rich; all his undertakings prospered; and he often blesses the day that he met with O'Donoghue, the great prince that lives down under the lake of Killarney.

Loughleagh (Lake of Healing)*

"Do you see that bit of lake," said my companion, turning his eyes towards the acclivity that overhung Loughleagh. "Troth, and as little as you think of it, and as ugly as it looks with its weeds and its flags, it is the most famous one in all Ireland. Young and ould, rich and poor, far and near, have come to that lake to get cured of all kinds of scurvy and sores. The Lord keep us our limbs whole and sound, for it's a sorrowful thing not to have the use o' them. 'Twas but last week we had a great grand Frenchman here; and, though he came upon crutches, faith he went home sound as a bell; and well he paid Billy Reily for curing him."

"And, pray, how did Billy Reily cure him?"

"Oh, well enough. He took his long pole, dipped it down to the bottom of the lake, and brought up on the top of it as much plaster as would do for a thousand sores!"

"What kind of plaster?"

"What kind of plaster? why black plaster to be sure; for isn't the bottom of the lake filled with a kind of black mud which cures all the world?"

"Then it ought to be a famous lake indeed."

"Famous, and so it is," replied my companion, "but it isn't for its cures neather that it is famous; for, sure, doesn't all the world know there is a fine beautiful city at the bottom of it, where the good people live just like Christians. Troth, it is the truth I tell you; for *Shemus-a-sneidh* saw it all when he followed his dun cow that was stolen."

"Who stole her?"

"I'll tell you about it:—Shemus was a poor gossoon, who lived on the brow of the hill, in a cabin with his ould mother. They lived by hook and by crook, one

Dublin and London Magazine, 1825.

204

way and another, in the best way they could. They had a bit of ground that gave 'em the preaty, and a little dun cow that gave 'em the drop o' milk; and, considering how times go, they weren't badly off, for Shemus was a handy gossoon to boot; and, while minden the cow, cut heath and made brooms, which his mother sould on a market-day, and brought home the bit o' tobaccy, the grain of salt, and other nic-nackeness, which a poor body can't well do widout. Once upon a time, however, Shemus went farther than usual up the mountain, looken for long heath, for townspeople don't like to stoop and so like long handles to their brooms. The little dun cow was a'most as cunning as a Christian sinner, and followed Shemus like a lap-dog everywhere he'd go, so that she required little or no herden. On this day she found nice picken on a round spot as green as a leek; and, as poor Shemus was weary, as a body would be on a fine summer's day, he lay down on the grass to rest himself, just as we're resten ourselves on the cairn here. Begad, he hadn't long lain there, sure enough, when, what should he see but whole loads of ganconers*[11] dancing about the place. Some o' them were hurlen, some kicking a football, and others leaping a kick-step-and-a-lep. They were so soople and so active that Shemus was highly delighted with the sport, and a little tanned-skinned chap in a red cap pleased him better than any o' them, bekase he used to tumble the other fellows like mushrooms. At one time he had kept the ball up for as good as half-an-hour, when Shemus cried out, 'Well done, my hurler!' The word wasn't well out of his mouth when whap went the ball on his eye, and flash went the fire. Poor Shemus thought he was blind, and roared out, 'Mille murdher!'† but the only thing he heard was a loud laugh. 'Cross o' Christ about us,'says he to himself, 'what is this for?' and afther rubbing his eyes they came to a little, and he could see the sun and the sky, and, by-and-by, he could see everything but his cow and the mischievous ganconers. They were gone to their rath or mote; but where was the little dun cow? He looked and he looked, and he might have looked from that day to this, bekase she wasn't to be found, and good reason why—the ganconers took her away with 'em.

"Shemus-a-sneidh, however, didn't think so, but ran home to his mother.

" 'Where is the cow, Shemus?' axed the ould woman.

" 'Och, musha, bad luck to her,' said Shemus, 'I donna where she is!'

*Ir. *gean-canach*—i.e., love-talker, a kind of fairy appearing in lonesome valleys, a dudeen (tobacco-pipe) in his mouth, making love to milk-maids, etc.
†A thousand murders.

" 'Is that an answer, you big blaggard, for the likes o' you to give your poor ould mother?' said she.

" 'Och, musha,' said Shemus, 'don't kick up saich a *bollhous* about nothing. The ould cow is safe enough, I'll be bail, some place or other, though I could find her if I put my eyes upon *kippeens*,* and, speaking of eyes, faith, I had very good luck o' my side, or I had naver a one to look after her.'

" 'Why, what happened your eyes, agrah?' axed the ould woman.

" 'Oh! didn't the ganconers—the Lord save us from all hurt and harm!—drive their hurlen ball into them both! and sure I was stone blind for an hour.'

" 'And may be,' said the mother, 'the good people took our cow?'

" 'No, nor the devil a one of them,' said Shemus, 'for, by the powers, that same cow is as knowen as a lawyer, and wouldn't be such a fool as to go with the ganconers while she could get such grass as I found for her today.'

"In this way," continued my informant, "they talked about the cow all that night, and next mornen both o' them set off to look for her. After searching every place, high and low, what should Shemus see sticking out of a bog-hole but something very like the horns of his little beast!

" 'Oh, mother, mother,' said he, 'I've found her!'

" 'Where, alanna?' axed the ould woman.

" 'In the bog-hole, mother,' answered Shemus.

"At this the poor ould creathure set up such a *pullallue* that she brought the seven parishes about her; and the neighbours soon pulled the cow out of the bog-hole. You'd swear it was the same, and yet it wasn't, as you shall hear by-and-by.

"Shemus and his mother brought the dead beast home with them; and, after skinnen her, hung the meat up in the chimney. The loss of the drop o' milk was a sorrowful thing, and though they had a good deal of meat, that couldn't last always; besides, the whole parish *faughed* upon them for eating the flesh of a beast that died without bleeden. But the pretty thing was, they couldn't eat the meat after all, for when it was boiled it was as tough as carrion, and as black as a turf. You might as well think of sinking your teeth in an oak plank as into a piece of it, and then you'd want to sit a great piece from the wall for fear of knocking your head against it when pulling it through your teeth. At last and at long run they were

*Ir. *cipín*—i.e., a stick, a twig.

forced to throw it to the dogs, but the dogs wouldn't smell to it, and so it was thrown into the ditch, where it rotted. This misfortune cost poor Shemus many a salt tear, for he was now obliged to work twice as hard as before, and be out cutten heath on the mountain late and early. One day he was passing by this cairn with a load of brooms on his back, when what should he see but the little dun cow and two red-headed fellows herding her.

" 'That's my mother cow,' said Shemus-a-sneidh.

" 'No, it is not,' said one of the chaps.

" 'But I say it is,' said Shemus, throwing the brooms on the ground, and seizing the cow by the horns. At that the red fellows drove her as fast as they could to this steep place, and with one leap she bounced over, with Shemus stuck fast to her horns. They made only one splash in the lough when the waters closed over 'em, and they sunk to the bottom. Just as Shemus-a-sneidh thought that all was over with him, he found himself before a most elegant palace built with jewels and all manner of fine stones. Though his eyes were dazzled with the splendour of the place, faith he had gomsh* enough not to let go his holt, but in spite of all they could do he held his little cow by the horns, He was axed into the palace, but wouldn't go.

"The hubbub at last grew so great that the door flew open and out walked a hundred ladies and gentlemen, as fine as any in the land.

" 'What does this boy want?' axed one o' them, who seemed to be the masther.

" 'I want my mother's cow,' said Shemus.

" 'That's not your mother's cow,' said the gentleman.

" 'Bethershin!'† cried Shemus-a-sneidh; 'don't I know her as well as I know my right hand?'

" 'Where did you lose her?' axed the gentleman. And so Shemus up and tould him all about it how he was on the mountain—how he saw the good people hurlen—how the ball was knocked in his eye, and his cow was lost.

" 'I believe you are right,' said the gentleman, pulling out his purse, 'and here is the price of twenty cows for you.'

" 'No, no,' said Shemus, 'you'll not catch ould birds wid chaff. I'll have my cow and nothen else.'

" 'You're a funny fellow,' said the gentleman; 'stop here and live in a palace.'

*Otherwise "gumshun—" i.e., sense, cuteness.
†Ir. *B'éidir sin*—i.e., "that is possible".

" 'I'd rather live with my mother.'

" 'Foolish boy!' said the gentleman; 'stop here and live in a palace.'

" 'I'd rather live in my mother's cabin.'

" 'Here you can walk through gardens loaded with fruit and flowers.'

" 'I'd rather,' said Shemus, 'be cutting heath on the mountain.'

" 'Here you can eat and drink of the best.'

" 'Since I've got my cow, I can have milk once more with the praties.'

" 'Oh!' cried the ladies, gathering round him, 'sure you wouldn't take away the cow that gives us milk for our tea?'

" 'Oh!' said Shemus, 'my mother wants milk as bad as anyone, and she must have it; so there is no use in your palaver—I must have my cow.'

"At this they all gathered about him and offered him bushels of gould, but he wouldn't have anything but his cow. Seeing him as obstinate as a mule, they began to thump and beat him; but still he held fast by the horns, till at length a great blast of wind blew him out of the place, and in a moment he found himself and the cow standing on the side of the lake, the water of which looked as if it hadn't been disturbed since Adam was a boy—and that's a long time since.

"Well, Shemus-a-sneidh drove home his cow, and right glad his mother was to see her; but the moment she said 'God bless the beast', she sunk down like the *breesha** of a turf rick. That was the end of Shemus-a-sneidh's dun cow.

"And, sure," continued my companion, standing up, "it is now time for me to look after my brown cow, and God send the ganconers haven't taken her!"

Of this I assured him there could be no fear; and so we parted.

*Ir. *briseadh*—i.e., breaking.

Hy-Brasail—The Isle of the Blest

GERALD GRIFFIN

On the ocean that hollows the rocks where ye dwell,
A shadowy land has appeared, as they tell;
Men thought it a region of sunshine and rest,
And they called it *Hy-Brasail*, the isle of the blest.
From year unto year on the ocean's blue rim,
The beautiful spectre showed lovely and dim;
The golden clouds curtained the deep where it lay,
And it looked like an Eden, away, far away!

A peasant who heard of the wonderful tale,
In the breeze of the Orient loosened his sail;
From Ara, the holy, he turned to the west,
For though Ara was holy, *Hy-Brasail* was blest.
He heard not the voices that called from the shore—
He heard not the rising wind's menacing roar;
Home, kindred, and safety, he left on that day,
And he sped to *Hy Brasail*, away, far away!

Morn rose on the deep, and that shadowy isle,
O'er the faint rim of distance, reflected its smile;
Noon burned on the wave, and that shadowy shore
Seemed lovelily distant, and faint as before;
Lone evening came down on the wanderer's track,
And to Ara again he looked timidly back;
Oh! far on the verge of the ocean it lay,
Yet the isle of the blest was away, far away!

Rash dreamer, return! O, ye winds of the main,
Bear him back to his own peaceful Ara again.
Rash fool! for a vision of fanciful bliss,
To barter thy calm life of labour and peace.
The warning of reason was spoken in vain;
He never revisited Ara again!
Night fell on the deep, amidst tempest and spray,
And he died on the waters, away, far away!

The Phantom Isle

GIRALDUS CAMBRENSIS*

Among the other islands is one newly formed, which they call the Phantom Isle, which had its origin in this manner. One calm day a large mass of earth rose to the surface of the sea, where no land had ever been seen before, to the great amazement of islanders who observed it. Some of them said that it was a whale, or other immense sea-monster; others, remarking that it continued motionless, said, "No; it is land". In order, therefore, to reduce their doubts to certainty, some picked young men of the island determined to approach nearer the spot in a boat. When, however, they came so near to it that they thought they should go on shore, the island sank in the water and entirely vanished from sight. The next day it re-appeared, and again mocked the same youths with the like delusion. At length, on their rowing towards it on the third day, they followed the advice of an older man, and let fly an arrow, barbed with red-hot steel, against the island; and then landing, found it stationary and habitable.

This adds one to the many proofs that fire is the greatest of enemies to every sort of phantom; in so much that those who have seen apparitions, fall into a swoon as soon as they are sensible of the brightness of fire. For fire, both from its position and nature, is the noblest of the elements, being a witness of the secrets of the heavens.

The sky is fiery; the planets are fiery; the bush burnt with fire, but was not consumed; the Holy Ghost sat upon the apostles in tongues of fire.

*"Giraldus Cambrensis" was born in 1146, and wrote a celebrated account of Ireland.

SAINTS, PRIESTS

Everywhere in Ireland are the holy wells. People as they pray by them make little piles of stones, that will be counted at the last day and the prayers reckoned up. Sometimes they tell stories. These following are their stories. They deal with the old times, whereof King Alfred of Northumberland wrote—

> "I found in Innisfail the fair,
> In Ireland, while in exile there,
> Women of worth, both grave and gay men,
> Many clericks and many laymen.
>
> Gold and silver I found, and money,
> Plenty of wheat, and plenty of honey;
> I found God's people rich in pity,
> Found many a feast, and many a city."

There are no martyrs in the stories. That ancient chronicler Giraldus taunted the Archbishop of Cashel because no one in Ireland had received the crown of martyrdom. "Our people may be barbarous," the prelate answered, "but they have never lifted their hands against God's saints; but now that a people have come amongst us who know how to make them (it was just after the English invasion), we shall have martyrs plentifully."

The bodies of saints are fastidious things. At a place called Four-mile-Water, in Wexford, there is an old graveyard full of saints. Once it was on the other side of the river, but they buried a rogue there, and the whole graveyard moved across in the night, leaving the rogue-corpse in solitude. It would have been easier to move merely the rogue-corpse, but they were saints, and had to do things in style.

213

The Priest's Soul*

LADY WILDE

In former days there were great schools in Ireland, where every sort of learning was taught to the people, and even the poorest had more knowledge at that time than many a gentleman has now. But as to the priests, their learning was above all, so that the fame of Ireland went over the whole world, and many kings from foreign lands used to send their sons all the way to Ireland to be brought up in the Irish schools.

Now, at this time there was a little boy learning at one of them who was a wonder to everyone for his cleverness. His parents were only labouring people, and of course poor; but young as he was, and as poor as he was, no king's or lord's son could come up to him in learning. Even the masters were put to shame; for when they were trying to teach him he would tell them something they never heard of before, and show them their ignorance. One of his great triumphs was in argument; and he would go on till he proved to you that black was white, and then when you gave in, for no one could beat him in talk, he would turn round and show you that white was black, or maybe that there was no colour at all in the world. When he grew up his poor father and mother were so proud of him that they resolved to make him a priest, which they did at last, though they nearly starved themselves to get the money. Well, such another learned man was not in Ireland, and he was as great in argument as ever, so that no one could stand before him. Even the bishops tried to talk to him, but he showed them at once they knew nothing at all.

Now, there were no schoolmasters in those times, but it was the priests taught the people; and as this man was the cleverest in Ireland, all the foreign kings sent their sons to him, as long as he had house-room to give them. So he grew very proud, and began to forget how low he had been, and worst of all, even to forget God, who had made him what he was. And the pride of arguing got hold of him,

*Ancient Legends of Ireland.

214

so that from one thing to another he went on to prove that there was no Purgatory, and then no Hell, and then no Heaven, and then no God; and at last that men had no souls, but were no more than a dog or a cow, and when they died there was an end of them. "Whoever saw a soul?" he would say. "If you can show me one, I will believe." No one could make any answer to this; and at last they all came to believe that as there was no other world, everyone might do what they liked in this; the priest setting the example, for he took a beautiful young girl to wife. But as no priest or bishop in the whole land could be got to marry them, he was obliged to read the service for himself. It was a great scandal, yet no one dared to say a word, for all the king's sons were on his side, and would have slaughtered anyone who tried to prevent his wicked goings-on. Poor boys; they all believed in him, and thought every word he said was the truth. In this way his notions began to spread about, and the whole world was going to the bad, when one night an angel came down from Heaven, and told the priest he had but twenty-four hours to live. He began to tremble, and asked for a little more time.

But the angel was stiff, and told him that could not be.

"What do you want time for, you sinner?" he asked.

"Oh sir, have pity on my poor soul!" urged the priest.

"Oh no! You have a soul then," said the angel. "Pray, how did you find that out?"

"It has been fluttering in me ever since you appeared," answered the priest. "What a fool I was not to think of it before."

"A fool, indeed," said the angel. "What good was all your learning, when it could not tell you that you had a soul?"

"Ah, my lord," said the priest, "If I am to die, tell me how soon I may be in Heaven?"

"Never," replied the angel. "You denied there was a Heaven."

"Then, my lord, may I go to Purgatory?"

"You denied Purgatory also; you must go straight to Hell," said the angel.

"But, my lord, I denied Hell also," answered the priest, "so you can't send me there either."

The angel was a little puzzled.

"Well," said he, "I'll tell you what I can do for you. You may either live now on earth for a hundred years, enjoying every pleasure, and then be cast into Hell for ever; or you may die in twenty-four hours in the most horrible torments, and pass through Purgatory, there to remain till the Day of Judgment, if only you can find some one person that believes, and through his belief mercy will be vouchsafed to you, and your soul will be saved."

The priest did not take five minutes to make up his mind.

"I will have death in the twenty-four hours," he said, "so that my soul may be saved at last."

On this the angel gave him directions as to what he was to do, and left him.

Then immediately the priest entered the large room where all the scholars and the kings' sons were seated, and called out to them—

"Now, tell me the truth, and let none fear to contradict me; tell me what is your belief—have men souls?"

"Master," they answered, "once we believed that men had souls; but thanks to your teaching, we believe so no longer. There is no Hell, and no Heaven, and no God. This is our belief, for it is thus you taught us."

Then the priest grew pale with fear, and cried out—

"Listen! I taught you a lie. There is a God, and man has an immortal soul. I believe now all I denied before."

But the shouts of laughter that rose up drowned the priest's voice, for they thought he was only trying them for argument.

"Prove it, master," they cried. "Prove it. Who has ever seen God? Who has ever seen the soul?"

And the room was stirred with their laughter.

The priest stood up to answer them, but no word could he utter. All his eloquence, all his powers of argument had gone from him; and he could do nothing but wring his hands and cry out, "There is a God! there is a God! Lord have mercy on my soul!"

And they all began to mock him! and repeat his own words that he had taught them—

"Show him to us; show us your God." And he fled from them, groaning with agony, for he saw that none believed; and how, then, could his soul be saved?

But he thought next of his wife "She will believe," he said to himself; "women never give up God."

And he went to her; but she told him that she believed only what he taught her, and that a good wife should believe in her husband first and before and above all things in Heaven or earth.

Then despair came on him, and he rushed from the house, and began to ask every one he met if they believed. But the same answer came from one and all—"We believe only what you have taught us", for his doctrine had spread far and wide through the country.

Then he grew half mad with fear, for the hours were passing, and he flung himself down on the ground in a lonesome spot, and wept and groaned in terror, for the time was coming fast when he must die.

Just then a little child came by. "God save you kindly," said the child to him. The priest started up.

"Do you believe in God?" he asked.

"I have come from a far country to learn about him," said the child. "Will your honour direct me to the best school they have in these parts?"

"The best school and the best teacher is close by," said the priest, and he named himself.

"Oh, not to that man," answered the child, "for I am told he denies God, and Heaven, and Hell, and even that man has a soul, because he cannot see it; but I would soon put him down."

The priest looked at him earnestly. "How?" he inquired.

"Why," said the child, "I would ask him if he believed he had life to show me his life."

"But he could not do that, my child," said the priest. "Life cannot be seen; we have it, but it is invisible."

"Then if we have life, though we cannot see it, we may also have a soul, though it is invisible," answered the child.

When the priest heard him speak these words, he fell down on his knees before him, weeping for joy, for now he knew his soul was safe; he had met one at last that believed. And he told the child his whole story—all his wickedness, and pride, and blasphemy against the great God; and how the angel had come to him, and told him of the only way in which he could be saved, through the faith and prayers of someone that believed.

"Now, then," he said to the child, "take this penknife and strike it into my breast, and go on stabbing the flesh until you see the paleness of death on my face. Then watch—for a living thing will soar from my body as I die, and you will then know that my soul has ascended to the presence of God. And when you see this thing, make haste and run to my school, and call on all my scholars to come and see that the soul of their master has left the body, and that all he taught them was a lie, for that there is a God who punishes sin, and a Heaven and a Hell, and that man has an immortal soul destined for eternal happiness or misery."

"I will pray," said the child, "to have courage to do this work."

And he kneeled down and prayed. Then when he rose up he took the penknife and struck it into the priest's heart, and struck and struck again till all the flesh was lacerated; but still the priest lived, though the agony was horrible, for he could not die until the twenty-four hours had expired.

At last the agony seemed to cease, and the stillness of death settled on his face. Then the child, who was watching, saw a beautiful living creature, with four snow-white wings, mount from the dead man's body into the air and go fluttering round his head.

. So he ran to bring the scholars; and when they saw it, they all knew it was the soul of their master; and they watched with wonder and awe until it passed from sight into the clouds.

And this was the first butterfly that was ever seen in Ireland; and now all men know that the butterflies are the souls of the dead, waiting for the moment when they may enter Purgatory, and so pass through torture to purification and peace.

But the schools of Ireland were quite deserted after that time, for people said, What is the use of going so far to learn, when the wisest man in all Ireland did not know if he had a soul till he was near losing it, and was only saved at last through the simple belief of a little child.

The Priest of Coloony

W. B. YEATS

Good Father John O'Hart
   In penal days rode out
To a *shoneen** in his freelands,
   With his snipe marsh and his trout.

In trust took he John's lands,
   —*Sleiveens*† were all his race—
And he gave them as dowers to his daughters,
   And they married beyond their place.

But Father John went up,
   And Father John went down;
And he wore small holes in his shoes,
   And he wore large holes in his gown.

All loved him, only the *shoneen*,
   Whom the devils have by the hair,
From their wives and their cats and their children,
   To the birds in the white of the air.

The birds, for he opened their cages,
   As he went up and down;
And he said with a smile, "Have peace, now,"
   And went his way with a frown.

Shoneen—i.e., upstart
†*Sleiveen*—i.e., mean fellow.

But if when anyone died,
Came keeners hoarser than rooks,
He bade them give over their keening,
    For he was a man of books.

And these were the works of John,
When weeping score by score,
People came into Coloony,
    For he'd died at ninety-four.

There was no human keening;
The birds from Knocknarea,
And the world round Knocknashee,
    Came keening in that day,—

Keening from Innismurry,
Nor stayed for bit or sup;
This way were all reproved
    Who dig old customs up.

[Coloony is a few miles south of the town of Sligo. Father O'Hart lived there in the last century, and was greatly beloved. These lines accurately record the tradition. No one who has held the stolen land has prospered. It has changed owners many times.]

The Story of the Little Bird*

T. CROFTON CROKER

Many years ago there was a very religious and holy man, one of the monks of a convent, and he was one day kneeling at his prayers in the garden of his monastery, when he heard a little bird singing in one of the rose-trees of the garden, and there never was anything that he had heard in the world so sweet as the song of that little bird.

And the holy man rose up from his knees where he was kneeling at his prayers to listen to its song; for he thought he never in all his life heard anything so heavenly.

And the little bird, after singing for some time longer on the rose-tree, flew away to a grove at some distance from the monastery, and the holy man followed it to listen to its singing, for he felt as if he would never be tired of listening to the sweet song it was singing out of its throat.

And the little bird after that went away to another distant tree, and sung there for a while, and then to another tree, and so on in the same manner, but ever farther and farther away from the monastery, and the holy man still following it farther, and farther, and farther still listening delighted to its enchanting song.

But at last he was obliged to give up, as it was growing late in the day, and he returned to the convent; and as he approached it in the evening, the sun was setting in the west with all the most heavenly colours that were ever seen in the world, and when he came into the convent, it was nightfall.

And he was quite surprised at everything he saw, for they were all strange faces about him in the monastery that he had never seen before, and the very place itself, and everything about it, seemed to be strangely altered; and, altogether, it seemed entirely different from what it was when he had left in the morning; and the garden

*Amulet, 1827. T. C. Croker wrote this, he says, word for word as he heard it from an old woman at a holy well.

221

was not like the garden where he had been kneeling at his devotion when he first heard the singing of the little bird.

And while he was wondering at all he saw, one of the monks of the convent came up to him, and the holy man questioned him, "Brother, what is the cause of all these strange changes that have taken place here since the morning?"

And the monk that he spoke to seemed to wonder greatly at his question, and asked him what he meant by the change since morning? for, sure, there was no change; that all was just as before. And then he said, "Brother, why do you ask these strange questions, and what is your name? for you wear the habit of our order, though we have never seen you before."

So upon this the holy man told his name, and said that he had been at mass in the chapel in the morning before he had wandered away from the garden listening to the song of a little bird that was singing among the rose-trees, near where he was kneeling at his prayers.

And the brother, while he was speaking, gazed at him very earnestly, and then told him that there was in the convent a tradition of a brother of his name, who had left it two hundred years before, but that what was become of him was never known.

And while he was speaking, the holy man said, "My hour of death is come; blessed be the name of the Lord for all his mercies to me, through the merits of his only-begotten Son."

And he kneeled down that very moment, and said, "Brother, take my confession, for my soul is departing."

And he made his confession, and received his absolution, and was anointed, and before midnight he died.

The little bird, you see, was an angel, one of the cherubims or seraphims; and that was the way the Almighty was pleased in His mercy to take to Himself the soul of that holy man.

Conversion of King Laoghaire's Daughters

Once when Patrick and his clericks were sitting beside a well in the Rath of Croghan, with books open on their knees, they saw coming towards them the two young daughters of the King of Connaught. 'Twas early morning, and they were going to the well to bathe.

The young girls said to Patrick, "Whence are ye, and whence come ye?" and Patrick answered, "It were better for you to confess to the true God than to inquire concerning our race."

"Who is God?" said the young girls, "and where is God, and of what nature is God, and where is His dwelling-place? Has your God sons and daughters, gold and silver? Is he everlasting? Is he beautiful? Did Mary foster her son? Are His daughters dear and beauteous to men of the world? Is He in heaven, or on earth, in the sea, in rivers, in mountainous places, in valleys?"

Patrick answered them, and made known who God was, and they believed and were baptised, and a white garment put upon their heads; and Patrick asked them would they live on or would they die and behold the face of Christ? They chose death, and died immediately, and were buried near the well Clebach.

King O'Toole and His Goose

S. LOVER

"By Gor, I thought all the world, far and near, heerd o' King O'Toole—well, well, but the darkness of mankind is ontellible! Well, sir, you must know, as you didn't hear it afore, that there was a king called King O'Toole, who was a fine ould king in the ould ancient times, long ago; and it was him that owned the churches in the early days. The king, you see, was the right sort; he was the rale boy, and loved sport as he loved his life, and huntin' in partic'lar; and from the risin' o' the sun, up he got, and away he wint over the mountains beyant afther the deer; and the fine times them wor.

"Well, it was all mighty good, as long as the king had his health; but, you see, in coorse of time the king grew ould, by raison he was stiff in his limbs, and when he got sthriken in years, his heart failed him, and he was lost intirely for want o' divarshin, bekase he couldn't go a huntin' no longer; and, by dad, the poor king was obleeged at last for to get a goose to divart him. Oh, you may laugh, if you like, but it's truth I'm tellin' you; and the way the goose divarted him was this-a-way: You see, the goose used for to swim acrass the lake, and go divin' for throut, and cotch fish on a Friday for the king, and flew every other day round about the lake, divartin' the poor king. All went on mighty well, antil, by dad, the goose got sthriken in years like her master, and couldn't divart him no longer, and then it was that the poor king was lost complate. The king was walkin' one mornin' by the edge of the lake lamentin' his cruel fate, and thinkin' o' drownin' himself, that could get no divarshun in life, when all of a suddint, turnin' round the corner beyant, who should he meet but a mighty dacent young man comin' up to him.

" 'God save you,' says the king to the young man.

" 'God save you kindly, King O'Toole,' says the young man. 'Thrue for you,' says the king. 'I am King O'Toole,' says he, 'prince and plennypennytinchery o'

224

these parts,' says he; 'but how kem ye to know that?' says he, 'Oh, never mind,' says Saint Kavin.

"You see it was Saint Kavin, sure enough—the saint himself in disguise, and nobody else. 'Oh, never mind,' says he, 'I know more than that. May I make bowld to ax how is your goose, King O'Toole?' says he. 'Blur-an-agers, how kem ye to know about my goose?' says the king. 'Oh, no matther; I was given to understand it,' says Saint Kavin. After some more talk the king says, 'What are you?' 'I'm an honest man,' says Saint Kavin. 'Well, honest man,' says the king, 'and how is it you make your money so aisy?' 'By makin' ould things as good as new,' says Saint Kavin. 'Is it a tinker you are?' says the king. 'No,' says the saint; 'I'm no tinker by thrade, King O'Toole; I've a betther thrade than a tinker,' says he—'what would you say,' says he, 'if I made your ould goose as good as new?'

"My dear, at the word o' making his goose as good as new, you'd think the poor ould king's eyes was ready to jump out iv his head. With that the king whistled, and down kem the poor goose, all as one as a hound, waddlin' up to the poor cripple, her mastther, and as like him as two pays. The minute the saint clapt his eyes on the goose, 'I'll do the job for you,' says he, 'King O'Toole.' 'By *Jaminee!*' says King O'Toole, 'if you do, bud I'll say you're the cleverest fellow in the sivin parishes.' 'Oh, by dad,' says Saint Kavin, 'you must say more nor that—my horn's not so soft all out,' says he, 'as to repair your ould goose for nothin'; what'll you gi' me if I do the job for you?—that's the chat,' says Saint Kavin. 'I'll give you whatever you ax,' says the king; 'isn't that fair?' 'Divil a fairer,' says the saint; 'that's the way to do business. Now,' says he, 'this is the bargain I'll make with you, King O'Toole: will you gi' me all the ground the goose flies over, the first offer, afther I make her as good as new?' 'I will,' says the king. 'You won't go back o' your word?' says Saint Kavin. 'Honour bright!' says King O'Toole, howldin' out his fist. 'Honour bright!' says Saint Kavin, back agin, 'it's a bargain. Come here!' says he to the poor ould goose—'come here, you unfort'nate ould cripple, and it's I that'll make you the sportin' bird.' With that, my dear, he took up the goose by the two wings—'Criss o' my crass an you,' says he, markin' her to grace with the blessed sign at the same minute—and throwin' her up in the air, 'whew,' says he, jist givin' her a blast to help her; and with that, my jewel, she tuk to her heels, flyin' like one o' the aigles themselves, and cuttin' as many capers as a swallow before a shower of rain.

"Well, my dear, it was a beautiful sight to see the king standin' with his mouth open, lookin' at his poor ould goose flyin' as light as a lark, and betther nor ever she was: and when she lit at his fut, patted her an the head, and, 'Ma *vourneen,*' says he, 'but you are the *darlint* o' the world.' 'And what do you say to me,' says Saint Kavin, 'for makin' her the like?' 'By gor,' says the king, 'I say nothin' bates the art o' man, barrin' the bees.' 'And do you say no more nor that?' says Saint Kavin. 'And that I'm behoulden to you,' says the king. 'But will you gi'e me all the ground the goose flew over?' says Saint Kavin. 'I will,' says King O'Toole, 'and you're welkim to it,' says he, 'though it's the last acre I have to give.' 'But you'll keep your word thrue?' says the saint. 'As thrue as the sun,' says the king. 'It's well for you, King O'Toole, that you said that word,' says he; 'for if you didn't say that word, *the devil receave the bit o' your goose id ever fly agin.*' Whin the king was as good as his word, Saint Kavin was *plazed* with him, and thin it was that he made himself known to the king. 'And,' says he, 'King O'Toole, you're a decent man, for I only kem here to *thry you.* You don't know me,' says he, 'bekase I'm disguised.' 'Musha! thin,' says the king, 'who are you?' 'I'm Saint Kavin,' said the saint, blessin' himself. 'Oh, queen iv heaven!' says the king, makin' the sign o' the crass betune his eyes, and fallin' down on his knees before the saint; 'is it the great Saint Kavin,' says he, 'that I've been discoorsin' all this time without knowin' it,' says he, 'all as one as if he was a lump iv a *gossoon?*—and so you're a saint?' says the king. 'I am,' says Saint Kavin. 'By gor, I thought I was only talking to a dacent boy,' says the king. 'Well, you know the differ now,' says the saint. 'I'm Saint Kavin,' says he, 'the greatest of all the saints.' And so the king had his goose as good as new, to divart him as long as he lived: and the saint supported him afther he kem into his property, as I tould you, until the day iv his death—and that was soon afther; for the poor goose thought he was ketchin' a throut one Friday; but, my jewel, it was a mistake he made—and instead of a throut, it was a thievin' horse-eel; and by gor, instead iv the goose killin' a throut for the king's supper,—by dad, the eel killed the king's goose—and small blame to him; but he didn't ate her, bekase he darn't ate what Saint Kavin laid his blessed hands on."

THE DEVIL

The Demon Cat*

LADY WILDE

There was a woman in Connemara, the wife of a fisherman; as he had always good luck, she had plenty of fish at all times stored away in the house ready for market. But, to her great annoyance, she found that a great cat used to come in at night and devour all the best and finest fish. So she kept a big stick by her, and determined to watch.

One day, as she and a woman were spinning together, the house suddenly became quite dark; and the door was burst open as if by the blast of the tempest, when in walked a huge black cat, who went straight up to the fire, then turned round and growled at them.

"Why, surely this is the devil," said a young girl, who was by, sorting fish.

"I'll teach you how to call me names," said the cat; and, jumping at her, he scratched her arm till the blood came. "There, now," he said, "you will be more civil another time when a gentleman comes to see you." And with that he walked over to the door and shut it close, to prevent any of them going out, for the poor young girl, while crying loudly from fright and pain, had made a desperate rush to get away.

Just then a man was going by, and hearing the cries, he pushed open the door and tried to get in; but the cat stood on the threshold, and would let no one pass. On this the man attacked him with his stick, and gave him a sound blow; the cat, however, was more than a match in the fight, for it flew at him and tore his face and hands so badly that the man at last took to his heels and ran away as fast as he could.

"Now, it's time for my dinner," said the cat, going up to examine the fish that was laid out on the tables. "I hope the fish is good today. Now, don't disturb me,

*Ancient Legends of Ireland.

229

nor make a fuss; I can help myself." With that he jumped up, and began to devour all the best fish, while he growled at the woman.

"Away, out of this, you wicked beast," she cried, giving it a blow with the tongs that would have broken its back only it was a devil; "out of this, no fish you have today."

But the cat only grinned at her, and went on tearing and spoiling and devouring the fish, evidently not a bit the worse for the blow. On this, both the women attacked it with sticks, and struck hard blows enough to kill it, on which the cat glared at them, and spit fire; then, making a leap, it tore their heads and arms till the blood came, and the frightened women rushed shrieking from the house.

But presently the mistress returned, carrying with her a bottle of holy water; and, looking in, she saw the cat still devouring the fish, and not minding. So she crept over quietly and threw holy water on it without a word. No sooner was this done than a dense black smoke filled the place, through which nothing was seen but the two red eyes of the cat, burning like coals of fire. Then the smoke gradually cleared away, and she saw the body of the creature burning slowly till it became shrivelled and black like a cinder, and finally disappeared. And from that time the fish remained untouched and safe from harm, for the power of the evil one was broken, and the demon cat was seen no more.

The Long Spoon*

PATRICK KENNEDY

The devil and the hearth-money collector for Bantry set out one summer morning to decide a bet they made the night before over a jug of punch. They wanted to see which would have the best load at sunset, and neither was to pick up anything that wasn't offered with the good-will of the giver. They passed by a house, and they heard the poor ban-a-t'yee[†] cry out to her lazy daughter, "Oh, musha——take you for a lazy sthronsuch[††] of a girl! do you intend to get up today?" "Oh, oh," says the taxman, "there's a job for you, Nick." "Ovock," says the other, "it wasn't from her heart she said it; we must pass on." The next cabin they were passing, the woman was on the bawnditch[‡] crying out to her husband that was mending one of his brogues inside: "Oh, tattheration to you, Nick! you never rung them pigs, and there they are in the potato drills rootin' away; the——run to Lusk with them." "Another windfall for you," says the man of the ink-horn, but the old thief shook his horns and wagged his tail. So they went on, and ever so many prizes were offered to the black fellow without him taking one. Here it was a gorsoon playing *marvels* when he should be using his clappers in the corn-field; and then it was a lazy drone of a servant asleep with his face to the sod when he ought to be weeding. No one thought of offering the hearth-money man even a drink of butter-milk, and at last the sun was within half a foot of the edge of Cooliagh. They were just then passing Monamolin, and a poor woman that was straining her supper in a skeeoge outside her cabin-door, seeing the two standing at the bawn gate, bawled out, "Oh, here's the hearth-money man—run away wid him." "Got a

*Legendary Fictions of the Irish Celts.
†Woman of the house.
††Ir. Stróinse—i.e., a lazy thing.
‡Ir. bádhun—i.e., enclosure, or wall round a house. From ba, cows, and dún, a fortress. Properly, cattle-fortress.

bite at last," says Nick. "Oh, no, no! it wasn't from her heart," says the collector. "Indeed, an' it was from the very foundation-stones it came. No help for misfortunes; in with you," says he, opening the mouth of his big black bag; and whether the devil was ever after seen taking the same walk or not, nobody ever laid eyes on his fellow-traveller again.

The Countess Kathleen O'Shea*

A very long time ago, there suddenly appeared in old Ireland two unknown merchants of whom nobody had ever heard, and who nevertheless spoke the language of the country with the greatest perfection. Their locks were black, and bound round with gold, and their garments were of rare magnificence.

Both seemed of like age; they appeared to be men of fifty, for their foreheads were wrinkled and their beards tinged with grey.

In the hostelry where the pompous traders alighted it was sought to penetrate their designs; but in vain—they led a silent and retired life. And whilst they stopped there, they did nothing but count over and over again out of their money-bags pieces of gold, whose yellow brightness could be seen through the windows of their lodging.

"Gentlemen," said the landlady one day, "how is it that you are so rich, and that, being able to succour the public misery, you do no good works?"

"Fair hostess," replied one of them, "we didn't like to present alms to the honest poor, in dread we might be deceived by make-believe paupers. Let want knock at our door, we shall open it."

The following day, when the rumour spread that two rich strangers had come, ready to lavish their gold, a crowd besieged their dwelling; but the figures of those who came out were widely different. Some carried pride in their mien; others were shamefaced.

The two chapmen traded in souls for the demon. The souls of the aged was worth twenty pieces of gold, not a penny more; for Satan had had time to make his valuation. The soul of a matron was valued at fifty, when she was handsome, and a hundred when she was ugly. The soul of a young maiden fetched an extravagant sum; the freshest and purest flowers are the dearest.

*This was quoted in a London-Irish newspaper. I am unable to find out the original source.

233

At that time there lived in the city an angel of beauty the Countess Kathleen O'Shea. She was the idol of the people and the providence of the indigent. As soon as she learned that these miscreants profited to the public misery to steal away hearts from God, she called to her butler.

"Patrick," said she to him, "how many pieces of gold in my coffers?"

"A hundred thousand."

"How many jewels?"

"The money's worth of gold."

"How much property in castles, forests, and lands?"

"Double the rest."

"Very well, Patrick; sell all that is not gold; and bring me the account. I only wish to keep this mansion and the demesne that surrounds it."

Two days afterwards the orders of the pious Kathleen were executed, and the treasure was distributed to the poor in proportion to their wants. This, says the tradition, did not suit the purposes of the Evil Spirit, who found no more souls to purchase. Aided by an infamous servant, they penetrated into the retreat of the noble dame, and purloined from her the rest of her treasure. In vain she struggled with all her strength to save the contents of her coffers; the diabolical thieves were the stronger. If Kathleen had been able to make the sign of the Cross, adds the legend, she would have put them to flight, but her hands were captive. The larceny was effected.

Then the poor called for aid to the plundered Kathleen, alas, to no good: she was able to succour their misery no longer; she had to abandon them to the temptation.

Meanwhile, but eight days had to pass before the grain and provender would arrive in abundance from the western lands. Eight such days were an age. Eight days required an immense sum to relieve the exigencies of the dearth, and the poor should either perish in the agonies of hunger, or, denying the holy maxims of the Gospel, vend, for base lucre, their souls, the richest gift from the bounteous hand of the Almighty. And Kathleen hadn't anything, for she had given up her mansion to the unhappy. She passed twelve hours in tears and mourning, rending her sun-tinted hair, and bruising her breast, of the whiteness of the lily; afterwards she stood up, resolute, animated by a vivid sentiment of despair.

She went to the traders in souls.

"What do you want?" they said.

"You buy souls?"

"Yes, a few still, in spite of you. Isn't that so, saint, with the eyes of sapphire?"

"Today I am come to offer you a bargain," replied she.

"What?"

"I have a soul to sell, but it is costly."

"What does that signify if it is precious? The soul, like the diamond, is appraised by its transparency."

"It is mine."

The two emissaries of Satan started. Their claws were clutched under their gloves of leather; their grey eyes sparkled; the soul, pure, spotless, virginal of Kathleen—it was a priceless acquisition!

"Beauteous lady, how much do you ask?"

"A hundred and fifty thousand pieces of gold."

"It's at your service," replied the traders, and they tendered Kathleen a parchment sealed with black, which she signed with a shudder.

The sum was counted out to her.

As soon as she got home she said to the butler, "Here distribute this: with this money that I give you the poor can tide over the eight days that remain, and not one of their souls will be delivered to the demon."

Afterwards she shut herself up in her room, and gave orders that none should disturb her.

Three days passed; she called nobody, she did not come out.

When the door was opened, they found her cold and stiff; she was dead of grief.

But the sale of this soul, so adorable in its charity, was declared null by the Lord; for she had saved her fellow-citizens from eternal death.

After the eight days had passed, numerous vessels brought into famished Ireland immense provisions in grain. Hunger was no longer possible. As to the traders, they disappeared from their hotel without anyone knowing what became of them. But the fishermen of the Blackwater pretend that they are enchained in a subterranean prison by order of Lucifer, until they shall be able to render up the soul of Kathleen, which escaped from them.

The Three Wishes

W. CARLETON

In ancient times there lived a man called Billy Dawson, and he was known to be a great rogue. They say he was descended from the family of the Dawsons, which was the reason, I suppose, of his carrying their name upon him.

Billy, in his youthful days, was the best hand at doing nothing in all Europe; devil a mortal could come next or near him at idleness; and, in consequence of his great practice that way, you may be sure that if any man could make a fortune by it he would have done it.

Billy was the only son of his father, barring two daughters; but they have nothing to do with the story I'm telling you. Indeed it was kind father and grandfather for Billy to be handy at the knavery as well as the idleness; for it was well known that not one of their blood ever did an honest act, except with a roguish intention. In short, they were altogether a *dacent* connection, and a credit to the name. As for Billy, all the villainy of the family, both plain and ornamental, came down to him by way of legacy; for it so happened that the father, in spite of all his cleverness, had nothing but his roguery to *lave* him.

Billy, to do him justice, improved the fortune he got: every day advanced him farther into dishonesty and poverty, until, at the long run, he was acknowledged on all hands to be the completest swindler and the poorest vagabond in the whole parish.

Billy's father, in his young days, had often been forced to acknowledge the inconvenience of not having a trade, in consequence of some nice point in law, called the "Vagrant Act", that sometimes troubled him. On this account he made up his mind to give Bill an occupation, and he accordingly bound him to a blacksmith; but whether Bill was to *live* or *die* by *forgery* was a puzzle to his father—though the neighbours said that *both* was most likely. At all events, he was put apprentice to a smith for seven years, and a hard card his master had to play

236

in managing him. He took the proper method, however, for Bill was so lazy and roguish that it would vex a saint to keep him in order.

"Bill," says his master to him one day that he had been sunning himself about the ditches, instead of minding his business, "Bill, my boy, I'm vexed to the heart to see you in such a bad state of health. You're very ill with that complaint called an *All-overness*; however," says he, "I think I can cure you. Nothing will bring you about but three or four sound doses every day of a medicine called 'the oil o' the hazel'. Take the first dose now," says he; and he immediately banged him with a hazel cudgel until Bill's bones ached for a week afterwards.

"If you were my son," said his master, "I tell you that, as long as I could get a piece of advice growing convenient in the hedges, I'd have you a different youth from what you are. If working was a sin, Bill, not an innocenter boy ever broke bread than you would be. Good people's scarce you think; but however that may be, I throw it out as a hint, that you must take your medicine till you're cured, whenever you happen to get unwell in the same way."

From this out he kept Bill's nose to the grinding-stone; and whenever his complaint returned, he never failed to give him a hearty dose for his improvement.

In the course of time, however, Bill was his own man and his own master; but it would puzzle a saint to know whether the master or the man was the more precious youth in the eyes of the world.

He immediately married a wife, and devil a doubt of it, but if *he* kept *her* in whiskey and sugar, *she* kept *him* in hot water. Bill drank and she drank; Bill fought and she fought; Bill was idle and she was idle; Bill whacked her and she whacked Bill. If Bill gave her one black eye, she gave him another; *just to keep herself in countenance*. Never was there a blessed pair so well met; and a beautiful sight it was to see them both at breakfast-time, blinking at each other across the potato-basket, Bill with his right eye black, and she with her left.

In short, they were the talk of the whole town: and to see Bill of a morning staggering home drunk, his shirt sleeves rolled up on his smutted arms, his breast open, and an old tattered leather apron, with one corner tucked up under his belt, singing one minute, and fighting with his wife the next—she, reeling beside him, with a discoloured eye, as aforesaid, a dirty ragged cap on one side of her head a pair of Bill's old slippers on her feet, a squalling child on her arm—now cuffing and dragging Bill, and again kissing and hugging him! Yes, it was a pleasant picture to see this loving pair in such a state!

This might do for a while, but it could not last. They were idle, drunken, and ill-conducted; and it was not to be supposed that they would get a farthing candle on their words. They were, of course, *dhruv* to great straits; and faith, they soon found that their fighting, and drinking, and idleness made them the laughing-sport of the neighbours; but neither brought food to their *childhre*, put a coat upon their backs, nor satisfied their landlord when he came to look for his own. Still, the never a one of Bill but was a funny fellow with strangers, though, as we said, the greatest rogue unhanged.

One day he was standing against his own anvil, completely in a brown study—being brought to his wit's end how to make out a breakfast for the family. The wife was scolding and cursing in the house, and the naked creatures of childhre squalling about her knees for food. Bill was fairly at an amplush, and knew not where or how to turn himself, when a poor withered old beggar came into the forge, tottering on his staff. A long white beard fell from his chin, and he looked as thin and hungry that you might blow him, one would think, over the house. Bill at this moment had been brought to his senses by distress, and his heart had a touch of pity towards the old man; for, on looking at him a second time, he clearly saw starvation and sorrow in his face.

"God save you, honest man!" said Bill.

The old man gave a sigh, and raising himself with great pain, on his staff, he looked at Bill in a very beseeching way.

"Musha, God save you kindly!" says he; "maybe you could give a poor, hungry, helpless ould man a mouthful of something to ait? You see yourself I'm not able to work; if I was, I'd scorn to be behoulding to anyone."

"Faith, honest man," said Bill, "if you knew who you're speaking to, you'd as soon ask a monkey for a churn-staff as me for either mate or money. There's not a blackguard in the three kingdoms so fairly on the *shaughran* as I am for both the one and the other. The wife within is sending the curses thick and heavy on me, and the childhre's playing the cat's melody to keep her in comfort. Take my word for it, poor man, if I had either mate or money I'd help you, for I know particularly well what it is to want them at the present spaking; an empty sack won't stand, neighbour."

So far Bill told him truth. The good thought was in his heart, because he found himself on a footing with the beggar; and nothing brings down pride, or softens the heart, like feeling what it is to want.

"Why, you are in a worse state than I am," said the old man; "you have a family to provide for, and I have only myself to support."

"You may kiss the book on that, my old worthy," replied Bill; "but come, what I can do for you I will; plant yourself up here beside the fire, and I'll give it a blast or two of my bellows that will warm the old blood in your body. It's a cold, miserable, snowy day, and a good heat will be of service."

"Thank you kindly," said the old man; "I *am* cold, and a warming at your fire will do me good, sure enough. Oh, it *is* a bitter, bitter day; God bless it!"

He then sat down, and Bill blew a rousing blast that soon made the stranger edge back from the heat. In a short time he felt quite comfortable, and when the numbness was taken out of his joints, he buttoned himself up and prepared to depart.

"Now," says he to Bill, "you hadn't the food to give me, but *what you could you did*. Ask any three wishes you choose, and be they what they may, take my word for it, they shall be granted."

Now, the truth is, that Bill, though he believed himself a great man in point of 'cuteness, wanted, after all, a full quarter of being square; for there is always a great difference between a wise man and a knave. Bill was so much of a rogue that he could not, for the blood of him, ask an honest wish, but stood scratching his head in a puzzle.

"Three wishes!" said he. "Why, let me see—did you say *three?*"

"Ay," replied the stranger, "three wishes—that was what I said."

"Well," said Bill, "here goes—aha!—let me alone, my old worthy!—faith I'll overreach the parish, if what you say is true. I'll cheat them in dozens, rich and poor, old and young: let me alone, man—I have it here;" and he tapped his forehead with great glee. "Faith, you're the sort to meet of a frosty morning, when a man wants his breakfast; and I'm sorry that I have neither money nor credit to get a bottle of whiskey, that we might take our *morning* together."

"Well, but let us hear the wishes," said the old man; "my time is short, and I cannot stay much longer."

"Do you see this sledge-hammer?" said Bill, "I wish in the first place, that whoever takes it up in their hands may never be able to lay it down till I give them lave; and that whoever begins to sledge with it may never stop sledging till it's my pleasure to release him."

"Secondly—I have an arm-chair, and I wish that whoever sits down in it may never rise out of it till they have my consent."

"And, thirdly—that whatever money I put into my purse, nobody may have power to take it out of it but myself!"

"You devil's rip!" says the old man in a passion, shaking his staff across Bill's nose, "why did you not ask something that would sarve you both here and hereafter? Sure it's as common as the market-cross, that there's not a vagabone in his Majesty's dominions stands more in need of both."

"Oh! by the elevens," said Bill, "I forgot that altogether! Maybe you'd be civil enough to let me change one of them? The sorra purtier wish ever was made than I'll make, if you'll give me another chance."

"Get out, you reprobate," said the old fellow, still in a passion. "Your day of grace is past. Little you knew who was speaking to you all this time. I'm St Moroky, you blackguard, and I gave you an opportunity of doing something for yourself and your family; but you neglected it, and now your fate is cast, you dirty, bog-trotting profligate. Sure, it's well known what you are! Aren't you a by-word in everybody's mouth, you and your scold of a wife? By this and by that, if ever you happen to come across me again, I'll send you to where you won't freeze, you villain!"

He then gave Bill a rap of his cudgel over the head, and laid him at his length beside the bellows, kicked a broken coal-scuttle out of his way, and left the forge in a fury.

When Billy recovered himself from the effects of the blow, and began to think on what had happened, he could have quartered himself with vexation for not asking great wealth as one of the wishes at least; but now the die was cast on him, and he could only make the most of the three he pitched upon.

He now bethought him how he might turn them to the best account, and here his cunning came to his aid. He began by sending for his wealthiest neighbours on pretence of business; and when he got them under his roof, he offered them the armchair to sit down in. He now had them safe, nor could all the art of man relieve them except worthy Bill was willing. Bill's plan was to make the best bargain he could before he released his prisoners; and let him alone for knowing how to make their purses bleed. There wasn't a wealthy man in the country he did not fleece. The parson of the parish bled heavily; so did the lawyer; and a rich attorney, who had retired from practice, swore that the Court of Chancery itself was paradise compared to Bill's chair.

This was all very good for a time. The fame of his chair, however, soon spread;

so did that of his sledge. In a short time neither man, woman, nor child would darken his door; all avoided him and his fixtures as they would a spring-gun or man-trap. Bill, so long as he fleeced his neighbours, never wrought a hand's turn; so that when his money was out, he found himself as badly off as ever. In addition to all this, his character was fifty times worse than before; for it was the general belief that he had dealings with the old boy. Nothing now could exceed his misery, distress, and ill-temper. The wife and he and their children all fought among one another. Everybody hated them, cursed them, and avoided them. The people thought they were acquainted with more than Christian people ought to know. This, of course, came to Bill's ears, and it vexed him very much.

One day he was walking about the fields, thinking of how he could raise the wind once more; the day was dark, and he found himself, before he stopped, in the bottom of a lonely glen covered by great bushes that grew on each side. "Well," thought he, when every other means of raising money failed him, "it's reported that I'm in league with the old boy, and as it's a folly to have the name of the connection without the profit, I'm ready to make a bargain with him any day—so," said he, raising his voice, "Nick, you sinner, if you be convenient and willing, why stand out here; show your best leg—here's your man."

The words were hardly out of his mouth when a dark, sober-looking old gentleman, not unlike a lawyer, walked up to him. Bill looked at the foot and saw the hoof. "Morrow, Nick," says Bill.

"Morrow, Bill," says Nick. "Well, Bill, what's the news?"

"Devil a much myself hears of late," says Bill; "is there anything *fresh* below?"

"I can't exactly say, Bill; I spend little of my time down now; the Tories are in office, and my hands are consequently too full of business here to pay much attention to anything else."

"A fine place this, sir," says Bill, "to take a constitutional walk in; when I want an appetite I often come this way myself—hem! *High* feeding is very bad without exercise."

"High feeding! Come, come, Bill, you know you didn't taste a morsel these four-and-twenty hours."

"You know that's a bounce, Nick. I eat a breakfast this morning that would put a stone of flesh on you, if you only smelt at it."

"No matter; this is not to the purpose. What's that you were muttering to yourself awhile ago? If you want to come to the brunt, here I'm for you."

241

"Nick," said Bill, "you're complate; you want nothing barring a pair of Brian O'Lynn's breeches."

Bill, in fact, was bent on making his companion open the bargain, because he had often heard that, in that case, with proper care on his own part, he might defeat him in the long run. The other, however, was his match.

"What was the nature of Brian's garment," inquired Nick. "Why, you know the song," said Bill—

> " 'Brian O'Lynn had no breeches to wear,
> So he got a sheep's skin for to make him a pair;
> With the fleshy side out and the woolly side in,
> They'll be pleasant and *cool*, says Brian O'Lynn.'

"A *cool* pare would sarve you, Nick."

"You're mighty waggish today, Misther Dawson."

"And good right I have," said Bill; "I'm a man snug and well to do in the world; have lots of money, plenty of good eating and drinking, and what more need a man wish for?"

"True," said the other; "in the meantime it's rather odd that so respectable a man should not have six inches of unbroken cloth in his apparel. You are as naked a tatter-demalion as I ever laid my eyes on; in full dress for a party of scare-crows, William."

"That's my own fancy, Nick; I don't work at my trade like a gentleman. This is my forge dress, you know."

"Well, but what did you summon me here for?" said the other; "you may as well speak out, I tell you; for, my good friend, unless *you* do, *I* shan't. Smell that."

"I smell more than that," said Bill; "and by the way, I'll thank you to give me the windy side of you—curse all sulphur, I say. There, that's what I call an improvement in my condition. But as you *are* so stiff," says Bill, "why, the short and long of it is—that—hem—you see I'm—tut—sure you know I have a thriving trade of my own, and that if I like I needn't be at a loss; but in the meantime I'm rather in a kind of a so—so—don't you *take*?"

And Bill winked knowingly, hoping to trick him into the first proposal.

"You must speak above-board, my friend," says the other. "I'm a man of few words, blunt and honest. If you have anything to say, be plain. Don't think I can be losing my time with such a pitiful rascal as you are."

"Well," says Bill, "I want money, then, and am ready to come into terms. What have you to say to that, Nick?"

"Let me see—let me look at you," says his companion, turning him about. "Now, Bill, in the first place, are you not as finished a scare-crow as ever stood upon two legs?"

"I play second fiddle to you there again," says Bill.

"There you stand, with the blackguards' coat of arms quartered under your eye, and—"

"Don't make little of *blackguards*," said Bill, "nor spake disparagingly of *your own* crest."

"Why, what would you bring, you brazen rascal, if you were fairly put up at auction?"

"Faith, I'd bring more bidders than you would," said Bill, "if you were to go off at auction tomorrow. I tell you they should bid *downwards* to come to your value, Nicholas. We have no coin *small* enough to purchase you."

"Well, no matter," said Nick. "If you are willing to be mine at the expiration of seven years, I will give you more money than ever the rascally breed of you was worth."

"Done!" said Bill; "but no disparagement to my family, in the meantime; so down with the hard cash, and don't be a *neger*."

The money was accordingly paid down! but as nobody was present, except the giver and receiver, the amount of what Bill got was never known.

"Won't you give me a luck-penny?" said the old gentleman.

"Tut," said Billy, "so prosperous an old fellow as you cannot want it; however, bad luck to you, with all my heart! and it's rubbing grease to a fat pig to say so. Be off now, or I'll commit suicide on you. Your absence is a cordial to most people, you infernal old profligate. You have injured my morals even for the short time you have been with me; for I don't find myself so virtuous as I was."

"Is that your gratitude, Billy?"

"Is it gratitude *you* speak of, man? I wonder you don't blush when you name it. However, when you come again, if you bring a third eye in your head you will see what I mane, Nicholas, ahagur."

The old gentleman, as Bill spoke, hopped across the ditch, on his way to *Downing*-street, where of late 'tis thought he possesses much influence.

Bill now began by degrees to show off; but still wrought a little at his trade to blindfold the neighbours. In a very short time, however, he became a great man. So long indeed as he was a *poor* rascal, no decent person would speak to him; even the proud serving-men at the "Big House" would turn up their noses at him. And he well deserved to be made little of by others, because he was mean enough to make little of himself. But when it was seen and known that he had oceans of money, it was wonderful to think, although he was *now* a greater blackguard than ever, how those who despised him before began to come round him and court his company. Bill, however, had neither sense nor spirit to make those sunshiny friends know their distance; not he—instead of that he was proud to be seen in decent company, and so long as the money lasted, it was, "hail fellow, well met", between himself and every fair-faced *spunger* who had a horse under him, a decent coat to his back, and a good appetite to eat his dinners. With riches and all, Bill was the same man still; but, somehow or other, there is a great difference between a rich profligate and a poor one, and Bill found it so to his cost in *both* cases.

Before half the seven years was passed, Bill had his carriage, and his equipages; was hand and glove with my Lord This, and my Lord That; kept hounds and hunters; was the first sportsman at the Curragh; patronised every boxing ruffian he could pick up; and betted night and day on cards, dice and horses. Bill, in short, *should* be a blood, and except he did all this, he could not presume to mingle with the fashionable bloods of his time.

It's an old proverb, however, that "what is got over the devil's back is sure to go off under it"; and in Bill's case this proved true. In short, the old boy himself could not supply him with money so fast as he made it fly; it was "come easy, go easy", with Bill, and so sign was on it, before he came within two years of his time he found his purse empty.

And now came the value of his summer friends to be known. When it was discovered that the cash was no longer flush with him—that stud, and carriage, and hounds were going to the hammer—whish! off they went, friends, relations, pot-companions, dinner-eaters, black-legs, and all, like a flock of crows that had smelt gunpowder. Down Bill soon went, week after week, and day after day, until at last he was obliged to put on the leather apron, and take to the hammer again; and not only that, for as no experience could make him wise, he once more began his tap-room brawls, his quarrels with Judy, and took to his "high feeding" at the dry potatoes and salt. Now, too, came the cutting tongues of all who knew him, like razors upon him. Those that he scorned because they were poor and himself rich, now paid him back his own with interest; and those that he measured himself with, because they were rich, and who only countenanced him in consequence of his wealth, gave him the hardest word in their cheeks. The devil mend him! He deserved it all, and more if he had got it.

Bill, however, who was a hardened sinner, never fretted himself down an ounce of flesh by what was said to him, or of him. Not he; he cursed, and fought, and swore, and schemed away as usual, taking in every one he could; and surely none could match him at villainy of all sorts, and sizes.

At last the seven years became expired, and Bill was one morning sitting in his forge, sober and hungry, the wife cursing him, and childhre squalling, as before; he was thinking how he might defraud some honest neighbour out of a breakfast to stop their mouths and his own too, when who walks in to him but old Nick, to demand his bargain.

"Morrow, Bill!" says he with a sneer.

"The devil welcome you!" says Bill; "but you have a fresh memory."

"A bargain's a bargain between two *honest* men, any day," says Satan; "when I speak of *honest* men, I mean *yourself* and *me*, Bill;" and he put his tongue in his cheek to make game of the unfortunate rogue he had come for.

"Nick, my worthy fellow," said Bill, "have bowels; you wouldn't do a shabby thing; you wouldn't disgrace your own character by putting more weight upon a falling man. You know what it is to get a *come down* yourself, my worthy; so just keep your toe in your pump, and walk off with yourself somewhere else. A *cool* walk will sarve you better than my company, Nicholas."

"Bill, it's no use in shirking," said his friend; "your swindling tricks may enable you to cheat others, but you won't cheat *me*, I guess. You want nothing to make you perfect in your way but to travel; and travel you shall under my guidance, Billy. No, no—*I'm* not to be swindled, my good fellow. I have rather a—a—better opinion of myself, Mr D., than to think that you could outwit one Nicholas Clutie, Esq.—ahem!"

"You may sneer, you sinner," replied Bill; "but I tell you that I have outwitted men who could buy and sell you to your face. Despair, you villain, when I tell you that *no attorney* could stand before me."

Satan's countenance got blank when he heard this; he wriggled and fidgeted about, and appeared to be not quite comfortable.

245

"In that case, then," says he, "the sooner I *deceive* you the better; so turn out for the *Low Countries*."

"Is it come to that in earnest?" said Bill, "are you going to act the rascal at the long run?"

" 'Pon honour, Bill."

"Have patience, then, you sinner, till I finish this horse shoe—it's the last of a set I'm finishing for one of your friend the attorney's horses. And here, Nick, I hate idleness, you know it's the mother of mischief; take this sledge-hammer, and give a dozen strokes or so, till I get it out of hands, and then here's with you, since it must be so."

He then gave the bellows a puff that blew half a peck of dust in Club-foot's face, whipped out the red-hot iron, and set Satan sledging away for bare life.

"Faith," says Bill to him, when the shoe was finished, "it's a thousand pities ever the sledge should be out of your hand; the great *Parra Gow* was a child to you at sledging, you're such an able tyke. Now just exercise yourself till I bid the wife and childhre good-bye, and then I'm off."

Out went Bill, of course, without the slightest notion of coming back; no more than Nick had that he could not give up the sledging, and indeed neither could he, but was forced to work away as if he was sledging for a wager. This was just what Bill wanted. He was now compelled to sledge on until it was Bill's pleasure to release him; and so we leave him very industriously employed, while we look after the worthy who outwitted him.

In the meantime, Bill broke cover, and took to the country at large; wrought a little journey-work wherever he could get it, and in this way went from one place to another, till, in the course of a month, he walked back very coolly into his own forge, to see how things went on in his absence. There he found Satan in a rage, the perspiration pouring from him in torrents, hammering with might and main upon the naked anvil. Bill calmly leaned his back against the wall, placed his hat upon the side of his head, put his hands into his breeches pockets, and began to whistle *Shaun Gow's* hornpipe. At length he says, in a very quiet and good-humoured way—

"Morrow, Nick!"

"Oh!" says Nick, still hammering away—"Oh! you double-distilled villain (hech!), may the most refined, ornamental (hech!), double-rectified, super-extra, and original (hech!) collection of curses that ever was gathered (hech!) into a single nosegay of ill-fortune (hech!), shine in the button-hole of your conscience (hech!) while your name is Bill Dawson! I denounce you (hech!) as a double-milled villain, a finished, hot-pressed knave (hech!), in comparison of whom all the other knaves I ever knew (hech!), attorneys included, are honest men. I brand you (hech!) as the pearl of cheats, a tip-top take-in (hech!). I denounce you, I say again, for the villainous treatment (hech!) I have received at your hands in this most untoward (hech!) and unfortunate transaction between us; for (hech!) unfortunate, in every sense, is he that has anything to do with (hech!) such a prime and finished impostor."

"You're very warm, Nicky," says Bill; "what puts you into a passion, you old sinner? Sure if it's your own will and pleasure to take exercise at my anvil, *I'm* not to be abused for it. Upon my credit, Nicky, you ought to blush for using such blackguard language, so unbecoming your grave character. You cannot say that it was I set you a hammering at the empty anvil, you profligate. However, as you are so industrious, I simply say it would be a thousand pities to take you from it. Nick, I love industry in my heart, and I always encourage it; so work away, its not often you spend your time so creditably. I'm afraid if you weren't at that you'd be worse employed."

"Bill, have bowels," said the operative; "you wouldn't go to lay more weight on a falling man, you know; you wouldn't disgrace your character by such a piece of iniquity as keeping an inoffensive gentleman, advanced in years, at such an unbecoming and rascally job as this. Generosity's your top virtue, Bill; not but that you have many other excellent ones, as well as that, among which, as you say yourself, I reckon industry; but still it is in generosity you *shine*. Come, Bill, honour bright, and release me."

"Name the terms, you profligate."

"You're above terms, William; a generous fellow like you never thinks of terms."

"Goodbye, old gentleman!" said Bill, very coolly; "I'll drop in to see you once a month."

"No, no, Bill, you infern—a—a—you excellent, worthy, delightful fellow, not so fast; not so fast. Come, name your terms, you sland—my dear Bill, name your terms."

"Seven years more."

"I agree; but—"

"And the same supply of cash as before, down on the nail here."

247

"Very good; very good. You're rather simple, Bill; rather soft, I must confess. Well, no matter. I shall yet turn the tab—a—hem! You are an exceedingly simple fellow, Bill; still there will come a day, my *dear* Bill—there will come—"

"Do you grumble, you vagrant? Another word, and I double the terms."

"Mum, William—mum; *tace* is Latin for a candle."

"Seven years more of grace, and the same measure of the needful that I got before. Ay or no?"

"Of grace, Bill! Ay! ay! ay! There's the cash. I accept the terms. Oh blood! the rascal—of grace!! Bill!"

"Well, now drop the hammer, and vanish," says Billy; "but what would you think to take this sledge, while you stay, and give me a—eh! why in such a hurry?" he added, seeing that Satan withdrew in double-quick time.

"Hollo! Nicholas!" he shouted, "come back; you forget something!" and when the old gentleman looked behind him, Billy shook the hammer at him, on which he vanished altogether.

Billy now got into his old courses; and what shows the kind of people the world is made of, he also took up with his old company. When they saw that he had the money once more, and was sowing it about him in all directions, they immediately began to find excuses for his former extravagance.

"Say what you will," said one, "Bill Dawson's a spirited fellow, and bleeds like a prince."

"He's a hospitable man in his own house, or out of it, as ever lived," said another.

"His only fault is," observed a third, "that he is, if anything, too generous, and doesn't know the value of money; his fault's on the right side, however."

"He has the spunk in him," said a fourth; "keeps a capital table, prime wines, and a standing welcome for his friends."

"Why," said a fifth, "if he doesn't enjoy his money while he lives, he won't when he's dead; so more power to him, and a wider throat to his purse."

Indeed, the very persons who were cramming themselves at his expense despised him at heart. They knew very well however, how to take him on the weak side. Praise his generosity, and he would do anything; call him a man of spirit, and you might fleece him to his face. Sometimes he would toss a purse of guineas to this knave, another to that flatterer, a third to a bully, and a fourth to some broken-down rake—and all to convince them that *he* was a sterling friend—a man of mettle and liberality. But never was he known to help a virtuous and struggling

248

family—to assist the widow or the fatherless, or to do any other act that was *truly* useful. It is to be supposed the reason of this was, that as he spent it, as most of the world do, in the service of the devil, by whose aid he got it, he was prevented from turning it to a good account. Between you and me, dear reader, there are more persons acting after Bill's fashion in the same world than you dream about.

When his money was out again, his friends played him the same rascally game once more. No sooner did his poverty become plain, than the knaves began to be troubled with small fits of modesty, such as an unwillingness to come to his place when there was no longer anything to be got there. A kind of virgin bashfulness prevented them from speaking to him when they saw him getting out on the wrong side of his clothes. Many of them would turn away from him in the prettiest and most delicate manner when they thought he wanted to borrow money from them—all for fear of putting him to the blush by asking it. Others again, when they saw him coming towards their houses about dinner hour, would become so confused, from mere gratitude, as to think themselves in another place; and their servants, seized, as it were, with the same feeling, would tell Bill that their masters were "not at home".

At length, after travelling the same villainous round as before, Bill was compelled to betake himself, as the last remedy, to the forge; in other words, he found that there is, after all, nothing in this world that a man can rely on so firmly and surely as his own industry. Bill, however, wanted the organ of common sense; for his experience—and it was sharp enough to leave an impression—ran off him like water off a duck.

He took to his employment sorely against his grain; but he had now no choice. He must either work or starve, and starvation is like a great doctor—nobody tries it till every other remedy fails them. Bill had been twice rich; twice a gentleman among blackguards, but always a blackguard among gentlemen; for no wealth or acquaintance with decent society could rub the rust of his native vulgarity off him. He was now a common blinking sot in his forge; a drunken bully in the tap-room, cursing and brow-beating every one as well as his wife; boasting of how much money he had spent in his day; swaggering about the high doings he carried on; telling stories about himself and Lord This at the Curragh; the dinners he gave—how much they cost him, and attempting to extort credit upon the strength of his former wealth. He was too ignorant, however, to know that he was publishing his own disgrace, and that it was a mean-spirited thing to be proud of what ought to make him blush through a deal board nine inches thick.

He was one morning industriously engaged in a quarrel with his wife, who, with a three-legged stool in her hand, appeared to mistake his head for his own anvil; he, in the meantime, paid his addresses to her with his leather apron, when who steps in to jog his memory about the little agreement that was between them, but old Nick. The wife, it seems, in spite of all her extortions to the contrary, was getting the worst of it; and Sir Nicholas, willing to appear a gentleman of great gallantry, thought he could not do less than take up the lady's quarrel, particularly as Bill had laid her in a sleeping posture. Now Satan thought this too bad; and as he felt himself under many obligations to the sex, he determined to defend one of them on the present occasion; so as Judy rose, he turned upon the husband, and floored him by a clever facer.

"You unmanly villain," said he, "is this the way you treat your wife? 'Pon honour, Bill, I'll chastise you on the spot. I could not stand by, a spectator of such ungentlemanly conduct without giving up all claim to gallant—" Whack! the word was divided in his mouth by the blow of a churn-staff from Judy, who no sooner saw Bill struck, than she nailed Satan, who "fell" once more.

"What, you villain! that's for striking my husband like a murderer behind his back," said Judy, and she suited the action to the word, "that's for interfering between man and wife. Would you murder the poor man before my face? eh? If *he* bates me, you shabby dog you, who has a better right? I'm sure it's nothing out of your pocket. Must you have your finger in every pie?"

This was anything but *idle* talk; for at every word she gave him a remembrance, hot and heavy. Nicholas backed, danced, and hopped; she advanced, still drubbing him with great perseverance, till at length he fell into the redoubtable arm-chair, which stood exactly behind him. Bill, who had been putting in two blows for Judy's one, seeing that his enemy was safe, now got between the devil and his wife, *a situation that few will be disposed to envy him.*

"Tenderness, Judy," said the husband, "I hate cruelty. Go put the tongs in the fire, and make them red hot. Nicholas, you have a nose," said he.

Satan began to rise, but was rather surprised to find that he could not budge.

"Nicholas," says Bill, "how is your pulse? you don't look well; that is to say, you look worse than usual."

The other attempted to rise, but found it a mistake.

"I'll thank you to come along," said Bill. "I have a fancy to travel under your guidance, and we'll take the *Low Countries* in our way, won't we? Get to your legs, you sinner; you know a bargain's a bargain between two *honest men*, Nicholas; meaning *yourself* and *me*. Judy, are the tongs hot?"

Satan's face was worth looking at, as he turned his eyes from the husband to the wife, and then fastened them on the tongs, now nearly at a furnace heat in the fire, conscious at the same time that he could not move out of the chair.

"Billy," said he, "you won't forget that I rewarded your generosity the last time I saw you, in the way of business." "Faith, Nicholas, it fails me to remember any generosity I ever showed you. Don't be womanish. I simply want to see what kind of stuff your nose is made of, and whether it will stretch like a rogue's conscience. If it does, we will flatter it up the *chimly* with red-hot tongs, and when this old hat is fixed on the top of it, let us alone for a weather-cock." "Have a *fellow-feeling*, Mr Dawson; you know *we* ought not to dispute. Drop the matter, and I give you the next seven years." "We know all that," says Billy, opening the red-hot tongs very coolly. "Mr Dawson," said Satan, "if you cannot remember my friendship to yourself, don't forget how often I stood your father's friend, your grandfather's friend, and the friend of all your relations up to the tenth generation. I intended, also, to stand by your children after you, so long as the name of Dawson, and a respectable one it is, might last." "Don't be blushing, Nick," says Bill, "you are too modest; that was ever your failing; hould up your head, there's money bid for you. I'll give you such a nose, my good friend, that you will have to keep an outrider before you, to carry the end of it on his shoulder." "Mr Dawson, I pledge my honour to raise your children in the world as *high* as they can go; no matter whether they desire it or not." "That's very kind of you," says the other, "and I'll do as much for your nose."

He gripped it as he spoke, and the old boy immediately sung out; Bill pulled, and the nose went with him like a piece of warm wax. He then transferred the tongs to Judy, got a ladder, resumed the tongs, ascended the chimney, and tugged stoutly at the nose until he got it five feet above the roof. He then fixed the hat upon the top of it, and came down.

"There's a weather-cock," said Billy; "I defy Ireland to show such a beauty. Faith, Nick, it would make the purtiest steeple for a church, in all Europe, and the old hat fits it to a shaving."

In this state, with his nose twisted up the chimney, Satan sat for some time, experiencing the novelty of what might be termed a peculiar sensation. At last the worthy husband and wife began to relent.

"I think," said Bill, "that we have made the most of the nose, as well as the joke; I believe, Judy, it's long enough." "What is?" says Judy.

"Why, the joke," said the husband.

"Faith, and I think so is the nose," said Judy.

"What do you say yourself, Satan?" said Bill.

"Nothing at all, William," said the other; "but that—ha! ha!—it's a good joke—an excellent joke, and a goodly nose, too, as it *stands*. You were always a gentlemanly man, Bill, and did things with a grace; still, if I might give an opinion on such a trifle—"

"It's no trifle at all," says Bill, "if you spake of the nose." "Very well, it is not," says the other; "still, I am decidedly of opinion, that if you could shorten both the joke and the nose without further violence, you would lay me under very heavy obligations, which I shall be ready to acknowledge and *repay* as I ought." "Come," said Bill, "shell out once more, and be off for seven years. As much as you came down with the last time, and vanish."

The words were scarcely spoken, when the money was at his feet, and Satan invisible. Nothing could surpass the mirth of Bill and his wife at the result of this adventure. They laughed till they fell down on the floor.

It is useless to go over the same ground again. Bill was still incorrigible. The money went as the devil's money always goes. Bill caroused and squandered, but could never turn a penny of it to a good purpose. In this way, year after year went, till the seventh was closed, and Bill's hour come. He was now, and had been for some time past, as miserable a knave as ever. Not a shilling had he, nor a shilling's worth, with the exception of his forge, his cabin, and a few articles of crazy furniture. In this state he was standing in his forge as before, straining his ingenuity how to make out a breakfast, when Satan came to look after him. The old gentleman was sorely puzzled how to get at him. He kept skulking and sneaking about the forge for some time, till he saw that Bill hadn't a cross to bless himself with. He immediately changed himself into a guinea, and lay in an open place where he knew Bill would see him. "If," said he. "I once get into his possession, I can manage him." The honest smith took the bait, for it was well gilded; he clutched the guinea put it into his purse, and closed it up. "Ho! Ho!" shouted the devil out of the purse, "you're caught, Bill; I've secured you at last, you knave you. Why don't you despair, you villain, when you think of what's before you?" "Why, you unlucky ould dog," said Bill, "is it there you are? Will you always drive your

252

head into every loophole that's set for you? Faith, Nick achora, I never had you bagged till now."

Satan then began to tug and struggle with a view of getting out of the purse, but in vain.

"Mr Dawson," said he, "we understand each other. I'll give the seven years additional, and the cash on the nail." "Be aisey, Nicholas. You know the weight of the hammer, that's enough. It's not a whipping with feathers you're going to get, anyhow. Just be aisey." "Mr Dawson, I grant I'm not your match. Release me, and I double the cash. I was merely trying your temper when I took the shape of a guinea."

"Faith and I'll try your's before I lave it, I've a notion." He immediately commenced with the sledge, and Satan sang out with a considerable want of firmness. "Am I heavy enough!" said Bill.

"Lighter, lighter, William, if you love me. I haven't been well latterly, Mr Dawson—I have been delicate—my health, in short, is in a very precarious state, Mr Dawson." "I can believe *that*," said Bill, "and it will be more so before I have done with you. Am I doing it right?" "Bill," said Nick, "is this gentlemanly treatment in your own respectable shop? Do you think, if you dropped into my little place, that I'd act this rascally part towards you? Have you no compunction?" "I know," replied Bill, sledging away with vehemence, "that you're notorious for giving your friends a *warm* welcome. Divil an ould youth more so; but you must be daling in bad coin, must you? However, good or bad, you're in for a sweat now, you sinner. Am I doin' it purty?"

"Lovely, William—but if possible, a little more delicate."

"Oh, how delicate you are! Maybe a cup o' tay would sarve you, or a little small gruel to compose your stomach."

"Mr Dawson," said the gentleman in the purse, "hold your hand and let us understand one another. I have a proposal to make." "Hear the sinner anyhow," said the wife. "Name your own sum," said Satan, "only set me free." "No, the sorra may take the toe you'll budge till you let Bill off," said the wife; "hould him hard, Bill, barrin' he sets *you* clear of your engagement." "There it is, my posy," said Bill; "that's the condition. If you don't give *me* up, here's at you once more—and you must double the cash you gave the last time, too. So, if you're of that opinion, say *ay*—leave the cash and be off."

The money again appeared in a glittering heap before Bill, upon which he exclaimed—"The *ay* has it, you dog. Take to pour pumps now, and fair weather after you, you vagrant; but Nicholas—Nick—here—" The other looked back, and saw Bill, with a broad grin upon him, shaking the purse at him—"Nicholas come back," said he. "I'm short a guinea." Nick shook his fist, and disappeared.

It would be useless to stop now, merely to inform our readers that Bill was beyond improvement. In short, he once more took to his old habits, and lived on exactly in the same manner as before. He had two sons—one as great a blackguard as himself, and who was also named after him; the other was a well-conducted, virtuous young man, called James, who left his father, and having relied upon his own industry and honest perseverance in life, arrived afterwards to great wealth, and built the town called Castle Dawson; which is so called from its founder until this day.

Bill, at length, in spite of all his wealth, was obliged, as he himself said, "to travel",—in other words, he fell asleep one day, and forgot to awaken; or, in still plainer terms, he died.

Now, it is usual, when a man dies, to close the history of his life and adventures at once; but with our hero this cannot be the case. The moment Bill departed, he very naturally bent his steps towards the residence of St Moroky, as being, in his opinion, likely to lead him towards the snuggest berth he could readily make out. On arriving, he gave a very humble kind of a knock, and St Moroky appeared.

"God save your Reverence!" said Bill, very submissively.

"Be off; there's no admittance here for so poor a youth as you are," said St Moroky.

He was now so cold and fatigued that he cared little where he went, provided only, as he said himself, "he could rest his bones, and get an air of the fire." Accordingly, after arriving at a large black gate, he knocked, as before, and was told he would get *instant* admittance the moment he gave his name.

"Billy Dawson," he replied.

"Off, instantly," said the porter to his companions, "and let his Majesty know that the rascal he dreads so much is here at the gate."

Such a racket and tumult were never heard as the very mention of Billy Dawson created.

In the meantime, his old acquaintance came running towards the gate with such haste and consternation, that his tail was several times nearly tripping up his heels.

"Don't admit that rascal," he shouted; "bar the gate—make every chain, and lock the bolt, fast—I won't be safe—and I won't stay here, nor none of us need stay here, if he gets in—my bones are sore yet after him. No, no—begone you villain—you'll get no entrance here—I know you too well."

Bill could not help giving a broad, malicious grin at Satan, and, putting his nose through the bars, he exclaimed—"Ha! you ould dog, I have you afraid of me at last, have I?"

He had scarcely uttered the words, when his foe, who stood inside, instantly tweaked him by the nose, and Bill felt as if he had been gripped by the same red-hot tongs with which he himself had formerly tweaked the nose of Nicholas.

Bill then departed, but soon found that in consequence of the inflammable materials which strong drink had thrown into his nose, that organ immediately took fire, and, indeed, to tell the truth, kept burning night and day, winter and summer, without ever once going out, from that hour to this.

Such was the sad fate of Billy Dawson, who has been walking without stop or stay, from place to place, ever since; and in consequence of the flame on his nose, and his beard being tangled like a wisp of hay, he has been christened by the country folk Will-o'-the-Wisp, while, as it were, to show the mischief of his disposition, the circulating knave, knowing that he must seek the coldest bogs and quagmires in order to cool his nose, seizes upon that opportunity of misleading the unthinking and tipsy night travellers from their way, just that he may have the satisfaction of still taking in as many as possible.

GIANTS

When the pagan gods of Ireland—the *Tuath-De-Danān*—robbed of worship and offerings, grew smaller and smaller in the popular imagination, until they turned into the fairies, the pagan heroes grew bigger and bigger, until they turned into the giants.

The Giant's Stairs*

T. CROFTON CROKER

On the road between Passage and Cork there is an old mansion called Ronayne's Court. It may be easily known from the stack of chimneys and the gable-ends, which are to be seen, look at it which way you will. Here it was that Maurice Ronayne and his wife Margaret Gould kept house, as may be learned to this day from the great old chimney-piece, on which is carved their arms. They were a mighty worthy couple, and had but one son, who was called Philip, after no less a person than the King of Spain.

Immediately on his smelling the cold air of this world the child sneezed, which was naturally taken to be a good sign of his having a clear head; and the subsequent rapidity of his learning was truly amazing, for on the very first day a primer was put into his hands he tore out the A, B, C page and destroyed it, as a thing quite beneath his notice. No wonder, then, that both father and mother were proud of their heir, who gave such indisputable proofs of genius, or, as they called it in that part of the world, "*genus*".

One morning, however, Master Phil, who was then just seven years old, was missing, and no one could tell what had become of him: servants were sent in all directions to seek him, on horseback and on foot, but they returned without any tidings of the boy, whose disappearance altogether was most unaccountable. A large reward was offered, but it produced them no intelligence, and years rolled away without Mr and Mrs Ronayne having obtained any satisfactory account of the fate of their lost child.

There lived at this time, near Carrigaline, one Robert Kelly, a blacksmith by trade. He was what is termed a handy man, and his abilities were held in much estimation by the lads and the lasses of the neighbourhood; for independent of shoeing horses, which he did to great perfection, and making plough-irons, he

Fairy Legends of the South of Ireland.

258

interpreted dreams for the young women, sung "Arthur O'Bradley" at their weddings, and was so good-natured a fellow at a christening, that he was gossip to half the country round.

Now it happened that Robin had a dream himself, and young Philip Ronayne appeared to him in it, at the dead hour of the night. Robin thought he saw the boy mounted upon a beautiful white horse, and that he told him how he was made a page to the giant Mahon MacMahon, who had carried him off, and who held his court in the hard heart of the rock. "The seven years—my time of service—are clean out, Robin," said he, "and if you release me this night I will be the making of you for ever after."

"And how will I know," said Robin—cunning enough, even in his sleep—"but this is all a dream?"

"Take that," said the boy, "for a token"—and at the word the white horse struck out with one of his hind legs, and gave poor Robin such a kick in the forehead that, thinking he was a dead man, he roared as loud as he could after his brains, and woke up, calling a thousand murders. He found himself in bed, but he had the mark of the blow, the regular print of a horse-shoe, upon his forehead as red as blood; and Robin Kelly, who never before found himself puzzled at the dream of any other person, did not know what to think of his own.

Robin was well acquainted with the Giant's Stairs—as, indeed, who is not that knows the harbour? They consist of great masses of rock, which, piled one above another, rise like a flight of steps from very deep water, against the bold cliff of Carrigmahon. Nor are they badly suited for stairs to those who have legs of sufficient length to stride over a moderate-sized house, or to enable them to clear the space of a mile in a hop, step, and jump. Both these feats the giant MacMahon was said to have performed in the days of Finnian glory; and the common tradition of the country placed his dwelling within the cliff up whose side the stairs led.

Such was the impression which the dream made on Robin, that he determined to put its truth to the test. It occurred to him, however, before setting out on his adventure, that a plough-iron may be no bad companion, as, from experience, he knew that it was an excellent knock-down argument, having on more occasions than one settled a little disagreement very quietly: so, putting one on his shoulder, off he marched, in the cool of the evening, through Glaun a Thowk (the Hawk's Glen) to Monkstown. Here an old gossip of his (Tom Clancey by name) lived, who on hearing Robin's dream, promised him the use of his skiff, and moreover, offered to assist in rowing it to the Giant's Stairs.

After supper, which was of the best, they embarked. It was a beautiful still night, and the little boat glided swiftly along. The regular dip of the oars, the distant song of the sailor, and sometimes the voice of a belated traveller at the ferry of Carrigaloe, alone broke the quietness of the land and sea and sky. The tide was in their favour, and in a few minutes Robin and his gossip rested on their oars under the dark shadow of the Giant's Stairs. Robin looked anxiously for the entrance to the Giant's palace, which, it was said, may be found by any one seeking it at midnight; but no such entrance could he see. His impatience had hurried him there before that time, and after waiting a considerable space in a state of suspense not to be described, Robin, with pure vexation, could not help exclaiming to his companion, "'Tis a pair of fools we are, Tom Clancey, for coming here at all on the strength of a dream."

"And whose doing is it," said Tom, "but your own?"

At the moment he spoke they perceived a faint glimmering of light to proceed from the cliff, which gradually increased until a porch big enough for a king's palace unfolded itself almost on a level with the water. They pulled the skiff towards the opening, and Robin Kelly, seizing his plough-iron, boldly entered with a strong hand and a stout heart. Wild and strange was that entrance, the whole of which appeared formed of grim and grotesque faces, blending so strangely each with the other that it was impossible to define any: the chin of one formed the nose of another; what appeared to be a fixed and stern eye, if dwelt upon, changed to a gaping mouth; and the lines of the lofty forehead grew into a majestic and flowing beard. The more Robin allowed himself to contemplate the forms around him, the more terrific they became; and the stony expression of this crowd of faces assumed a savage ferocity as his imagination converted feature after feature into a different shape and character. Losing the twilight in which these indefinite forms were visible, he advanced through a dark and devious passage, whilst a deep and rumbling noise sounded as if the rock was about to close upon him, and swallow him up alive for ever. Now, indeed, poor Robin felt afraid.

"Robin, Robin," said he, "if you were a fool for coming here, what in the name of fortune are you now?" But, as before, he had scarcely spoken, when he saw a small light twinkling through the darkness of the distance, like a star in the midnight sky. To retreat was out of the question; for so many turnings and windings were in the passage, that he considered he had but little chance of making his way back. He, therefore, proceeded towards the bit of light, and came at last into a spacious chamber, from the roof of which hung the solitary lamp that had guided him. Emerging from such profound gloom the single lamp afforded Robin abundant light to discover several gigantic figures seated round a massive stone table, as if in serious deliberation, but no word disturbed the breathless silence which prevailed. At the head of this table sat Mahon MacMahon himself, whose majestic beard had taken root, and in the course of ages grown into the stone slab. He was the first who perceived Robin; and instantly starting up, drew his long beard from out the huge piece of rock in such haste and with so sudden a jerk that it was shattered into a thousand pieces.

"What seek you?" he demanded in a voice of thunder.

"I come," answered Robin, with as much boldness as he could put on, for his heart was almost fainting within him; "I come," said he, "to claim Philip Ronayne, whose time of service is out this night."

"And who sent you here?" said the giant.

" 'Twas of my own accord I came," said Robin.

"Then you must single him out from among my pages," said the giant; "and if you fix on the wrong one, your life is forfeit. Follow me." He led Robin into a hall of vast extent and filled with lights; along either side of which were rows of beautiful children, all apparently seven years old, and none beyond that age, dressed in green, and every one exactly dressed alike.

"Here," said Mahon, "you are free to take Philip Ronayne, if you will; but, remember, I give you but one choice."

Robin was sadly perplexed; for there were hundreds upon hundreds of children; and he had no very clear recollection of the boy he sought. But he walked along the hall, by the side of Mahon, as if nothing was the matter, although his great iron dress clanked fearfully at every step, sounding louder than Robin's own sledge battering on his anvil.

They had nearly reached the end without speaking, when Robin, seeing that the only means he had was to make friends with the giant, determined to try what effect a few soft words might have.

" 'Tis a fine wholesome appearance the poor children carry," remarked Robin, "although they have been here so long shut out from the fresh air and the blessed light of heaven. 'Tis tenderly your honour must have reared them!"

"Ay," said the giant, "that is true for you; so give me your hand; for you are, I believe, a very honest fellow for a blacksmith."

Robin at the first look did not much like the huge size of the hand, and, therefore, presented his plough-iron, which the giant seizing, twisted in his grasp round and round again as if it had been a potato stalk. On seeing this all the children set up a shout of laughter. In the midst of their mirth Robin thought he heard his name called; and all ear and eye, he put his hand on the boy who he fancied had spoken, crying out at the same time, "Let me live or die for it, but this is young Phil Ronayne."

"It is Philip Ronayne—happy Philip Ronayne," said his young companions; and in an instant the hall became dark. Crashing noises were heard, and all was in strange confusion; but Robin held fast his prize, and found himself lying in the grey dawn of the morning at the head of the Giant's Stairs with the boy clasped in his arms.

Robin had plenty of gossips to spread the story of his wonderful adventure: Passage, Monkstown, Carrigaline—the whole barony of Kerricurrihy rung with it.

"Are you quite sure, Robin, it is young Phil Ronayne you have brought back with you?" was the regular question; for although the boy had been seven years away, his appearance now was just the same as on the day he was missed. He had neither grown taller nor older in look, and he spoke of things which had happened before he was carried off as one awakened from sleep, or as if they had occurred yesterday.

"Am I sure? Well, that's a queer question," was Robin's reply; "seeing the boy has the blue eye of the mother, with the foxy hair of the father; to say nothing of the *purty* wart on the right side of his little nose."

However Robin Kelly may have been questioned, the worthy couple of Ronayne's Court doubted not that he was the deliverer of their child from the power of the giant MacMahon; and the reward they bestowed on him equalled their gratitude.

Philip Ronayne lived to be an old man; and he was remarkable to the day of his death for his skill in working brass and iron, which it was believed he had learned during his seven years' apprenticeship to the giant Mahon MacMahon.

A Legend of Knockmany

WILLIAM CARLETON

What Irish man, woman, or child has not heard of our renowned Hibernian Hercules, the great and glorious Fin M'Coul? Not one, from Cape Clear to the Giant's Causeway, nor from that back again to Cape Clear. And, by the way, speaking of the Giant's Causeway brings me at once to the beginning of my story. Well, it so happened that Fin and his gigantic relatives were all working at the Causeway, in order to make a bridge, or what was still better, a good stout pad-road, across to Scotland; when Fin, who was very fond of his wife Oonagh, took it into his head that he would go home and see how the poor woman got on in his absence. To be sure, Fin was a true Irishman, and so the sorrow thing in life brought him back, only to see that she was snug and comfortable, and, above all things, that she got her rest well at night; for he knew that the poor woman, when he was with her, used to be subject to nightly qualms and configurations, that kept him very anxious, decent man, striving to keep her up to the good spirits and health that she had when they were first married. So, accordingly, he pulled up a fir-tree, and, after lopping off the roots and branches, made a walking-stick of it, and set out on his way to Oonagh.

Oonagh, or rather Fin, lived at this time on the very tip-top of Knockmany Hill, which faces a cousin of its own called Cullamore, that rises up, half-hill, half-mountain, on the opposite side—east-east by south, as the sailors say, when they wish to puzzle a landsman.

Now, the truth is, for it must come out, that honest Fin's affection for his wife, though cordial enough in itself, was by no manner of means the real cause of his journey home. There was at that time another giant, named Cucullin—some say he was Irish, and some say he was Scotch—but whether Scotch or Irish, sorrow doubt of it but he was a *targer*. No other giant of the day could stand before him; and such was his strength, that, when well vexed, he could give a stamp that shook

263

the country about him. The fame and name of him went far and near; and nothing in the shape of a man, it was said, had any chance with him in a fight. Whether the story is true or not, I cannot say, but the report went that, by one blow of his fists he flattened a thunderbolt, and kept it in his pocket, in the shape of a pancake, to show to all his enemies, when they were about to fight him. Undoubtedly he had given every giant in Ireland a considerable beating, barring Fin M'Coul himself; and he swore, by the solemn contents of Moll Kelly's Primer, that he would never rest, night or day, winter or summer, till he would serve Fin with the same sauce, if he could catch him. Fin, however, who no doubt was the cock of the walk on his own dunghill, had a strong disinclination to meet a giant who could make a young earthquake, or flatten a thunderbolt when he was angry; so accordingly kept dodging about from place to place, not much to his credit as a Trojan, to be sure, whenever he happened to get the hard word that Cucullin was on the scent of him. This, then, was the marrow of the whole movement, although he put it on his anxiety to see Oonagh; and I am not saying but there was some truth in that too. However, the short and long of it was, with reverence be it spoken, that he heard Cucullin was coming to the Causeway to have a trial of strength with him; and he was naturally enough seized, in consequence, with a very warm and sudden fit of affection for his wife, poor woman, who was delicate in her health, and leading, besides, a very lonely, uncomfortable life of it (he assured them) in his absence. He accordingly pulled up the fir-tree, as I said before, and having snedded it into a walking-stick, set out on his affectionate travels to see his darling Oonagh on the top of Knockmany, by the way.

In truth, to state the suspicions of the country at the time, the people wondered very much why it was that Fin selected such a windy spot for his dwelling-house, and they even went so far as to tell him as much.

"What can you mane, Mr M'Coul," said they, "by pitching your tent upon the top of Knockmany, where you never are without a breeze, day or night, winter or summer, and where you're often forced to take your nightcap* without either going to bed or turning up your little finger; ay, an' where, besides this, there's the sorrow's own want of water?"

"Why," said Fin, "ever since I was the height of a round tower, I was known to be fond of having a good prospect of my own; and where the dickens, neighbours,

---

*A common name for the cloud or rack that hangs, as a forerunner of wet weather, about the peak of a mountain.

could I find a better spot for a good prospect than the top of Knockmany? As for water, I am sinking a pump*, and, please goodness, as soon as the Causeway's made, I intend to finish it."

Now, this was more of Fin's philosophy; for the real state of the case was, that he pitched upon the top of Knockmany in order that he might be able to see Cucullin coming towards the house, and, of course, that he himself might go to look after his distant transactions in other parts of the country, rather than—but no matter—we do not wish to be too hard on Fin. All we have to say is, that if he wanted a spot from which to keep a sharp look-out—and, between ourselves, he did want it grievously—barring Slieve Croob, or Slieve Donard, or its own cousin, Cullamore, he could not find a neater or more convenient situation for it in the sweet and sagacious province of Ulster.

"God save all here!" said Fin, good-humouredly, on putting his honest face into his own door.

"Musha, Fin, avick, an' you're welcome home to your own Oonagh, you darlin' bully." Here followed a smack that is said to have made the waters of the lake at the bottom of the hill curl, as it were, with kindness and sympathy.

"Faith," said Fin, "beautiful; an' how are you, Oonagh—and how did you sport your figure during my absence, my bilberry?"

"Never a merrier—as bouncing a grass widow as ever there was in sweet 'Tyrone among the bushes'."

Fin gave a short, good-humoured cough, and laughed most heartily, to show her how much he was delighted that she made herself happy in his absence.

"An' what brought you home so soon, Fin?" said she.

"Why, avourneen," said Fin, putting in his answer in the proper way, "never the thing but the purest of love and affection for yourself. Sure you know that's truth, anyhow, Oonagh."

Fin spent two or three happy days with Oonagh, and felt himself very comfortable, considering the dread he had of Cucullin. This, however, grew upon him so much that his wife could not but perceive something lay on his mind which he kept altogether to himself. Let a woman alone, in the meantime, for ferreting, or wheedling a secret out of her good man, when she wishes. Fin was a proof of this.

*There *is* upon the top of this hill an opening that bears a very strong resemblance to the crater of an extinct volcano.

"It's this Cucullin," said he, "that's troubling me. When the fellow gets angry, and begins to stamp, he'll shake you a whole townland; and it's well known that he can stop a thunderbolt, for he always carries one about him in the shape of a pancake, to show to anyone that might misdoubt it."

As he spoke, he clapped his thumb in his mouth, which he always did when he wanted to prophesy, or to know anything that happened in his absence; and the wife, who knew what he did it for, said, very sweetly,

"Fin, darling, I hope you don't bite your thumb at me, dear?"

"No," said Fin; "but I bite my thumb, acushla," said he.

"Yes, jewel; but take care and don't draw blood," said she. "Ah, Fin! don't, my bully—don't."

"He's coming," said Fin; "I see him below Dungannon."

"Thank goodness, dear! an' who is it, avick? Glory be to God!"

"That baste, Cucullin," replied Fin; "and how to manage I don't know. If I run away, I am disgraced; and I know that sooner or later I must meet him, for my thumb tells me so."

"When will he be here?" said she.

"Tomorrow, about two o'clock," replied Fin, with a groan.

"Well, my bully, don't be cast down," said Oonagh; "depend on me, and maybe I'll bring you better out of this scrape than ever you could bring yourself, by your rule o' thumb."

This quieted Fin's heart very much, for he knew that Oonagh was hand and glove with the fairies; and, indeed, to tell the truth, she was supposed to be a fairy herself. If she was, however, she must have been a kind-hearted one, for, by all accounts, she never did anything but good in the neighbourhood.

Now it so happened that Oonagh had a sister named Granua, living opposite them, on the very top of Cullamore, which I have mentioned already, and this Granua was quite as powerful as herself. The beautiful valley that lies between them is not more than about three or four miles broad, so that of a summer's evening, Granua and Oonagh were able to hold many an agreeable conversation across it, from the one hill-top to the other. Upon this occasion Oonagh resolved to consult her sister as to what was best to be done in the difficulty that surrounded them.

"Granua," said she, "are you at home?"

"No," said the other; "I'm picking bilberries in Althadhawan" (*Anglicé* the Devil's Glen).

"Well," said Oonagh, "get up to the top of Cullamore, look about you, and then tell us what you see."

"Very well," replied Granua; after a few minutes, "I am there now."

"What do you see?" asked the other.

"Goodness be about us!" exclaimed Granua, "I see the biggest giant that ever was known coming up from Dungannon."

"Ay," said Oonagh, "there's our difficulty. That giant is the great Cucullin; and he's now commin' up to leather Fin. What's to be done?"

"I'll call to him," she replied, "to come up to Cullamore and refresh himself, and maybe that will give you and Fin time to think of some plan to get yourselves out of the scrape. But," she proceeded, "I'm short of butter, having in the house only half-a-dozen firkins, and as I'm to have a few giants and giantesses to spend the evenin' with me, I'd feel thankful, Oonagh, if you'd throw me up fifteen or sixteen tubs, or the largest miscaun you have got, and you'll oblige me very much."

"I'll do that with a heart and a half," replied Oonagh; "and, indeed, Granua, I feel myself under great obligations to you for your kindness in keeping him off of us till we see what can be done; for what would become of us all if anything happened to Fin, poor man."

She accordingly got the largest miscaun of butter she had—which might be about the weight of a couple a dozen mill-stones, so that you may easily judge of its size—and calling up to her sister, "Granua," said she, "are you ready? I'm going to throw you up a miscaun, so be prepared to catch it."

"I will," said the other; "a good throw now, and take care it does not fall short."

Oonagh threw it; but in consequence of her anxiety about Fin and Cucullin, she forgot to say the charm that was to send it up, so that, instead of reaching Cullamore, as she expected, it fell about half-way between the two hills, at the edge of the Broad Bog near Augher.

"My curse upon you!" she exclaimed; "you've disgraced me. I now change you into a grey stone. Lie there as a testimony of what has happened; and may evil betide the first living man that will ever attempt to remove or injure you!"[15]

And, sure enough, there it lies to this day, with the mark of the four fingers and thumb imprinted in it, exactly as it came out of her hand.

"Never mind," said Granua, "I must only do the best I can with Cucullin. If all fail, I'll give him a cast of heather broth to keep the wind out of his stomach, or panada of oak-bark to draw it in a bit; but, above all things, think of some plan to get Fin out of the scrape he's in, otherwise he's a lost man. You know you used to be sharp and ready-witted; and my own opinion, Oonagh, is, that it will go hard with you, or you'll outdo Cucullin yet."

She then made a high smoke on the top of the hill, after which she put her finger in her mouth, and gave three whistles, and by that Cucullin knew he was invited to Cullamore—for this was the way that the Irish long ago gave a sign to all strangers and travellers, to let them know they were welcome to come and take share of whatever was going.

In the meantime, Fin was very melancholy, and did not know what to do, or how to act at all. Cucullin was an ugly customer, no doubt, to meet with; and, moreover, the idea of the confounded "cake" aforesaid flattened the very heart within him. What chance could he have, strong and brave though he was, with a man who could, when put in a passion, walk the country into earthquakes and knock thunderbolts into pancakes? The thing was impossible; and Fin knew not on what hand to turn him. Right or left—backward or forward—where to go he could form no guess whatsoever.

"Oonagh," said he, "can you do nothing for me? Where's all your invention? Am I to be skivered like a rabbit before your eyes, and to have my name disgraced forever in the sight of all my tribe, and me the best man among them? How am I to fight this man-mountain—this huge cross between an earthquake and a thunderbolt?—with a pancake in his pocket that was once—"

"Be easy Fin," replied Oonagh; "troth, I'm ashamed of you. Keep your toe in your pump, will you? Talking of pancakes, maybe we'll give him as good as any he brings with him—thunderbolt or otherwise. If I don't treat him to as smart feeding as he's got this many a day, never trust Oonagh again. Leave him to me, and do just as I bid you."

This relieved Fin very much; for, after all, he had great confidence in his wife, knowing, as he did, that she had got him out of many a quandary before. The present, however, was the greatest of all; but still be began to get courage, and was able to eat his victuals as usual. Oonagh then drew the nine woollen threads of different colours, which she always did to find out the best way of succeeding in anything of importance she went about. She then platted them into three plats with three colours in each, putting one on her right arm, one round her heart, and the third round her right ankle, for then she knew that nothing could fail with her that she undertook.

Having everything prepared, she sent round to the neighbours and borrowed one-and-twenty iron griddles, which she took and kneaded into the hearts of one-and-twenty cakes of bread, and these she baked on the fire in the usual way, setting them aside in the cupboard according as they were done. She then put down a large pot of new milk, which she made into curds and whey, and gave Fin due instructions how to use the curds when Cucullin should come. Having done all this, she sat down quite contented, waiting for his arrival on the next day about two o'clock, that being the hour at which he was expected—for Fin knew as much by the sucking of his thumb. Now, this was a curious property that Fin's thumb had; but, notwithstanding all the wisdom and logic he used, to suck out of it, it could never have stood to him here were it not for the wit of his wife. In this very thing, moreover, he was very much resembled by his great foe, Cucullin; for it was well known that the huge strength he possessed all lay in the middle finger of his right hand, and that, if he happened by any mischance to lose it, he was no more, notwithstanding his bulk, than a common man.

At length, the next day, he was seen coming across the valley, and Oonagh knew that it was time to commence operations. She immediately made the cradle, and desired Fin to lie down in it, and cover himself up with the clothes.

"You must pass for your own child," said she; "so just lie there snug, and say nothing, but be guided by me." This, to be sure, was wormwood to Fin—I mean going into the cradle in such a cowardly manner—but he knew Oonagh well; and finding that he had nothing else for it, with a very rueful face he gathered himself into it, and lay snug, as she had desired him.

About two o'clock, as he had been expected, Cucullin came in. "God save all here!" said he; "is this where the great Fin M'Coul lives?"

"Indeed it is, honest man," replied Oonagh; "God save you kindly—won't you be sitting?"

"Thank you, ma'am," says he, sitting down; "you're Mrs M'Coul, I suppose?"

"I am," said she; "and I have no reason, I hope, to be ashamed of my husband."

"No," said the other, "he has the name of being the strongest and bravest man in Ireland; but for all that, there's a man not far from you that's very desirous of taking a shake with him. Is he at home?"

"Why, then, no," she replied; "and if ever a man left his house in a fury, he did. It appears that some one told him of a big basthoon of a giant called Cucullin being down at the Causeway to look for him, and so he set out there to try if he could catch him. Troth, I hope, for the poor giant's sake, he won't meet him, for if he does, Fin will make paste of him at once."

"Well," said the other, "I am Cucullin, and I have been seeking him these twelve months, but he always kept clear of me; and I will never rest night or day till I lay my hands on him."

At this Oonagh set up a loud laugh, of great contempt, by the way, and looked at him as if he was only a mere handful of a man.

"Did you ever see Fin?" said she, changing her manner all at once.

"How could I?" said he; "he always took care to keep his distance."

"I thought so," she replied; "I judged as much; and if you take my advice, you poor-looking creature, you'll pray night and day that you may never see him, for I tell you it will be a black day for you when you do. But, in the meantime, you perceive that the wind's on the door, and as Fin himself is from home, maybe you'd be civil enough to turn the house, for it's always what Fin does when he's here."

This was a startler even to Cucullin; but he got up, however, and after pulling the middle finger of his right hand until it cracked three times, he went outside, and getting his arms about the house, completely turned it as she had wished. When Fin saw this, he felt a certain description of moisture, which shall be nameless, oozing out through every pore of his skin; but Oonagh, depending upon her woman's wit, felt not a whit daunted.

"Arrah, then," said she, "as you are so civil, maybe you'd do another obliging turn for us, as Fin's not here to do it himself. You see, after this long stretch of dry weather we've had, we feel very badly off for want of water. Now, Fin says there's a fine spring-well somewhere under the rocks behind the hill here below, and it was his intention to pull them asunder; but having heard of you, he left the place in such a fury, that he never thought of it. Now, if you try to find it, troth I'd feel it a kindness."

She then brought Cucullin down to see the place, which was then all one solid rock; and, after looking at it for some time, he cracked his right middle finger nine times, and, stooping down, tore a cleft about four hundred feet deep, and a quarter of a mile in length, which has since been christened by the name of Lumford's Glen. This feat nearly threw Oonagh herself off her guard; but what won't a woman's sagacity and presence of mind accomplish?

"You'll now come in," said she, "and eat a bit of such humble fare as we can give you. Fin, even although he and you are enemies, would scorn not to treat you kindly in his own house; and, indeed, if I didn't do it even in his absence, he would not be pleased with me."

She accordingly brought him in, and placing half-a-dozen of the cakes we spoke of before him, together with a can or two of butter, a side of boiled bacon, and a stack of cabbage, she desired him to help himself—for this, be it known, was long before the invention of potatoes. Cucullin, who, by the way, was a glutton as well as a hero, put one of the cakes in his mouth to take a huge whack out of it, when both Fin and Oonagh were stunned with a noise that resembled something between a growl and a yell. "Blood and fury!" he shouted; "how is this? Here are two of my teeth out! What kind of bread is this you gave me?"

"What's the matter?" said Oonagh coolly.

"Matter!" shouted the other again; "why, here are the two best teeth in my head gone."

"Why," said she, "that's Fin's bread—the only bread he ever eats when at home; but, indeed, I forgot to tell you nobody can eat it but himself, and that child in the cradle there. I thought, however, that, as you were reported to be rather a stout little fellow of your size, you might be able to manage it, and I did not wish to affront a man that thinks himself able to fight Fin. Here's another cake—maybe it's not so hard as that."

Cucullin at the moment was not only hungry, but ravenous, so he accordingly made a fresh set at the second cake, and immediately another yell was heard twice as loud as the first. "Thunder and giblets!" he roared, "take your bread out of this, or I will not have a tooth in my head; there's another pair of them gone!"

"Well, honest man," replied Oonagh, "if you're not able to eat the bread, say so quietly, and don't be wakening the child in the cradle there. There, now, he's awake upon me."

Fin now gave a skirl that startled the giant, as coming from such a youngster as he was represented to be. "Mother," said he, "I'm hungry—get me something to eat." Oonagh went over, and putting into his hand a cake *that had no griddle in it*, Fin, whose appetite in the meantime was sharpened by what he saw going forward, soon made it disappear. Cucullin was thunderstruck, and secretly thanked his stars that he had the good fortune to miss meeting Fin, for, as he said to himself, I'd have no chance with a man who could eat such bread as that, which even his son that's in his cradle can munch before my eyes.

"I'd like to take a glimpse at the lad in the cradle," said he to Oonagh; "for I can tell you that the infant who can manage that nutriment is no joke to look at, or to feed of a scarce summer."

"With all the veins of my heart," replied Oonagh; "get up, acushla, and show this decent little man something that won't be unworthy of your father, Fin M'Coul."

Fin, who was dressed for the occasion as much like a boy as possible, got up, and bringing Cucullin out, "Are you strong?" said he.

"Thunder an' ounds!" exclaimed the other, "what a voice in so small a chap!"

"Are you strong?" said Fin again; "are you able to squeeze water out of that white stone?" he asked, putting one into Cucullin's hand. The latter squeezed and squeezed the stone, but to no purpose; he might pull the rocks of Lumford's Glen asunder, and flatten a thunderbolt, but to squeeze water out of a white stone was beyond his strength. Fin eyed him with great contempt, as he kept straining and squeezing and squeezing and straining, till he got black in the face with the efforts.

"Ah, you're a poor creature!" said Fin. "You a giant! Give me the stone here, and when I'll show what Fin's little son can do; you may then judge of what my daddy himself is."

Fin then took the stone, and slyly exchanging it for the curds, he squeezed the latter until the whey, as clear as water, oozed out in a little shower from his hand.

"I'll now go in," said he "to my cradle; for I scorn to lose my time with any one that's not able to eat my daddy's bread, or squeeze water out of a stone. Bedad, you had better be off out of this before he comes back; for if he catches you, it's in flummery he'd have you in two minutes."

Cucullin, seeing what he had seen, was of the same opinion himself; his knees knocked together with the terror of Fin's return, and he accordingly hastened in to bid Oonagh farewell, and to assure her, that from that day out, he never wished to hear of, much less to see, her husband. "I admit fairly that I'm not a match for him," said he, "strong as I am; tell him I will avoid him as I would the plague, and that I will make myself scarce in this part of the country while I live."

Fin, in the meantime, had gone into the cradle, where he lay very quietly, his heart at his mouth with delight that Cucullin was about to take his departure, without discovering the tricks that had been played off on him.

"It's well for you," said Oonagh, "that he doesn't happen to be here, for it's nothing but hawk's meat he'd make of you."

"I know that," says Cucullin; "divil a thing else he'd make of me; but before I go, will you let me feel what kind of teeth they are that can eat griddle-bread like *that?*"—and he pointed to it as he spoke.

"With all pleasure in life," said she; "only, as they're far back in his head, you must put your finger a good way in."

Cucullin was surprised to find such a powerful set of grinders in one so young; but he was still much more so on finding, when he took his hand from Fin's mouth, that he had left the very finger upon which his whole strength depended, behind him. He gave one loud groan, and fell down at once with terror and weakness. This was all Fin wanted, who now knew that his most powerful and bitterest enemy was completely at his mercy. He instantly started out of the cradle, and in a few minutes the great Cucullin, that was for such a length of time the terror of him and all his followers, lay a corpse before him. Thus did Fin, through the wit and invention of Oonagh, his wife, succeed in overcoming his enemy by stratagem, which he never could have done by force: and thus also is it proved that the women, if they bring us *into* many an unpleasant scrape, can sometimes succeed in getting us *out* of others that are as bad.

KINGS, QUEENS, PRINCESSES, EARLS, ROBBERS

The Twelve Wild Geese*

PATRICK KENNEDY

There was once a King and Queen that lived very happily together, and they had twelve sons and not a single daughter. We are always wishing for what we haven't, and don't care for what we have, and so it was with the Queen. One day in winter, when the bawn was covered with snow, she was looking out of the parlour window, and saw there a calf that was just killed by the butcher, and a raven standing near it. "Oh," says she, "if I had only a daughter with her skin as white as that snow, her cheeks as red as that blood, and her hair as black as that raven, I'd give away every one of my twelve sons for her." The moment she said the word, she got a great fright, and a shiver went through her, and in an instant after a severe-looking old woman stood before her. "That was a wicked wish you made," said she, "and to punish you it will be granted. You will have such a daughter as you desire, but the very day of her birth you will lose your other children." She vanished the moment she said the words.

And that very way it turned out. When she expected her delivery, she had her children all in a large room of the palace, with guards all round it, but the very hour her daughter came into the world, the guards inside and outside heard a great whirling and whistling, and the twelve princes were seen flying one after another out through the open window, and away like so many arrows over the woods. Well, the king was in great grief for the loss of his sons, and he would be very enraged with his wife if he only knew that she was so much to blame for it.

Everyone called the little princess Snow-white-and-Rose-red on account of her beautiful complexion. She was the most loving and lovable child that could be seen anywhere. When she was twelve years old she began to be very sad and lonely, and to torment her mother, asking her about her brothers that she thought were dead, for none up to that time ever told her the exact thing that happened to them. The secret was weighing very heavy on the Queen's conscience, and as the little

*The Fireside Stories of Ireland (Gill & Sons, Dublin).

277

girl persevered in her questions, at last she told her. "Well, mother," said she, "it was on my account my poor brothers were changed into wild geese, and are now suffering all sorts of hardship; before the world is a day older, I'll be off to seek them, and try to restore them to their own shapes."

The King and Queen had her well watched, but all was no use. Next night she was getting through the woods that surrounded the palace, and she went on and on that night, and till the evening of next day. She had a few cakes with her, and she got nuts, and *mugoreens* (fruit of the sweet briar), and some sweet crabs, as she went along. At last she came to a nice wooden house just at sunset. There was a fine garden round it, full of the handsomest flowers, and a gate in the hedge. She went in, and saw a table laid out with twelve plates, and twelve knives and forks, and twelve spoons, and there were cakes, and cold wild fowl, and fruit along with the plates, and there was a good fire, and in another long room there were twelve beds. Well, while she was looking about her she heard the gate opening, and footsteps along the walk, and in came twelve young men, and there was great grief on all their faces when they laid eyes on her. "Oh, what misfortune sent you here?" said the eldest. "For the sake of a girl we were obliged to leave our father's court, and be in the shape of wild geese all day. That's twelve years ago, and we took a solemn oath that we would kill the first young girl that came into our hands. It's a pity to put such an innocent and handsome girl as you are out of the world, but we must keep our oath." "But," said she, "I'm your only sister, that never knew anything about this till yesterday; and I stole away from our father's and mother's palace last night to find you out and relieve you if I can." Every one of them clasped his hands, and looked down on the floor, and you could hear a pin fall till the eldest cried out, "A curse light on our oath! what shall we do?" "I'll tell you that," said an old woman that appeared at the instant among them. "Break your wicked oath, which no one should keep. If you attempted to lay an uncivil finger on her I'd change you into twelve *booliaun buis* (stalks of ragweed), but I wish well to you as well as to her. She is appointed to be your deliverer in this way. She must spin and knit twelve shirts for you out of bog-down, to be gathered by her own hands on the moor just outside of the wood. It will take her five years to do it, and if she once speaks, or laughs, or cries the whole time, you will have to remain wild geese by day till you're called out of the world. So take care of your sister; it is worth your while." The fairy then vanished, and it was only strife with the brothers to see who would be first to kiss and hug their sister.

So for three long years the poor young princess was occupied pulling bog-down, spinning it, and knitting it into shirts, and at the end of the three years she had eight made. During all that time, she never spoke a word, nor laughed, nor cried: the last was the hardest to refrain from. One fine day she was sitting in the garden spinning, when in sprung a fine greyhound and bounded up to her, and laid his paws on her shoulder, and licked her forehead and her hair. The next minute a beautiful young prince rode up to the little garden gate, took off his hat, and asked for leave to come in. She gave him a little nod, and in he walked. He made ever so many apologies for intruding, and asked her ever so many questions, but not a word could he get out of her. He loved her so much from the first moment that he could not leave her till he told her he was king of a country just bordering on the forest, and he begged her to come home with him, and be his wife. She couldn't help loving him as much as he did her, and though she shook her head very often, and was very sorry to leave her brothers, at last she nodded her head, and put her hand in his. She knew well enough that the good fairy and her brothers would be able to find her out. Before she went she brought out a basket holding all her bog-down, and another holding the eight shirts. The attendants took charge of these, and the prince placed her before him on his horse. The only thing that disturbed him while riding along was the displeasure his stepmother would feel at what he had done. However, he was full master at home, and as soon as he arrived he sent for the bishop, got his bride nicely dressed and the marriage was celebrated, the bride answering by signs. He knew by her manners she was of high birth, and no two could be fonder of each other.

The wicked stepmother did all she could to make mischief, saying she was sure she was only a woodman's daughter; but nothing could disturb the young king's opinion of his wife. In good time the young queen was delivered of a beautiful boy, and the king was so glad he hardly knew what to do for joy. All the grandeur of the christening and the happiness of the parents tormented the bad woman more than I can tell you, and she determined to put a stop to all their comfort. She got a sleeping posset given to the young mother, and while she was thinking and thinking how she could best make away with the child, she saw a wicked-looking wolf in the garden, looking up at her, and licking his chops. She lost no time, but snatched the child from the arms of the sleeping woman, and pitched it out. The beast caught it in his mouth, and was over the garden fence in a minute. The wicked woman then pricked her own fingers, and dabbled the blood round the mouth of the sleeping mother.

Well, the young king was just then coming into the big bawn from hunting, and as soon as he entered the house, she beckoned to him, shed a few crocodile tears, began to cry and wring her hands, and hurried him along the passage to the bed-chamber.

Oh, wasn't the poor king frightened when he saw the queen's mouth bloody, and missed his child? It would take two hours to tell you the devilment of the old queen, the confusion and fright, and grief of the young king and queen, the bad opinion he began to feel of his wife, and the struggle she had to keep down her bitter sorrow, and not give way to it by speaking or lamenting. The young king would not allow any one to be called, and ordered his stepmother to give out that the child fell from the mother's arms at the window, and that a wild beast ran off with it. The wicked woman pretended to do so, but she told underhand to everybody she spoke to what the king and herself saw in the bed-chamber.

The young queen was the most unhappy woman in the three kingdoms for a long time, between sorrow for her child and her husband's bad opinion; still she neither spoke nor cried, and she gathered bog-down and went on with the shirts. Often the twelve wild geese would be seen lighting on the trees in the park or on the smooth sod, and looking in at her windows. So she worked on to get the shirts finished, but another year was at an end, and she had the twelfth shirt finished except one arm, when she was obliged to take to her bed, and a beautiful girl was born.

Now the king was on his guard, and he would not let the mother and child be left alone for a minute; but the wicked woman bribed some of the attendants, set others asleep, gave the sleepy posset to the queen, and had a person watching to snatch the child away, and kill it. But what should she see but the same wolf in the garden looking up, and licking his chops again? Out went the child, and away with it flew the wolf, and she smeared the sleeping mother's mouth and face with blood, and then roared, and bawled, and cried out to the king and to everybody she met, and the room was filled, and everyone was sure the young queen had just devoured her own babe.

The poor mother thought now her life would leave her. She was in such a state she could neither think nor pray, but she sat like a stone, and worked away at the arm of the twelfth shirt.

The king was for taking her to the house in the wood where he found her, but the stepmother, and the lords of the court, and the judges would not hear of it, and she was condemned to be burned in the big bawn at three o'clock the same day. When the hour drew near, the king went to the farthest part of his palace, and there was no more unhappy man in his kingdom at that hour.

When the executioners came and led her off, she took the pile of shirts in her arms. There was still a few stitches wanted, and while they were tying her to the stakes she still worked on. At the last stitch she seemed overcome and dropped a tear on her work, but the moment after she sprang up, and shouted out, "I am innocent; call my husband!" The executioners stayed their hands, except one wicked-disposed creature, who set fire to the faggot next him, and while all were struck in amaze, there was a rushing of wings, and in a moment the twelve wild geese were standing around the pile. Before you could count twelve, she flung a shirt over each bird, and there in the twinkling of an eye were twelve of the finest young men that could be collected out of a thousand. While some were untying their sister, the eldest, taking a strong stake in his hand, struck the busy executioner such a blow that he never needed another.

While they were comforting the young queen, and the king was hurrying to the spot, a fine-looking woman appeared among them holding the babe on one arm and the little prince by the hand. There was nothing but crying for joy, and laughing for joy, and hugging and kissing, and when any one had time to thank the good fairy, who in the shape of a wolf, carried the child away, she was not to be found. Never was such happiness enjoyed in any palace that ever was built, and if the wicked queen and her helpers were not torn by wild horses, they richly deserved it.

The Lazy Beauty and her Aunts*

PATRICK KENNEDY

There was once a poor widow woman, who had a daughter that was as handsome as the day, and as lazy as a pig, saving your presence. The poor mother was the most industrious person in the townland, and was a particularly good hand at the spinning-wheel. It was the wish of her heart that her daughter should be as handy as herself; but she'd get up late, eat her breakfast before she'd finished her prayers, and then go about dawdling, and anything she handled seemed to be burning her fingers. She drawled her words as if it was a great trouble to her to speak, or as if her tongue was as lazy as her body. Many a heart-scald her poor mother got with her, and still she was only improving like dead fowl in August.

Well, one morning that things were as bad as they could be, and the poor woman was giving tongue at the rate of a millclapper, who should be riding by but the king's son. "Oh dear, oh dear, good woman!" said he, "you must have a very bad child to make you scold so terribly. Sure it can't be this handsome girl that vexed you!" "Oh, please your Majesty, not at all," says the old dissembler. "I was only checking her for working herself too much. Would your majesty believe it? She spins three pounds of flax in a day, weaves it into linen the next, and makes it all into shirts the day after." "My gracious," says the prince, "she's the very lady that will just fill my mother's eye, and herself's the greatest spinner in the kingdom. Will you put on your daughter's bonnet and cloak, if you please, ma'am, and set her behind me? Why, my mother will be so delighted with her, that perhaps she'll make her her daughter-in-law in a week, that is, if the young woman herself is agreeable."

Well, between the confusion, and the joy, and the fear of being found out, the women didn't know what to do; and before they could make up their minds, young Anty (Anastasia) was set behind the prince, and away he and his attendants went,

The Fireside Stories of Ireland.

282

and a good heavy purse was left behind with the mother. She *pullillued* a long time after all was gone, in dread of something bad happening to the poor girl.

The prince couldn't judge of the girl's breeding or wit from the few answers he pulled out of her. The queen was struck in a heap when she saw a young country girl sitting behind her son, but when she saw her handsome face, and heard all she could do, she didn't think she could make too much of her. The prince took an opportunity of whispering her that if she didn't object to be his wife she must strive to please his mother. Well, the evening went by, and the prince and Anty were getting fonder and fonder of one another, but the thought of the spinning used to send the cold to her heart every moment. When bed-time came, the old queen went along with her to a beautiful bedroom, and when she was bidding her good-night, she pointed to a heap of fine flax, and said, "You may begin as soon as you like tomorrow morning, and I'll expect to see these three pounds in nice thread the morning after." Little did the poor girl sleep that night. She kept crying and lamenting that she didn't mind her mother's advice better. When she was left alone next morning, she began with a heavy heart; and though she had a nice mahogany wheel and the finest flax you ever saw, the thread was breaking every moment. One while it was as fine as a cobweb, and the next as coarse as a little boy's whipcord. At last she pushed her chair back, let her hands fall in her lap, and burst out a-crying.

A small, old woman with surprising big feet appeared before her at the same moment, and said, "What ails you, you handsome colleen?" "An' haven't I all that flax to spin before tomorrow morning, and I'll never be able to have even five yards of fine thread of it put together." "An' would you think bad to ask poor *Colliagh Cushmōr* (Old woman Big-foot) to your wedding with the young prince? If you promise me that, all your three pounds will be made into the finest of thread while you're taking your sleep tonight." "Indeed, you must be there and welcome, and I'll honour you all the days of your life." "Very well; stay in your room till tea-time, and tell the queen she may come in for her thread as early as she likes tomorrow morning." It was all as she said; and the thread was finer and evener than the gut you see with fly-fishers. "My brave girl you were!" says the queen. "I'll get my own mahogany loom brought into you, but you needn't do anything more today. Work and rest, work and rest, is my motto. Tomorrow you'll weave all this thread, and who knows what may happen?"

The poor girl was more frightened this time than the last, and she was so afraid

283

to lose the prince. She didn't even know how to put the warp in the gears, nor how to use the shuttle, and she was sitting in the greatest grief, when a little woman, who was mighty well-shouldered about the hips, all at once appeared to her, told her her name was *Colliach Cromanmōr* and made the same bargain with her as Colliach Cushmōr. Great was the queen's pleasure when she found early in the morning a web as fine and white as the finest paper you ever saw. "The darling you were!" says she. "Take your ease with the ladies and gentlemen today, and if you have all this made into nice shirts tomorrow you may present one of them to my son, and be married to him out of hand."

Oh, wouldn't you pity poor Anty the next day, she was now so near the prince, and, maybe, would be soon so far from him. But she waited as patiently as she could with scissors, needle, and thread in hand, till a minute after noon. Then she was rejoiced to see the third woman appear. She had a big red nose, and informed Anty that people called her *Shron Mor Rua* on that account. She was up to her as good as others, for a dozen fine shirts were lying on the table when the queen paid her an early visit.

Now there was nothing talked of but the wedding, and I needn't tell you it was grand. The poor mother was there along with the rest, and at the dinner the old queen could talk of nothing but the lovely shirts, and how happy herself and the bride would be after the honeymoon, spinning, and weaving, and sewing shirts and shifts without end. The bridegroom didn't like the discourse, and the bride liked it less, and he was going to say something, when the footman came up to the head of the table and said to the bride, "Your ladyship's aunt, Colliach Cushmōr, bade me ask might she come in." The bride blushed and wished she was seven miles under the floor, but well became the prince. "Tell Mrs Cushmōr," said he, "that any relation of my bride's will be always heartily welcome wherever she and I are." In came the woman with the big foot, and got a seat near the prince. The old queen didn't like it much, and after a few words she asked rather spitefully, "Dear ma'am, what's the reason your foot is so big?" "*Musha*, faith, your majesty, I was standing almost all my life at the spinning-wheel, and that's the reason." "I declare to you, my darling," said the prince, "I'll never allow you to spend one hour at the same spinning-wheel." The same footman said again, "Your ladyship's aunt, Colliach Cromanmōr, wishes to come in, if the genteels and yourself have no objection." Very *sharoose* (displeased) was Princess Anty, but the prince sent her welcome, and she took her seat, and drank healths apiece to the company. "May I ask, ma'am?" says the old queen, "why you're so wide half-way between the head and the feet?" "That, your majesty, is owing to sitting all my life at the loom." "By my sceptre," says the prince, "my wife shall never sit there an hour." The footman again came up. "Your ladyship's aunt, Colliach Shron Mor Rua, is asking leave to come into the banquet." More blushing on the bride's face, but the bridegroom spoke out cordially, "Tell Mrs Shron Mor Rua she's doing us an honour." In came the old woman, and great respect she got near the top of the table, but the people down low put up their tumblers and glasses to their noses to hide the grins. "Ma'am," says the old queen, "will you tell us, if you please, why your nose is so big and red?" "Throth, your majesty, my head was bent down over the stitching all my life, and all the blood in my body ran into my nose." "My darling," said the prince to Anty, "if ever I see a needle in your hand, I'll run a hundred miles from you."

"And in troth, girls and boys, though it's a diverting story, I don't think the moral is good; and if any of you *thuckeens* go about imitating Anty in her laziness, you'll find it won't thrive with you as it did with her. She was beautiful beyond compare, which none of you are, and she had three powerful fairies to help her besides. There's no fairies now, and no prince or lord to ride by, and catch you idling or working; and maybe, after all, the prince and herself were not so very happy when the cares of the world or old age came on them."

Thus was the tale ended by poor old *Shebale* (Sybilla), Father Murphy's housekeeper, in Coolbawn, Barony of Bantry, about half a century since.

The Haughty Princess*

PATRICK KENNEDY

There was once a very worthy king, whose daughter was the greatest beauty that could be seen far or near, but she was as proud as Lucifer, and no king or prince would she agree to marry. Her father was tired out at last, and invited every king and prince, and duke, and earl that he knew or didn't know to come to his court to give her one trial more. They all came, and next day after breakfast they stood in a row in the lawn, and the princess walked along in the front of them to make her choice. One was fat, and says she, "I won't have you, Beer-barrel!" One was tall and thin, and to him she said, "I won't have you, Ramrod!" To a white-faced man she said, "I won't have you, Pale Death;" and to a red-cheeked man she said, "I won't have you, Cockscomb!" She stopped a little before the last of all for he was a fine man in face and form. She wanted to find some defect in him, but he had nothing remarkable but a ring of brown curling hair under his chin. She admired him a little, and then carried it off with, "I won't have you, Whiskers!"

So all went away, and the king was so vexed, he said to her, "Now to punish your *impedence*, I'll give you to the first beggarman or singing *sthronshuch* that calls;" and, as sure as the hearth-money, a fellow all over rags, and hair that came to his shoulders, and a bushy red beard all over his face, came next morning, and began to sing before the parlour window.

When the song was over, the hall-door was opened, the singer asked in, the priest brought, and the princess married to Beardy. She roared and she bawled, but her father didn't mind her. "There," says he to the bridegroom, "is five guineas for you. Take your wife out of my sight, and never let me lay eyes on you or her again."

Off he led her, and dismal enough she was. The only thing that gave her relief was the tones of her husband's voice and his genteel manners. "Whose wood is this?" said she, as they were going through one. "It belongs to the king you called

*Fireside Stories of Ireland.

286

Whiskers yesterday." He gave her the same answer about meadows and cornfields and at last a fine city. "Ah, what a fool I was!" said she to herself. "He was a fine man, and I might have him for a husband." At last they were coming up to a poor cabin. "Why are you bringing me here?" says the poor lady. "This was my house," said he, "and now it's yours." She began to cry, but she was tired and hungry, and she went in with him.

Ovoch! there was neither a table laid out, nor a fire burning, and she was obliged to help her husband to light it, and boil their dinner, and clean up the place after; and next day he made her put on a stuff gown and a cotton handkerchief. When she had her house readied up, and no business to keep her employed, he brought home *sallies* (willows), peeled them, and showed her how to make baskets. But the hard twigs bruised her delicate fingers, and she began to cry. Well, then he asked her to mend their clothes, but the needle drew blood from her fingers, and she cried again. He couldn't bear to see her tears, so he bought a creel of eathenware, and sent her to the market to sell them. This was the hardest trial of all, but she looked so handsome and sorrowful, and had such a nice air about her, that all her pans, and jugs, and plates, and dishes were gone before noon, and the only mark of her old pride she showed was a slap she gave a buckeen across the face when he *axed* her to go in an' take share of a quart.

Well, her husband was so glad, he sent her with another creel the next day; but faith! her luck was after deserting her. A drunken huntsman came up riding, and his beast got in among her ware, and made *brishe* of every mother's son of 'em. She went home cryin', and her husband wasn't at all pleased. "I see," said he, "you're not fit for business. Come along, I'll get you a kitchenmaid's place in the palace. I know the cook."

So the poor thing was obliged to stifle her pride once more. She was kept busy, and the footman and the butler would be very impudent about looking for a kiss, but she let a screech out of her the first attempt was made, and the cook gave the fellow such a lambasting with the besom that he made no second offer. She went home to her husband every night, and she carried broken victuals wrapped in papers in her side pockets.

A week after she got service there was great bustle in the kitchen. The king was going to be married, but no one knew who the bride was to be. Well, in the evening the cook filled the princess's pockets with cold meat and puddings, and, says she, "Before you go, let us have a look at the great doings in the big parlour."

So they came near the door to get a peep, and who should come out but the king himself, as handsome as you please, and no other but King Whiskers himself. "Your handsome helper must pay for her peeping," said he to the cook, "and dance a jig with me." Whether she would or no, he held her hand and brought her into the parlour. The fiddlers struck up, and away went *him* with *her*. But they hadn't danced two steps when the meat and the *puddens* flew out of her pockets. Every one roared out, and she flew to the door, crying piteously. But she was soon caught by the king, and taken into the back parlour. "Don't you know me, my darling?" said he. "I'm both King Whiskers, your husband the ballad-singer, and the drunken huntsman. Your father knew me well enough when he gave you to me, and all was to drive your pride out of you." Well, she didn't know how she was with fright, and shame, and joy. Love was uppermost anyhow, for she laid her head on her husband's breast and cried like a child. The maids-of-honour soon had her away and dressed her as fine as hands and pins could do it; and there were her mother and father, too; and while the company were wondering what end of the handsome girl and the king, he and his queen, who they didn't know in her fine clothes, and the other king and queen, came in, and such rejoicings and fine doings as there was, none of us will ever see, any way.

The Enchantment of Gearoidh Iarla

PATRICK KENNEDY

In old times in Ireland there was a great man of the Fitzgeralds. The name on him was Gerald, but the Irish, that always had a great liking for the family, called him *Gearoidh Iarla* (Earl Gerald). He had a great castle or rath at *Mullymast* (Mullaghmast); and whenever the English Government were striving to put some wrong on the country, he was always the man that stood up for it. Along with being a great leader in a fight, and very skilful at all weapons, he was deep in the *black art*, and could change himself into whatever shape he pleased. His lady knew that he had this power, and often asked him to let her into some of his secrets, but he never would gratify her.

She wanted particularly to see him in some strange shape, but he put her off and off on one pretence or other. But she wouldn't be a woman if she hadn't perseverance; and so at last he let her know that if she took the least fright while he'd be out of his natural form, he would never recover it till many generations of men would be under the mould. "Oh! she wouldn't be a fit wife for Gearoidh Iarla if she could be easily frightened. Let him but gratify her in this whim, and he'd see what a hero she was!" So one beautiful summer evening, as they were sitting in their grand drawing-room, he turned his face away from her and muttered some words, and while you'd wink he was clever and clean out of sight, and a lovely *goldfinch* was flying about the room.

The lady, as courageous as she thought herself, was a little startled, but she held her own pretty well, especially when he came and perched on her shoulder, and shook his wings, and put his little beak to her lips, and whistled the delightfullest tune you ever heard. Well, he flew in circles round the room, and played *hide and go seek* with his lady, and flew out into the garden, and flew back again, and lay down in her lap as if he was asleep, and jumped up again.

Legendary Fiction of the Irish Celts (Macmillan).

289

Well, when the thing had lasted long enough to satisfy both, he took one flight more into the open air; but by my word he was soon on his return. He flew right into his lady's bosom, and the next moment a fierce hawk was after him. The wife gave one loud scream, though there was no need, for the wild bird came in like an arrow, and struck against a table with such force that the life was dashed out of him. She turned her eyes from his quivering body to where she saw the goldfinch an instant before, but neither goldfinch nor Earl Gerald did she ever lay eyes on again.

Once every seven years the Earl rides round the Curragh of Kildare on a steed, whose silver shoes were half an inch thick the time he disappeared; and when these shoes are worn as thin as a cat's ear he will be restored to the society of living men, fight a great battle with the English, and reign king of Ireland for two-score years.*

Himself and his warriors are now sleeping in a long cavern under the Rath of Mullaghmast. There is a table running along through the middle of the cave. The Earl is sitting at the head, and his troopers down along in complete armour both sides of the table, and their heads resting on it. Their horses, saddled and bridled, are standing behind their masters in their stalls at each side; and when the day comes, the miller's son that's to be born with six fingers on each hand, will blow his trumpet, and the horses will stamp and whinny, and the knights awake and mount their steeds, and go forth to battle.

Some night that happens once in every seven years, while the Earl is riding round the Curragh, the entrance may be seen by any one chancing to pass by. About a hundred years ago, a horsedealer that was late abroad and a little drunk, saw the lighted cavern, and went in. The lights, and the stillness, and the sight of the men in armour, cowed him a good deal, and he became sober. His hands began to tremble, and he let a bridle fall on the pavement. The sound of the bit echoed through the long cave, and one of the warriors that was next him lifted his head a little, and said, in a deep hoarse voice, "Is it time yet?" He had the wit to say, "Not yet, but soon will," and the heavy helmet sunk down on the table. The horse-dealer made the best of his way out, and I never heard of any other one having got the same opportunity.

---

*The last time *Gearoidh Iarla* appeared the horse-shoes were as thin as a sixpence.

Munachar and Manachar

Translated Literally From The Irish By Douglas Hyde

There once lived a Munachar and a Manachar, a long time ago, and it is a long time since it was, and if they were alive then they would not be alive now. They went out together to pick raspberries, and as many as Munachar used to pick Manachar used to eat. Munachar said he must go look for a rod to make a gad (a withy band) to hang Manachar, who ate his raspberries every one; and he came to the rod. "God save you," said the rod. "God and Mary save you." "How far are you going?" "Going looking for a rod, a rod to make a gad, a gad to hang Manachar, who ate my raspberries every one."

"You will not get me," said the rod, "until you get an axe to cut me." He came to the axe. "God save you," said the axe. "God and Mary save you." "How far are you going?" "Going looking for an axe, an axe to cut a rod, a rod to make a gad to hang Manachar, who ate my raspberries every one."

"You will not get me," said the axe, "until you get a flag to edge me." He came to the flag. "God save you," says the flag. "God and Mary save you." "How far are you going?" "Going looking for an axe, axe to cut a rod, a rod to make a gad, a gad to hang Manachar, who ate my raspberries every one."

"You will not get me," says the flag. "till you get water to wet me." He came to the water. "God save you," says the water. "God and Mary save you." "How far are you going?" "Going looking for water, water to wet flag to edge axe, axe to cut a rod, a rod to make a gad, a gad to hang Manachar, who ate my raspberries every one."

"You will not get me," said the water, "until you get a deer who will swim me." He came to the deer. "God save you," says the deer. "God and Mary save you." "How far are you going?" "Going looking for a deer, deer to swim water, water to wet flag, flag to edge axe, axe to cut a rod, a rod to make a gad, a gad to hang Manachar, who ate my raspberries every one."

"You will not get me," said the deer, "until you get a hound who will hunt me." He came to the hound. "God save you," says the hound. "God and Mary save you." "How far are you going?" "Going looking for a hound, hound to hunt deer, deer to swim water, water to wet flag, flag to edge axe, axe to cut a rod, a rod to make a gad, a gad to hang Manachar, who ate my raspberries every one."

"You will not get me," said the hound, "until you get a bit of butter to put in my claw." He came to the butter. "God save you," says the butter. "God and Mary save you." "How far are you going?" "Going looking for butter, butter to go in claw of hound, hound to hunt deer, deer to swim water, water to wet flag, flag to edge axe, axe to cut a rod, a rod to make a gad, a gad to hang Manachar, who ate my raspberries every one."

"You will not get me," said the butter, "until you get a cat who shall scrape me." He came to the cat. "God save you," said the cat. "God and Mary save you." "How far are you going?" "Going looking for a cat, cat to scrape butter, butter to go in claw of hound, hound to hunt deer, deer to swim water, water to wet flag, flag to edge axe, axe to cut a rod, a rod to make a gad, a gad to hang Manachar, who ate my raspberries every one."

"You will not get me," said the cat, "until you will get milk which you will give me." He came to the cow. "God save you," said the cow. "God and Mary save you." "How far are you going?" "Going looking for a cow, cow to give me milk, milk I will give to the cat, cat to scrape butter, butter to go in claw of hound, hound to hunt deer, deer to swim water, water to wet flag, flag to edge axe, axe to cut a rod, a rod to make a gad, a gad to hang Manacher, who ate my raspberries every one."

"You will not get any milk from me," said the cow, "until you bring me a whisp of straw from those threshers yonder." He came to the threshers. "God save you," said the threshers. "God and Mary save ye." "How far are you going?" "Going looking for a whisp of straw from ye to give to the cow, the cow to give me milk, milk I will give to the cat, cat to scrape butter, butter to go in claw of hound, hound to hunt deer, deer to swim water, water to wet flag, flag to edge axe, axe to cut a rod, a rod to make a gad, a gad to hang Manachar, who ate my raspberries every one."

"You will not get any whisp of straw from us," said the threshers, "until you bring us the makings of a cake from the miller over yonder." He came to the miller. "God save you." "God and Mary save you." "How far are you going?" "Going looking for the makings of a cake, which I will give to the threshers, the threshers to give me a whisp of straw, the whisp of straw I will give to the cow, the cow to give me milk, milk I will give to the cat, cat to scrape butter, butter to go in claw of hound, hound to hunt deer, deer to swim water, water to wet flag, flag to edge axe, axe to cut a rod, a rod to make a gad, a gad to hang Manachar, who ate my raspberries every one."

"You will not get any makings of a cake from me," said the miller, "till you bring me the full of that sieve of water from the river over there."

He took the sieve in his hand and went over to the river, but as often as ever he would stoop and fill it with water, the moment he raised it the water would run out of it again, and sure, if he had been there from that day till this, he never could have filled it. A crow went flying by him, over his head. "Daub! daub!" said the crow. "My soul to God, then," said Munachar, "but it's the good advice you have," and he took the red clay and the daub that was by the brink, and he rubbed it to the bottom of the sieve, until all the holes were filled, and then the sieve held the water, and he brought the water to the miller, and the miller gave him the makings of a cake, and he gave the makings of the cake to the threshers, and the threshers gave him a whisp of straw, and he gave the whisp of straw to the cow, and the cow gave him milk, the milk he gave to the cat, the cat scraped the butter, the butter went into the claw of the hound, the hound hunted the deer, the deer swam the water, the water wet the flag, the flag sharpened the axe, the axe cut the rod, and the rod made a gad, and when he had it ready—I'll go bail that Manachar was far enough away from him.

There is some tale like this in almost every language. It resembles that given in that splendid work of industry and patriotism, Campbell's *Tales of the West Highlands* under the name of *Moonachug and Meenachug*. "The English House that Jack built," says Campbell, "has eleven steps, the Scotch Old Woman with the Silver Penny has twelve, the Novsk Cock and Hen A-nutting has twelve, ten of which are double. The German story in Grimm has five or six, all single ideas." This, however, is longer than any of them. It sometimes varies a little in the telling, and the actors' names are sometimes *Suracha* and *Muracha*, and the crow is sometimes a gull, who, instead of *daub! daub!* says *cuir cré rua lesh!*]

Donald and his Neighbours

*From Hibernian Tales**

Hudden and Dudden and Donald O'Nery were near neighbours in the barony of Balinconlig, and ploughed with three bullocks; but the two former, envying the present prosperity of the latter, determined to kill his bullock, to prevent his farm being properly cultivated and laboured, that going back in the world he might be induced to sell his lands, which they meant to get possession of. Poor Donald finding his bullock killed, immediately skinned it, and throwing the skin over his shoulder, with the fleshy side out, set off to the next town with it, to dispose of it to the best of his advantage. Going along the road a magpie flew on the top of the hide, and began picking it, chattering all the time. The bird had been taught to speak, and imitate the human voice, and Donald, thinking he understood some words it was saying, put round his hand and caught hold of it. Having got possession of it, he put it under his great-coat, and so went to town. Having sold the hide, he went into an inn to take a dram, and following the landlady into the cellar, he gave the bird a squeeze which made it chatter some broken accents that surprised her very much. "What is that I hear?" said she to Donald. "I think it is talk, and yet I do not understand." "Indeed," said Donald, "it is a bird I have that tells me everything, and I always carry it with me to know when there is any danger. Faith," says he, "it says you have far better liquor than you are giving me." "That is strange," said she, going to another cask of better quality, and asking him if he would sell the bird. "I will," said Donald, "if I get enough for it. I will fill your hat with silver if you leave it with me." Donald was glad to hear the news, and taking the silver, set off, rejoicing at his good luck. He had not been long at home until he met with Hudden and Dudden. "Mr," said he, "you thought you had done me a bad turn, but you could not have done me a better; for look here, what I have got for the hide," showing them a hatful of silver; "you never saw such a demand for hides in your life as there is at present." Hudden and Dudden that very night killed their bullocks,

*A chap-book mentioned by Thackeray in his *Irish Sketch Book*.

and set out the next morning to sell their hides. On coming to the place they went through all the merchants, but could only get a trifle for them; at last they had to take what they could get, and came home in a great rage, and vowing revenge on poor Donald. He had a pretty good guess how matters would turn out, and he being under the kitchen window, he was afraid they would rob him, or perhaps kill him when asleep, and on that account when he was going to bed he left his old mother in his place, and lay down in her bed, which was in the other side of the house, and they taking the old woman for Donald, choked her in her bed, but he making some noise, they had to retreat, and leave the money behind them, which grieved them very much. However, by daybreak, Donald got his mother on his back, and carried her to town. Stopping at a well, he fixed his mother with her staff, as if she was stooping for a drink, and then went into a public-house convenient and called for a dram. "I wish," said he to a woman that stood near him, "you would tell my mother to come in; she is at yon well trying to get a drink, and she is hard of hearing; if she does not observe you, give her a little shake and tell her that I want her." The woman called her several times, but she seemed to take no notice; at length she went to her and shook her by the arm, but when she let her go again, she tumbled on her head into the well, and, as the woman thought, was drowned. She, in her great surprise and fear at the accident, told Donald what had happened. "O mercy," said he, "what is this?" He ran and pulled her out of the well, weeping and lamenting all the time, and acting in such a manner that you would imagine that he had lost his senses. The woman, on the other hand, was far worse than Donald, for his grief was only feigned, but she imagined herself to be the cause of the old woman's death. The inhabitants of the town hearing what had happened, agreed to make Donald up a good sum of money for his loss, as the accident happened in their place, and Donald brought a greater sum home with him than he got for the magpie. They buried Donald's mother, and as soon as he saw Hudden he showed them the last purse of money he had got. "You thought to kill me last night," said he, "but it was good for me it happened on my mother, for I got all the purse for her to make gunpowder."

That very night Hudden and Dudden killed their mothers, and the next morning set off with them to town. On coming to the town with their burthen on their backs, they went up and down crying, "Who will buy old wives for gunpowder," so that everyone laughed at them, and the boys at last clotted them out of the place. They then saw the cheat, and vowed revenge on Donald, buried the old women, and set off in pursuit of him. Coming to his house they found him sitting at his breakfast, and seizing him, put him in a sack, and went to drown him in a river at some distance. As they were going along the highway they raised a hare, which they saw had but three feet, and throwing off the sack, ran after her, thinking by her appearance she would be easily taken. In their absence there came a drover that way, and hearing Donald singing in the sack, wondered greatly what could be the matter. "What is the reason," said he, "that you are singing, and you confined?" "O, I am going to heaven," said Donald, "and in a short time I expect to be free from trouble." "O dear," said the drover, "what will I give you if you let me to your place?" "Indeed, I do not know," said he, "it would take a good sum." "I have not much money," said the drover, "but I have twenty head of fine cattle, which I will give you to exchange places with me." "Well," says Donald, "I do not care if I should lose the sack, and I will come out." In a moment the drover liberated him, and went into the sack himself, and Donald drove home the fine heifers, and left them in his pasture.

Hudden and Dudden having caught the hare, returned, and getting the sack on one of their backs, carried Donald, as they thought, to the river and threw him in, where he immediately sank. They then marched home, intending to take immediate possession of Donald's property, but how great was their surprise when they found him safe at home before them, with such a fine head of cattle, whereas they knew he had none before. "Donald," said they, "what is all this? We thought you were drowned, and yet you are here before us." "Ah!" said he, "if I had but help along with me when you threw me in, it would have been the best job ever I met with, for of all the sight of cattle and gold that ever was seen is there, and no one to own them, but I was not able to manage more than what you see, and I could show you the spot where you might get hundreds." They both swore they would be his friend, and Donald accordingly led them to a very deep part of the river, and lifted up a stone. "Now," said he, "watch this," throwing it into the stream; "there is the very place, and go in, one of you first, and if you want help, you have nothing to do but call." Hudden jumping in, and sinking to the bottom, rose up again, and making a bubbling noise, as those do that are drowning, attempted to speak, but could not. "What is that he is saying now?" says Dudden. "Faith," says Donald, "he is calling for help; don't you hear him? Stand about," said he, running back, "till I leap in. I know how to do it better than any of you." Dudden, to have the advantage of him, jumped in off the bank, and was drowned along with Hudden, and this was the end of Hudden and Dudden.

The Jackdaw

Tom Moor was a linen draper in Sackville Street. His father, when he died, left him an affluent fortune, and a shop of excellent trade.

As he was standing at his door one day a countryman came up to him with a nest of jackdaws, and accosting him, says, "Master, will you buy a nest of daws?" "No, I don't want any." "Master," replied the man, "I will sell them all cheap; you shall have the whole nest for ninepence." "I don't want them," answered Tom Moor, "so go about your business."

As the man was walking away one of the daws popped out his head, and cried, "Mawk, mawk." "Damn it," says Tom Moor, "that bird knows my name; halloo, countryman, what will you take for the bird?" "Why, you shall have him for threepence." Tom Moor bought him, had a cage made, and hung him up in the shop.

The journeymen took much notice of the bird, and would frequently tap at the bottom of the cage, and say, "Who are you? who are you? Tom Moor of Sackville Street."

In a short time the jackdaw learned these words, and if he wanted victuals or water, would strike his bill against the cage, turn up the white of his eyes, cock his head and cry, "Who are you? who are you? Tom Moor of Sackville Street."

Tom Moor was fond of gaming, and often lost large sums of money; finding his business neglected in his absence, he had a small hazard table set up in one corner of his dining-room, and invited a party of friends to play at it.

The jackdaw had by this time become familiar; his cage was left open, and he hopped into every part of the house; sometimes he got into the dining-room, where the gentlemen were at play, and one of them being a constant winner, the others would say, "Damn it, how he nicks them." The bird learned these words also, and adding them to the former, would call, "Who are you? who are you? Tom Moor of Sackville Street. Damn it, how he nicks them."

Tom Moor, from repeated losses and neglect of business failed in trade, and became a prisoner in the Fleet; he took his bird with him, and lived on the master's side, supported by friends, in a decent manner. They would sometimes ask what brought you here? when he used to lift up his hands and answer, "Bad company, by G——." The bird learned these likewise, and at the end of the former words, would say, "What brought you here? Bad company by G——."

Some of Tom Moor's friends died, others went abroad, and by degrees he was totally deserted, and removed to the common side of the prison, where the jail distemper soon attacked him; and in the last stage of life, lying on a straw bed; the poor bird had been for two days without food or water, came to his feet, and striking his bill on the floor, calls out, "Who are you? Tom Moor of Sackville Street; damn it, how he nicks them. What brought you here? bad company, by G——, bad company, by G——."

Tom Moor, who had attended to the bird, was struck with his words, and reflecting on himself, cried out, "Good God, to what a situation am I reduced! my father, when he died, left me a good fortune and an established trade. I have spent my fortune, ruined my business, and am now dying in a loathsome jail; and to complete all, keeping that poor thing confined without support. I will endeavour to do one piece of justice before I die, by setting him at liberty."

He made a struggle to crawl from his straw bed, opened the casement, and out flew the bird. A flight of jackdaws from the Temple were going over the jail, and Tom Moor's bird mixed among them. The gardener was then laying the plats of the Temple gardens, and as often as he placed them in the day the jackdaws pulled them up by night. They got a gun and attempted to shoot some of them, but, being cunning birds, they always placed one as a watch in the stump of a hollow tree; who, as soon as the gun was levelled cried "Mawk", and away they flew.

The gardeners were advised to get a net, and the first night it was spread they caught fifteen; Tom Moor's bird was amongst them. One of the men took the net into a garret of an uninhabited house, fastens the doors and windows, and turns the birds loose. "Now," said he, "you black rascals, I will be revenged of you." Taking hold of the first at hand, he twists her neck, and throwing him down, cries, "There goes one." Tom Moor's bird, who had hopped up to a beam at one corner of the room unobserved, as the man lays hold of the second, calls out, "Damn it, how he nicks them." The man alarmed, cries, "Sure I heard a voice, but the house is uninhabited, and the door is fast; it could only be imagination." On laying hold of the third, and twisting his neck, Tom's bird again says, "Damn it, how he nicks them." The man dropped the bird in his hand, and turning to where the voice came from, seeing the other with his mouth open, cries out, "Who are you?" to which the bird answered, "Tom Moor of Sackville Street, Tom Moor of Sackville Street." "The devil you are; and what brought you here." Tom Moor's bird, lifting up his pinions, answered, "Bad company, by G——, bad company by G——." The fellow, frightened almost out of his wits, opened the door, ran down stairs, and out of the house, followed by all the birds, who by this means regained their liberty.

The Story Of Conn-eda; Or The Golden Apples Of Lough Erne*

~~~~

Translated from the original Irish of the Story-teller Abraham M'Coy, by Nicholas O'Kearney

It was long before the time the western districts of *Innis Fodhla*† had any settled name, but were indiscriminately called after the person who took possession of them, and whose name they retained only as long as his sway lasted, that a powerful king reigned over this part of the sacred island. He was a puissant warrior, and no individual was found able to compete with him either on land or sea, or question his right to his conquest. The great king of the west held uncontrolled sway from the island of Rathlin to the mouth of the Shannon by sea, and far as the glittering length by land. The ancient king of the west, whose name was Conn, was good as well as great, and passionately loved by his people. His queen was a *Breaton* (British) princess, and was equally beloved and esteemed, because she was the great counterpart of the king in every respect; for whatever good qualification was wanting in the one, the other was certain to indemnify the omission. It was plainly manifest that heaven approved of the career in life of the virtuous couple; for during their reign the earth produced exuberant crops, the trees fruit ninefold commensurate with their usual bearing, the rivers, lakes, and surrounding sea teemed with abundance of choice fish, while herds and flocks were unusually prolific, and kine and sheep yielded such abundance of rich milk that they shed it in torrents upon the pastures; and furrows and cavities were always filled with the pure lacteal produce of the dairy. All these were blessings heaped by heaven upon the western districts of *Innis Fodhla*, over which the benignant and just Conn swayed his sceptre, in

*Printed first in the *Cambrian Journal*, 1855; reprinted and re-edited in the *Folk-Lore Record*, vol.ii.
†*Innis Fodhla*—Island of Destiny, an old name for Ireland.

300

approbation of the course of government he had marked out for his own guidance. It is needless to state that the people who owned the authority of this great and good sovereign were the happiest on the face of the wide expanse of earth. It was during his reign, and that of his son and successor, that Ireland acquired the title of the "happy isle of the west" among foreign nations. Con Mór and his good Queen Eda reigned in great glory during many years; they were blessed with an only son, whom they named Conn-eda, after both his parents, because the Druids foretold at his birth that he would inherit the good qualities of both. According as the young prince grew in years, his amiable and benignant qualities of mind, as well as his great strength of body and manly bearing, became more manifest. He was the idol of his parents, and the boast of his people; he was beloved and respected to that degree that neither prince, lord, nor plebeian swore an oath by the sun, moon, stars, or elements, except by the head of Conn-eda. This career of glory, however, was doomed to meet a powerful but temporary impediment, for the good Queen Eda took a sudden and severe illness, of which she died in a few days, thus plunging her spouse, her son, and all her people into a depth of grief and sorrow from which it was found difficult to relieve them.

The good king and his subjects mourned the loss of Queen Eda for a year and a day, and at the expiration of that time Conn Mór reluctantly yielded to the advice of his Druids and counsellors, and took to wife the daughter of his Arch-Druid. The new queen appeared to walk in the footsteps of the good Eda for several years, and gave great satisfaction to her subjects. But, in course of time, having had several children, and perceiving that Conn-eda was the favourite son of the king and the darling of the people, she clearly foresaw that he would become successor to the throne after the demise of his father, and that her son would certainly be excluded. This excited the hatred and inflamed the jealousy of the Druid's daughter against her stepson to such an extent, that she resolved in her own mind to leave nothing in her power undone to secure his death, or even exile from the kingdom. She began by circulating evil reports of the prince; but, as he was above suspicion the king only laughed at the weakness of the queen; and the great princes and chieftains, supported by the people in general, gave an unqualified contradiction; while the prince himself bore all his trials with the utmost patience, and always repaid her bad and malicious acts towards him with good and benevolent ones. The enmity of the queen towards Conn-eda knew no bounds when she saw that the false reports she circulated could not injure him. As a last resource, to carry out her wicked projects, she determined to consult her Cailleach-chearc (hen-wife), who was a reputed enchantress.

Pursuant to her resolution, by the early dawn of morning she hied to the cabin of the Cailleach-chearc, and divulged to her the cause of her trouble. "I cannot render you any help," said the Cailleach, "until you name the duais" (reward). "What duais do you require?" asked the queen, impatiently. "My duais," replied the enchantress, "is to fill the cavity of my arm with wool, and the hole I shall bore with my distaff with red wheat." "Your duais is granted, and shall be immediately given you," said the queen. The enchantress thereupon stood in the door of her hut, and bending her arm into a circle with her side, directed the royal attendants to thrust the wool into her house through her arm, and she never permitted them to cease until all the available space within was filled with wool. She then got on the roof of her brother's house, and, having made a hole through it with her distaff caused red wheat to be spilled through it, until that was filled up to the roof with red wheat, so that there was no room for another grain within. "Now," said the queen, "since you have received your duais, tell me how I can accomplish my purpose." "Take this chess-board and chess, and invite the prince to play with you; you shall win the first game. The condition you shall make is, that whoever wins a game shall be at liberty to impose whatever geasa (conditions) the winner pleases on the loser. When you win, you must bid the prince, under the penalty either to go into ionarbadh (exile), or procure for you, within the space of a year and a day, the three golden apples that grew in the garden, the each dubh (black steed), and coileen con na mbuadh (hound of supernatural powers), called Samer, which are in the possession of the king of the Firbolg race, who resides in Lough Erne*. Those two things are so precious, and so well guarded, that he can never attain them by his own power; and, if he would rashly attempt to seek them, he should lose his life."

The queen was greatly pleased at the advice, and lost no time in inviting Conn-eda to play a game at chess, under the conditions she had been instructed to arrange by the enchantress. The queen won the game, as the enchantress foretold, but so great was her anxiety to have the prince completely in her power, that she was tempted to challenge him to play a second game, which Conn-eda, to her astonishment, and no less mortification, easily won. "Now," said the prince, "since you won the first game, it is your duty to impose your geis first." "My geis," said the queen, "which I impose upon you, is to procure me the three golden apples that grow in the garden, the *each dubh* (black steed), and *cuileen con na mbuadh* (hound of supernatural powers),which are in the keeping of the king of the Firbolgs, in Lough Erne, within the space of a year and a day; or, in case you fail, to go into *ionarbadh* (exile), and never return, except you surrender yourself to lose your head and *comhead beatha*" (preservation of life). "Well, then," said the prince, "the *geis* which I bind you by, is to sit upon the pinnacle of yonder tower until my return, and to take neither food nor nourishment of any description, except what red-wheat you can pick up with the point of your bodkin; but if I do not return, you are at perfect liberty to come down at the expiration of the year and a day."

In consequence of the severe *geis* imposed upon him Conn-eda was very much troubled in mind; and, well knowing he had a long journey to make before he would reach his destination, immediately prepared to set out on his way, not, however, before he had the satisfaction of witnessing the ascent of the queen to the place where she was obliged to remain exposed to the scorching sun of the summer and the blasting storms of winter, for the space of one year and a day, at least. Conn-eda being ignorant of what steps he should take to procure the *each dubh* and *cuileen con na mbuadh*, though he was well aware that human energy would prove unavailing, thought proper to consult the great Druid, Fionn Dadhna, of Sleabh Badhna, who was a friend of his, before he ventured to proceed to Lough Erne. When he arrived at the bruighean of the Druid, he was received with cordial friendship, and the *failte* (welcome), as usual, was poured out before him, and when he was seated, warm water was fetched, and his feet bathed, so that the fatigue he felt after his journey was greatly relieved. The Druid, after he had partaken of refreshments, consisting of the newest of food and oldest of liquors, asked him the reason for paying the visit, and more particularly the cause of his sorrow; for the prince appeared exceedingly depressed in spirit. Conn-eda told his friend the whole history of the transaction with his stepmother from the beginning to end. "Can you not assist me?" asked the Prince, with downcast countenance. "I cannot, indeed, assist you at present," replied the Druid; "but I will retire to my *grianan* (green place) at sun-rising on the morrow, and learn by virtue of my Druidism what can be done to assist you." The Druid, accordingly, as the sun rose on the following morning, retired to his *grianan*, and consulted the god he adored, through the power

*The firbolgs believed their elysium to be under water. The peasantry still believe many lakes to be peopled.—See section on *Tír-na-n-Og*.

of his *draoidheacht*.* When he returned, he called Conn-eda aside on the plain, and addressed him thus: "My dear son, I find you have been under a severe—an almost impossible—*geis* intended for your destruction; no person on earth could have advised the queen to impose it except the Cailleach of Lough Corrib, who is the greatest Druidess now in Ireland, and sister to the Firbolg, King of Lough Erne. It is not in my power, nor in that of the Deity I adore, to interfere in your behalf; but go directly to Sliabh Mis, and consult *Eánchinn-duine* (the bird of the human head), and if there be any possibility of relieving you, that bird can do it, for there is not a bird in the western world so celebrated as that bird, because it knows all things that are past, all things that are present and exist, and all things that shall hereafter exist. It is difficult to find access to his place of concealment, and more difficult still to obtain an answer from him; but I will endeavour to regulate that matter for you; and that is all I can do for you at present."

The Arch-Druid then instructed him thus: "Take," said he, "yonder little shaggy steed, and mount him immediately, for in three days the bird will make himself visible, and the little shaggy steed will conduct you to his place of abode. But lest the bird should refuse to reply to your queries, take this precious stone (*leag lorgmhar*), and present it to him, and then little danger and doubt exist but that he will give you a ready answer." The prince returned heartfelt thanks to the Druid, and, having saddled and mounted the little shaggy horse without much delay, received the precious stone from the Druid, and, after having taken his leave of him, set out on his journey. He suffered the reins to fall loose upon the neck of the horse according as he had been instructed, so that the animal took whatever road he chose.

It would be tedious to relate the numerous adventures he had with the little shaggy horse, which had the extraordinary gift of speech, and was a *draoidheacht* horse during his journey.

The Prince having reached the hiding-place of the strange bird at the appointed time, and having presented him with the *leag lorgmhar*, according to Fionn Badhna's instructions, and proposed his questions relative to the manner he could best arrange for the fulfilment of his *geis*, the bird took up in his mouth the jewel from the stone on which it was placed, and flew to an inaccessible rock at some distance, and, when there perched, he thus addressed the prince, "Conn-eda, son of the King of Cruachan," said he, in a loud, croaking human voice, "remove the

Draoidheacht, i.e., the Druidic worship; magic, sorcery, divination.

stone just under your right foot, and take the ball of iron and *corna* (cup) you shall find under it; then mount your horse cast the ball before you, and having so done, your horse will tell you all the other things necessary to be done." The bird, having said this, immediately flew out of sight.

Conn-eda took great care to do everything according to the instructions of the bird. He found the iron ball and *corna* in the place which had been pointed out. He took them up, mounted his horse, and cast the ball before him. The ball, rolled on at a regular gait, while the little shaggy horse followed on the way it led until they reached the margin of Lough Erne. Here the ball rolled in the water and became invisible. "Alight now," said the *draoidheacht* pony, "and put your hand into mine ear; take from thence the small bottle of *íce* (all-heal) and the little wicker basket which you will find there, and remount with speed, for just now your great dangers and difficulties commence." Conn-eda, ever faithful to the kind advice of his *draoidheacht* pony, did what he had been advised. Having taken the basket and bottle of *íce* from the animal's ear, he remounted and proceeded on his journey, while the water of the lake appeared only like an atmosphere above his head. When he entered the lake the ball again appeared, and rolled along until it came to the margin, across which was a causeway, guarded by three frightful serpents; the hissings of the monsters were heard at a great distance, while, on a nearer approach, their yawning mouths and formidable fangs were quite sufficient to terrify the stoutest heart. "Now," said the horse, "open the basket and cast a piece of the meat you find in it into the mouth of each serpent; when you have done this, secure yourself in your seat in the best manner you can, so that we may make all due arrangements to pass those *draoidheacht peists*. If you cast the pieces of meat into the mouth of each *peist* unerringly, we shall pass them safely, otherwise we are lost." Conn-eda flung the pieces of meat into the jaws of the serpents with unerring aim. "Bare a benison and victory," said the *draoidheacht* steed, "for you are a youth that will win and prosper." And, on saying these words, he sprang aloft, and cleared in his leap the river and ford, guarded by the serpents, seven measures beyond the margin. "Are you still mounted, prince Conn-eda?" said the steed. "It has taken only half my exertion to remain so," replied Conn-eda. "I find," said the pony, "that you are a young prince that deserves to succeed; one danger is now over, but two others remain." They proceeded onwards after the ball until they came in view of a great mountain flaming with fire. "Hold yourself in readiness for another dangerous leap," said the horse. The trembling prince had no answer to make, but seated himself as securely as the magnitude of the danger before him would permit. The horse in the next instant sprang from the earth, and flew like an arrow over the burning mountain. "Are you still alive, Conn-eda, son of Conn-mór?" inquired the faithful horse. "I'm just alive, and no more, for I'm greatly scorched," answered the prince. "Since you are yet alive, I feel assured that you are a young man destined to meet supernatural success and benisons," said the Druidic steed. "Our greatest dangers are over," added he, "and there is hope that we shall overcome the next and last danger." After they had proceeded a short distance, his faithful steed, addressing Conn-eda, said, "Alight, now, and apply a portion of the little bottle of *íce* to your wounds." The prince immediately followed the advice of his monitor, and, as soon as he rubbed the *íce* (all-heal) to his wounds, he became as whole and fresh as ever he had been before. After having done this, Conn-eda remounted, and following the track of the ball, soon came in sight of a great city surrounded by high walls. The only gate that was visible was not defended by armed men, but by two great towers that emitted flames that could be seen at a great distance. "Alight on this plain," said the steed, "and take a small knife from my other ear; and with this knife you shall kill and flay me. When you have done this, envelop yourself in my hide, and you can pass the gate unscathed and unmolested. When you get inside you can come out at pleasure; because when once you enter there is no danger, and you can pass and repass whenever you wish; and let me tell you that all I have to ask of you in return is that you, when once inside the gates, will immediately return and drive away the birds of prey that may be fluttering round to feed on my carcass; and more, that you will pour any drop of that powerful *íce*, if such still remain in the bottle, upon my flesh, to preserve it from corruption. When you do this in memory of me, if it be not too troublesome, dig a pit, and cast my remains into it."

"Well," said Conn-eda, "my noblest steed, because you have been so faithful to me hitherto, and because you still would have rendered me further service, I consider such a proposal insulting to my feelings as a man, and totally in variance with the spirit which can feel the value of gratitude, not to speak of my feelings as a prince. But as a prince I am able to say, Come what may—come death itself in its most hideous forms and terrors—I never will sacrifice private friendship to personal interest. Hence, I am, I swear by my arms of valour, prepared to meet the worst—even death itself—sooner than violate the principles of humanity, honour, and friendship! What a sacrifice do you propose!" "Pshaw, man! heed not that; do what I advise you, and prosper." "Never! never!" exclaimed the prince. "Well, then, son of the great western monarch," said the horse, with a tone of sorrow, "if you do not follow my advice on this occasion, I tell you that both you and I shall perish, and shall never meet again; but, if you act as I have instructed you, matters shall assume a happier and more pleasing aspect than you may imagine. I have not misled you heretofore, and, if I have not, what need have you to doubt the most important portion of my counsel? Do exactly as I have directed you, else you will cause a worse fate than death to befall me. And, moreover, I can tell you that, if you persist in your resolution, I have done with you for ever."

When the prince found that his noble steed could not be persuaded from his purpose, he took the knife out of his ear with reluctance, and with a faltering and trembling hand essayed experimentally to point the weapon at his throat. Conn-eda's eyes were bathed in tears; but no sooner had he pointed the Druidic *scian* to the throat of his good steed than the dagger, as if impelled by some Druidic power, stuck in his neck, and in an instant the work of death was done, and the noble animal fell dead at his feet. When the prince saw his noble steed fall dead by his hand, he cast himself on the ground, and cried aloud until his consciousness was gone. When he recovered, he perceived that the steed was quite dead; and, as he thought there was no hope of resuscitating him, he considered it the most prudent course he could adopt to act according to the advice he had given him. After many misgivings of mind and abundant showers of tears, he essayed the task of flaying him, which was only that of a few minutes. When he found he had the hide separated from the body, he, in the derangement of the moment, enveloped himself in it, and proceeding towards the magnificent city in rather a demented state of mind, entered it without any molestation or opposition. It was a surprisingly populous city, and an extremely wealthy place; but its beauty, magnificence, and wealth had no charms for Conn-eda, because the thoughts of the loss he sustained in his dear steed were paramount to those of all other earthly considerations.

He scarcely proceeded more than fifty paces from the gate, when the last request of his beloved *draoidheacht* steed forced itself upon his mind, and compelled him to return to perform the last solemn injunctions upon him. When he came to the spot upon which the remains of his beloved *draoidheacht* steed lay, an appalling sight presented itself; ravens and other carnivorous birds of prey were tearing and devouring the flesh of his dear steed. It was but short work to put them to flight; and having uncorked his little jar of *íce*, he deemed it a labour of love to embalm

307

the now mangled remains with the precious ointment. The potent *íce* had scarcely touched the inanimate flesh, when, to the surprise of Conn-eda, it commenced to undergo some strange change, and in a few minutes, to his unspeakable astonishment and joy, it assumed the form of one of the handsomest and noblest young men imaginable, and in the twinkling of an eye the prince was locked in his embrace, smothering him with kisses, and drowning him with tears of joy. When one recovered from his ecstasy of joy, the other from his surprise, the strange youth thus addressed the prince: "Most noble and puissant prince, you are the best sight I ever saw with my eyes, and I am the most fortunate being in existence for having met you! Behold in my person, changed to the natural shape, your little shaggy *draoidheacht* steed! I am brother of the king of the city; and it was the wicked, Druid, Fionn Badhna, who kept me so long in bondage; but he was forced to give me up when you came to *consult* him, for my *geis* was then broken; yet I could not recover my pristine shape and appearance unless you had acted as you have kindly done. It was my own sister that urged the queen, your step-mother, to send you in quest of the steed and powerful puppy hound, which my brother has now in keeping. My sister, rest assured, had no thought of doing you the least injury, but much good, as you will find hereafter; because, if she were maliciously inclined towards you, she could have accomplished her end without any trouble. In short, she only wanted to free you from all future danger and disaster, and recover me from my relentless enemies through your instrumentality. Come with me, my friend and deliverer, and the steed and the puppy-hound of extraordinary powers, and the golden apples, shall be yours, and a cordial welcome shall greet you in my brother's abode; for you will deserve all this and much more."

The exciting joy felt on the occasion was mutual, and they lost no time in idle congratulations, but proceeded on to the royal residence of the King of Lough Erne. Here they were both received with demonstrations of joy by the king and his chieftains; and, when the purpose of Conn-eda's visit became known to the king, he gave a free consent to bestow on Conn-eda the black steed, the *coileen con-na-mbuadh*, called Samer, and the three apples of health that were growing in his garden, under the special condition, however, that he would consent to remain as his guest until he could set out on his journey in proper time to fulfil his *geis*. Conn-eda, at the earnest solicitation of his friends, consented, and remained in the royal residence of the Firbolg, King of Lough Erne, in the enjoyment of the most delicious and fascinating pleasures during that period.

When the time of his departure came, the three golden apples were plucked from the crystal tree in the midst of the pleasure-garden, and deposited in his bosom; the puppy-hound, Samer, was leashed, and the leash put into his hand; and the black steed, richly harnessed, was got in readiness for him to mount. The king himself helped him on horseback, and both he and his brother assured him that he might not fear burning mountains or hissing serpents, because none would impede him, as his steed was always a passport to and from his subaqueous kingdom. And both he and his brother extorted a promise from Conn-eda, that he would visit them once every year at least.

Conn-eda took leave of his dear friend, and the king his brother. The parting was a tender one, soured by regret on both sides. He proceeded on his way without meeting anything to obstruct him, and in due time came in sight of the *dún* of his father, where the queen had been placed on the pinnacle of the tower, in full hope that, as it was the last day of her imprisonment there, the prince would not make his appearance, and thereby forfeit all pretensions and right to the crown of his father for ever. But her hopes were doomed to meet a disappointment, for when it had been announced to her by her couriers, who had been posted to watch the arrival of the prince, that he approached, she was incredulous; but when she saw him mounted on a foaming black steed, richly harnessed, and leading a strange kind of animal by a silver chain, she at once knew he was returning in triumph, and that her schemes laid for his destruction were frustrated. In the excess of grief at her disappointment, she cast herself from the top of the tower, and was instantly dashed to pieces. Conn-eda met a welcome reception from his father, who mourned him as lost to him for ever, during his absence; and, when the base conduct of the queen became known, the king and his chieftains ordered her remains to be consumed to ashes for her perfidy and wickedness.

Conn-eda planted the three golden apples in his garden, and instantly a great tree, bearing similar fruit, sprang up. This tree caused all the district to produce an exuberance of crops and fruits, so that it became as fertile and plentiful as the dominions of the Firbolgs, in consequence of the extraordinary powers possessed by the golden fruit. The hound Samer and the steed were of the utmost utility to him; and his reign was long and prosperous, and celebrated among the old people for the great abundance of corn, fruit, milk, fowl, and fish that prevailed during this happy reign. It was after the name Conn-eda the province of Connaucht, or *Conneda*, or *Connacht*, was so called.

Irish Fairy Tales

WHERE MY BOOKS GO

All the words that I gather,
  And all the words that I write,
Must spread out their wings untiring,
  And never rest in their flight,
Till they come where your sad, sad heart is,
  And sing to you in the night,
Beyond where the waters are moving,
  Storm darkened or starry bright.

W. B. Yeats

LONDON, January 1892

NOTE

I have to thank Lady Wilde for leave to give "Seanchan the Bard" from her *Ancient Legends of Ireland* (Ward and Downey), the most poetical and ample collection of Irish folk-lore yet published; Mr Standish O'Grady for leave to give "The Knighting of Cuculain" from that prose epic he has curiously named *History of Ireland, Heroic Period*; Professor Joyce for his "Fergus O'Mara and the Air Demons"; and Mr Douglas Hyde for his unpublished story, "The Man who never knew Fear".

I have included no story that has already appeared in my *Fairy and Folk Tales of the Irish Peasantry* (Camelot Series).

The two volumes make, I believe, a fairly representative collection of Irish folk tales.

INTRODUCTION

An Irish Story-Teller

I am often doubted when I say that the Irish peasantry still believe in fairies. People think I am merely trying to bring back a little of the old dead beautiful world of romance into this century of great engines and spinning-jinnies. Surely the hum of wheels and clatter of printing presses, to let alone the lecturers with their black coats and tumblers of water, have driven away the goblin kingdom and made silent the feet of the little dancers.

Old Biddy Hart at any rate does not think so. Our bran-new opinions have never been heard of under her brown-thatched roof tufted with yellow stone-crop. It is not so long since I sat by the turf fire eating her griddle cake in her cottage on the slope of Benbulben and asking after her friends, the fairies, who inhabit the green thorn-covered hill up there behind her house. How firmly she believed in them! how greatly she feared offending them! For a long time she would give me no answer but "I always mind my own affairs and they always mind theirs". A little talk about my great-grandfather who lived all his life in the valley below, and a few words to remind her how I myself was often under her roof when but seven or eight years old loosened her tongue, however. It would be less dangerous at any rate to talk to me of the fairies than it would be to tell some "Towrow" of them, as she contemptuously called English tourists, for I had lived under the shadow of their own hillsides. She did not forget, however, to remind me to say after we had finished, "God bless them, Thursday" (that being the day), and so ward off their displeasure, in case they were angry at our notice, for they love to live and dance unknown of men.

Once started, she talked on freely enough, her face glowing in the firelight as she bent over the griddle or stirred the turf, and told how such a one was stolen away from near Coloney village and made to live seven years among "the gentry", as she calls the fairies for politeness' sake, and how when she came home she had no toes, for she had danced them off; and how such another was taken from the neighbouring village of Grange and compelled to nurse the child of the queen of the fairies a few months before I came. Her news about the creatures is always quite matter-of-fact and detailed, just as if she dealt with any common occurrence: the late fair, or the dance at Rosses last year, when a bottle of whiskey was given to the best man, and a cake tied up in ribbons to the best woman dancer. They are, to her, people not so different from herself, only grander and finer in every way. They have the most beautiful parlours and drawing-rooms, she would tell you, as an old man told me once. She has endowed them with all she knows of splendour, although that is not such a great deal, for her imagination is easily pleased. What does not seem to us so very wonderful is wonderful to her, there, where all is so homely under her wood rafters and her thatched ceiling covered with whitewashed canvas. We have pictures and books to help us imagine a splendid fairy world of gold and silver, of crowns and marvellous draperies; but she has only that little picture of St Patrick over the fireplace, the bright-coloured crockery on the dresser, and the sheet of ballads stuffed by her young daughter behind the stone dog on the mantelpiece. Is it strange, then, if her fairies have not the fantastic glories of the fairies you and I are wont to see in picture-books and read of in stories? She will tell you of peasants who met the fairy cavalcade and thought it but a troop of peasants like themselves until it vanished into shadow and night, and of great fairy palaces that were mistaken, until they melted away, for the country seats of rich gentlemen.

Her views of heaven itself have the same homeliness, and she would be quite as naïve about its personages if the chance offered as was the pious Clondalkin laundress who told a friend of mine that she had seen a vision of St Joseph, and that he had "a lovely shining hat upon him and a shirt-buzzom that was never starched in this world". She would have mixed some quaint poetry with it, however; for there is a world of difference between Benbulben and Dublinised Clondalkin.

Heaven and Fairyland—to these has Biddy Hart given all she dreams of magnificence, and to them her soul goes out—to the one in love and hope, to the other in love and fear—day after day and season after season; saints and angels, fairies and witches, haunted thorn-trees and holy wells, are to her what books, and plays, and pictures are to you and me. Indeed they are far more; for too many among us grow prosaic and commonplace, but she keeps ever a heart full of music. "I stand here in the doorway," she said once to me on a fine day, "and look at the mountain and think of the goodness of God"; and when she talks of the fairies I have noticed a touch of tenderness in her voice. She loves them because they are always young, always making festival, always far off from the old age that is coming upon her and filling her bones with aches, and because, too, they are so like little children.

Do you think the Irish peasant would be so full of poetry if he had not his fairies? Do you think the peasant girls of Donegal; when they are going to service inland, would kneel down as they do and kiss the sea with their lips if both sea and land were not made lovable to them by beautiful legends and wild sad stories? Do you think the old men would take life so cheerily and mutter their proverb, "The lake is not burdened by its swan, the steed by its bridle, or a man by the soul that is in him," if the multitude of spirits were not near them?

W. B. YEATS

CLONDALKIN, *July 1891*

LAND AND WATER FAIRIES

The Fairies' Dancing-place

WILLIAM CARLETON

Lanty M'Clusky had married a wife, and, of course, it was necessary to have a house in which to keep her. Now, Lanty had taken a bit of a farm, about six acres; but as there was no house on it, he resolved to build one; and that it might be as comfortable as possible, he selected for the site of it one of those beautiful green circles that are supposed to be the play-ground of the fairies. Lanty was warned against this; but as he was a headstrong man, and not much given to fear, he said he would not change such a pleasant situation for his house to oblige all the fairies in Europe. He accordingly proceeded with the building, which he finished off very neatly; and, as it is usual on these occasions to give one's neighbours and friends a house-warming, so, in compliance with this good and pleasant old custom, Lanty having brought home the wife in the course of the day, got a fiddler and a lot of whiskey, and gave those who had come to see him a dance in the evening. This was all very well, and the fun and hilarity were proceeding briskly, when a noise was heard after night had set in, like a crushing and straining of ribs and rafters on the top of the house. The folks assembled all listened, and, without doubt, there was nothing heard but crushing, and heaving, and pushing, and groaning, and panting, as if a thousand little men were engaged in pulling down the roof.

"Come," said a voice which spoke in a tone of command, "work hard: you know we must have Lanty's house down before midnight."

This was an unwelcome piece of intelligence to Lanty, who, finding that his enemies were such as he could not cope with, walked out, and addressed them as follows:

"Gintlemen, I humbly ax yer pardon for buildin' on any place belongin' to you; but if you'll have the civilitude to let me alone this night, I'll begin to pull down and remove the house tomorrow morning."

This was followed by a noise like the clapping of a thousand tiny little hands,

319

and a shout of "Bravo, Lanty! build half-way between the two White-thorns above the boreen"; and after another hearty little shout of exultation, there was a brisk rushing noise, and they were heard no more.

The story, however, does not end here; for Lanty, when digging the foundation of his new house, found the full of a *kam** of gold: so that in leaving to the fairies their play-ground, he became a richer man than ever he otherwise would have been, had he never come in contact with them at all.

*Kam—a metal vessel in which peasantry dip rushlights.

The Rival Kempers

WILLIAM CARLETON

In the north of Ireland there are spinning meetings of unmarried females frequently held at the houses of farmers, called *kemps*. Every young woman who has got the reputation of being a quick and expert spinner attends where the kemp is to be held, at an hour usually before daylight, and on these occasions she is accompanied by her sweetheart or some male relative, who carries her wheel, and conducts her safely across the fields or along the road, as the case may be. A kemp, is, indeed, an animated and joyous scene, and one, besides, which is calculated to promote industry and decent pride. Scarcely anything can be more cheering and agreeable than to hear at a distance, breaking the silence of morning, the light-hearted voices of many girls either in mirth or song, the humming sound of the busy wheels—jarred upon a little, it is true, by the stridulous noise and checkings of the reels, and the voices of the reelers, as they call aloud the checks, together with the name of the girl and the quantity she has spun up to that period; for the contest is generally commenced two or three hours before daybreak. This mirthful spirit is also sustained by the prospect of a dance—with which, by the way, every kemp closes; and when the fair victor is declared, she is to be looked upon as the queen of the meeting, and treated with the necessary respect.

But to our tale. Every one knew Shaun Buie M'Gaveran to be the cleanest, best-conducted boy, and the most industrious too, in the whole parish of Faugh-a-ballagh. Hard was it to find a young fellow who could handle a flail, spade, or reaping-hook in better style, or who could go through his day's work in a more creditable or workmanlike manner. In addition to this, he was a fine, well-built, handsome young man as you could meet in a fair; and so, sign was on it, maybe the pretty girls weren't likely to pull each other's caps about him. Shaun, however, was as prudent as he was good-looking; and although he wanted a wife, yet the sorrow one of him but preferred taking a well-handed, smart girl, who was known to be

321

well-behaved and industrious, like himself. Here, however, was where the puzzle lay on him; for instead of one girl of that kind, there were in the neighbourhood no less than a dozen of them—all equally fit and willing to become his wife, and all equally good-looking. There were two, however, whom he thought a trifle above the rest; but so nicely balanced were Biddy Corrigan and Sally Gorman, that for the life of him he could not make up his mind to decide between them. Each of them had won her kemp; and it was currently said by them who ought to know, that neither of them could overmatch the other. No two girls in the parish were better respected, or deserved to be so; and the consequence was, they had every one's good word and good wish. Now it so happened that Shaun had been pulling a cord with each; and as he knew not how to decide between, he thought he would allow them to do that themselves if they could. He accordingly gave out to the neighbours that he would hold a kemp on that day week, and he told Biddy and Sally especially that he had made up his mind to marry whichever of them won the kemp, for he knew right well, as did all the parish, that one of them must. The girls agreed to this very good-humouredly, Biddy telling Sally that she (Sally) would surely win it; and Sally not to be outdone in civility, telling the same thing to her.

Well, the week was nearly past, there being but two days till that of the kemp, when, about three o'clock, there walks into the house of old Paddy Corrigan a little woman dressed in high-heeled shoes and a short red cloak. There was no one in the house but Biddy at the time, who rose up and placed a chair near the fire, and asked the little red woman to sit down and rest herself. She accordingly did so, and in a short time a lively chat commenced between them.

"So," said the strange woman, "there's to be a great kemp in Shaun Buie M'Gaveran's?"

"Indeed there is that, good woman," replied Biddy, smiling and blushing to back of that again, because she knew her own fate depended on it.

"And," continued the little woman, "whoever wins the kemp wins a husband?"

"Ay, so it seems."

"Well, whoever gets Shaun will be a happy woman, for he's the moral of a good boy."

"That's nothing but the truth, anyhow," replied Biddy, sighing, for fear, you may be sure, that she herself might lose him; and indeed a young woman might sigh from many a worse reason. "But," said she, changing the subject, "you appear to be tired, honest woman, an' I think you had better eat a bit, an' take a good drink of *buinnhe ramwher* (thick milk) to help you on your journey."

"Thank you kindly, a colleen," said the woman; "I'll take a bit, of you plase, hopin', at the same time, that you won't be the poorer of it this day twelve months."

"Sure," said the girl, "you know that what we give from kindness ever an' always leaves a blessing behind it."

"Yes, acushla, when it *is* given from kindness."

She accordingly helped herself to the food that Biddy placed before her, and appeared, after eating, to be very much refreshed.

"Now," said she, rising up, "you're a very good girl, an' if you are able to find out my name before Tuesday morning, the kemp-day, I tell you that you'll win it, and gain the husband."

"Why," said Biddy, "I never saw you before. I don't know who you are, nor where you live; how then can I ever find out your name?"

"You never saw me before, sure enough," said the old woman, "an' I tell you that you never will see me again but once; an' yet if you have not my name for me at the close of the kemp, you'll lose all, an' that will leave you a sore heart, for well I know you love Shaun Buie."

So saying, she went away, and left poor Biddy quite cast down at what she had said, for, to tell the truth, she loved Shaun very much, and had no hopes of being able to find out the name of the little woman, on which, it appeared, so much to her depended.

It was very near the same hour of the same day that Sally Gorman was sitting alone in her father's house, thinking of the kemp, when who should walk in to her but our friend the little red woman.

"God save you, honest woman," said Sally, "this is a fine day that's in it, the Lord be praised!"

"It is," said the woman, "as fine a day as one could wish for: indeed it is."

"Have you no news on your travels?" asked Sally.

"The only news in the neighbourhood," replied the other, "is this great kemp that's to take place at Shaun Buie M'Gaveran's. They say you're either to win him or lose him then," she added, looking closely at Sally as she spoke.

"I'm not very much afraid of that," said Sally, with confidence; "but even if I do lose him, I may get as good."

"It's not easy gettin' as good," rejoined the old woman, "an' you ought to be very glad to win him, if you can."

"Let me alone for that," said Sally. "Biddy's a good girl, I allow; but as for spinnin', she never saw the day she could leave me behind her. Won't you sit an' rest you?" she added; "maybe you're tired."

"It's time for you to think of it," *thought* the woman, but she spoke nothing: "but," she added to herself on reflection, "it's better late than never—I'll sit awhile, till I see a little closer what she's made of."

She accordingly sat down and chatted upon several subjects, such as young women like to talk about, for about half an hour; after which she arose, and taking her little staff in hand, she bade Sally good-bye, and went her way. After passing a little from the house she looked back, and could not help speaking to herself as follows:

> "She's smooth and smart,
> But she wants the heart;
> She's tight and neat,
> But she gave no meat."

Poor Biddy now made all possible inquiries about the old woman, but to no purpose. Not a soul she spoke to about her had ever seen or heard of such a woman. She felt very dispirited, and began to lose heart, for there is no doubt that if she missed Shaun it would have cost her many a sorrowful day. She knew she would never get his equal, or at least any one that she loved so well. At last the kemp day came, and with it all the pretty girls of the neighbourhood to Shaun Buie's. Among the rest, the two that were to decide their right to him were doubtless the handsomest pair by far, and every one admired them. To be sure, it was a blythe and merry place, and many a light laugh and sweet song rang out from pretty lips that day. Biddy and Sally, as every one expected, were far ahead of the rest, but so even in their spinning that the reelers could not for the life of them declare which was the better. It was neck-and-neck and head-and-head between the pretty creatures, and all who were at the kemp felt themselves wound up to the highest pitch of interest and curiosity to know which of them would be successful.

The day was now more than half gone, and no difference was between them, when, to the surprise and sorrow of every one present, Biddy Corrigan's *heck* broke in two, and so to all appearance ended the contest in favour of her rival; and what added to her mortification, she was ignorant of the little red woman's name as ever. What was to be done? All that could be done was done. Her brother, a boy of about fourteen years of age, happened to be present when the accident took place, having been sent by his father and mother to bring them word how the match went on between the rival spinsters. Johnny Corrigan was accordingly despatched with all speed to Donnel M'Cusker's, the wheelwright, in order to get the heck mended, that being Biddy's last but hopeless chance. Johnny's anxiety that his sister should win was of course very great, and in order to lose as little time as possible he struck across the country, passing through, or rather close by, Kilrudden forth, a place celebrated as a resort of the fairies. What was his astonishment, however, as he passed a white-thorn tree, to hear a female voice singing, in accompaniment to the sound of a spinning-wheel, the following words:

> "There's a girl in this town doesn't know my name;
> But my name's Even Trot—Even Trot."

"There's a girl in this town," said the lad, "who's in great distress, for she has broken her heck, and lost a husband. I'm now goin' to Donnel M'Cusker's to get it mended."

"What's her name?" said the little red woman.

"Biddy Corrigan."

The little woman immediately whipped out the heck from her own wheel, and giving it to the boy, desired him to take it to his sister, and never mind Donnel M'Cusker.

"You have little time to lose," she added, "so go back and give her this; but don't tell her how you got it, nor, above all things, that it was Even Trot that gave it to you."

The lad returned, and after giving the heck to his sister, as a matter of course told her that it was a little red woman called Even Trot that sent it to her, a circumstance which made tears of delight start to Biddy's eyes, for she knew now that Even Trot was the name of the old woman, and having known that she felt that something good would happen to her. She now resumed her spinning, and never did human fingers let down the thread so rapidly. The whole kemp were amazed at the quantity which from time to time filled her pirn. The hearts of her friends began to rise, and those of Sally's party to sink, as hour after hour she was fast approaching her rival, who now spun if possible with double speed on finding Biddy coming up with her. At length they were again even, and just at that moment in came her friend the little red woman, and asked aloud, "Is there any one in this kemp that knows my name?" This question she asked three times before Biddy could pluck up courage to answer her. She at last said,

> " There's a girl in this town does know your name—
> Your name is Even Trot—Even Trot."

"Aye," said the old woman, "and so it is; and let that name be your guide and your husband's through life. Go steadily along, but let your step be even; stop little; keep always advancing; and you'll never have cause to rue the day that you first saw Even Trot."

We need scarcely add that Biddy won the kemp and the husband, and that she and Shaun lived long and happily together; and I have only now to wish, kind reader, that you and I may live longer and more happily still.

The Young Piper

CROFTON CROKER

There lived not long since, on the borders of the county Tipperary, a decent honest couple, whose names were Mick Flannigan and Judy Muldoon. These poor people were blessed, as the saying is, with four children, all boys: three of them were as fine, stout, healthy, good-looking children as ever the sun shone upon; and it was enough to make any Irishman proud of the breed of his countrymen to see them about one o'clock on a fine summer's day standing at their father's cabin door, with their beautiful flaxen hair hanging in curls about their head, and their cheeks like two rosy apples, and a big laughing potato smoking in their hand. A proud man was Mick of these fine children, and a proud woman, too, was Judy; and reason enough they had to be so. But it was far otherwise with the remaining one, which was third eldest: he was the most miserable, ugly, ill-conditioned brat that ever God put life into; he was so ill-thriven that he never was able to stand alone, or to leave his cradle; he had long, shaggy, matted, curled hair, as black as the soot; his face was of a greenish-yellow colour; his eyes were like two burning coals, and were for ever moving in his head, as if they had the perpetual motion. Before he was a twelvemonth old he had a mouth full of great teeth; his hands were like kites' claws, and his legs were no thicker than the handle of a whip, and about as straight as a reaping-hook: to make the matter worse, he had the appetite of a cormorant, and the whinge, and the yelp, and the screech, and the yowl, was never out of his mouth.

The neighbours all suspected that he was something not right, particularly as it was observed, when people, as they do in the country, got about the fire, and began to talk of religion and good things, the brat, as he lay in the cradle, which his mother generally put near the fireplace that he might be snug, used to sit up, as they were in the middle of their talk, and begin to bellow as if the devil was in him in right earnest; this, as I said, led the neighbours to think that all was not right, and there was a general consultation held one day about what would be best to do with him. Some advised to put him out on the shovel, but Judy's pride was up at that. A pretty thing indeed, that a child of hers should be put on a shovel and flung out on the dunghill just like a dead kitten or a poisoned rat; no, no, she would not hear to that at all. One old woman, who was considered very skilful and knowing in fairy matters, strongly recommended her to put the tongs in the fire, and heat them red hot, and to take his nose in them, and that would beyond all manner of doubt make him tell what he was and where he came from (for the general suspicion was, that he had been changed by the good people); but Judy was too soft-hearted, and too fond of the imp, so she would not give in to this plan, though everybody said she was wrong, and maybe she was, but it's hard to blame a mother. Well, some advised one thing, and some another; at last one spoke of sending for the priest who was a very holy and a very learned man, to see it. To this Judy of course had no objection; but one thing or other always prevented her doing so, and the upshot of the business was that the priest never saw him.

Things went on in the old way for some time longer. The brat continued yelping and yowling, and eating more than his three brothers put together, and playing all sorts of unlucky tricks, for he was mighty mischievously inclined, till it happened one day that Tim Carrol, the blind piper, going his rounds, called in and sat down by the fire to have a bit of chat with the woman of the house. So after some time Tim, who was no churl of his music, yoked on the pipes, and began to bellows away in high style; when the instant he began, the young fellow, who had been lying as still as a mouse in his cradle, sat up, began to grin and twist his ugly face, to swing about his long tawny arms, and to kick out his crooked legs, and to show signs of great glee at the music. At last nothing would serve him but he should get the pipes into his own hands, and to humour him his mother asked Tim to lend them to the child for a minute. Tim, who was kind to children, readily consented; and as Tim had not his sight, Judy herself brought them to the cradle, and went to put them on him; but she had no occasion, for the youth seemed quite up to the business. He buckled on the pipes, set the bellows under one arm, and the bag under the other, worked them both as knowingly as if he had been twenty years at the business, and lilted up "Sheela na guira" in the finest style imaginable.

All were in astonishment: the poor woman crossed herself. Tim, who, as I said before, was *dark*, and did not well know who was playing, was in great delight; and when he heard that it was a little prechan not five years old, that had never seen a set of pipes in his life, he wished the mother joy of her son; offered to take him off her hands if she would part with him, swore he was a born piper, a natural genus, and declared that in a little time more, with the help of a little good instruction from himself, there would not be his match in the whole country. The poor woman was greatly delighted to hear all this, particularly as what Tim said about natural genus quieted some misgivings that were rising in her mind, lest what the neighbours said about his not being right might be too true; and it gratified her moreover to think that her dear child (for she really loved the whelp) would not be forced to turn out and beg, but might earn decent bread for himself. So when Mick came home in the evening from his work, she up and told him all that had happened, and all that Tim Carrol had said; and Mick, as was natural, was very glad to hear it, for the helpless condition of the poor creature was a great trouble to him. So next day he took the pig to the fair, and with what it brought set off to Clonmel, and bespoke a bran-new set of pipes, of the proper size for him.

In about a fortnight the pipes came home, and the moment the chap in his cradle laid eyes on them he squealed with delight and threw up his pretty legs, and bumped himself in his cradle, and went on with a great many comical tricks; till at last, to quiet him, they gave him the pipes, and he immediately set to and pulled away at "Jig Polthog", to the admiration of all who heard him.

The fame of his skill on the pipes soon spread far and near, for there was not a piper in the six next counties could come at all near him, in "Old Moderagh Rue", or "The Hare in the Corn", or "The Fox-hunter's Jig", or "The Rakes of Cashel", or "The Piper's Maggot", or any of the fine Irish jigs which make people dance whether they will or no: and it was surprising to hear him rattle away "The Foxhunter"; you'd really think you heard the hounds giving tongue, and the terriers yelping behind, and the huntsman and the whippers-in cheering or correcting the dogs; it was, in short, the very next thing to seeing the hunt itself.

The best of him was, he was noways stingy of his music, and many a merry dance the boys and girls of the neighbourhood used to have in his father's cabin; and he would play up music for them, that they said used as it were to put quicksilver in their feet; and they all declared they never moved so light and so airy to any piper's playing that ever they danced to.

But besides all this fine Irish music, he had one queer tune of his own, the oddest that ever was heard; for the moment he began to play it everything in the house

329

seemed disposed to dance; the plates and porringers used to jingle on the dresser, the pots and pot-hooks used to rattle in the chimney, and people used to fancy they felt the stools moving from under them; but, however it might be with the stools, it is certain that no one could keep long sitting on them, for both old and young always fell to capering as hard as ever they could. The girls complained that when he began this tune it always threw them out in their dancing, and that they never could handle their feet rightly, for they felt the floor like ice under them, and themselves every moment ready to come sprawling on their backs or their faces. The young bachelors who wished to show off their dancing and their new pumps, and their bright red or green and yellow garters, swore that it confused them so that they never could go rightly through the *heel and toe* or *cover the buckle*, or any of their best steps, but felt themselves always all bedizzied and bewildered, and then old and young would go jostling and knocking together in a frightful manner; and when the unlucky brat had them all in this way, whirligigging about the floor, he'd grin and chuckle and chatter, for all the world like Jacko the monkey when he has played off some of his roguery.

The older he grew the worse he grew, and by the time he was six years old there was no standing the house for him; he was always making his brothers burn or scald themselves, or break their shins over the pots and stools. One time, in harvest, he was left at home by himself, and when his mother came in she found the cat a-horseback on the dog, with her face to the tail, and her legs tied round him, and the urchin playing his queer tune to them; so that the dog went barking and jumping about, and puss was mewing for the dear life, and slapping her tail backwards and forwards, which, as it would hit against the dog's chaps, he'd snap and bite, and then there was the philliloo. Another time, the farmer with whom Mick worked, a very decent, respectable man, happened to call in, and Judy wiped a stool with her apron, and invited him to sit down and rest himself after his walk. He was sitting with his back to the cradle, and behind him was a pan of blood, for Judy was making pig's puddings. The lad lay quite still in his nest, and watched his opportunity till he got ready a hook at the end of a piece of twine, which he contrived to fling so handily that it caught in the bob of the man's nice new wig, and soused it in the pan of blood. Another time his mother was coming in from milking the cow, with the pail on her head: the minute he saw her he lilted up his infernal tune, and the poor woman, letting go the pail, clapped her hands aside, and began to dance a jig, and tumbled the milk all a-top of her husband, who was bringing in some turf to boil the supper. In short, there would be no end to telling all his pranks, and all the mischievous tricks he played.

Soon after, some mischances began to happen to the farmer's cattle. A horse took the staggers, a fine veal calf died of the black-leg, and some of his sheep of the red-water; the cows began to grow vicious, and to kick down the milk-pails, and the roof of one end of the barn fell in; and the farmer took it into his head that Mick Flannigan's unlucky child was the cause of all the mischief. So one day he called Mick aside, and said to him, "Mick, you see things are not going on with me as they ought, and to be plain with you, Mick, I think that child of yours is the cause of it. I am really falling away to nothing with fretting, and I can hardly sleep on my bed at night for thinking of what may happen before the morning. So I'd be glad if you'd look out for work somewhere else; you're as good a man as any in the country, and there's no fear but you'll have your choice of work." To this Mick replied, "that he was sorry for his losses, and still sorrier that he or his should be thought to be the cause of them; that for his own part he was not quite easy in his mind about that child, but he had him and so must keep him"; and he promised to look out for another place immediately.

Accordingly, next Sunday at chapel Mick gave out that he was about leaving the work at John Riordan's, and immediately a farmer who lived a couple of miles off, and who wanted a ploughman (the last one having just left him), came up to Mick, and offered him a house and garden, and work all the year round. Mick, who knew him to be a good employer, immediately closed with him; so it was agreed that the farmer should send a car* to take his little bit of furniture, and that he should remove on the following Thursday.

When Thursday came, the car came according to promise, and Mick loaded it, and put the cradle with the child and his pipes on the top, and Judy sat beside it to take care of him, lest he should tumble out and be killed. They drove the cow before them, the dog followed, but the cat was of course left behind; and the other three children went along the road picking skeehories (haws) and blackberries, for it was a fine day towards the latter end of harvest.

They had to cross a river, but as it ran through a bottom between two high banks, you did not see it till you were close on it. The young fellow was lying pretty quiet in the bottom of the cradle, till they came to the head of the bridge, when hearing the roaring of the water (for there was a great flood in the river, as it had

*Car, a cart.

331

rained heavily for the last two or three days), he sat up in his cradle and looked about him; and the instant he got a sight of the water, and found they were going to take him across it, oh, how he did bellow and how he did squeal! no rat caught in a snap-trap ever sang out equal to him. "Whist! A lanna," said Judy, "there's no fear of you; sure it's only over the stone bridge we're going."—"Bad luck to you, you old rip!" cried he, "what a pretty trick you've played me to bring me here?" and still went on yelling, and the farther they got on the bridge the louder he yelled; till at last Mick could hold out no longer, so giving him a great skelp of the whip he had in his hand, "Devil choke you, you brat?" said he, "will you never stop bawling? a body can't hear their ears for you." The moment he felt the thong of the whip he leaped up in the cradle, clapped the pipes under his arm, gave a most wicked grin at Mick, and jumped clean over the battlements of the bridge down into the water. "Oh, my child, my child!" shouted Judy, "he's gone for ever from me." Mick and the rest of the children ran to the other side of the bridge, and looking over, they saw him coming out from under the arch of the bridge, sitting cross-legged on the top of a white-headed wave, and playing away on the pipes as merrily as if nothing had happened. The river was running very rapidly, so he was whirled away at a great rate; but he played as fast, ay, and faster, than the river ran; and though they set off as hard as they could along the bank, yet, as the river made a sudden turn round the hill, about a hundred yards below the bridge, by the time they got there he was out of sight, and no one ever laid eyes on him more; but the general opinion was that he went home with the pipes to his own relations, the good people, to make music for them.

A Fairy Enchantment

STORY-TELLER: MICHAEL HART
RECORDER: W. B. YEATS

In the times when we used to travel by canal I was coming down from Dublin. When we came to Mullingar the canal ended, and I began to walk, and stiff and fatigued I was after the slowness. I had some friends with me, and now and then we walked, now and then we rode in a cart. So on till we saw some girls milking a cow, and stopped to joke with them. After a while we asked them for a drink of milk. "We have nothing to put it in here," they said, "but come to the house with us." We went home with them and sat round the fire talking. After a while the others went, and left me loath to stir from the good fire. I asked the girls for something to eat. There was a pot on the fire and they took the meat out and put it on a plate and told me to eat only the meat that came from the head. When I had eaten, the girls went out and I did not see them again.

It grew darker and darker, and there I still sat, loath as ever to leave the good fire; and after a while two men came in, carrying between them a corpse. When I saw them I hid behind the door. Says one to the other, "Who'll turn the spit?" Says the other, "Michael Hart, come out of that and turn the meat!" I came out in a tremble and began turning the spit. "Michael Hart," says the one who spoke first, "if you let it burn we will have to put you on the spit instead," and on that they went out. I sat there trembling and turning the corpse until midnight. The men came again, and the one said it was burnt, and the other said it was done right, but having fallen out over it, they both said they would do me no harm that time; and sitting by the fire one of them cried out, "Michael Hart, can you tell a story?" "Never a one," said I. On that he caught me by the shoulders and put me out like a shot.

It was a wild, blowing night; never in all my born days did I see such a night—the darkest night that ever came out of the heavens. I did not know where I was for the life of me. So when one of the men came after me and touched me

333

on the shoulder with a "Michael Hart, can you tell a story now?"—"I can," says I. In he brought me, and, putting me by the fire, says "Begin." "I have no story but the one," says I, "that I was sitting here, and that you two men brought in a corpse and put it on the spit and set me turning it." "That will do," says he; "you may go in there and lie down on the bed." And in I went, nothing loath, and in the morning where was I but in the middle of a green field.

Teigue of the Lee

CROFTON CROKER

"I can't stop in the house—I won't stop in it for all the money that is buried in the old castle of Carrigrohan. If ever there was such a thing in the world!—to be abused to my face night and day, and nobody to the fore doing it! and then, if I'm angry, to be laughed at with a great roaring ho, ho, ho! I won't stay in the house after tonight, if there was not another place in the country to put my head under." This angry soliloquy was pronounced in the hall of the old manor-house of Carrigrohan by John Sheehan. John was a new servant; he had been only three days in the house, which had the character of being haunted, and in that short space of time he had been abused and laughed at by a voice which sounded as if a man spoke with his head in a cask; nor could he discover who was the speaker, or from whence the voice came. "I'll not stop here," said John; "and that ends the matter."

"Ho, ho, ho! be quiet, John Sheehan, or else worse will happen to you."

John instantly ran to the hall window, as the words were evidently spoken by a person immediately outside, but no one was visible. He had scarcely placed his face at the pane of glass when he heard another loud "Ho, ho, ho!" as if behind him in the hall; as quick as lightning he turned his head, but no living thing was to be seen.

"Ho, ho, ho, John!" shouted a voice that appeared to come from the lawn before the house: "do you think you'll see Teigue?—oh, never! as long as you live! so leave alone looking after him, and mind your business; there's plenty of company to dinner from Cork to be here today, and 'tis time you had the cloth laid."

"Lord bless us! there's more of it!—I'll never stay another day here," repeated John.

"Hold your tongue, and stay where you are quietly, and play no tricks on Mr Pratt, as you did on Mr Jervois about the spoons."

John Sheehan was confounded by this address from his invisible persecutor, but

335

nevertheless he mustered courage enough to say, "Who are you? come here, and let me see you, if you are a man"; but he received in reply only a laugh of unearthly derision, which was followed by a "Good-bye—I'll watch you at dinner, John!"

"Lord between us and harm! this beats all! I'll watch you at dinner! maybe you will! 'tis the broad daylight, so 'tis no ghost; but this is a terrible place, and this is the last day I'll stay in it. How does he know about the spoons? if he tells it I'm a ruined man! there was no living soul could tell it to him but Tim Barrett, and he's far enough off in the wilds of Botany Bay now, so how could he know it? I can't tell for the world! But what's that I see there at the corner of the wall! 'tis not a man! oh, what a fool I am! 'tis only the old stump of a tree! But this is a shocking place—I'll never stop in it, for I'll leave the house tomorrow; the very look of it is enough to frighten any one."

The mansion had certainly an air of desolation; it was situated in a lawn, which had nothing to break its uniform level save a few tufts of narcisses and a couple of old trees coeval with the building. The house stood at a short distance from the road, it was upwards of a century old, and Time was doing his work upon it; its walls were weather-stained in all colours, its roof showed various white patches, it had no look of comfort; all was dim and dingy without, and within there was an air of gloom, of departed and departing greatness, which harmonised well with the exterior. It required all the exuberance of youth and of gaiety to remove the impression, almost amounting to awe, with which you trod the huge square hall, paced along the gallery which surrounded the hall, or explored the long rambling passages below stairs. The ballroom, as the large drawing-room was called, and several other apartments, were in a state of decay; the walls were stained with damp, and I remember well the sensation of awe which I felt creeping over me when, boy as I was, and full of boyish life and wild and ardent spirits, I descended to the vaults; all without and within me became chilled beneath their dampness and gloom—their extent, too, terrified me; nor could the merriment of my two schoolfellows, whose father, a respectable clergyman, rented the dwelling for a time, dispel the feelings of a romantic imagination until I once again ascended to the upper regions.

John had pretty well recovered himself as the dinner-hour approached, and several guests arrived. They were all seated at the table, and had begun to enjoy the excellent repast, when a voice was heard in the lawn.

"Ho, ho, ho! Mr Pratt, won't you give poor Teigue some dinner? ho, ho! a fine company you have there, and plenty of everything that's good; sure you won't forget poor Teigue?"

John dropped the glass he had in his hand.

"Who is that?" said Mr Pratt's brother, an officer of the artillery.

"That is Teigue," said Mr Pratt, laughing, "whom you must often have heard me mention."

"And pray, Mr Pratt," inquired another gentleman, "who *is* Teigue?"

"That," he replied, "is more than I can tell. No one has ever been able to catch even a glimpse of him. I have been on the watch for a whole evening with three of my sons, yet, although his voice sometimes sounded almost in my ear, I could not see him. I fancied, indeed, that I saw a man in a white frieze jacket pass into the door from the garden to the lawn, but it could be only fancy, for I found the door locked, while the fellow, whoever he is, was laughing at our trouble. He visits us occasionally, and sometimes a long long interval passes between his visits, as in the present case; it is now nearly two years since we heard that hollow voice outside the window. He has never done any injury that we know of, and once when he broke a plate, he brought one back exactly like it."

"It is very extraordinary," exclaimed several of the company.

"But," remarked a gentleman to young Mr Pratt, "your father said he broke a plate; how did he get it without your seeing him?"

"When he asks for some dinner we put it outside the window and go away; whilst we watch he will not take it, but no sooner have we withdrawn than it is gone."

"How does he know that you are watching?"

"That's more than I can tell, but he either knows or suspects. One day my brothers Robert and James with myself were in our back parlour, which has a window into the garden, when he came outside and said, 'Ho, ho, ho! Master James and Robert and Henry, give poor Teigue a glass of whiskey.' James went out of the room, filled a glass with whiskey, vinegar, and salt, and brought it to him. 'Here, Teigue,' said he, 'come for it now.'—'Well, put it down, then, on the step outside the window.' This was done, and we stood looking at it. 'There, now, go away,' he shouted. We retired, but still watched it. 'Ho, ho! you are watching Teigue go out of the room, now, or I won't take it.' We went outside the door and returned, the glass was gone, and a moment after we heard him roaring and cursing frightfully. He took away the glass, but the next day it was on the stone step under the window, and there were crumbs of bread in the inside, as if he had put it in his pocket; from that time he has not been heard till today."

"Oh," said the colonel, "I'll get a sight of him; you are not used to these things; an old soldier has the best chance, and as I shall finish my dinner with this wing, I'll be ready for him when he speaks next—Mr Bell, will you take a glass of wine with me?"

"Ho, ho! Mr Bell," shouted Teigue. "Ho, ho! Mr Bell, you were a Quaker long ago. Ho, ho! Mr Bell, you're a pretty boy! a pretty Quaker you were; and now you're no Quaker, nor anything else: ho, ho! Mr Bell. And there's Mr Parkes: to be sure, Mr Parkes looks mighty fine today, with his powdered head, and his grand silk stockings and his bran new rakish-red waistcoat. And there's Mr Cole: did you ever see such a fellow? A pretty company you've brought together, Mr Pratt: kiln-dried Quakers, butter-buying buckeens from Mallow Lane, and a drinking exciseman from the Coal Quay, to meet the great thundering artillery general that is come out of the Indies, and is the biggest dust of them all."

"You scoundrel!" exploded the colonel, "I'll make you show yourself"; and snatching up his sword from a corner of the room, he sprang out of the window upon the lawn. In a moment a shout of laughter, so hollow, so unlike any human sound, made him stop, as well as Mr Bell, who with a huge oak stick was close at the colonel's heels; others of the party followed to the lawn, and the remainder rose and went to the windows. "Come on, colonel," said Mr Bell; "let us catch this impudent rascal."

"Ho, ho! Mr Bell, here I am—here's Teigue—why don't you catch him? Ho, ho! Colonel Pratt, what a pretty soldier you are to draw your sword upon poor Teigue, that never did anybody harm."

"Let us see your face, you scoundrel," said the colonel.

"Ho, ho, ho!—look at me—look at me: do you see the wind, Colonel Pratt? you'll see Teigue as soon; so go in and finish your dinner."

"If you're upon the earth, I'll find you, you villain!" said the colonel, whilst the same unearthly shout of derision seemed to come from behind an angle of the building. "He's round that corner," said Mr Bell, "run, run."

They followed the sound, which was continued at intervals along the garden wall, but could discover no human being; at last both stopped to draw breath, and in an instant, almost at their ears, sounded the shout—

"Ho, ho, ho! Colonel Pratt, do you see Teigue now? do you hear him? Ho, ho, ho! you're a fine colonel to follow the wind."

338

"Not that way, Mr Bell—not that way; come here," said the colonel.

"Ho, ho, ho! what a fool you are; do you think Teigue is going to show himself to you in the field, there? But, colonel, follow me if you can: you a soldier! ho, ho, ho!" The colonel was enraged: he followed the voice over hedge and ditch, alternately laughed at and taunted by the unseen object of his pursuit (Mr Bell, who was heavy, was soon thrown out); until at length, after being led a weary chase, he found himself at the top of the cliff, over that part of the river Lee, which, from its great depth, and the blackness of its water, has received the name of Hell-hole. Here, on the edge of the cliff, stood the colonel out of breath, mopping his forehead with his handkerchief, while the voice, which seemed close at his feet, exclaimed, "Now, Colonel Pratt, now, if you're a soldier, here's a leap for you! Now look at Teigue—why don't you look at him? Ho, ho, ho! Come along; you're warm, I'm sure, Colonel Pratt, so come in and cool yourself; Teigue is going to have a swim!" The voice seemed as if descending amongst the trailing ivy and brushwood which clothes this picturesque cliff nearly from top to bottom, yet it was impossible that any human being could have found footing. "Now, colonel, have you courage to take the leap? Ho, ho, ho! what a pretty soldier you are. Good-bye; I'll see you again in ten minutes above, at the house—look at your watch, colonel: there's a dive for you"; and a heavy plunge into the water was heard. The colonel stood still, but no sound followed, and he walked slowly back to the house, not quite half a mile from the Crag.

"Well, did you see Teigue?" said his brother, whilst his nephews, scarcely able to smother their laughter, stood by.

"Give me some wine," said the colonel. "I never was led such a dance in my life; the fellow carried me all round and round till he brought me to the edge of the cliff, and then down he went into Hell-hole, telling me he'd be here in ten minutes; 'tis more than that now, but he's not come."

"Ho, ho, ho! colonel, isn't he here? Teigue never told a lie in his life: but, Mr Pratt, give me a drink and my dinner, and then good-night to you all, for I'm tired; and that's the colonel's doing." A plate of food was ordered; it was placed by John, with fear and trembling, on the lawn under the window. Every one kept on the watch, and the plate remained undisturbed for some time.

"Ah! Mr Pratt, will you starve poor Teigue? Make every one go away from the windows, and Master Henry out of the tree, and Master Richard off the garden wall."

339

The eyes of the company were turned to the tree and the garden wall the two boys' attention was occupied in getting down; the visitors were looking at them; and "Ho, ho, ho!—good luck to you, Mr Pratt! 'tis a good dinner, and there's the plate, ladies and gentlemen. Good-bye to you, colonel!—good-bye, Mr Bell! good-bye to you all!" brought their attention back, when they saw the empty plate lying on the grass; and Teigue's voice was heard no more for that evening. Many visits were afterwards paid by Teigue; but never was he seen, nor was any discovery ever made of his person or character.

The Fairy Greyhound

Paddy M'Dermid was one of the most rollicking boys in the whole county of Kildare. Fair or pattern* wouldn't be held barring he was in the midst of it. He was in every place, like bad luck, and his poor little farm was seldom sowed in season; and where he expected barley, there grew nothing but weeds. Money became scarce in poor Paddy's pocket; and the cow went after the pig, until nearly all he had was gone. Lucky however for him, if he had *gomch* (sense) enough to mind it, he had a most beautiful dream one night as he lay tossicated (drunk) in the Rath† of Monogue because he wasn't able to come home. He dreamt that, under the place where he lay, a pot of money was buried since long before the memory of man. Paddy kept the dream to himself until the next night, when, taking a spade and pickaxe, with a bottle of holy water, he went to the Rath, and, having made a circle round the place, commenced diggin' sure enough, for the bare life and sowl of him thinkin' that he was made up for ever and ever. He had sunk about twice the depth of his knees, when *whack* the pickaxe struck against a flag, and at the same time Paddy heard something breathe quite near him. He looked up, and just fornent him there sat on his haunches a comely-looking greyhound.

"God save you," said Paddy, every hair in his head standing up as straight as a sally twig.

"Save you kindly," answered the greyhound—leaving out God, the beast, bekase he was the divil. Christ defend us from ever seeing the likes o' him.

"Musha, Paddy M'Dermid," said he, "what would you be looking after in that grave of a hole you're diggin' there?"

*A merry-making in the honour of some patron saint.
†Raths are little fields enclosed by circular ditches. They are thought to be the sheep-folds and dwellings of an ancient people.

"Faith, nothing at all, at all," answered Paddy; bekase you see he didn't like the stranger.

"Arrah, be easy now, Paddy M'Dermid," said the greyhound; "don't I know very well what you are looking for?"

"Why then in truth, if you do, I may as well tell you at wonst, particularly as you seem a civil-looking gentleman, that's not above speaking to a poor gossoon like myself." (Paddy wanted to butter him up a bit.)

"Well then," said the greyhound, "come out here and sit down on this bank," and Paddy, like a gomulagh (fool), did as he was desired, but had hardly put his brogue outside of the circle made by the holy water, when the beast of a hound set upon him, and drove him out of the Rath; for Paddy was frightened, as well he might, at the fire that flamed from his mouth. But next night he returned, full sure the money was there. As before, he made a circle, and touched the flag, when my gentleman, the greyhound, appeared in the ould place.

"Oh ho," said Paddy, "you are there, are you? But it will be a long day, I promise you, before you trick me again"; and he made another stroke at the flag.

"Well, Paddy M'Dermid," said the hound, "since you will have money, you must; but say, how much will satisfy you?"

Paddy scratched his conlaan, and after a while said—

"How much will your honour give me?" for he thought it better to be civil.

"Just as much as you consider reasonable, Paddy M'Dermid."

"Egad," says Paddy to himself, "there's nothing like axin' enough."

"Say fifty thousand pounds," said he. (He might as well have said a hundred thousand, for I'll be bail the beast had money gulloure.)

"You shall have it" said the hound; and then after trotting away a little bit, he came back with a crock full of guineas between his paws.

"Come here and reckon them," said he; but Paddy was up to him, and refused to stir, so the crock was shoved alongside the blessed and holy circle, and Paddy pulled it in, right glad to have it in his clutches, and never stood still until he reached his own home, where his guineas turned into little bones, and his ould mother laughed at him. Paddy now swore vengeance against the deceitful beast of a greyhound, and went next night to the Rath again, where, as before, he met Mr Hound.

"So you are here again, Paddy?" said he.

"Yes, you big blaggard," said Paddy, "and I'll never leave this place until I pull out the pot of money that's buried here."

"Oh, you won't," said he. "Well, Paddy M'Dermid, since I see you are such a brave venturesome fellow I'll be after making you up if you walk downstairs with me out of the could"; and sure enough it was snowing like murder.

"Oh may I never see Athy if I do," returned Paddy, "for you only want to be loading me with ould bones, or perhaps breaking my own, which would be just as bad."

" 'Pon honour," said the hound, "I am your friend; and so don't stand in your own light; come with me and your fortune is made. Remain where you are and you'll die a beggar-man." So bedad, with one palaver and another, Paddy consented; and in the middle of the Rath opened up a beautiful staircase, down which they walked; and after winding and turning they came to a house much finer than the Duke of Leinster's, in which all the tables and chairs were solid gold. Paddy was delighted; and after sitting down, a fine lady handed him a glass of something to drink; but he had hardly swallowed a spoonful when all around set up a horrid yell, and those who before appeared beautiful now looked like what they were—enraged "good people" (fairies). Before Paddy could bless himself, they seized him, legs and arms, carried him out to a great high hill that stood like a wall over a river, and flung him down. "Murder!" cried Paddy; but it was no use; he fell upon a rock, and lay there as dead until next morning, where some people found him in the trench that surrounds the *mote* of Coulhall, the "good people" having carried him there; and from that hour to the day of his death he was the greatest object in the world. He walked double, and had his mouth (God bless us) where his ear should be.

The Lady of Gollerus

CROFTON CROKER

On the shore of Smerwick harbour, one fine summer's morning, just at daybreak, stood Dick Fitzgerald "shoghing the dudeen", which may be translated, smoking his pipe. The sun was gradually rising behind the lofty Brandon, the dark sea was getting green in the light, and the mists clearing away out of the valleys went rolling and curling like the smoke from the corner of Dick's mouth.

" 'Tis just the pattern of a pretty morning," said Dick, taking the pipe from between his lips, and looking towards the distant ocean, which lay as still and tranquil as a tomb of polished marble. "Well, to be sure," continued he, after a pause, " 'tis mighty lonesome to be talking to one's self by way of company, and not to have another soul to answer one—nothing but the child of one's own voice, the echo! I know this, that if I had the luck, or may be the misfortune," said Dick, with a melancholy smile, "to have the woman it would not be this way with me! and what in the wide world is a man without a wife? He's no more surely than a bottle without a drop of drink in it, or dancing without music, or the left leg of a scissors, or a fishing-line without a hook, or any other matter that is no ways complete. Is it not so?" said Dick Fitzgerald, casting his eyes towards a rock upon the strand, which, though it could not speak, stood up as firm and looked as bold as ever Kerry witness did.

But what was his astonishment at beholding, just at the foot of that rock, a beautiful young creature combing her hair, which was of a sea-green colour; and now the salt water shining on it appeared, in the morning light, like melted butter upon cabbage.

Dick guessed at once that she was a Merrow,* although he had never seen one before, for he spied the *cohuleen driuth*, or little enchanted cap, which the sea people use for diving down into the ocean, lying upon the strand near her; and he had

*Sea fairy.

344

heard that, if once he could possess himself of the cap she would lose the power of going away into the water: so he seized it with all speed, and she, hearing the noise, turned her head about as natural as any Christian.

When the Merrow saw that her little diving-cap was gone, the salt tears—doubly salt, no doubt, from her—came trickling down her cheeks, and she began a low mournful cry with just the tender voice of a new-born infant. Dick, although he knew well enough what she was crying for, determined to keep the *cohuleen driuth*, let her cry never so much, to see what luck would come out of it. Yet he could not help pitying her; and when the dumb thing looked up in his face, with her cheeks all moist with tears, 'twas enough to make any one feel, let alone Dick, who had ever and always, like most of his countrymen, a mighty tender heart of his own.

"Don't cry, my darling," said Dick Fitzgerald; but the Merrow, like any bold child, only cried the more for that.

Dick sat himself down by her side, and took hold of her hand by way of comforting her. 'Twas in no particular an ugly hand, only there was a small web between the fingers, as there is in a duck's foot; but 'twas as thin and as white as the skin between egg and shell.

"What's your name, my darling?" says Dick, thinking to make her conversant with him; but he got no answer; and he was certain sure now, either that she could not speak, or did not understand him: he therefore squeezed her hand in his, as the only way he had of talking to her. It's the universal language; and there's not a woman in the world, be she fish or lady, that does not understand it.

The Merrow did not seem much displeased at this mode of conversation; and making an end of her whining all at once, "Man," says she, looking up in Dick Fitzgerald's face; "man, will you eat me?"

"By all the red petticoats and check aprons between Dingle and Tralee," cried Dick, jumping up in amazement, "I'd as soon eat myself, my jewel! Is it I eat you, my pet? Now, 'twas some ugly ill-looking thief of a fish put that notion into your own pretty head, with the nice green hair down upon it, that is so cleanly combed out this morning!"

"Man," said the Merrow, "what will you do with me if you won't eat me?"

Dick's thoughts were running on a wife: he saw, at the first glimpse, that she was handsome; but since she spoke, and spoke too like any real woman, he was fairly in love with her. 'Twas the neat way she called him man that settled the matter entirely.

"Fish," says Dick, trying to speak to her after her own short fashion; "fish," says he, "here's my word, fresh and fasting, for you this blessed morning, that I'll make you Mistress Fitzgerald before all the world, and that's what I'll do."

"Never say the word twice," says she; "I'm ready and willing to be yours, Mister Fitzgerald; but stop, if you please, till I twist up my hair." It was some time before she had settled it entirely to her liking; for she guessed, I suppose, that she was going among strangers, where she would be looked at. When that was done, the Merrow put the comb in her pocket, and then bent down her head and whispered some words to the water that was close to the foot of the rock.

Dick saw the murmur of the words upon the top of the sea, going out towards the wide ocean, just like a breath of wind rippling along, and, says he, in the greatest wonder, "Is it speaking you are, my darling, to the salt water?"

"It's nothing else," says she, quite carelessly; "I'm just sending word home to my father not to be waiting breakfast for me; just to keep him from being uneasy in his mind."

"And who's your father, my duck?" said Dick.

"What!" said the Merrow, "did you never hear of my father? he's the king of the waves to be sure!"

"And yourself, then, is a real king's daughter?" said Dick, opening his two eyes to take a full and true survey of his wife that was to be. "Oh, I'm nothing else but a made man with you, and a king your father; to be sure he has all the money that's down at the bottom of the sea!"

"Money," repeated the Merrow, "what's money?"

" 'Tis no bad thing to have when one wants it," replied Dick; "and may be now the fishes have the understanding to bring up whatever you bid them?"

"Oh yes," said the Merrow, "they bring me what I want."

"To speak the truth then," said Dick, " 'tis a straw bed I have at home before you, and that, I'm thinking, is no ways fitting for a king's daughter; so if 'twould not be displeasing to you, just to mention a nice feather bed, with a pair of new blankets—but what am I talking about? may be you have not such things as beds down under the water?"

"By all means," said she, "Mr. Fitzgerald—plenty of beds at your service. I've fourteen oyster-beds of my own, not to mention one just planting for the rearing of young ones."

"You have?" says Dick, scratching his head and looking a little puzzled. " 'Tis a feather bed I was speaking of; but, clearly, yours is the very cut of a decent plan to have bed and supper so handy to each other, that a person when they'd have the one need never ask for the other."

However, bed or no bed, money or no money, Dick Fitzgerald determined to marry the Merrow, and the Merrow had given her consent. Away they went, therefore, across the strand, from Gollerus to Ballinrunnig, where Father Fitzgibbon happened to be that morning.

"There are two words to this bargain, Dick Fitzgerald," said his Reverence, looking mighty glum. "And is it a fishy woman you'd marry? The Lord preserve us! Send the scaly creature home to her own people; that's my advice to you, wherever she came from."

Dick had the *cohuleen driuth* in his hand, and was about to give it back to the Merrow, who looked covetously at it, but he thought for a moment, and then says he, "Please your Reverence, she's a king's daughter."

"If she was the daughter of fifty kings," said Father Fitzgibbon, "I tell you, you can't marry her, she being a fish."

"Please your Reverence," said Dick again, in an undertone, "she is as mild and as beautiful as the moon."

"If she was as mild and as beautiful as the sun, moon, and stars, all put together, I tell you, Dick Fitzgerald," said the Priest, stamping his right foot, "you can't marry her, she being a fish."

"But she has all the gold that's down in the sea only for the asking, and I'm a made man if I marry her; and," said Dick, looking up slily, "I can make it worth any one's while to do the job."

"Oh! that alters the case entirely," replied the Priest; "why there's some reason now in what you say: why didn't you tell me this before? marry her by all means, if she was ten times a fish. Money you know, is not to be refused in these bad times, and I may as well have the hansel of it as another, that may be would not take half the pains in counselling you that I have done."

So Father Fitzgibbon married Dick Fitzgerald to the Merrow, and like any loving couple, they returned to Gollerus well pleased with each other. Everything prospered with Dick—he was at the sunny side of the world; the Merrow made the best of wives, and they lived together in the greatest contentment.

It was wonderful to see, considering where she had been brought up, how she would busy herself about the house, and how well she nursed the children; for, at the end of three years there were as many young Fitzgeralds—two boys and a girl.

In short, Dick was a happy man, and so he might have been to the end of his days if he had only had the sense to take care of what he had got; many another man, however, beside Dick, has not had wit enough to do that.

One day, when Dick was obliged to go to Tralee, he left the wife minding the children at home after him, and thinking she had plenty to do without disturbing his fishing-tackle.

Dick was no sooner gone than Mrs Fitzgerald set about cleaning up the house, and chancing to pull down a fishing-net, what should she find behind it in a hole in the wall but her own *cohuleen driuth*. She took it out and looked at it, and then she thought of her father the king, and her mother the queen, and her brothers and sisters, and she felt a longing to go back to them.

She sat down on a little stool and thought over the happy days she had spent under the sea; then she looked at her children, and thought on the love and affection of poor Dick, and how it would break his heart to lose her. "But," says she, "he won't lose me entirely, for I'll come back to him again, and who can blame me for going to see my father and my mother after being so long away from them?"

She got up and went towards the door, but came back again to look once more at the child that was sleeping in the cradle. She kissed it gently, and as she kissed it a tear trembled for an instant in her eye and then fell on its rosy cheek. She wiped away the tear, and turning to the eldest little girl, told her to take good care of her brothers, and to be a good child herself until she came back. The Merrow then went down to the strand. The sea was lying calm and smooth, just heaving and glittering in the sun, and she thought she heard a faint sweet singing, inviting her to come down. All her old ideas and feelings came flooding over her mind, Dick and her children were at the instant forgotten, and placing the *cohuleen driuth* on her head she plunged in.

Dick came home in the evening, and missing his wife he asked Kathleen, his little girl, what had become of her mother, but she could not tell him. He then inquired of the neighbours, and he learned that she was seen going towards the strand with a strange-looking thing like a cocked hat in her hand. He returned to his cabin to search for the *cohuleen driuth*. It was gone, and the truth now flashed upon him.

Year after year did Dick Fitzgerald wait expecting the return of his wife, but he never saw her more. Dick never married again, always thinking that the Merrow would sooner or later return to him, and nothing could ever persuade him but that her father the king kept her below by main force; "for," said Dick, "she surely would not of herself give up her husband and her children."

While she was with him she was so good a wife in every respect that to this day she is spoken of in the tradition of the country as the pattern for one, under the name of THE LADY OF GOLLERUS.

EVIL SPIRITS

The Devil's Mill

SAMUEL LOVER

You see, sir, there was a colonel wanst, in times back, that owned a power of land about here—but God keep uz, they said he didn't come by it honestly, but did a crooked turn whenever 'twas to sarve himself.

Well, the story goes that at last the divil (God bless us) kem to him, and promised him hapes o' money, and all his heart could desire and more, too, if he'd sell his sowl in exchange.

He was too cunnin' for that; bad as he was—and he was bad enough God knows—he had some regard for his poor sinful sowl, and he would not give himself up to the divil, all out; but, the villian, he thought he might make a bargain with the *old chap*, and get all he wanted, and keep himself out of harm's way still: for he was mighty 'cute—and, throth, he was able for Owld Nick any day.

Well, the bargain was struck, and it was this-a-way: the divil was to give him all the goold ever he'd ask for, and was to let him alone as long as he could; and the timpter promised him a long day, and said 'twould be a great while before he'd want him at all, at all; and whin that time kem, he was to keep his hands aff him, as long as the other could give him some work he couldn't do.

So, when the bargain was made, "Now," says the colonel to the divil, "give me all the money I want."

"As much as you like," says Owld Nick; "how much will you have?"

"You must fill me that room," says he, pointin' into a murtherin' big room that he emptied out on purpose—"you must fill that room," says he, "up to the very ceilin' with goolden guineas."

"And welkem," says the divil.

With that, sir, he began to shovel the guineas into the room like mad; and the colonel towld him, that as soon as he was done, to come to him in his own parlour below, and that he would then go up and see if the divil was as good as his word,

353

and had filled the room with the goolden guineas. So the colonel went downstairs, and the owld fellow worked away as busy as a nailer, shovellin' in the guineas by hundherds and thousands.

Well, he worked away for an hour and more, and at last he began to get tired; and he thought it *mighty odd* that the room wasn't fillin' fasther. Well, afther restin' for awhile, he began agin, and he put his shouldher to the work in airnest; but still the room was no fuller at all, at all.

"Och! bad luck to me," says the divil, "but the likes of this I never seen," says he, "far and near, up and down—the dickens a room I ever kem across afore," says he, "I couldn't cram while a cook would be crammin' a turkey, till now; and here I am," says he, "losin' my whole day, and I with such a power o' work an my hands yit, and this room no fuller than five minutes ago."

Begor, while he was spakin' he seen the hape o' guineas in the middle of the flure growing *littler and littler* every minit; and at last they wor disappearing, for all the world like corn in the hopper of a mill.

"Ho! ho!" says Owld Nick, "is that the way wid you?" says he; and wid that, he ran over to the hape of goold—and what would you think, but it was runnin' down through a great big hole in the flure, that the colonel made through the ceilin' in the room below; and that was the work he was at afther he left the divil, though he purtended he was only waitin' for him in his parlour; and there the divil, when he looked down the hole in the flure, seen the colonel, not content with the *two* rooms full of guineas, but with a big shovel throwin' them into a closet a' one side of him as fast as they fell down. So, putting his head through the hole, he called down to the colonel:

"Hillo, neighbour!" says he.

The colonel looked up, and grew as white as a sheet, when he seen he was found out, and the red eyes starin' down at him through the hole.

"Musha, bad luck to your impudence!" says Owld Nick: "it is sthrivin' to chate *me* you are," says he, "you villian!"

"Oh, forgive me for this wanst!" says the colonel, "and, upon the honour of a gintleman," says he, "I'll never—"

"Whisht whisht! you thievin' rogue," says the divil, "I'm not angry with you at all, at all, but ony like you the betther, bekase you're so cute;—lave off slaving yourself there," says he, "you have got goold enough for this time; and whenever you want more, you have only to say the word, and it shall be yours to command."

So with that, the divil and he parted for that time: and myself doesn't know whether they used to meet often afther or not; but the colonel never wanted money, anyhow, but went on prosperous in the world—and, as the saying is, if he took the dirt out o' the road, it id turn to money wid him; and so, in course of time, he bought great estates, and was a great man entirely—not a greater in Ireland, throth.

At last, afther many years of prosperity, the owld colonel got stricken in years, and he began to have misgivings in his conscience for his wicked doings and his heart was heavy as the fear of death came upon him; and sure enough while he had such murnful thoughts, the divil kem to him, and towld him *he should go wid him.*

Well to be sure, the owld man was frekened, but he plucked up his courage and his cuteness and towld the divil, in a bantherin' way, jokin' like, that he had partic'lar business thin, that he was goin' to a party and hoped an *owld friend* wouldn't inconvaynience him that-a-way.

The divil said he'd call the next day and that he must be ready; and sure enough in the evenin' he kem to him; and when the colonel seen him, he reminded him of his bargain that as long as he could give him some work he couldn't do, he wasn't obleeged to go.

"That's thrue," says the devil.

"I'm glad you're as good as your word anyhow," says the colonel.

"I never bruk my word yit," says the owld chap, cocking up his horns consaitedly; "honour bright," says he.

"Well then" says the colonel, "build me a mill, down there, by the river," says he, "and let me have it finished by tomorrow mornin'."

"Your will is my pleasure," says the owld chap, and away he wint; and the colonel thought he had nicked Owld Nick at last, and wint to bed quite aisy in his mind.

But, *jewel machree*, sure the first thing he heerd the next mornin' was that the whole counthry round was runnin' to see a fine bran new mill that was an the river-side, where the evening before not a thing at all, at all, but rushes was standin', and all, of coorse, wonderin' what brought it there; and some sayin' 'twas not lucky, and many more throubled in their mind, but one and all agreein' it was no *good*; and that's the very mill forninst you.

But when the colonel heerd it he was more throubled than any, of coorse, and began to conthrive what else he could think iv to keep himself out iv the claws of the *owld one*. Well, he often heerd tell that there was one thing the divil never could do, and I darsay you heerd it too, sir,—that is, that he couldn't make a rope out of the sands of the say; and so when the *owld one* kem to him next day and said his job was done, and that now the mill was built he must either tell him somethin' else he wanted done, or come away wid him.

So the colonel said he saw it was all over wid him. "But," says he, "I wouldn't like to go wid you alive, and sure it's all the same to you, alive or dead?"

"Oh, that won't do," says his frind; "I can't wait no more," says he.

"I don't want you to wait, my dear frind," says the colonel; "all I want is, that you'll be plased to kill me before you take me away."

"With pleasure," says Owld Nick.

"But will you promise me my choice of dyin' one partic'lar way?" says the colonel.

"Half a dozen ways, if it plazes you," says he.

"You're mighty obleegin'," says the colonel; "and so," says he, "I'd rather die by bein' hanged with a rope *made out of the sands of the say*," says he, lookin' mighty knowin' at the *owld fellow*.

"I've always one about me," says the divil, "to obleege my frinds," says he; and with that he pulls out a rope made of sand, sure enough.

"Oh, it's game you're makin'," says the colonel, growin' as white as a sheet.

"The *game is mine*, sure enough," says the owld fellow, grinnin', with a terrible laugh.

"That's not a sand-rope at all," says the colonel.

"Isn't it?" says the divil, hittin' him across the face with the ind iv the rope, and the sand (for it *was* made of sand, sure enough) went into one of his eyes, and made the tears come with the pain.

"That bates all I ever seen or heerd," says the colonel, sthrivin' to rally and make another offer; "is there anything you *can't* do?"

"Nothing you can tell me," says the divil, "so you may as well leave off your palaverin' and come along at wanst."

"Will you give me one more offer," says the colonel.

"You don't desarve it," says the divil; "but I don't care if I do"; for you see, sir, he was only playin' wid him, and tantalising the owld sinner.

"All fair," says the colonel, and with that he ax'd him could he stop a woman's tongue.

"Thry me," says Owld Nick.

"Well then," says the colonel, "make my lady's tongue be quiet for the next month and I'd thank you."

"She'll never trouble you agin," says Owld Nick; and with that the colonel heerd roarin' and cryin', and the door of his room was thrown open and in ran his daughter, and fell down at his feet, telling him her mother had just dhropped dead.

The minit the door opened, the divil runs and hides himself behind a big elbow-chair; and the colonel was frekened almost out of his siven sinses by raison of the sudden death of his poor lady, let alone the jeopardy he was in himself, seein' how the divil had *forestalled* him every way; and after ringin' his bell and callin' to his sarvants and recoverin' his daughter out of her faint, he was goin' away wid her out of the room, whin the divil caught howld of him by the skirt of the coat, and the colonel was obleeged to let his daughter be carried out by the sarvants, and shut the door afther them.

"Well," says the divil, and he grinn'd and wagg'd his tail, all as one as a dog when he's plaised; "what do you say now?" says he.

"Oh," says the colonel, "only lave me alone until I bury my poor wife," says he, "and I'll go with you then, you villain," say he.

"Don't call names," says the divil; "you had better keep a civil tongue in your head," says he; "and it doesn't become a gintleman to forget good manners."

Well, sir, to make a long story short, the divil purtended to let him off, out of kindness, for three days antil his wife was buried; but the raison of it was this, that when the lady his daughter fainted, he loosened the clothes about her throat, and in pulling some of her dhress away, he tuk off a goold chain that was on her neck and put it in his pocket, and the chain had a diamond crass on it (the Lord be praised!) and the divil darn't touch him while he had *the sign of the crass* about him.

Well, the poor colonel (God forgive him!) was grieved for the loss of his lady, and she had an *illigant berrin*—and they say that when the prayers was readin' over the dead, the owld colonel took it to heart like anything, and the word o' God kem home to his poor sinful sowl at last.

Well, sir, to make a long story short, the ind of it was, that for the three days o' grace that was given to him the poor deluded owld sinner did nothin' at all but read the Bible from mornin' till night, and bit or sup didn't pass his lips all the time, he was so intint upon the Holy Book, but he sat up in an owld room in the far ind of the house, and bid no one disturb him an no account, and struv to make

357

his heart bould with the words iv life; and sure it was somethin' strinthened him at last, though as the time drew nigh that the *inimy* was to come, he didn't feel aisy, and no wondher; and, bedad the three days was past and gone in no time, and the story goes that at the dead hour o' the night, when the poor sinner was readin' away as fast as he could, my jew'l, his heart jumped up to his mouth at gettin' a tap on the shoulder.

"Oh murther!" says he, "who's there?" for he was afeard to look up.

"It's me," says the *owld one*, and he stood right forninst him, and his eyes like coals o' fire, lookin' him through, and he said, with a voice that almost split his owld heart, "Come!" says he.

"Another day!" cried out the poor colonel.

"Not another hour," says Sat'n.

"Half an hour!"

"Not a quarther," says the divil, grinnin' with a bitther laugh; "give over your readin', I bid you," says he, "and come away wid me."

"Only gi' me a few minits," says he.

"Lave aff your palaverin', you snakin' owld sinner," says Sat'n; "you know you're bought and sould to me, and a purty bargain I have o' you, you owld baste," says he; "So come along at wanst," and he put out his claw to ketch him; but the colonel tuk a fast hould o' the Bible, and begged hard that he'd let him alone, and wouldn't harm him antil the bit o' candle that was just blinkin' in the socket before him was burned out.

"Well, have it so, you dirty coward," says Owld Nick, and with that he spit an him.

But the poor owld colonel didn't lose a minit (for he was cunnin' to the ind), but snatched the little taste o' candle that was forninst him out o' the candlestick, and puttin' it an the Holy Book before him, he shut down the cover of it and quinched the light. With that the divil gave a roar like a bull, and vanished in a flash o' fire, and the poor colonel fainted away in his chair; but the sarvants heerd the noise (for the divil tore off the roof o' the house when he left it), and run into the room, and brought their master to himself agin. And from that day he was an althered man, and used to have the Bible read to him every day, for he couldn't read himself any more, by raison of losin' his eyesight when the divil hit him with the rope of sand in the face, and afther spit an him—for the sand wint into one eye, and he lost the other that-a-way, savin' your presence.

Fergus O'Mara and the Air-demons

Dr P.W. JOYCE

Of all the different kinds of goblins that haunted the lonely places of Ireland in days of old, air-demons were most dreaded by the people. They lived among the clouds, and mists, and rocks, and they hated the human race with the utmost malignity. In those times lived in the north of Desmond (the present county of Cork) a man named Fergus O'Mara. His farm lay on the southern slope of the Ballyhoura Mountains, along which ran the open road that led to his house. This road was not shut in by walls or fences; but on both sides there were scattered trees and bushes that sheltered it in winter, and made it dark and gloomy when you approached the house at night. Beside the road, a little way off from the house, there was a spot that had an evil name all over the country, a little hill covered closely with copsewood with a great craggy rock on top, from which, on stormy nights, strange and fearful sounds had often been heard—shrill voices, and screams, mingled with loud fiendish laughter; and the people believed that it was the haunt of air-demons. In some way it had become known that these demons had an eye on Fergus, and watched for every opportunity to get him into their power. He had himself been warned of this many years before, by an old monk from the neighbouring monastery of Buttevant, who told him, moreover, that so long as he led a blameless, upright life, he need have no fear of the demons; but that if ever he yielded to temptation or fell into any great sin, then would come the opportunity for which they were watching day and night. He never forgot this warning, and he was very careful to keep himself straight, both because he was naturally a good man, and for fear of the air-demons.

Some time before the occurrence about to be related, one of Fergus's children, a sweet little girl about seven years of age, fell ill and died. The little thing gradually wasted away, but suffered no pain; and as she grew weaker she became more loving and gentle than ever, and talked in a wonderful way, quite beyond her years, of the bright land she was going to. One thing she was particularly anxious about, that when she was dying they should let her hold a blessed candle in her hand. They thought it very strange that she should be so continually thinking and talking of this; and over and over again she made her father and mother promise that it should be done. And with the blessed candle in her hand she died so calmly and sweetly that those round her bed could not tell the exact moment.

About a year after this, on a bright Sunday morning in October, Fergus set out for Mass. The place was about three miles away, and it was not a chapel, but a lonely old fort, called to this day Lissanaffrin, the fort of the Mass. A rude stone altar stood at one side near the mound of the fort, under a little shed that sheltered the priest also; and the congregation worshipped in the open air on the green plot in the centre. For in those days there were many places that had no chapels; and the people flocked to these open-air Masses as faithfully as we do now to our stately comfortable chapels. The family had gone on before, the men walking and the women and children riding; and Fergus set out to walk alone.

Just as he approached the Demons' Rock he was greatly surprised to hear the eager yelping of dogs, and in a moment a great deer bounded from the covert beside the rock, with three hounds after her in full chase. No man in the whole country round loved a good chase better than Fergus, or had a swifter foot to follow, and without a moment's hesitation he started in pursuit. But in a few minutes he stopped up short; for he bethought him of the Mass, and he knew there was little time for delay. While he stood wavering, the deer seemed to slacken her pace, and the hounds gained on her, and in a moment Fergus dashed off at full speed, forgetting Mass and everything else in his eagerness for the sport. But it turned out a long and weary chase. Sometimes they slackened, and he was almost at the hounds' tails, but the next moment both deer and hounds started forward and left him far behind. Sometimes they were in full view, and again they were out of sight in thickets and deep glens, so that he could guide himself only by the cry of the hounds. In this way he was decoyed across hills and glens, but instead of gaining ground he found himself rather falling behind.

Mass was all over and the people dispersed to their homes, and all wondered that they did not see Fergus; for no one could remember that he was ever absent before. His wife returned, expecting to find him at home; but when she arrived there was trouble in her heart, for there were no tidings of him, and no one had seen him since he had set out for Mass in the morning.

Meantime Fergus followed up the chase till he was wearied out; and at last, just on the edge of a wild moor, both deer and hounds disappeared behind a shoulder of rock, and he lost them altogether. At the same moment the cry of the hounds became changed to frightful shrieks and laughter, such as he had heard more than once from Demons' Rock. And now, sitting down on a bank to rest, he had full time to reflect on what he had done, and he was overwhelmed with remorse and shame. Moreover, his heart sank within him, thinking of the last sounds he had heard; for he believed that he had been allured from Mass by the cunning wiles of the demons and he feared that the dangerous time had come foretold by the monk. He started up and set out for his home, hoping to reach it before night. But before he had got half-way night fell and a storm came on, great wind and rain and bursts of thunder and lightning. Fergus was strong and active, however, and knew every turn of the mountain, and he made his way through the storm till he approached the Demons' Rock.

Suddenly there burst on his ears the very same sounds that he had heard on losing sight of the chase—shouts and shrieks and laughter. A great black ragged cloud, whirling round and round with furious gusts of wind, burst from the rock and came sweeping and tearing towards him. Crossing himself in terror and uttering a short prayer, he rushed for home. But the whirlwind swept nearer, till at last, in a sort of dim, shadowy light, he saw the black cloud full of frightful faces, all glaring straight at him and coming closer and closer. At this moment a bright light dropped down from the sky and rested in front of the cloud; and when he looked up, he saw his little child floating in the air between him and the demons, holding a lighted candle in her hand. And although the storm was raging and roaring all round, she was quite calm—not a breath of air stirred her long yellow hair—and the candle burned quietly. Even in the midst of all his terror he could observe her pale gentle face and blue eyes just as when she was alive, not showing traces of sickness or sadness now, but lighted up with joy. The demons seemed to start back from the light, and with great uproar rushed round to the other side of Fergus, the black cloud still moving with them and wrapping them up in its ragged folds; but the little angel floated softly round, still keeping between them and her father. Fergus ran on for home, and the cloud of demons still kept furiously whirling round and round him, bringing with them a whirlwind that roared among the trees and bushes and tore them from the roots; but still the child, always holding the candle towards them, kept floating calmly round and shielded him.

361

At length he arrived at his house; the door lay half-open, for the family were inside expecting him home, listening with wonder and affright to the approaching noises; and he bounded in through the doorway and fell flat on his face. That instant the door—though no one was near—was shut violently, and the bolts were shot home. They hurried anxiously round him to lift him up, but found him in a death-like swoon. Meantime the uproar outside became greater than ever; round and round the house it tore, a roaring whirlwind with shouts and yells of rage, and great trampling, as if there was a whole company of horsemen. At length, however, the noises seemed to move away farther and farther off from the house, and gradually died away in the distance. At the same time the storm ceased, and the night became calm and beautiful.

The daylight was shining in through the windows when Fergus recovered from his swoon, and then he told his fearful story; but many days passed over before he had quite recovered from the horrors of that night. When the family came forth in the morning there was fearful waste all round and near the house, trees and bushes torn from the roots, and the ground all trampled and torn up. After this the revelry of the demons was never again heard from the rock; and it was believed that they had left it and betaken themselves to some other haunt.

The Man Who Never Knew Fear

Translated From The Gaelic By Douglas Hyde

There was once a lady, and she had two sons whose names were Louras (Lawrence) and Carrol. From the day that Lawrence was born nothing ever made him afraid, but Carrol would never go outside the door from the time the darkness of the night began.

It was the custom at that time when a person died for people to watch the dead person's grave in turn, one after another; for there used to be destroyers going about stealing the corpses.

When the mother of Carrol and Lawrence died, Carrol said to Lawrence—

"You say that nothing ever made you afraid yet, but I'll make a bet with you that you haven't courage to watch your mother's tomb tonight."

"I'll make a bet with you that I have," said Lawrence.

When the darkness of the night was coming, Lawrence put on his sword and went to the burying-ground. He sat down on a tombstone near his mother's grave till it was far in the night and sleep was coming upon him. Then he saw a big black thing coming to him, and when it came near him he saw that it was a head without a body that was in it. He drew the sword to give it a blow if it should come any nearer, but it didn't come. Lawrence remained looking at it until the light of the day was coming, then the head-without-body went, and Lawrence came home.

Carrol asked him, did he see anything in the graveyard.

"I did," said Lawrence, "and my mother's body would be gone, but that I was guarding it."

"Was it dead or alive, the person you saw?" said Carrol.

"I don't know was it dead or alive," said Lawrence; "there was nothing in it but a head without a body."

363

"Weren't you afraid?" says Carrol.

"Indeed I wasn't," said Lawrence; "don't you know that nothing in the world ever put fear on me."

"I'll bet again with you that you haven't the courage to watch tonight again," says Carrol.

"I would make that bet with you," said Lawrence, "but that there is a night's sleep wanting to me. Go yourself tonight."

"I wouldn't go to the graveyard tonight if I were to get the riches of the world," says Carrol.

"Unless you go your mother's body will be gone in the morning," says Lawrence.

"If only you watch tonight and tomorrow night, I never will ask of you to do a turn of work as long as you will be alive," said Carrol, "but I think there is fear on you."

"To show you that there's no fear on me," said Lawrence, "I will watch."

He went to sleep, and when the evening came he rose up, put on his sword, and went to the graveyard. He sat on a tombstone near his mother's grave. About the middle of the night he heard a great sound coming. A big black thing came as far as the grave and began rooting up the clay. Lawrence drew back his sword, and with one blow he made two halves of the big black thing, and with the second blow he made two halves of each half, and he saw it no more.

Lawrence went home in the morning, and Carrol asked him did he see anything.

"I did," said Lawrence, "and only that I was there my mother's body would be gone."

"Is it the head-without-body that came again?" said Carrol.

"It was not, but a big black thing, and it was digging up my mother's grave until I made two halves of it."

Lawrence slept that day, and when the evening came he rose up, and put on his sword, and went to the churchyard. He sat down on a tombstone until it was the middle of the night. Then he saw a thing as white as snow and as hateful as sin; it had a man's head on it, and teeth as long as a flax-carder. Lawrence drew back the sword and was going to deal it a blow, when it said:

"Hold your hand; you have saved your mother's body, and there is not a man in Ireland as brave as you. There is great riches waiting for you if you go looking for it."

Lawrence went home, and Carrol asked him did he see anything.

"I did," said Lawrence, "and but that I was there my mother's body would be gone, but there's no fear of it now."

In the morning, the day on the morrow, Lawrence said to Carrol—

"Give me my share of money, and I'll go on a journey, until I have a look round the country."

Carrol gave him the money, and he went walking. He went on until he came to a large town. He went into the house of a baker to get bread. The baker began talking to him, and asked him how far he was going.

"I am going looking for something that will put fear on me," said Lawrence.

"Have you much money?" said the baker.

"I have a half-hundred pounds," said Lawrence.

"I'll bet another half-hundred with you that there will be fear on you if you go to the place that I'll bid you," says the baker.

"I'll take your bet," said Lawrence, "if only the place is not too far away from me."

"It's not a mile from the place where you're standing," said the baker; "wait here till the night comes, and then go to the graveyard, and as a sign that you were in it, bring me the goblet that is upon the alter of the old church (cill) that is in the graveyard."

When the baker made the bet he was certain that he would win, for there was a ghost in the churchyard, and nobody went into it for forty years before that whom he did not kill.

When the darkness of the night came, Lawrence put on his sword and went to the burying-ground. He came to the door of the churchyard and struck it with his sword. The door opened, and there came out a great black ram, and two horns on him as long as flails. Lawrence gave him a blow, and he went out of sight, leaving him up to the ankles in blood. Lawrence went into the old church, got the goblet, came back to the baker's house, gave him the goblet, and got the bet. Then the baker asked him did he see anything in the churchyard.

"I saw a big black ram with long horns on him," said Lawrence, "and I gave him a blow which drew as much blood out of him as would swim a boat; sure he must be dead by this time."

In the morning, the day on the morrow, the baker and a lot of people went to the graveyard and they saw the blood of the black ram at the door. They went to the priest and told him that the black ram was banished out of the churchyard. The priest did not believe them, because the churchyard was shut up forty years before that on account of the ghost that was in it, and neither priest nor friar could banish him. The priest came with them to the door of the churchyard, and when he saw the blood he took courage and sent for Lawrence, and heard the story from his own mouth. Then he sent for his blessing-materials, and desired the people to come in till he read mass for them. The priest went in, and Lawrence and the people after him, and he read mass without the big black ram coming as he used to do. The priest was greatly rejoiced, and gave Lawrence another fifty pounds.

On the morning of the next day Lawrence went on his way. He travelled the whole day without seeing a house. About the hour of midnight he came to a great lonely valley, and he saw a large gathering of people looking at two men hurling. Lawrence stood looking at them, as there was a bright light from the moon. It was the good people that were in it, and it was not long until one of them struck a blow on the ball and sent it into Lawrence's breast. He put his hand in after the ball to draw it out, and what was there in it but the head of a man. When Lawrence got hold of it, it began screeching, and at last it asked Lawrence—

"Are you not afraid?"

"Indeed I am not," said Lawrence, and no sooner was the word spoken than both head and people disappeared, and he was left in the glen alone by himself.

He journeyed until he came to another town, and when he ate and drank enough, he went out on the road, and was walking until he came to a great house on the side of the road. As the night was closing in, he went in to try if he could get lodging. There was a young man at the door who said to him—

"How far are you going, or what are you in search of?"

"I do not know how far I am going, but I am in search of something that will put fear on me," said Lawrence.

"You have not far to go, then," said the young man; "if you stop in that big house on the other side of the road there will be fear put on you before morning, and I'll give you twenty pounds into the bargain."

"I'll stop in it," said Lawrence.

The young man went with him, opened the door, and brought him into a large room in the bottom of the house, and said to him, "Put down fire for yourself and I'll send you plenty to eat and drink." He put down a fire for himself, and there came a girl to him and brought him everything that he wanted.

He went on very well, until the hour of midnight came, and then he heard a great sound over his head, and it was not long until a stallion and a bull came in and commenced to fight. Lawrence never put to them nor from them, and when they were tired fighting they went out. Lawrence went to sleep, and he never awoke until the young man came in in the morning, and he was surprised when he saw Lawrence alive. He asked him had he seen anything.

"I saw a stallion and a bull fighting hard for about two hours," said Lawrence.

"And weren't you afraid?" said the young man.

"I was not," says Lawrence.

"If you wait tonight again, I'll give you another twenty pounds," says the young man.

"I'll wait, and welcome," says Lawrence.

The second night, about ten o'clock, Lawrence was going to sleep, when two black rams came in and began fighting hard. Lawrence neither put to them nor from them, and when twelve o'clock struck they went out. The young man came in the morning and asked him did he see anything last night.

"I saw two black rams fighting," said Lawrence.

"Were you afraid at all?" said the young man.

"I was not," said Lawrence.

"Wait tonight, and I'll give you another twenty pounds," says the young man.

"All right," says Lawrence.

The third night he was falling asleep, when there came in a grey old man and said to him—

"You are the best hero in Ireland; I died twenty years ago, and all that time I have been in search of a man like you. Come with me now till I show you your riches; I told you when you were watching your mother's grave that there was great riches waiting for you."

He took Lawrence to a chamber under ground, and showed him a large pot filled with gold, and said to him—

"You will have all that if you give twenty pounds to Mary Kerrigan the widow and get her forgiveness for me for a wrong I did her. Then buy this house, marry my daughter, and you will be happy and rich as long as you live."

The next morning the young man came to Lawrence and asked him did he see anything last night.

"I did," said Lawrence, "and it's certain that there will be a ghost always in it,

367

but nothing in the world would frighten me; I'll buy the house and the land round it, if you like."

"I'll ask no price for the house, but I won't part with the land under a thousand pounds, and I'm sure you haven't that much."

"I have more than would buy all the land and all the herds you have," said Lawrence.

When the young man heard that Lawrence was so rich, he invited him to come to dinner. Lawrence went with him, and when the dead man's daughter saw him she fell in love with him.

Lawrence went to the house of Mary Kerrigan and gave her twenty pounds, and got her forgiveness for the dead man. Then he married the young man's sister and spent a happy life. He died as he lived, without there being fear on him.

CATS

Seanchan the Bard and the King of the Cats

LADY WILDE

When Seanchan, the renowned Bard, was made *Ard-Filé*, or Chief Poet of Ireland, Guaire, the king of Connaught, to do him honour, made a great feast for him and the whole Bardic Association. And all the professors and learned men went to the king's house, the great ollaves of poetry and history and music, and of the arts and sciences; and the learned, aged females, Grug and Grag and Grangait; and all the chief poets and poetesses of Ireland, an amazing number. But Guaire the king entertained them all splendidly, so that the ancient pathway to his palace is still called "The Road of the Dishes".

And each day he asked, "How fares it with my noble guests?" But they were all discontented, and wanted things he could not get for them. So he was very sorrowful, and prayed to God to be delivered from "the learned men and women, a vexatious class".

Still the feast went on for three days and three nights. And they drank and made merry. And the whole Bardic Association entertained the nobles with the choicest music and professional accomplishments.

But Seanchan sulked and would neither eat nor drink, for he was jealous of the nobles of Connaught. And when he saw how much they consumed of the best meats and wine, he declared he would taste no food till they and their servants were all sent away out of the house.

And when Guaire asked him again, "How fares my noble guest, and this great and excellent people?" Seanchan answered, "I have never had worse days, nor worse nights, nor worse dinners in my life." And he ate nothing for three whole days.

Then the king was sorely grieved that the whole Bardic Association should be feasting and drinking while Seanchan, the chief poet of Erin, was fasting and weak. So he sent his favourite serving-man, a person of mild manners and cleanliness, to offer special dishes to the bard.

"Take them away," said Seanchan; "I'll have none of them."

"And why, O Royal Bard?" asked the servitor.

"Because thou art an uncomely youth," answered Seanchan. "Thy grandfather was chip-nailed—I have seen him; I shall eat no food from thy hands."

Then the king called a beautiful maiden to him, his foster-daughter, and said, "Lady, bring thou this wheaten cake and this dish of salmon to the illustrious poet, and serve him thyself." So the maiden went.

But when Seanchan saw her he asked: "Who sent thee hither, and why hast thou brought me food?"

"My lord the king sent me, O Royal Bard," she answered, "because I am comely to look upon, and he bade me serve thee with food myself."

"Take it away," said Seanchan, "thou art an unseemly girl, I know of none more ugly. I have seen thy grandmother; she sat on a wall one day and pointed out the way with her hand to some travelling lepers. How could I touch thy food?" So the maiden went away in sorrow.

And then Guaire the king was indeed angry, and he exclaimed, "My malediction on the mouth that uttered that! May the kiss of a leper be on Seanchan's lips before he dies!"

Now there was a young serving-girl there, and she said to Seanchan, "There is a hen's egg in the place, my lord, may I bring it to thee, O Chief Bard?"

"It will suffice," said Seanchan; "bring it that I may eat."

But when she went to look for it, behold the egg was gone.

"Thou hast eaten it," said the bard, in wrath.

"Not so, my lord," she answered; "but the mice, the nimble race, have carried it away."

"Then I will satirise them in a poem," said Seanchan; and forthwith he chanted so bitter a satire against them that ten mice fell dead at once in his presence.

" 'Tis well," said Seanchan; "but the cat is the one most to blame, for it was her duty to suppress the mice. Therefore I shall satirise the tribe of the cats, and their chief lord, Irusan, son of Arusan; for I know where he lives with his wife Spit-fire, and his daughter Sharp-tooth, with her brothers the Purrer and the Growler. But I shall begin with Irusan himself, for he is king, and answerable for all the cats."

And he said: "Irusan, monster of claws, who strikes at the mouse but lets it go; weakest of cats. The otter did well who bit off the tips of the progenitor's ears, so that every cat since is jagged-eared. Let thy tail hang down; it is right, for the mouse jeers at thee."

Now Irusan heard these words in his cave, and he said to his daughter Sharp-tooth: "Seanchan has satirised me, but I will be avenged."

"Nay, father," she said, "bring him here alive that we may all take our revenge."

"I shall go then and bring him," said Irusan; "so send thy brothers after me."

Now when it was told to Seanchan that the King of the Cats was on his way to come and kill him, he was timorous, and besought Guaire and all the nobles to stand by and protect him. And before long a vibrating, impressive, impetuous sound was heard, like a raging tempest of fire in full blaze. And when the cat appeared he seemed to them of the size of a bullock; and this was his appearance—rapacious, panting, jagged-eared, snub-nosed, sharp-toothed, nimble, angry, vindictive, glare-eyed, terrible, sharp-clawed. Such was his similitude. But he passed on amongst them, not minding till he came to Seanchan; and him he seized by the arm and jerked him up on his back, and made off the way he came before any one could touch him; for he had no other object in view but to get hold of the poet.

Now Seanchan, being in evil plight, had recourse to flattery. "O Irusan," he exclaimed, "how truly splendid thou art: such running, such leaps, such strength, and such agility! But what evil have I done, O Irusan, son of Arusan? spare me, I entreat. I invoke the saints between thee and me, O great King of the Cats."

But not a bit did the cat let go his hold for all this fine talk, but went straight on to Clonmacnoise, where there was a forge; and St Kieran happened to be there standing at the door.

"What!" exclaimed the saint; "is that the Chief Bard of Erin on the back of the cat? Has Guaire's hospitality ended in this?" And he ran for a red-hot bar of iron that was in the furnace, and struck the cat on the side with it, so that the iron passed through him, and he fell down lifeless.

"Now my curse on the hand that gave that blow!" said the bard, when he got to his feet.

"And wherefore?" asked St Kieran.

"Because," answered Seanchan, "I would rather Irusan had killed me, and eaten me every bit, that so I might bring disgrace on Guaire for the bad food he gave me; for it was all owing to his wretched dinners that I got into this plight."

And when all the other kings heard of Seanchan's misfortunes, they sent to beg he would visit their courts. But he would have neither kiss nor welcome from them, and went on his way to the bardic mansion, where the best of good living was always to be had. And ever after the kings were afraid to offend Seanchan.

So long as he lived he had the chief place at the feast, and all the nobles there were made to sit below him, and Seanchan was content. And in time he and Guaire were reconciled; and Seanchan and all the ollaves, and the whole Bardic Association, were feasted by the king for thirty days in noble style, and had the choicest of viands and the best of French wines to drink, served in goblets of silver. And in return for his splendid hospitality the Bardic Association decreed unanimously a vote of thanks to the king. And they praised him in poems as "Guaire the Generous", by which name he was ever known in history, for the words of the poet are immortal.

Owney and Owney-na-peak

GERALD GRIFFIN

When Ireland had kings of her own—when there was no such thing as a coat made of red cloth in the country—when there was plenty in men's houses, and peace and quietness at men's doors (and that is a long time since)—there lived, in a village not far from the great city of Lumneach,* two young men, cousins: one of them named Owney, a smart, kind-hearted, handsome youth, with limb of a delicate form, and a very good understanding. His cousin's name was Owney too, and the neighbours christened him Owney-na-peak (Owney of the nose), on account of a long nose he had got—a thing so out of all proportion, that after looking at one side of his face, it was a smart morning's walk to get round the nose and take a view of the other (at least, so the people used to say). He was a stout, able-bodied fellow, as stupid as a beaten hound, and he was, moreover, a cruel tyrant to his young cousin, with whom he lived in a kind of partnership.

Both of them were of a humble station. They were smiths—whitesmiths—and they got a good deal of business to do from the lords of the court, and the knights, and all the grand people of the city. But one day young Owney was in town, he saw a great procession of lords, and ladies, and generals, and great people, among whom was the king's daughter of the court—and surely it is not possible for the young rose itself to be so beautiful as she was. His heart fainted at her sight, and he went home desperately in love, and not at all disposed to business.

Money, he was told, was the surest way of getting acquainted with the king, and so he began saving until he had put together a few hogs,† but Owney-na-peak, finding where he had hid them, seized on the whole, as he used to do on all young Owney's earnings.

One evening young Owney's mother found herself about to die, so she called

*Limerick.
†A hog ls. 1d.

her son to her bedside and said to him: "You have been a most dutiful good son, and 'tis proper you should be rewarded for it. Take this china cup to the fair—there is a fairy gift upon it—use your own wit, look about you, and let the highest bidder have it—and so, my white-headed boy,* God bless you!"

The young man drew his little bedcurtain down over his dead mother, and in a few days after, with a heavy heart, he took his china cup, and set off to the fair of Garryowen.

The place was merry enough. The field that is called Gallows Green now was covered with tents. There was plenty of wine (poteen not being known in these days, let alone *parliament*), a great many handsome girls, and 'tis unknown all the *keoh* that was with the boys and themselves. Poor Owney walked all the day through the fair, wishing to try his luck, but ashamed to offer his china cup among all the fine things that were there for sale. Evening was drawing on at last, and he was thinking of going home, when a strange man tapped him on the shoulder, and said: "My good youth, I have been marking you through the fair the whole day, going about with that cup in your hand, speaking to nobody, and looking as if you would be wanting something or another."

"I'm for selling it," said Owney.

"What is it you're for selling, you say?" said a second man, coming up and looking at the cup.

"Why then," said the first man, "and what's that to you, for a prying meddler? what do you want to know what it is he's for selling?"

"Bad manners to you (and where's the use of my wishing you what you have already?), haven't I a right to ask the price of what's in the fair?"

"E'then, the knowledge o' the price is all you'll have for it," says the first. "Here, my lad, is a golden piece for your cup."

"That cup shall never hold drink or diet in your house, please Heaven," says the second; "here's two gold pieces for the cup, lad."

"Why then, see this now—if I was forced to fill it to the rim with gold before I could call it mine, you shall never hold that cup between your fingers. Here, boy, do you mind me, give me that, once for all, and here's ten gold pieces for it, and say no more."

"Ten gold pieces for a china cup!" said a great lord of the court, who just rode

*White-haired boy, a curious Irish phrase for the favourite child.

up at that minute, "it must surely be a valuable article. Here, boy, here are twenty pieces for it, and give it to my servant."

"Give it to mine," cried another lord of the party, "and here's my purse, where you will find ten more. And if any man offers another fraction for it to outbid that, I'll spit him on my sword like a snipe."

"I outbid him," said a fair young lady in a veil, by his side, flinging twenty golden pieces more on the ground.

There was no voice to outbid the lady, and young Owney, kneeling, gave the cup into her hands.

"Fifty gold pieces for a china cup," said Owney to himself, as he plodded on home, "that was not worth two! Ah! mother, you knew that vanity had an open hand."

But as he drew near home he determined to hide his money somewhere, knowing, as he well did, that his cousin would not leave him a single cross to bless himself with. So he dug a little pit, and buried all but two pieces, which he brought to the house. His cousin, knowing the business on which he had gone, laughed heartily when he saw him enter, and asked him what luck he had got with his punch-bowl.

"Not so bad, neither," says Owney. "Two pieces of gold is not a bad price for an article of old china."

"Two gold pieces, Owney, honey! Erra, let us see 'em, maybe you would?" He took the cash from Owney's hand, and after opening his eyes in great astonishment at the sight of so much money, he put them into his pocket.

"Well, Owney, I'll keep them safe for you, in my pocket within. But tell us, maybe you would, how come you to get such a *mort* o' money for an old cup o' painted chaney, that wasn't worth, maybe, a fi-penny bit?"

"To get into the heart o' the fair, then, free and easy, and to look about me, and to cry old china, and the first man that *come* up, he to ask me, what is it I'd be asking for the cup, and I to say out bold: 'A hundred pieces of gold,' and he to laugh hearty, and we to huxter together till he beat me down to two, and there's the whole way of it all."

Owney-na-peak made as if he took no note of this, but next morning early he took an old china saucer himself had in his cupboard, and off he set, without saying a word to anybody, to the fair. You may easily imagine that it created no small surprise in the place when they heard a great big fellow with a china saucer in his hand crying out: "A raal *chaney* saucer going for a hundred pieces of goold! raal chaney—who'll be buying?"

"Erra, what's that you're saying, you great gomeril?" says a man, coming up to him, and looking first at the saucer and then in his face. "Is it thinking anybody would go make a *muthaun* of himself to give the like for that saucer?" But Owney-na-peak had no answer to make, only to cry out: "Raal chaney! one hundred pieces of goold"

A crowd soon collected about him, and finding he would give no account of himself, they fell upon him, beat him within an inch of his life, and after having satisfied themselves upon him, they went their way laughing and shouting. Towards sunset he got up, and crawled home as well as he could, without saucer or money. As soon as Owney saw him, he helped him into the forge, looking very mournful, although, if the truth must be told, it was to revenge himself for former good deeds of his cousin that he set him about this foolish business.

"Come here, Owney, eroo," said his cousin, after he had fastened the forge door and heated two irons in the fire. "You child of mischief!" said he, when he had caught him, "you shall never see the fruits of your roguery again, for I will put out your eyes." And so saying he snatched one of the red-hot irons from the fire.

It was all in vain for poor Owney to throw himself on his knees, and ask mercy, and beg and implore forgiveness; he was weak, and Owney-na-peak was strong; he held him fast, and burned out both his eyes. Then taking him, while he was yet fainting from the pain, upon his back, he carried him off to the bleak hill of Knockpatrick,* a great distance, and there laid him under a tombstone, and went his ways. In a little time after, Owney came to himself.

"Oh sweet light of day! what is to become of me now?" thought the poor lad, as he lay on his back under the tomb. "Is this to be the fruit of that unhappy present? Must I be dark for ever? and am I never more to look upon that sweet countenance, that even in my blindness is not entirely shut out from me?" He would have said a great deal more in this way, and perhaps more pathetic still, but just then he heard a great mewing, as if all the cats in the world were coming up the hill together in one faction. He gathered himself up, and drew back under the stone, and remained quite still, expecting what would come next. In a very short time he heard all the cats purring and mewing about the yard, whisking over the

*A hill in the west of the County of Limerick on the summit of which are the ruins of an old church, with a burying-ground still in use. The situation is exceedingly singular and bleak.

tombstones and playing all sorts of pranks among the graves. He felt the tails of one or two brush his nose; and well for him it was that they did not discover him there, as he afterwards found. At last—

"Silence!" said one of the cats, and they were all as mute as so many mice in an instant. "Now, all you cats of this great country, small and large, grey, red, yellow, black, brown, mottled, and white, attend to what I'm going to tell you in the name of your king and the master of all the cats. The sun is down, and the moon is up, and the night is silent, and no mortal hears us, and I may tell you a secret. You know the king of Munster's daughter?"

"O yes, to be sure, and why wouldn't we? Go on with your story," said all the cats together.

"I have heard of her for one," said a little dirty-faced black cat, speaking after they had all done, "for I'm the cat that sits upon the hob of Owney and Owney-na-peak, the whitesmiths, and I know many's the time young Owney does be talking of her, when he sits by the fire alone, rubbing me down and planning how he can get into her father's court."

"Whist, you natural!" says the cat that was making the speech, "what do you think we care for your Owney, or Owney-na-peak?"

"Murther, murther!" thinks Owney to himself, "did anybody ever hear the aiqual of this?"

"Well, gentlemen," says the cat again, "what I have to say is this. The king was last week struck with blindness, and you all know well, how blindness may be cured. You know there is no disorder that can ail mortal frame, that may not be removed by praying a round at the well of Barrygowen* yonder, and the king's disorder is such, that no other cure whatever can be had for it. Now, beware, don't let the secret pass one o' yer lips, for there's a great-grandson of Simon Magus, that is coming down to try his skill, and he it is that must use the water and marry the princess, who is to be given to any one so fortunate as to heal her father's eyes; and on that day, gentlemen, we are all promised a feast of the fattest mice that ever walked the ground." This speech was wonderfully applauded by all the cats, and presently after, the whole crew scampered off, jumping, and mewing, and purring, down the hill.

*The practice of praying rounds, with the view of healing diseases, at Barrygowen Well, in the County of Limerick, is still continued, notwithstanding the exertions of the neighbouring Catholic priesthood, which have diminished, but not abolished it.

Owney, being sensible that they were all gone, came from his hiding-place, and knowing the road to Barrygowen well, he set off, and groped his way out, and shortly knew, by the rolling of the waves,* coming in from the point of Foynes, that he was near the place. He got to the well, and making a round like a good Christian, rubbed his eyes with the well-water, and looking up, saw day dawning in the east. Giving thanks,he jumped up on his feet, and you may say that Owney-na-peak was much astonished on opening the door of the forge to find him there, his eyes as well or better than ever, and his face as merry as a dance.

"Well, cousin," said Owney, smiling, "you have done me the greatest service that one man can do another; you put me in the way of getting two pieces of gold," said he, showing two he had taken from his hiding-place. "If you could only bear the pain of suffering me just to put out your eyes, and lay you in the same place as you laid me, who knows what luck you'd have?"

"No, there's no occasion for putting out eyes at all, but could not you lay me, just as I am, tonight, in that place, and let me try my own fortune, if it be a thing you tell thruth; and what else could put the eyes in your head, after I burning them out with irons?"

"You'll know all that in time," says Owney, stopping him in his speech, for just at that minute, casting his eye towards the hob, he saw the cat sitting upon it, and looking very hard at him. So he made a sign to Owney-na-peak to be silent, or talk of something else; at which the cat turned away her eyes, and began washing her face, quite simple, with her two paws, looking now and then sideways into Owney's face, just like a Christian. By and by, when she had walked out of the forge, he shut the door after her, and finished what he was going to say, which made Owney-na peak still more anxious than before to be placed under the tombstone. Owney agreed to it very readily, and just as they were done speaking, cast a glance towards the forge window, where he saw the imp of a cat, just with her nose and one eye peeping in through a broken pane. He said nothing, however, but prepared to carry his cousin to the place; where, towards nightfall, he laid him as he had been laid himself, snug under the tombstone, and went his way down the hill, resting in Shanagolden that night, to see what would come of it in the morning.

Owney-na peak had not been more than two or three hours or so lying down, when he heard the very same noises coming up the hill, that had puzzled Owney

*Of the Shannon.

the night before. Seeing the cats enter the churchyard, he began to grow very uneasy, and strove to hide himself as well as he could, which was tolerably well too, all being covered by the tombstone excepting part of the nose, which was so long that he could not get it to fit by any means. You may say to yourself, that he was not a little surprised, when he say the cats all assemble like a congregation going to hear mass, some sitting, some walking about, and asking one another after the kittens and the like, and more of them stretching themselves upon the tombstones, and waiting the speech of their commander.

Silence was proclaimed at length, and he spoke: "Now all you cats of this great county, small and large, grey, red, yellow, black, brown, mottled, or white, attend—"

"Stay! stay!" said a little cat with a dirty face, that just then came running into the yard. "Be silent, for there are mortal ears listening to what you say. I have run hard and fast to say that your words were overheard last night. I am the cat that sits upon the hob of Owney and Owney-na-peak. And I saw a bottle of the water of Barrygowen hanging up over the chimbley this morning in their house."

In an instant all the cats began screaming, and mewing, and flying, as if they were mad, about the yard, searching every corner, and peeping under every tombstone. Poor Owney-na-peak endeavoured as well as he could to hide himself from them, and began to thump his breast and cross himself, but it was all in vain, for one of the cats saw the long nose peeping from under the stone, and in a minute they dragged him, roaring and bawling, into the very middle of the churchyard, where they flew upon him all together, and made *smithereens* of him, from the crown of his head to the soles of his feet.

The next morning very early, young Owney came to the churchyard, to see what had become of his cousin. He called over and over again upon his name, but there was no answer given. At last, entering the place of tombs, he found his limbs scattered over the earth.

"So that is the way with you, is it?" said he, clasping his hands, and looking down on the bloody fragments; "why then, though you were no great things in the way of kindness to me when your bones were together, that isn't the reason why I'd be glad to see them torn asunder this morning early." So gathering up all the pieces that he could find, he put them into a bag he had with him, and away with him to the well of Barrygowen, where he lost no time in making a round, and throwing them in, all in a heap. In an instant, he saw Owney-na-peak as well as ever, scrambling out of the well, and helping him to get up, he asked him how he felt himself.

"Oh is it how I'd feel myself you'd want to know?" said the other; "easy and I'll tell you. Take that for a specimen!" giving him at the same time a blow on the head, which you may say wasn't long in laying Owney sprawling on the ground. Then without giving him a minute's time to recover, he thrust him into the very bag from which he had been just shaken himself, resolving within himself to drown him in the Shannon at once, and put an end to him for ever.

Growing weary by the way, he stopped at a shebeen house *over-right* Robertstown Castle, to refresh himself with a *morning*, before he'd go any farther. Poor Owney did not know what to do when he came to himself, if it might be rightly called coming to himself, and the great bag tied up about him. His wicked cousin shot him down behind the door in the kitchen, and telling him he'd have his life surely if he stirred, he walked in to take something that's good in the little parlour.

Owney could not for the life of him avoid cutting a hole in the bag, to have a peep about the kitchen, and see whether he had no means of escape. He could see only one person, a simple-looking man, who was counting his beads in the chimney-corner, and now and then striking his breast, and looking up as if he was praying greatly.

"Lord" says he, "only give me death, death, and a favourable judgment! I haven't anybody now to look after, nor anybody to look after me. What's a few tinpennies to save a man from want? Only a quiet grave is all I ask."

"Murther, murther!" says Owney to himself, "here's a man wants death and can't have it, and here am I going to have it, and, in troth, I don't want it at all, see." So, after thinking a little what he had best do, he began to sing out very merrily, but lowering his voice, for fear he should be heard in the next room:

"To him that tied me here,
    Be thanks and praises given!
I'll bless him night and day,
    For packing me to Heaven.
Of all the roads you'll name,
    He surely will not lag,
Who takes his way to Heaven
    By travelling in a bag!"

"To Heaven, *ershishin?*"* said the man in the chimney-corner, opening his mouth and his eyes; "why then, you'd be doing a Christian turn, if you'd take a neighbour with you, that's tired of this bad and villainous world."

"You're a fool, you're a fool!" said Owney.

"I know I am, at least so the neighbours always tell me—but what hurt? Maybe I have a Christian soul as well as another; and fool or no fool, in a bag or out of a bag, I'd be glad and happy to go the same road it is you are talking of."

After seeming to make a great favour of it, in order to allure him the more to the bargain, Owney agreed to put him into the bag instead of himself; and cautioning him against saying a word, he was just going to tie him, when he was touched with a little remorse for going to have the innocent man's life taken: and seeing a slip of a pig that was killed the day before, in a corner, hanging up, the thought struck him that it would do just as well to put it in the bag in their place. No sooner said than done, to the great surprise of the natural, he popped the pig into the bag and tied it up.

"Now," says he, "my good friend, go home, say nothing, but bless the name in Heaven for saving your life; and you were as near losing it this morning as ever man was that didn't know."

They left the house together. Presently out comes Owney-na-peak, very hearty; and being so, he was not able to perceive the difference in the contents of the bag, but hoisting it upon his back, he sallied out of the house. Before he had gone far, he came to the rock of Foynes, from the top of which he flung his burden into the salt waters.

Away he went home, and knocked at the door of the forge, which was opened to him by Owney. You may fancy him to yourself crossing and blessing himself over and over again, when he saw, as he thought, the ghost standing before him. But Owney looked very merry, and told him not to be afraid. "You did many is the good turn in your life," says he, "but the equal of this never." So he up and told him that he found the finest place in the world at the bottom of the waters, and plenty of money. "See these four pieces for a specimen," showing him some he had taken from his own hiding hole: "what do you think of that for a story?"

"Why then that it's a droll one, no less; sorrow bit av I wouldn't have a mind to try my luck in the same way; how did you come home here before me that took

*Does he say?

383

the straight road, and didn't stop for so much as my *gusthah** since I left Knockpatrick?"

"Oh, there's a short cut under the waters," said Owney. "Mind and only be civil while you're in Thiernaoge,† and you'll make a sight o' money."

Well became Owney, he thrust his cousin into the bag, tied it about him, and putting it into a car that was returning after leaving a load of oats at a corn-store in the city, it was not long before he was at Foynes again. Here he dismounted, and going to the rock, he was, I am afraid, half inclined to start his burden into the wide water, when he saw a small skiff making towards the point. He hailed her, and learned that she was about to board a great vessel from foreign parts, that was sailing out of the river. So he went with his bag on board, and making his bargain with the captain of the ship, he left Owney-na-peak along with the crew, and never was troubled with him after, from that day to this.

As he was passing by Barrygowen well, he filled a bottle with the water; and going home, he bought a fine suit of clothes with the rest of the money he had buried, and away he set off in the morning to the city of Lumneach. He walked through the town, admiring everything he saw, until he came before the palace of the king. Over the gates of this he saw a number of spikes, with a head of a man stuck upon each, grinning in the sunshine.

Not at all daunted, he knocked very boldly at the gate, which was opened by one of the guards of the palace. "Well! who are you, friend?"

"I am a great doctor that's come from foreign parts to cure the king's eyesight. Lead me to his presence this minute."

"Fair and softly," said the soldier. "Do you see all those heads that are stuck up there? Yours is very likely to be keeping company by them, if you are so foolish as to come inside these walls. They are the heads of all the doctors in the land who came before you; and that's what makes the town so fine and healthy this time past, praised be Heaven for the same!"

"Don't be talking, you great gomeril," says Owney; "only bring me to the king at once."

He was brought before the king. After being warned of his fate if he should fail to do all that he undertook, the place was made clear of all but a few guards, and Owney was informed once more, that if he should restore the king's eyes, he should

---

*Literally—*walk in.*
†The abode of the fairies.

wed with the princess, and have the crown after her father's death. This put him in great spirits, and after making a round upon his bare knees about the bottle he took a little of the water, and rubbed it into the king's eyes. In a minute he jumped up from his throne and looked about him as well as ever. He ordered Owney to be dressed out like a king's son, and sent word to his daughter that she should receive him that instant for her husband.

You may say to yourself that the princess, glad as she was of her father's recovery, did not like this message. Small blame to her, when it is considered that she never set her eyes upon the man himself. However, her mind was changed wonderfully when he was brought before her, covered with gold and diamonds, and all sorts of grand things. Wishing, however, to know whether he had as good a wit as he had a person, she told him that he should give her, on the next morning, an answer to two questions, otherwise she would not hold him worthy of her hand. Owney bowed, and she put the questions as follows:

"What is that which is the sweetest thing in the world?"

"What are the three most beautiful objects in the creation?"

These were puzzling questions; but Owney having a small share of brains of his own, was not long in forming an opinion upon the matter. He was very impatient for the morning; but it came just as slow and regular as if he were not in the world. In a short time he was summoned to the courtyard, where all the nobles of the land assembled, with flags waving, and trumpets sounding, and all manner of glorious doings going on. The princess was placed on a throne of gold near her father, and there was a beautiful carpet spread for Owney to stand upon while he answered her questions. After the trumpets were silenced, she put the first, with a clear sweet voice, and he replied:

"It's salt!" says he, very stout, out.

There was a great applause at the answer; and the princess owned, smiling, that he had judged right.

"But now," said she, "for the second. What are the three most beautiful things in the creation?"

"Why," answered the young man, "here they are. A ship in full sail—a field of wheat in ear—and—"

What the third most beautiful thing was, all the people didn't hear; but there was a great blushing and laughing among the ladies, and the princess smiled and nodded at him, quite pleased with his wit. Indeed, many said that the judges of the land themselves could not have answered better, had they been in Owney's place; nor could there be anywhere found a more likely or well-spoken young man. He was brought first to the king, who took him in his arms, and presented him to the princess. She could not help acknowledging to herself that his understanding was quite worthy of his handsome person. Orders being immediately given for the marriage to proceed, they were made one with all speed; and it is said, that before another year came round, the fair princess was one of the most beautiful objects in the creation.

KINGS AND WARRIORS

The Knighting of Cuculain*

STANDISH O'GRADY

One night in the month of the fires of Bel, Cathvah, the Druid and star-gazer, was observing the heavens through his astrological instruments. Beside him was Cuculain, just then completing his sixteenth year. Since the exile of Fergus MacRoy, Cuculain had attached himself most to the Ard-Druid, and delighted to be along with him in his studies and observations. Suddenly the old man put aside his instruments and meditated a long time in silence.

"Setanta," said he at length, "art thou yet sixteen years of age?"

"No, father," replied the boy.

"It will then be difficult to persuade the king to knight thee and enrol thee among his knights," said Cathvah. "Yet this must be done tomorrow, for it has been revealed to me that he whom Concobar MacNessa shall present with arms tomorrow, will be renowned to the most distant ages, and to the ends of the earth. Thou shalt be presented with arms tomorrow, and after that thou mayest retire for a season among thy comrades, nor go out among the warriors until thy strength is mature."

The next day Cathvah procured the king's consent to the knighting of Cuculain. Now on the same morning, one of his grooms came to Concobar MacNessa and said: "O chief of the Red Branch, thou knowest how no horse has eaten barley, or ever occupied the stall where stood the divine steed which, with another of mortal breed, in the days of Kimbay MacFiontann, was accustomed to bear forth to the battle the great war-queen, Macha Monga-Rue; but ever since that stall has been empty, and no mortal steed hath profaned the stall in which the deathless Lia Macha was wont to stand. Yet, O Concobar, as I passed into the great stables on the east side of the courtyard, wherein are the steeds of thy own ambus, and in which is that spot since held sacred, I saw in the empty stall a mare,

*Cuculain was the great hero of legendary Ireland.

grey almost to whiteness, and of a size and beauty such as I have never seen, who turned to look upon me as I entered the stable, having very gentle eyes, but such as terrified me, so that I let fall the vessel in which I was bearing curds for the steed of Konaul Clareena; and she approached me, and laid her head upon my shoulder, making a strange noise."

Now as the groom was thus speaking, Cowshra Mend Macha, a younger son of Concobar, came before the king, and said: "Thou knowest, O my father, that house in which is preserved the chariot of Kimbay MacFiontann, wherein he and she, whose name I bear, the great queen that protects our nation, rode forth to the wars in the ancient days, and how it has been preserved ever since, and that it is under my care to keep bright and clean. Now this day at sunrise I approached the house, as is my custom, and approaching, I heard dire voices, clamorous and terrible, that came from within, and noises like the noise of battle, and shouts as of warriors in the agony of the conflict, that raise their voices with short intense cries as they ply their weapons, avoiding or inflicting death. Then I went back terrified, but there met me Minrowar, son of Gerkin, for he came but last night from Moharne, in the east, and he went to look at his own steeds; but together we opened the gate of the chariot-house, and the bronze of the chariot burned like glowing fire, and the voices cried out in acclaim, when we stood in the doorway, and the light streamed into the dark chamber. Doubtless, a great warrior will appear amongst the Red Branch, for men say that not for a hundred years have these voices been heard, and I know not for whom Macha sends these portents, if it be not for the son of Sualtam, though he is not yet of an age to bear arms."

Thus was Concobar prepared for the knighting of Cuculain.

Then in the presence of his court, and his warriors, and the youths who were the comrades and companions of Cuculain, Concobar presented the young hero with his weapons of war, after he had taken the vows of the Red Branch, and having also bound himself by certain gæsa.* But Cuculain looked narrowly upon the weapons, and he struck the spears together and clashed the sword upon the shield, and he brake the spears in pieces, and the sword, and made chasms in the shield.

"These are not good weapons, O my King," said the boy.

Then the king presented him with others that were larger and stronger, and these too the boy brake into little pieces.

*Curious vows taken by the ancient warriors. Hardly anything definite is known of them.—ED.

"These are still worse, O son of Nessa," said the boy, "and it is not seemly, O chief of the Red Branch, that on the day that I am to receive my arms I should be made a laughing-stock before the Clanna Rury, being yet but a boy."

But Concobar MacNessa exulted exceedingly when he beheld the amazing strength and the waywardness of the boy, and beneath delicate brows his eyes glittered like gleaming swords as he glanced rapidly round on the crowd of martial men that surrounded him; but amongst them all he seemed himself a bright torch of valour and war, more pure and clear than polished steel. But he beckoned to one of his knights, who hastened away and returned, bringing Concobar's own shield and spears and the sword out of the Tayta Brac, where they were kept, an equipment in reserve. And Cuculain shook them and bent them, and clashed them together, but they held firm.

"These are good arms, O son of Nessa," said Cuculain.

Then there were led forward a pair of noble steeds and a warcar, and the king conferred them on Cuculain. Then Cuculain sprang into the chariot, and standing with legs apart, he stamped from side to side, and shook and shook, and jolted the car until the axle brake and the car itself was broken in pieces.

"This is not a good chariot, O my King," said the boy.

Then there were led forward three chariots, and all these he brake in succession.

"These are not good chariots. O chief of the Red Branch," said Cuculain. "No brave warrior would enter the battle or fight from such rotten foothold."

Then the king called to his son Cowshra Mead Macha and bade him take Læg, and harness to the war-chariot, of which he had the care, the wondrous grey steed, and that one which had been given him by Kelkar, the son of Uther, and to give Læg, a charioteering equipment, to be charioteers of Cuculain. For now it was apparent to all the nobles and to the king that a lion of war had appeared amongst them, and that it was for him Macha had sent these omens.

Then Cuculain's heart leaped in his breast when he heard the thunder of the great war-car and the mad whinnying of the horses that smelt the battle afar. Soon he beheld them with his eyes and the charioteer with the golden fillet of his office, erect in the car, struggling to subdue their fury. A grey, long-maned steed, whale-bellied, broad-chested, behind one yoke; a black, ugly-maned steed behind the other.

Like a hawk swooping along the face of a cliff when the wind is high, or like the rush of the March wind over the plain, or like the fleetness of the stag roused from his lair by the hounds and covering his first field, was the rush of those steeds when they had broken through the restraint of the charioteer, as though they galloped over fiery flags, so that the earth shook and trembled with the velocity of their motion, and all the time the great car brayed and shrieked as the wheels of solid and glittering bronze went round, for there were demons that had their abode in that car.

The charioteer restrained the steeds before the assembly, but nay-the-less a deep purr, like the purr of a tiger, proceeded from the axle. Then the whole assembly lifted up their voices and shouted for Cuculain, and he himself, Cuculain the son of Sualtam, sprang into his chariot, all armed, with a cry as of a warrior springing into his chariot in the battle, and he stood erect and brandished his spears, and the war-sprites of the Gaeil shouted along with them, to the Bocanahs and Bananahs and the Genitii Glindi, the wild people of the glens, and the demons of the air, roared around him, when first the great warrior of the Gæil, his battle-arms in his hands stood equipped for war in his chariot before all the warriors of his tribe, the kings of the Clanna Rury, and the people of Emain Macha.

The Little Weaver of Duleek Gate

SAMUEL LOVER

You see, there was a waiver lived, wanst upon a time, in Duleek here, hard by the gate, and a very honest, industherous man he was, by all accounts. He had a wife, and av coorse they had childhre, and small blame to them, and plenty of them, so that the poor little waiver was obleeged to work his fingers to the bone a'most to get them the bit and the sup; but he didn't begridge that, for he was an industherous craythur, as I said before, and it was up airly and down late with him, and the loom never standin' still. Well, it was one mornin' that his wife called to him, and he sitting very busy throwin' the shuttle; and says she, "Come here," says she, "jewel, and ate your brekquest, now that it's ready." But he never minded her, but wint an workin'. So in a minit or two more says she, callin' out to him agin, "Arrah, lave off slavin' yourself, my darlin' and ate your bit o' brekquest while it is hot."

"Lave me alone," says he, and he dhruv the shuttle fasther nor before.

Well, in a little time more, she goes over to him where he sot, and says she, coaxin' him like, "Thady, dear," says she, "the stirabout* will be stone cowld if you don't give over that weary work and come and ate it at wanst."

"I'm busy with a patthern here that is brakin' my heart," says the waiver; "and antil I complate it and masther it intirely I won't quit."

"O, think o' the iligant stirabout, that 'ill be spylte intirely."

"To the divil with the stirabout," says he.

"God forgive you," says she, "for cursin' your good brekquest."

"Ay, and you too," says he.

"Throth, you're as cross as two sticks this blessed morning, Thady," says the poor wife; "and it's a heavy handful I have of you when you are cruked in your temper; but stay there if you like, and let your stirabout grow cowld and not one o' me 'ill ax you agin;" and with that off she wint, and the waiver, sure enough,

*Porridge.

393

was mighty crabbed, and the more the wife spoke to him the worse he got, which, you know, is only nath'ral. Well, he left the loom, at last, and wint over to the stirabout, and what would you think but whin he looked at it, it was as black as a crow; for, you see, it was in the hoighth o' summer, and the flies lit upon it to that degree that the stirabout was fairly covered with them.

"Why, thin, bad luck to your impidence," says the waiver; "would no place sarve you but that? and is it spyling my brekquest yiz are, you dirty bastes?" And with that, bein' altogether cruked-tempered at the time, he lifted his hand, and he made one great slam at the dish o' stirabout, and killed no less than three score and tin flies at the one blow. It was three score and tin exactly, for he counted the carcasses one by one, and laid them out on a clane plate, for to view them.

Well, he felt a powerful sperit risin' in him, when he seen the slaughther he done, at one blow; and with that he got as consaited as the very dickens, and not a sthroke more work he'd do that day, but out he wint, and was fractious and impident to every one he met, and was squarin' up into their faces and sayin', "Look at that fist! that's the fist that killed three score and tin at one blow—Whoo!"

With that all the neighbours thought he was crack'd, and faith, the poor wife herself thought the same when he kem home in the evenin', afther spendin' every rap he had in dhrink, and swaggerin' about the place, and lookin' at his hand every minit.

"Indeed, an' your hand is very dirty, sure enough, Thady jewel," says the poor wife; and thrue for her, for he rowled into a ditch comin' home. "You had betther wash it, darlin'."

"How dar' you say dirty to the greatest hand in Ireland?" says he, going to bate her.

"Well, it's nat dirty," says she.

"It is throwin' away my time I have been all my life," says he; "livin' with you at all, and stuck at a loom, nothin' but a poor waiver, when it is Saint George or the Dhraggin I ought to be, which is two of the siven champions o' Christendom."

"Well, suppose they christened him twice as much," says the wife; "sure, what's that to uz?"

"Don't put in your prate," says he; "you ignorant sthrap," says he. "You're vulgar, woman—you're vulgar—mighty vulgar; but I'll have nothin' more to say to any dirty snakin' thrade again—divil a more waivin' I'll do."

"Oh, Thady dear, and what'll the children do then?"

"Let them go play marvels," says he.

"That would be but poor feedin' for them, Thady."

"They shan't want for feedin'," says he; "for it's a rich man I'll be soon, and a great man too."

"Usha, but I'm glad to hear it, darlin',—though I dunna how it's to be, but I think you had betther go to bed, Thady."

"Don't talk to me of any bed but the bed o' glory, woman," says he, lookin' mortial grand.

"Oh! God send we'll all be in glory yet," says the wife, crassin' herself; "but go to sleep, Thady, for this present."

"I'll sleep with the brave yit," says he.

"Indeed, an' a brave sleep will do you a power o' good, my darlin'," says she.

"And it's I that will be the knight!" says he.

"All night, if you plaze, Thady," says she.

"None o' your coaxin'," says he. "I'm determined on it, and I'll set off immediantly, and be a knight arriant."

"A what?" says she.

"A knight arriant, woman."

"Lord be good to me, what's that?" says she.

"A knight arriant is a rale gintleman," says he; "going round the world for sport, with a swoord by his side, takin' whatever he plazes for himself; and that's a knight arriant," says he.

Well, sure enough he wint about among his neighbours the next day, and he got an owld kittle from one, and a saucepan from another; and he took them to the tailor, and he sewed him up a shuit o' tin clothes like any knight arriant and he borrowed a pot lid, and *that* he was very partic'lar about, bekase it was his shield and he wint to a frind o' his, a painther and glazier, and made him paint an his shield in big letthers—

"I'M THE MAN OF ALL MIN
THAT KILL'D THREE SCORE AND TIN
AT A BLOW"

"When the people sees *that*," says the waiver to himself, "the sorra one will dar' for to come near me."

And with that he towld the wife to scour out the small iron pot for him "For," says he, "it will make an iligant helmet;" and when it was done he put it an his head, and his wife said, "Oh, murther, Thady jewel, is it puttin' a great heavy iron pot an your head you are, by way iv a hat?"

"Sartinly," says he; "for a knight arriant should always have a *woight an his brain*."

"But, Thady dear," says the wife, "there's a hole in it, and it can't keep out the weather."

"It will be the cooler," says he, puttin' it an him; "besides, if I don't like it, it is aisy to stop it with a wisp o' sthraw, or the like o' that."

"The three legs of it looks mighty quare, stickin' up," says she.

"Every helmet has a spike stickin' out o' the top of it," says the waiver; "and if mine has three, its only the grandher it is."

"Well," says the wife, getting bitther at last, "all I can say is, it isn't the first sheep's head was dhress'd in it."

"*Your sarvint ma'am*," says he; and off he set.

Well, he was in want of a horse, and so he wint to a field hard by, where the miller's horse was grazin', that used to carry the ground corn round the counthry.

"This is the idintical horse for me," says the waiver; "he is used to carryin' flour and male, and what am I but the *flower* o' shovelry in a coat o' *mail*; so that the horse won't be put out iv his way in the laste."

But as he was ridin' him out o' the field, who should see him but the miller.

"Is it stalin' my horse you are, honest man?" says the miller.

"No," says the waiver; "I'm only going to axercise him," says he, "in the cool o' the evenin'; it will be good for his health."

"Thank you kindly," says the miller; "but lave him where he is, and you'll obleege me."

"I can't afford it," says the waiver, runnin' the horse at the ditch.

"Bad luck to your impidence," says the miller; "you've as much tin about you as a thravellin' tinker, but you've more brass. Come back here, you vagabone," says he.

But he was too late; away galloped the waiver, and took the road to Dublin, for he thought the best thing he could do was to go to the King o' Dublin (for Dublin was a grate place thin, and had a king iv its own), and he thought, maybe, the King o' Dublin would give him work. Well, he was four days goin' to Dublin, for the baste was not the best and the roads worse, not all as one as now; but there was no turnpikes then, glory be to God! When he got to Dublin, he wint sthrait to the palace, and whin he got into the coortyard he let his horse go and graze about the place, for the grass was growin' out betune the stones; everything was flourishin' thin in Dublin, you see. Well, the king was lookin' out of his dhrawin'-room windy, for divarshin, whin the waiver kem in; but the waiver pretended not to see him, and he wint over to a stone sate, undher the windy—for, you see, there was stone sates all round about the place for the accommodation o' the people—for the king was a dacent, obleeging man; well, as I said, the waiver wint over and lay down an one o' the sates, just undher the king's windy, and purtended to go asleep; but he took care to turn out the front of his shield that had the letthers an it; well, my dear, with that, the king calls out to one of the lords of his coort that was standin' behind him, howldin' up the skirt of his coat, accordin' to rayson, and says he: "Look here," says he, "what do you think of a vagabone like that comin' undher my very nose to go sleep? It is thrue I'm a good king," says he, "and I 'commodate the people by havin' sates for them to sit down and enjoy the raycreation and contimplation of seein' me here, lookin' out a' my dhrawin'-room windy, for divarshin; but that is no rayson they are to *make a hotel* o' the place, and come and sleep here. Who is it at all?" says the king.

"Not a one o' me knows, plaze your majesty."

"I think he must be a furriner," says the King; "bekase his dhress is outlandish."

"And doesn't know manners, more betoken," says the lord.

"I'll go down and *circumspect* him myself," says the king; "folly me," says he to the lord, wavin' his hand at the same time in the most dignacious manner.

Down he wint accordingly, followed by the lord; and whin he wint over to where the waiver was lying, sure the first thing he seen was his shield with the big letthers an it, and with that says he to the lord, "Bedad," says he, "this is the very man I want."

"For what, plaze your majesty?" says the lord.

"To kill that vagabone dragghin, to be sure," says the king.

"Sure, do you think he could kill him," says the lord, "when all the stoutest knights in the land wasn't aiquil to it, but never kem back, and was ate up alive by the cruel desaiver."

"Sure, don't you see there," says the king, pointin' at the shield, "that he killed three score and tin at one blow? and the man that done *that*, I think, is a match for anything."

So, with that, he wint over to the waiver and shuck him by the shouldher for to wake him, and the waiver rubbed his eyes as if just wakened, and the king says to him, "God save you," said he.

"God save you kindly," says the waiver, *purtendin'* he was quite onknowst who he was spakin' to.

"Do you know who I am," says the king, "that you make so free, good man?"

"No, indeed," says the waiver; "you have the advantage o' me."

"To be sure I have," says the king, *moighty high*; "sure, ain't I the King o' Dublin?" says he.

The waiver dhropped down an his two knees forninst the king, and says he, "I beg God's pardon and yours for the liberty I tuk; plaze your holiness, I hope you'll excuse it."

"No offince," says the king; "get up, good man. And what brings you here?" says he.

"I'm in want o' work, plaze your riverence," says the waiver.

"Well, suppose I give you work?" says the king.

"I'll be proud to sarve you, my lord," says the waiver.

"Very well," says the king. "You killed three score and tin at one blow, I understan'," says the king.

"Yis," says the waiver: "that was the last thrifle o' work I done, and I'm afeard my hand'll go out o' practice if I don't get some job to do at wanst."

"You shall have a job immediantly," says the king. "It is not three score and tin or any fine thing like that; it is only a blaguard dhraggin that is disturbin' the counthry and ruinatin' my tinanthry wid aitin' their powlthry, and I'm lost for want of eggs," says the king.

"Throth, thin, plaze your worship," says the waiver, "you look as yollow as if you swallowed twelve yolks this minit."

"Well, I want this dhraggin to be killed," says the king. "It will be no throuble in life to you; and I am only sorry that it isn't betther worth your while, for he isn't worth fearin' at all; only I must tell you, that he lives in the County Galway, in the middle of a bog, and he has an advantage in that."

"Oh, I don't value it in the laste," says the waiver; "for the three score and tin I killed was in a *soft place*."

"When will you undhertake the job, then?" says the king.

"Let me at him at wanst," says the waiver.

"That's what I like," says the king; "you're the very man for my money," says he.

398

"Talkin' of money," says the waiver; "by the same token, I'll want a thrifle o' change from you for my thravellin charges."

"As much as you plaze," says the king; and with the word, he brought him into his closet, where there was an owld stockin' in an oak chest, burstin' wid goolden guineas.

"Take as many as you plaze," says the king; and sure enough, my dear, the little waiver stuffed his tin clothes as full as they could howld them.

"Now, I'm ready for the road," says the waiver.

"Very well," says the king; "but you must have a fresh horse," says he.

"With all my heart," says the waiver, who thought he might as well exchange the miller's owld garron for a betther.

And maybe it's wonderhin' you are that the waiver would think of goin' to fight the dhraggin afther what he heerd about him, when he was purtendin' to be asleep, but he had no sitch notion; all he intended was,—to fob the goold, and ride back again to Duleek with his gains and a good horse. But, you see, cute as the waiver was, the king was cuter still; for these high quolity, you see, is great desaivers; and so the horse the waiver was put an was larned on purpose; and sure, the minit he mounted, away powdhered the horse, and the divil a toe he'd go but right down to Galway. Well, for four days he was goin' evermore, until at last the waiver seen a crowd o' people runnin' as if owld Nick was at their heels, and they shoutin' a thousand murdhers and cryin', "The dhraggin, the dhraggin!" and he couldn't stop the horse nor make him turn back, but away he pelted right forninst the terrible baste that was comin' up to him, and there was the most *nefaarious* smell o' sulphur, savin' your presence, enough to knock you down; and, faith the waiver seen he had no time to lose, and so he threw himself off the horse and made to a tree that was growin' nigh hand, and away he clambered up into it as nimble as a cat; and not a minit had he to spare, for the dhraggin kem up in a powerful rage, and he devoured the horse body and bones, in less than no time; and then he began to sniffle and scent about for the waiver, and at last he clapt his eye an him, where he was, up in the three, and says he, "In throth, you might as well come down out o' that," says he; "for I'll have you as sure as eggs is mate."

"Divil a fut I'll go down,", says the waiver.

"Sorra care, I care," says the dhraggin; "for you're as good as ready money in my pocket this minit, for I'll lie undher this three," says he, "and sooner or later you must fall to my share;" and sure enough he sot down, and began to pick his teeth with his tail, afther the heavy brekquest he made that mornin' (for he ate a whole village, let alone the horse), and he got dhrowsy at last, and fell asleep; but before he wint to sleep, he wound himself all round about the three, all as one as a lady windin' ribbon round her finger, so that the waiver could not escape.

Well, as soon as the waiver knew he was dead asleep, by the snorin' of him—and every snore he let out of him was like a clap o' thunder—that minit the waiver began to creep down the three, as cautious as a fox; and he was very nigh hand the bottom, when, bad cess to it, a theivin' branch he was dipindin' an bruk and down he fell right a-top o' the dhraggin; but if he did, good luck was an his side, for where should he fall but with his two legs right acrass the dhraggin's neck, and my jew'l, he laid howlt o' the baste's ears, and there he kept his grip, for the dhraggin wakened and endayvoured for to bite him; but, you see, by rayson the waiver was behind his ears, he could not come at him, and, with that, he endayvoured for to shake him off; but the divil a stir could he stir the waiver; and though he shuk all the scales an his body, he could not turn the scale agin the waiver.

"By the hokey, this is too bad intirely," says the dhraggin; "but if you won't let go," says he, "by the powers o' wildfire, I'll give you a ride that 'ill astonish your siven small sinses, my boy;" and, with that, away he flew like mad; and where do you think he did fly?—bedad, he flew sthraight for Dublin, divil a less. But the waiver bein' an his neck was a great disthress to him, and he would rather have had him an *inside passenger*; but, anyway, he flew and he flew till he kem *slap* up agin the palace o' the king; for, bein' blind with the rage, he never seen it, and he knocked his brains out—that is, the small thrifle he had—and down he fell spacheless. An' you see, good luck would have it, that the King o' Dublin was lookin' out iv' his dhrawin'-room windy, for divarshin, that day also, and whin he seen the waiver ridin' an the fiery dhraggin (for he was blazin' like a tar-barrel), he called out to his coortyers to come and see the show. "By the powdhers o' war, here comes the knight arriant," says the king, "ridin' the dhraggin that's all afire, and if he gets *into the palace*, yiz must be ready wid the *fire ingines*," says he,"for to *put him out*." But when they seen the dhraggin fall outside, they all run down-stairs and scampered into the palace-yard for to circumspect the *curosity*; and by the time they got down, the waiver had got off o' the dhraggin's neck, and runnin' up to the king, says he, "Plaze your holiness," says he, "I did not think myself worthy of killin' this facetious baste, so I brought him to yourself for to do him the honour of decripitation by your own royal five fingers. But I tamed him first, before I allowed him the liberty for to *dar'* to appear in your royal prisince, and you'll oblige me if you'll just make your mark with your own hand upon the onruly baste's neck." And with that the King sure enough, dhrew out his swoord and took the head aff the *dirty* brute as *clane* as a new pin. Well, there was great rejoicin' in the coort that the dhraggin was killed; and says the king to the little waiver, says he, "You are a knight arriant as it is, and so it would be of no use for to knight you over agin; but I will make you a lord," says he.

"O Lord!" says the waiver, thunder-struck like at his own good luck.

"I will," says the king; "and as you are the first man I ever heer'd tell of that rode a dhraggin, you shall be called Lord *Mount* Dhraggin," says he.

"And where's my estates, plaze your holiness?" says the waiver, who always had a sharp look-out afther the main chance.

"Oh, I didn't forget that," says the king; "it is my royal pleasure to provide well for you, and for that rayson I make you a present of all the dhraggins in the world, and give you power over them from this out," says he.

"Is that all?" says the waiver.

"All!" says the king. "Why, you ongrateful little vagabone, was the like ever given to any man before?"

"I b'lieve not, indeed," says the waiver; "many thanks to your majesty."

"But that is not all I'll do for you," says the king; "I'll give you my daughther too in marriage," says he. Now, you see, that was nothin' more than what he promised the waiver in the first promise; for, by all accounts, the king's daughther was the greatest dhraggin ever was seen, and had the divil's own tongue, and a beard a yard long, which she *purtended* was put an her by way of a penance by Father Mulcahy, her confissor; but it was well known it was in the family for ages, and no wonder it was so long, by rayson of that same.

APPENDIX

CLASSIFICATION OF IRISH FAIRIES

Irish Fairies divide themselves into two great classes: the sociable and the solitary. The first are in the main kindly, and the second full of all uncharitableness.

The Sociable Fairies

These creatures who go about in troops, and quarrel, and make love, much as men and women do, are divided into land fairies or Sheoques (Ir. *Sidheog*, "a little fairy"), and water fairies or Merrows (Ir. *Moruadh*, "a sea maid"; the masculine is unknown). At the same time I am inclined to think that the term Sheoque may be applied to both upon occasion, for I have heard of a whole village turning out to hear two red-capped water fairies, who were very "little fairies" indeed, play upon the bagpipes.

1. *The Sheoques.* The Sheoques proper, however, are the spirits that haunt the sacred thorn bushes and the green raths. All over Ireland are little fields circled by ditches, and supposed to be ancient fortifications and sheepfolds. These are the raths, or forts, or "royalties", as they are variously called. Here marrying and giving in marriage, live the land fairies. Many a mortal they are said to have enticed down into their dim world. Many more have listened to their fairy music, till all human cares and joys drifted from their hearts and they became great peasant seers or "Fairy Doctors", or great peasant musicians or poets like Carolan, who gathered his tunes while sleeping on a fairy rath; or else they died in a year and a day, to live ever after among the fairies. These Sheoques are on the whole good; but one most malicious habit have they—a habit worthy of a witch. They steal children and leave a withered fairy a thousand or maybe two thousand years old, instead. Three or four years ago a man wrote to one of the Irish papers, telling of a case in his own

village, and how the parish priest made the fairies deliver the stolen child up again. At times full-grown men and women have been taken. Near the village of Coloney, Sligo, I have been told, lives an old woman who was taken in her youth. When she came home at the end of seven years she had no toes, for she had danced them off. Now and then one hears of some real injury being done a person by the land fairies, but then it is nearly always deserved. They are said to have killed two people in the last six months in the County Down district where I am now staying. But then these persons had torn up thorn bushes belonging to the Sheoques.

2. *The Merrows.* These water fairies are said to be common. I asked a peasant woman once whether the fishermen of her village had ever seen one. "Indeed, they don't like to see them at all," she answered, "for they always bring bad weather." Sometimes the Merrows come out of the sea in the shape of little hornless cows. When in our own shape they have fishes' tails and wear a red cap called in Irish *cohuleen driuth* (p. 344). The men among them have, according to Croker, green teeth, green hair, pigs' eyes, and red noses; but their women are beautiful, and sometimes prefer handsome fishermen to their green-haired lovers. Near Bantry, in the last century, lived a woman covered with scales like a fish, who was descended, as the story goes, from such a marriage. I have myself never heard tell of this grotesque appearance of the male Merrows, and think it probably a merely local Munster tradition.

The Solitary Fairies

These are nearly all gloomy and terrible in some way. There are, however, some among them who have light hearts and brave attire.

1. *The Lepracaun* (Ir. *Leith bhrogan*, i.e. the one shoemaker). This creature is seen sitting under a hedge mending a shoe, and one who catches him can make him deliver up his crocks of gold, for he is a miser of great wealth; but if you take your eyes off him the creature vanishes like smoke. He is said to be the child of an evil spirit and a debased fairy, and wears, according to M'Anally, a red coat with seven buttons in each row, and a cocked-hat on the point of which he sometimes spins like a top. In Donegal he goes clad in a great frieze coat.

2. *The Cluricaun* (Ir. *Clobhair-cean* in O'Kearney). Some writers consider this to be another name for the Lepracaun, given him when he has laid aside his shoemaking at night and goes on the spree. The Cluricauns' occupations are

403

robbing wine-cellars and riding sheep and shepherds' dogs for a livelong night, until the morning finds them panting and mud-covered.

3. *The Ganconer or Gancanagh* (Ir. *Gean-canogh*, i.e. love-talker). This is a creature of the Lepracaun type, but unlike him, is a great idler. He appears in lonely valleys, always with a pipe in his mouth, and spends his time in making love to shepherdesses and milkmaids.

4. *The Far Darrig* (Ir. *Fear Dearg*, i.e. red man). This is the practical joker of the other world. The wild Sligo story I give of "A Fairy Enchantment" was probably his work. Of these solitary and mainly evil fairies there is no more lubberly wretch than this same Far Darrig. Like the next phantom, he presides over evil dreams.

5. *The Pooka* (Ir. *Púca*, a word derived by some from *poc*, a he-goat). The Pooka seems of the family of the nightmare. He has most likely never appeared in human form, the one or two recorded instances being probably mistakes, he being mixed up with the Far Darrig. His shape is usually that of a horse, a bull, a goat, eagle, or ass. His delight is to get a rider, whom he rushes with through ditches and rivers and over mountains, and shakes off in the grey of the morning. Especially does he love to plague a drunkard: a drunkard's sleep is his kingdom. At times he takes more unexpected forms than those of beast or bird. The one that haunts the Dun of Coch-na-Phuca in Kilkenny takes the form of a fleece of wool, and at night rolls out into the surrounding fields, making a buzzing noise that so terrifies the cattle that unbroken colts will run to the nearest man and lay their heads upon his shoulder for protection.

6. *The Dullahan.* This is a most gruesome thing. He has no head, or carries it under his arm. Often he is seen driving a black coach called coach-a-bower (Ir. *Coite-bodhar*), drawn by headless horses. It rumbles to your door, and if you open it a basin of blood is thrown in your face. It is an omen of death to the houses where it pauses. Such a coach not very long ago went through Sligo in the grey of the morning, as was told me by a sailor who believed he saw it. In one village I know its rumbling is said to be heard many times in the year.

7. *The Leanhaun Shee* (Ir. *Leanhaun sidhe*, i.e. fairy mistress). This spirit seeks the love of men. If they refuse she is their slave; if they consent, they are hers, and can only escape by finding one to take their place. Her lovers waste away, for she lives on their life. Most of the Gaelic poets, down to quite recent times, have had a Leanhaun Shee, for she gives inspiration to her slaves and is indeed the Gaelic muse—this malignant fairy. Her lovers, the Gaelic poets, died young. She grew

restless, and carried them away to other worlds, for death does not destroy her power.

8. *The Far Gorta* (man of hunger). This is an emaciated fairy that goes through the land in famine time, begging and bringing good luck to the giver.

9. *The Banshee* (Ir. *Bean-sidhe*, i.e. fairy woman). This fairy, like the Far Gorta, differs from the general run of solitary fairies by its generally good disposition. She is perhaps not really one of them at all, but a sociable fairy grown solitary through much sorrow. The name corresponds to the less common Far Shee (Ir. *Fear Sidhe*), a man fairy. She wails, as most people know, over the death of a member of some old Irish family. Sometimes she is an enemy of the house and screams with triumph, but more often a friend. When more than one Banshee comes to cry, the man or woman who is dying must have been very holy or very brave. Occasionally she is most undoubtedly one of the sociable fairies. Cleena, once an Irish princess and then a Munster goddess, and now a Sheoque, is thus mentioned by the greatest of Irish antiquarians.

O'Donovan, writing in 1849 to a friend, who quotes his words in the *Dublin University Magazine*, says: "When my grandfather died in Leinster in 1798, Cleena came all the way from Ton Cleena to lament him; but she has not been heard ever since lamenting any of our race, though I believe she still weeps in the mountains of Drumaleaque in her own country, where so many of the race of Eoghan More are dying of starvation." The Banshee on the other hand who cries with triumph is often believed to be no fairy but a ghost of one wronged by an ancestor of the dying. Some say wrongly that she never goes beyond the seas, but dwells always in her own country. Upon the other hand, a distinguished writer on anthropology assures me that he has heard her on 1st December 1867, in Pital, near Libertad, Central America, as he rode through a deep forest. She was dressed in pale yellow, and raised a cry like the cry of a bat. She came to announce the death of his father. This is her cry, written down by him with the help of a Frenchman and a violin.

He saw and heard her again on 5th February 1871, at 16 Devonshire Street, Queen's Square, London. She came this time to announce the death of his eldest child; and in 1884 he again saw and heard her at 28 East Street, Queen's Square, the death of his mother being the cause.

The Banshee is called *badh* or *bowa* in East Munster, and is named *Bachuntha* by Banim in one of his novels.

10. *Other Fairies and Spirits.* Besides the foregoing, we have other solitary fairies, of which too little definite is known to give them each a separate mention. They are the House Spirits, of whom "Teigue of the Lee" is probably an instance; the Water Sherie, a kind of will-o'-the-wisp; the Sowlth, a formless luminous creature; the Pastha (*Piast-bestia*), the lake dragon, a guardian of hidden treasure; and the Bo men fairies, who live in the marshes of County Down and destroy the unwary. They may be driven away by a blow from a particular kind of seaweed. I suspect them of being Scotch fairies imported by Scotch settlers. Then there is the great tribe of ghosts called Thivishes in some parts.

These are all the fairies and spirits I have come across in Irish folk-lore. There are probably many others undiscovered.

W. B. YEATS

Co. Down, *June 1891*